KT-178-720

BINGE EATING

STRODE'S COLLEGE
LIBRARY

BINGE EATING

Nature, Assessment, and Treatment

Christopher G. Fairburn
G. Terence Wilson
Editors

THE GUILFORD PRESS

New York   London

© 1993 The Guilford Press
Chapter 15 © 1993 Christopher G. Fairburn and Zafra Cooper

Published by The Guilford Press
A Division of Guilford Publications, Inc.
72 Spring Street, New York, NY 10012

All rights reserved

No part of this book may be reproduced, stored in a retrieval
system, or transmitted, in any form or by any means,
electronic, mechanical, photocopying, microfilming, recording,
or otherwise, without written permission from the Publisher.

Printed in the United States of America

This book is printed on acid-free paper.

Last digit is print number: 9 8 7 6 5 4

Library of Congress Cataloging-in-Publication Data

Binge eating : nature, assessment, and treatment / edited by
  Christopher G. Fairburn, G. Terence Wilson.
      p. cm.
  Includes bibliographical references and index.
  ISBN 0-89862-995-0   ISBN 0-89862-858-X (pbk)
  1. Compulsive eating. I. Fairburn, Christopher G. II. Wilson,
G. Terence, 1944–
  [DNLM: 1. Compulsive Behavior. 2. Eating Disorders. WM 175
B6125]
RC552.C65B56 1993
616.85'26—dc20
DNLM/DLC
for Library of Congress   92-48235
                                                              CIP

Contributors

W. Stewart Agras, MD, Professor of Psychiatry, Department of Psychiatry and Behavioral Sciences, Stanford University, Stanford, Cal.

John Blundell, PhD, FBPsS, Reader in Biological Psychology, Department of Psychology, Leeds University, Leeds, U.K.

Zafra Cooper, DPhil, DipPsych, Senior Research Psychologist, Department of Psychiatry, University of Oxford, Oxford, U.K.

Christopher G. Fairburn, DM, FRCPsych, Wellcome Trust Senior Lecturer and Honorary Clinical Reader, Department of Psychiatry, University of Oxford, Oxford, U.K.

David M. Garner, PhD, Professor of Psychiatry, Department of Psychiatry, Michigan State University, East Lansing, Mich.

Phillipa J. Hay, FRANZCP, Nuffield Research Fellow, Department of Psychiatry, University of Oxford, Oxford, U.K.

C. Peter Herman, PhD. Professor of Psychology and Psychiatry, Department of Psychology, University of Toronto, Erindale Campus, Mississauga, Ont.

Andrew Hill, PhD, Lecturer in Behavioral Sciences, Department of Psychiatry, Leeds University, Leeds, U.K.

Marsha D. Marcus, PhD, Assistant Professor, Western Psychiatric Institute and Clinic, University of Pittsburgh, Pittsburgh, Pa.

James E. Mitchell MD, Professor of Psychiatry, Department of Psychiatry, University of Minnesota, Minneapolis, Mn.

Janet Polivy, PhD, Professor of Psychology and Psychiatry, Department of Psychology, University of Toronto, Erindale Campus, Mississauga, Ont.

Ruth H. Striegel-Moore, PhD, Assistant Professor, Wesleyan University, Middletown, Ct.

Albert J. Stunkard, MD, Professor of Psychiatry, University of Pennsylvania, Philadelphia, Pa.

David L. Tobin, PhD, Assistant Professor, Department of Psychiatry, Baystate Medical Center, Springfield, Mass.

B. Timothy Walsh, MD, Professor of Psychiatry, Department of Psychiatry, College of Physicians and Surgeons of Columbia University, New York, N.Y.

Sarah L. Welch, MA, BM, Research Senior House Officer, Department of Psychiatry, University of Oxford, Oxford, U.K.

G. Terence Wilson, PhD., Oscar K. Buros Professor of Psychology, Graduate School of Applied and Professional Psychology, Rutgers University, Piscataway, N.J.

Martina de Zwaan, MD, Assistant Professor, Department of Psychiatry, University of Vienna, Vienna, Austria.

Preface

Some books seem contrived: To us this book seemed almost a necessity. It was clear that to further our clinical and research work on eating disorders we needed a synthesis of what was known about binge eating, since the available literature was widely dispersed and specific to particular disorders. No such synthesis was available; hence this book was born.

In editing the book our goal has been to collect in one volume what is known about binge eating and its treatment. This has involved collaboration with colleagues from a variety of fields. Some have been asked to review what is known about binge eating from the perspective of a particular disorder, for example, obesity. Others have been asked to ignore diagnostic distinctions and consider all those who binge eat, but from a particular point of view, for example, treatment. The result is, we believe, a collection of original and important contributions to the understanding and treatment of this complex behavior.

The first section of the book opens with a consideration of definitional and classificatory issues, since the definition and diagnostic status of binge eating are still subjects of controversy. In Chapter 1 the American Psychiatric Association's DSM-IV scheme for classifying eating disorders is presented, including the proposal to introduce a "binge eating disorder" (American Psychiatric Association, 1993).* Chapter 2 presents a scholarly review of the history of binge eating. It is particularly apt that this chapter is written by Stunkard, since he has a unique perspective on binge eating, having written one of the first papers on the subject (Stunkard, 1959), and has also researched the behavior from the perspectives of both obesity and bulimia nervosa. Another strength of this chapter is that Stunkard brings to his historical review a knowledge

*The DSM-IV criteria cited in this volume are those that were approved as final by the DSM-IV Eating Disorders Work Group and the Task Force on DSM-IV (APA, 1993). These criteria may be subject to minor editorial revisions before the publication of DSM-IV.

of German. As a result, he makes available for the first time important sources that are unlikely to be familiar to most English-speaking readers.

The next section considers binge eating from the perspectives of bulimia nervosa, anorexia nervosa, obesity, and addictive disorders. To date, detailed laboratory studies of the behavior have mainly been in the context of bulimia nervosa. As Walsh points out in Chapter 3, these studies disconfirm the popular notion of "carbohydrate craving": The binges of patients with bulimia nervosa do not contain an unduly high proportion of carbohydrate. The binge eating of patients with anorexia nervosa has received remarkably little research attention. This is curious given the emphasis that is placed on the behavior in the DSM-IV diagnostic scheme. Preparing this chapter led Garner to reexamine available data on binge eating in anorexia nervosa, the result of which is his proposal in Chapter 4 that self-induced vomiting rather than binge eating be used as the basis for subtyping the disorder (Garner, Garner, & Rosen, 1993). Chapter 5 provides a valuable account of the work on binge eating in obesity. This is a highly active field, and the review by Marcus is both comprehensive and critical. Chapter 6 addresses the relationship between binge eating and addictive disorders. One major point to emerge is the folly of reasoning by analogy: The similarities between binge eating and the various forms of addictive behavior are superficial.

The third section opens with a review of the work on the incidence and prevalence of binge eating and bulimia nervosa. It is pointed out that although there are now good data on the distribution of bulimia nervosa, almost nothing is known about the distribution of binge eating, as defined by DSM-IV, since few studies have used the new contextual definition of what constitutes a large amount of food to eat. The second half of this chapter is concerned with the use of epidemiological methods to address etiological questions. In a broad-ranging review, binge eating is approached from a developmental perspective in Chapter 8, considering why it is young women who appear to be at greatest risk. In contrast, Chapter 9 provides a detailed analysis of the psychological factors and processes involved in the behavior itself. Section III closes with a review of the psychobiological processes involved in the control of appetite and their relevance to binge eating.

The fourth section of the book is concerned with the management of patients who binge eat. Chapter 11 provides a detailed account of the methods available for assessing binge eating. This chapter is followed by appraisals of the value of drug treatment (Chapter 12), short-term psychological treatments (Chapter 13), and psychodynamic psychotherapy (Chapter 14).

The final section of the book contains two manuals that we hope will be of value to clinicians and researchers. The first (Chapter 15), is devoted to the Eating Disorder Examination (EDE), the standardized interview for assessing eating disorders. This is the first time that the EDE has been made generally available. Chapter 16 describes in full the cognitive behavioral approach to the treatment of those who binge eat. The strength of this chapter lies in the fact that it has been written by three proponents of the approach, each drawing on his or her clinical experience treating specific subgroups of these patients.

Several acknowledgments are called for. The idea of editing this book emerged during a year we spent together as Fellows at the Center for Advanced Study in the Behavioral Sciences at Stanford. We are immensely grateful to Gardner Lindzey, Phil Converse, Bob Scott, and the staff at "The Center" for their unfailing support and encouragement throughout the year. Our views on binge eating were influenced by our close collaboration with Stewart Agras, another Center Fellow, during that year. We are also grateful to all those who have joined us in writing this book. Without exception they have produced original and important new contributions to the field. We are grateful to them for their efforts. Finally, we would like to acknowledge two funding agencies, the Wellcome Trust and the MacArthur Foundation. As a result of their farsighted funding policies and generous support, our work in this field has been greatly enhanced.

REFERENCES

American Psychiatric Association. (1993). *DSM-IV draft criteria (3/1/93)*. Washington, DC: Author.

Garner, D. M., Garner, M. V., & Rosen, L. W. (in press). Anorexia nervosa "restricters" who purge: Implications for subtyping anorexia nervosa. *International Journal of Eating Disorders*.

Stunkard, A. J. (1959). Eating patterns and obesity. *Psychiatry Quarterly, 33,* 284-295.

Contents

SECTION I

INTRODUCTION

Binge Eating: Definition and Classification

Christopher G. Fairburn
G. Terence Wilson

DEFINITION OF BINGE EATING

"Binge" and "binge eating" are technical terms in the clinical and research literature on eating disorders. They refer to a particular form of overeating. They are also in common use in the population at large, and this carries with it the potential for confusion. *Webster's Ninth New Collegiate Dictionary* defines "binge" as "unrestrained indulgence," and it is in this general and often vague sense of excess that people variously use the term. A systematic analysis of what young women mean when they describe their own eating as a binge revealed that it is primarily the experience of loss of control over eating, and not the amount consumed, which is the important feature (Beglin & Fairburn, 1992). This lay use of the term differs from formal professional usage, as we describe below, and underscores the need for ensuring an unambiguous and shared use of the term in both clinical practice and research.

Although binge eating occurs across the weight spectrum and has become a diagnostic criterion in the major disorders of anorexia nervosa and bulimia nervosa, the *Diagnostic and Statistical Manual of Mental Disorders* (DSM) of the American Psychiatric Association (1980, 1987, 1993) has addressed its definition only in the diagnostic criteria for bulimia nervosa.* Within this disorder, the definition of binge eating has changed over successive revisions of DSM as shown in Table 1.1. The

---

*The DSM-IV criteria cited in this volume are those that were approved as final by the DSM-IV Eating Disorders Work Group and the Task Force on DSM-IV (APA, 1993). These criteria may be subject to minor editorial revisions before the publication of DSM-IV.

TABLE 1.1. Evolving Definitions of Binge Eating across Successive Revisions of the *Diagnostic and Statistical Manual of Mental Disorders* of the American Psychiatric Association

DSM-III (1980)	Recurrent episodes of binge eating (rapid consumption of a large amount of food in a discrete period of time, usually less than 2 hours)
DSM-III-R (1987)	Recurrent episodes of binge eating (rapid consumption of large amount of food in a discrete period of time).
DSM-IV Draft Criteria (1993)	Recurrent episodes of binge eating. An episode of binge-eating is characterized by both of the following: (1) eating, in a discrete period of time (e.g., within any 2-hour period), an amount of food that is definitely larger than most people would eat during a similar period of time in similar circumstances; and (2) a sense of lack of control over eating during the episode (e.g., a feeling that one cannot stop eating or control what or how much one is eating)

definition in DSM-IV specifies that to be considered a binge, an episode of eating must be characterized by (1) the consumption of a large amount of food and (2) loss of control over the eating at the time.

Consumption of a Large Amount of Food

Whereas DSM-III-R provided no definition of what a *large* amount of food entailed, the criteria in DSM-IV specify that the amount of food consumed must be "definitely larger than most people would eat during a similar period of time in similar circumstances" (see Table 1.1). This guideline for what constitutes a "large amount" was adapted from the definition used in the Eating Disorder Examination (EDE) (Cooper & Fairburn, 1987; see Fairburn & Cooper, Chapter 15, this volume). It is important to note that the judgment is partly a function of the context within which the eating occurred. The question is whether the amount consumed was larger than most people would eat under similar circumstances (i.e., considering when, where, and with whom the eating took place).

The requirement that a binge consist of a large amount of food is consistent with the findings of laboratory studies and self-reports of the caloric size of the binges of patients with bulimia nervosa (as discussed by Walsh, Chapter 3, this volume). Nevertheless, several groups of investigators have challenged this definitional requirement, arguing that the amount of food consumed is not the cardinal characteristic of a binge. For example, Rosen, Leitenberg, Fisher, and Khazam (1986) found that one-third of their patients, who otherwise satisfied diagnostic criteria for bulimia nervosa, reported consuming fewer than 600 kcal per binge, with no relationship between the size of the self-reported binge and the accompanying anxiety. Similarly, Rossiter and Agras (1990) observed that a significant minority of their patients with bulimia nervosa reported binges of fewer than 500 kcal. Essentially the same pattern of results have also been obtained with overweight binge eaters (Rossiter, Agras, Telch, & Bruce, 1992). There are presently no data showing fundamental differences in the nature of binges, in associated psychopathology, or in predictive validity, as a function of the quantity of food consumed. The absence of persuasive evidence for the diagnostic significance of the amount of food eaten during overeating episodes has led Garner, Shafer, and Rosen (1992) to recommend that the distinction between large and small episodes be abandoned.

Loss of Control over Eating

The definition of a binge in DSM-IV, adapted from the EDE, specifies that loss of control over eating is a necessary feature. There is an impressive consensus on this point (e.g., Fairburn, 1987; Garner et al., 1992; Rossiter & Agras, 1990), and it is in line with the lay use of the term (Beglin & Fairburn, 1992). In the DSM-III and DSM-III-R criteria "lack of control" was required for the diagnosis of bulimia nervosa, but was not a defining feature of binge eating itself. Table 1.2 summarizes the evolution within DSM of the definition of "lack of control."

Other Defining Features

Both DSM-III and DSM-III-R required that a binge involve the rapid consumption of food. This feature has been eliminated from the DSM-IV criteria, as it is not thought to be central to the construct. Nevertheless, there is some evidence that in patients with bulimia nervosa food consumption during binge eating is more rapid than during nonbinge meals (Hadigan, Kissileff, & Walsh, 1989; Rossiter et al., 1992).

TABLE 1.2. Evolving Definitions of Loss of Control in the Diagnosis of Bulimia Nervosa across Successive Revisions of the *Diagnostic and Statistical Manual of Mental Disorders* of the American Psychiatric Associaton

DSM-III (1980)	Fear of not being able to stop eating voluntarily
DSM-III-R (1987)	A feeling of lack of control over eating behavior during the eating binges
DSM-IV Draft Criteria (1993)	A sense of lack of control over eating during the episode (e.g., a feeling that one cannot stop eating or control what or how much one is eating)

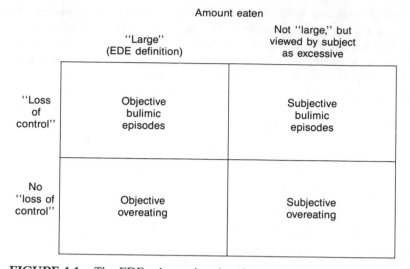

FIGURE 1.1.. The EDE scheme for classifying episodes of overeating.

Successive versions of the DSM criteria for bulimia nervosa have all specified that a binge involves overeating within a "discrete period of time." This refers to a discriminable period of time. Continual snacking throughout the day is not considered to be a binge. In practice, however, it can be difficult to identify the boundaries of individual binges, especially among those whose eating is not punctuated by episodes of "purging." This issue is taken up by Wilson (Chapter 11, this volume). The EDE approach to the identification of boundaries between episodes of eating is described in full by Fairburn and Cooper (Chapter 16, this volume).

Recurrent Overeating versus Binge Eating

The most comprehensive scheme for classifying episodes of overeating is provided by the EDE. As shown in Figure 1.1, "objective bulimic episodes" are what the DSM-IV criteria term binge eating. "Subjective bulimic episodes" are similar, except that the amount of food eaten is not objectively large. As discussed earlier, some critics of the DSM-IV criteria have recommended that no distinction be made between objective and subjective bulimic episodes, because they view the quantity eaten as immaterial to the definition of a binge (e.g., Garner et al., 1992; Rossiter & Agras, 1990). The EDE terms "objective overeating" and "subjective overeating" describe parallel episodes of perceived overeating except that there is no loss of control. These different patterns of actual and perceived overeating are not mutually exclusive, and the data indicate that both patients with bulimia nervosa and those who are obese binge eaters engage in both objective and subjective bulimic episodes (see Walsh, Chapter 3, this volume; Marcus, Chapter 5, this volume). The assessment of these different forms of overeating is discussed by Wilson (Chapter 11, this volume).

A significant strength of the EDE scheme for classifying episodes of overeating is that it is comprehensive, allowing the description of the full range of episodes of actual and perceived overeating. Given the absence of any compelling evidence bearing on the fundamentally important issue of whether differences in the size of "binges" are of diagnostic significance, it would be well for clinicians and researchers to assess all forms of overeating. Only in this way can the large versus small controversy be resolved on empirical grounds.

BINGE EATING AND THE CLASSIFICATION OF EATING DISORDERS

Binge eating is not confined to any one eating disorder. It is seen across all diagnostic categories. To describe the relationship between binge eating and the eating disorders, it is first necessary to review the current scheme for classifying eating disorders. This account is based upon DSM-IV (APA, 1993). The ICD-10 scheme is very similar (World Health Organization, 1992). At the heart of both schemes are the two well-established eating disorders, anorexia nervosa and bulimia nervosa. The relationship between the two diagnoses is represented by the Venn diagram shown in Figure 1.2.

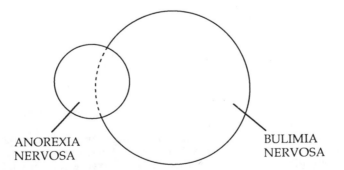

FIGURE 1.2. A schematic representation of the relationship between the diagnoses anorexia nervosa and bulimia nervosa.

Bulimia Nervosa

In principle three features are required to make a diagnosis of bulimia nervosa. The first is recurrent episodes of binge eating: Thus, by definition, all patients with bulimia nervosa binge eat. (Binge eating in bulimia nervosa is discussed by Walsh, Chapter 3, this volume.) The second feature is the regular practice of extreme behavior designed to control body shape and weight. This includes self-induced vomiting, the misuse of laxatives or diuretics, excessive exercising, and extreme dieting or fasting. The third feature is the presence of a characteristic form of overconcern with shape and weight, the essence of which is the tendency to judge self-worth largely or even exclusively in terms of shape or weight.

The DSM-IV criteria for bulimia nervosa include two additional refinements. First, it is specified that the individual does not currently meet diagnostic criteria for anorexia nervosa. This has the effect of restricting the diagnosis of bulimia nervosa to those of average or above average weight. The main argument for giving anorexia nervosa precedence over bulimia nervosa relates to the clear therapeutic implications of the former diagnosis, namely, the need for weight gain. In DSM-III-R no such ''trumping'' system operated: Therefore, some individuals were eligible for both diagnoses. The second refinement is that bulimia ner-

---

TABLE 1.3. DSM-IV Draft Criteria for Bulimia Nervosa

Bulimia Nervosa

A. Recurrent episodes of binge eating. An episode of binge eating is characterized by both of the following:
   (1) Eating, in a discrete period of time (e.g., within any two-hour period), an amount of food that is definitely larger than most people would eat during a similar period of time in similar circumstances
   (2) A sense of lack of control over eating during the episode (e.g., a feeling that one cannot stop eating or control what or how much one is eating).
B. Recurrent inappropriate compensatory behavior in order to prevent weight gain, such as: self-induced vomiting; misuse of laxatives, diuretics or other medications; fasting; or excessive exercise.
C. The binge eating and inappropriate compensatory behaviors both occur, on average, at least twice a week for three months.
D. Self-evaluation is unduly influenced by body shape and weight.
E. The disturbance does not occur exclusively during episodes of Anorexia Nervosa.

   Purging type: The person regularly engages in self-induced vomiting or the misuse of laxatives or diuretics.
   Non-purging type: The person uses other inappropriate compensatory behaviors, such as fasting or excessive exercise, but does not regularly engage in self-induced vomitinng or the misuse of laxatives or diuretics.

Note. From American Psychiatric Association (1993). Copyright 1993 by the American Psychiatric Association. Reprinted by permission.

vosa is subdivided into a ''purging type'' in which there is either regular self-induced vomiting or regular misuse of laxatives or diuretics, and a ''nonpurging type'' in which such behavior is not present. This distinction derives from the evidence, albeit weak, that these two groups differ in certain respects including their eating behavior (Mitchell, 1992). There is no evidence that they differ in their prognoses or responses to treatment. The full DSM-IV diagnostic criteria for bulimia nervosa are given in Table 1.3.

Anorexia Nervosa

In principle three features are also required to make a diagnosis of anorexia nervosa. The first is the active maintenance of an abnormally low weight (defined in DSM-IV as 15% below that expected); the second applies only to post-menarchal females and is amenorrhea (defined in DSM-IV as the absence of three consecutive menstrual cycles when otherwise expected to occur); and the third is the presence of concerns about shape and weight similar to those found in bulimia nervosa. Characteristically there is an intense fear of gaining weight, despite the low weight, and evidence that shape and weight are central to the subject's self-evaluation. A proportion of cases of anorexia nervosa overeat at times, and in some instances these episodes of overeating meet criteria for a binge. (Binge eating in anorexia nervosa is discussed by Garner, Chapter 4, this vol-

---

TABLE 1.4. DSM-IV Draft Criteria for Anorexia Nervosa

Anorexia Nervosa

A. Refusal to maintain body weight at or above a minimally normal weight for age and height (e.g., weight loss leading to maintenance of body weight less than 85% of that expected; or failure to make expected weight gain during period of growth, leading to body weight less than 85% of that expected).

B. Intense fear of gaining weight or becoming fat, even though underweight.

C. Disturbance in the way in which one's body weight or shape is experienced, undue influence of body shape or weight on self-evaluation, or denial of the seriousness of current low body weight.

D. In post-menarchal females, amenorrhea, i.e., the absence of at least three consecutive menstrual cycles. (A woman is considered to have amenorrhea if her periods occur only following hormone, e.g., estrogen, administration.)

   Restricting type: During the episode of Anorexia Nervosa, the person does not regularly engage in binge eating or purging behavior (i.e., self-induced vomiting or the misuse of laxatives or diuretics).

   Binge eating/purging type: During the episode of Anorexia Nervosa, the person regularly engages in binge eating or purging behavior (i.e., self-induced vomiting or the misuse of laxatives or diuretics).

Note. From American Psychiatric Association (1993). Copyright 1993 by the American Psychiatric Association. Reprinted by permission.

ume.) In DSM-IV anorexia nervosa is subdivided on the basis of the presence of binge eating and purging into a binge eating/purging type in which there are regular episodes of binge eating or purging and a restricting type in which binge eating and purging do not occur "regularly." ("Regularly" is not defined.) The basis for this distinction is the evidence that, compared with the restricting group, those who regularly binge or purge tend to have stronger personal and family histories of obesity and higher rates of so-called impulsive behaviors, including stealing, drug misuse, deliberate self-harm, and lability of mood (DaCosta & Halmi, 1992). The validity of this distinction is discussed by Garner (Chapter 4, this volume). Subjects who belong to the binge eating/purging subtype of anorexia nervosa occupy the area in Figure 1.2 where the anorexia nervosa and bulimia nervosa circles overlap. The full DSM-IV diagnostic criteria for anorexia nervosa are given in Table 1.4.

Eating Disorders Not Otherwise Specified and Binge Eating Disorder

A third category of eating disorder is recognized in DSM-IV. It is "eating disorders not otherwise specified" (EDNOS). This category is de-

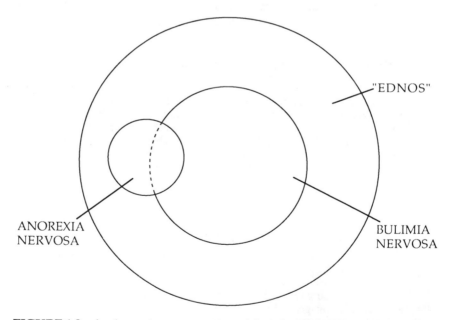

FIGURE 1.3. A schematic representation of the relationship between the diagnoses anorexia nervosa, bulimia nervosa and eating disorders not otherwise specified (EDNOS).

TABLE 1.5. DSM-IV Draft Critiera for Eating Disorders Not Otherwise Specified

Eating Disorders, NOS

Disorders of eating that do not meet the criteria for a specific Eating Disorder. Examples include:

(1) All of the criteria for Anorexia Nervosa are met except the individual has regular menses.

(2) All of the criteria for Anorexia Nervosa are met except, despite significant weight loss, the individual's current weight is in the normal range.

(3) All of the criteria for Bulimia Nervosa are met except binges occur at a frequency of less than twice a week for a duration of less than three months.

(4) An individual of normal body weight regularly engages in inappropriate compensatory behavior after eating small amounts of food (e.g., self-induced vomiting after the consumption of two cookies).

(5) An individual who repeatedly chews and spits out, but does not swallow, large amounts of food.

(6) Binge Eating Disorder: recurrent episodes of binge eating in the absence of inappropriate compensatory behaviors characteristic of Bulimia Nervosa[a]

[a]See Table 1.6 for the criteria for 'binge eating disorder'.
Note. From American Psychiatric Association (1993). Copyright 1993 by the American Psychiatric Association. Reprinted by permission.

signed to include those who have an eating disorder of clinical severity yet do not meet diagnostic criteria for anorexia nervosa or bulimia nervosa. The category tends to get overlooked despite common clinical experience that a sizable proportion of patients belong to it (e.g., Bunnell, Shenker, Nussbaum, Jacobson, & Cooper, 1990; Clinton & Glant, 1992; Mitrany, 1992). The relationship between the diagnoses EDNOS, anorexia nervosa, and bulimia nervosa is illustrated in Figure 1.3. The DSM-IV diagnostic criteria for EDNOS are given in Table 1.5.

One group within EDNOS comprises those with recurrent episodes of overeating. Such people present with a variety of clinical problems. A group that has been the subject of recent attention comprises those who have regular binges (as defined in DSM-IV) in the absence of extreme behavior designed to control body shape and weight of the type required to make a diagnosis of bulimia nervosa (Spitzer et al., 1991; Spitzer et al., 1992). The term "binge eating disorder" has been used to describe these people. DSM-IV includes binge eating disorder (BED) as an example within the general category of EDNOS, and provides specific diagnostic criteria for BED in the Appendix. The delineation of BED in DSM-IV has attracted criticism (Fairburn, Welch, & Hay, 1993). The diagnostic criteria for BED are given in Table 1.6. Binge eating disorder is discussed by Stunkard (Chapter 2, this volume), Marcus (Chapter 5, this volume), and Fairburn and colleagues (Chapter 7, this volume).

There are other groups within EDNOS in which binge eating is a

---

TABLE 1.6. DSM-IV Draft Criteria for "Binge Eating Disorder"

Binge Eating Disorder

A. Recurrent episodes of binge eating. An episode of binge eating is characterized by both of the following:
   (i) Eating, in a discrete period of time (e.g., within any 2 hour period), an
        amount of food that is definitely larger than most people would eat dur-
        ing a similar period of time in similar circumstances; and,
   (ii) A sense of lack of control over eating during the episode (e.g., a feeling
        that one can't stop eating or control what or how much one is eating).
B. The binge eating episodes are associated with at least three of the following:
   (1) Eating much more rapidly than normal
   (2) Eating until feeling uncomfortably full
   (3) Eating large amounts of food when not feeling physically hungry
   (4) Eating alone because of being embarrassed by how much one is eating
   (5) Feeling disgusted with oneself, depressed or feeling very guilty after over-
       eating.
C. Marked distress regarding binge eating.
D. The binge eating occurs, on average, at least two days a week[a] for six
   months.
E. The disturbance does not occur exclusively during the course of Anorexia
   Nervosa or Builimia Nervosa.

---

[a]The method of determining frequency differs from that used for Bulimia Nervosa; future research should address whether counting the number of days on which binges occur or the number of episodes of binge eating is the preferable method of setting a frequency
threshold.
Note. From American Psychiatric Association (1993). Copyright 1993 by the American Psychiatric Association. Reprinted by permission.

---

prominent feature. For example, there are individuals with all the features of bulimia nervosa, including regular purging, but the characteristic attitudinal disturbance is either not present or not of sufficient severity
to permit a diagnosis of bulimia nervosa. In addition, there are people
with all the features of bulimia nervosa, but the frequency of binge eating is too low for the diagnosis to be given.

Recurrent Overeating versus Binge Eating

As discussed earlier, the concept of binge eating, as defined in DSM-IV,
represents a particular form of overeating ("objective bulimic episodes"
in EDE terminology). Other forms of overeating are regularly encountered in clinical practice. Smaller "subjective bulimic episodes" are seen
in anorexia nervosa, and they often accompany the objective bulimic
episodes of patients with bulimia nervosa. In addition, they are present
in a sizable but neglected group of individuals within EDNOS. Such individuals typically have high levels of dietary restraint and may, or may
not, vomit or misuse laxatives or diuretics.

People with recurrent episodes of "objective overeating" are also seen. In such cases there is true overeating but no associated loss of control. This behavior is largely confined to individuals within EDNOS and tends not to be associated with extreme weight control behavior. It either occurs in isolation, when it is often associated with obesity, or it may be an aftermath of bulimia nervosa with subjects describing an attenuation of loss of control over time.

Much remains to be learned about those with recurrent episodes of overeating. The people who show this behavior are a varied group, and we do not know as yet whether there are clinically useful distinctions to be made among them. There have been no systematic studies of their clinical features, eating and weight histories, exposure to putative risk factors, course or response to treatment. At present, there is focus on the subgroup that shows one particular form of overeating, binge eating (objective bulimic episodes), while other groups are receiving relatively little attention. There are reasons to have misgivings about this narrow perspective. As has been argued with respect to binge eating disorder (Fairburn, Welch, & Hay, 1993), focusing prematurely on one very specific problem may impede acquisition of knowledge rather than enhance it, since other related problems tend to get ignored. In our view investigators should be encouraged to study broad samples of those who overeat rather than narrow ones, so that knowledge is acquired on all forms of clinically significant overeating.

ACKNOWLEDGMENTS

CGF is supported by a Senior Lectureship award from the Wellcome Trust. Our joint research on the classification of recurrent overeating is funded by grants from the Wellcome Trust, the Johann Jacobs Foundation, and the Health and Behavior Research Network of the John D. and Catherine T. MacArthur Foundation.

REFERENCES

American Psychiatric Association. (1980). *Diagnostic and statistical manual of mental disorders* (3rd ed.). Washington, DC: Author.

American Psychiatric Association. (1987). *Diagnostic and statistical manual of mental disorders* (3rd ed., rev.). Washington, DC: Author.

American Psychiatric Association. (1993). *DSM-IV draft criteria (3/1/93)*. Washington, DC: Author.

Beglin, S. J., & Fairburn, C. G. (1992). What is meant by the term "binge"? *American Journal of Psychiatry, 149*, 123–124.

Bunnell, D. W., Shenker, I. R., Nussbaum, M. P., Jacobson, M. S., & Cooper, P. J. (1990). Subclinical versus formal eating disorders: Differentiating psychological features. *International Journal of Eating Disorders, 9*, 357–362.

Clinton, D. N., & Glant, R. (1992). The eating disorders spectrum of DSM-III-R. Clinical features and psychosocial concomitants of 86 consecutive cases from a Swedish urban catchment area. *Journal of Nervous and Mental Disease, 180,* 244–250.

Cooper, Z., & Fairburn, C. G. (1987). The Eating Disorder Examination: A semi-structured interview for the assessment of the specific psychopathology of eating disorders. *International Journal of Eating Disorders, 6,* 1–8.

DaCosta, M., & Halmi, K. A. (1992). Classification of anorexia nervosa: Question of subtypes. *International Journal of Eating Disorders, 11,* 305–314.

Fairburn, C. G. (1987). The definition of bulimia nervosa: Guidelines for clinicians and research workers. *Annals of Behavioral Medicine, 9,* 3–7.

Fairburn, C. G., Welch, S. L., & Hay, P. J. (1993). The classification of recurrent overeating: The "Binge Eating Disorder" proposal. *International Journal of Eating Disorders, 13,* 155–160.

Garner, D. M., Shafer, C. L., & Rosen, L. W. (1992). Critical appraisal of the DSM-III-R diagnostic criteria for eating disorders. In S. R. Hooper, G. W. Hynd, & R. E. Mattison (Eds.), *Child psychopathology: Diagnostic criteria and clinical assessment.* Hillsdale, NJ: Erlbaum.

Hadigan, C. M., Kissileff, H. R., & Walsh, B. T. (1989). Patterns of food selection during meals in women with bulimia. *American Journal of Clinical Nutrition, 50,* 759–766.

Mitchell, J. E. (1992). Subtyping of bulimia nervosa. *International Journal of Eating Disorders, 11,* 327–332.

Mitrany, E. (1992). Atypical eating disorders. *Journal of Adolescent Health, 13,* 400–402.

Rosen, J. C., Leitenberg, H., Fisher, C., & Khazam, C. (1986). Binge-eating episodes in bulimia nervosa: The amount and type of food consumed. *International Journal of Eating Disorders, 5,* 255–257.

Rossiter, E. M., & Agras, W. S. (1990). An empirical test of the DSM-III-R definition of binge. *International Journal of Eating Disorders, 9,* 513–518.

Rossiter, E. M., Agras, W. S., Telch, C. F., & Bruce, B. (1992). The eating patterns of non-purging bulimic subjects. *International Journal of Eating Disorders, 11,* 111–120.

Spitzer, R. L., Devlin, M. J., Walsh, B. T., Hasin, D., Wing, R., Marcus, M. D., Stunkard, A., Wadden, T., Yanovski, S., Agras, S., Mitchell, J., & Nonas, C. (1991). Binge Eating Disorder: To be or not to be in DSM-IV? *International Journal of Eating Disorders, 10,* 627–629.

Spitzer, R. L., Devlin, M., Walsh, B. T., Hasin, D., Wing, R., Marcus, M., Stunkard, A., Wadden, T., Yanovski, S., Agras, S., Mitchell, J., & Nonas, C. (1992). Binge Eating Disorder: A multisite field trial of the diagnostic criteria. *International Journal of Eating Disorders, 11,* 191–203.

World Health Organization. (1992). *The ICD-10 classification of mental and behavioural disorders.* Geneva: Author.

A History
of Binge Eating

Albert J. Stunkard

A history of binge eating makes clear the importance of this term and of this volume, which is devoted to it. The term "binge eating" is of recent origin and its emergence from the ancient diagnosis of bulimia is a fascinating story. Furthermore, this history may even help to resolve current nosological problems affecting the eating disorders.

Bulimia is truly an ancient diagnosis and for the early history of this term I am indebted to the scholarly reviews of Beumont (1991), of Casper (1983), and of Stein and Laakso (1988) and particularly to the extensive writings in German of Habermas (1989, 1990) and of Ziolko and Schrader (1985).

EARLY REFERENCES TO BULIMIA

Ziolko and Schrader (1985) point out that the word for "hunger" in ancient Greek was "limos" and that it was characterized as "ravenous hunger" by the addition of either the prefix "bou-," which signifies "a great amount of," or "boul-," meaning ox or steer (Liddell & Scott, 1972). According to these authors this distinction was made by Homer as early as the 8th century B.C. and it continued to be made by subsequent authors. Thus, Hippocrates recognized *boulimos* as a sick hunger as distinct from ordinary hunger, and both Aristophanes and Xenophon referred to *boulimos* as "ravenous hunger" (Liddell & Scott, 1972). The ancient authors apparently referred to *boulimos* as episodes of overeating that were triggered by an unusual form of hunger. Xenophon, however, also identified *boulimos* with feelings of hunger, weakness, and faintness and described its occurrence among soldiers who had been on short rations during the "march up country" in the campaign against Artaxerxes.

Later authors, both Greek and Roman, apparently used the term *bou-limos* in an ambiguous manner, referring to both the feelings of hunger, weakness, and faintness and to the overeating that they aroused. In his writings Galen emphasized the aspect of faintness along with avidity for food, and the weight of his authority perpetuated this interpretation for more 1,000 years.

MORE MODERN DESCRIPTIONS OF BULIMIA

It was not until the 18th century that the influence of Galen waned sufficiently that new descriptions of binge eating began to appear and the Galenic criterion of faintness was abandoned. One of the earliest authors was James (1743). He described both "true boulimus" characterized by intense preoccupation with food and overeating at very short intervals, followed by fainting, and a variant, "caninus appetitus," in which the overeating was followed by vomiting. In 1772, W. Cullen reported on patients who suffered from "such strong hunger that more is eaten than can be digested," and he differentiated no less than seven forms of bulimia (cited in Ziolko & Schrader, 1985). A contemporary, Vogel (see Vogel, 1981), described a patient with an almost insatiable appetite who consumed not only vast amounts of food but even stones. And in 1785 Motherby distinguished three types of bulimia—bulimia of the pure hunger type, that associated with swooning, and that terminated by vomiting.

By the turn of the 19th century the concept of bulimia as binge eating was sufficiently well recognized to be included in the 1797 edition of the *Encyclopaedia Brittanica* and the *Dictionnaire de Medecine et Chirurgie*, published in Paris in 1830. In 1833, Descuret described a case of "congenital bulimia" in a girl who was expelled from school for taking food from her classmates and who, under later observation in the Salpetriere, was reported to have consumed 8 to 10 lb of bread a day. In 1867, Blachez described two forms of "boulimie." In each, food was the major preoccupation of the person, hunger might persist even after the consumption of enormous amounts of food, and torpor sometimes followed the binge. In the form that Blachez called "cynorexia," the binge was followed by vomiting. Bouveret (1893) and Soltmann (1894) described what they called "hyperorexia," characterized by the repeated ingestion of small amounts of food. Soltmann distinguished this form of overeating from "polyphagia," the consumption of large amounts of food without apparent satiety.

Ever since the reappearance of bulimia as binge eating during the past 2 centuries, it has been recognized as a distinctive form of behavior. Osler (1892), for example, referred to it in his textbook of medicine and

Janet (1903) in his monograph. More recently, however, it has received far less attention than that accorded other forms of disturbed eating, such as extensive dieting and self-induced vomiting. This relative lack of attention may be due to the sparsity of careful clinical descriptions. A search for such descriptions leads naturally to the neurological literature, where the automatic quality of binge eating should lend itself particularly well to neurological assessment. Four forms of overeating have been described in the neurological literature.

NEUROLOGICAL DESCRIPTIONS

1. The Kluver–Bucy syndrome (Kluver & Bucy, 1938) produced in monkeys by bilateral ablation of temporal lobes. Following such ablation, monkeys manifest ''psychic blindness'' and a variety of neurological disorders, including the mouthing and swallowing of inedible as well as edible materials. In 1962, Lilly, Cummmings, Beason, and Frankel (1983) reported human cases of temporal lobe blindness that were associated with disturbed eating behavior, but in no case could they be confused with binge eating.

2. The Klein–Levin syndrome, an episodic disorder characterized by somnolence and overeating. For days and even weeks, the patients, mostly adolescent boys, sleep for 18 or more hours a day, awakening only long enough to eat and attend to toilet activities. Periods of these attacks last for several weeks and may occur from 2 to 12 times a year. Interestingly, the disorder appears to remit during adulthood (Critchley, 1962).

3. The Prader–Willi syndrome. This disorder begins in infancy and is characterized by mental retardation, short stature, hypotonia, and hypogenitalism. During childhood these patients develop voracious appetites and obesity. The genetic basis of the disorder has been localized to microdeletions of chromosome 15, but the few autopsied cases have not identified the neurological deficit.

4. Damage to the ventromedial hypothalamus. In 1975 Bray and Gallagher (1975) reviewed the 69 cases of hypothalamic damage that had been reported in the world's literature. Although most of the patients were obese, eating behavior was described in only two. One was a patient of Bray and Gallagher in whom ''uncontrollable hyperphagia'' was observed during a 37-day hospital admission in which he gained 8 lb and was estimated to have consumed 400 kcal a day in excess of his metabolic needs. The second case, reported by Reeves and Plum (1969), was a woman who presented with ''hyperphagia, rage, and dementia'' and who was found at autopsy to have a neoplasm that had destroyed her ventromedial hypothalamus.

Less dramatic neurologically determined eating disorders may be far more common. Hope, Fairburn, and Goodwin (1989) reported overeating and weight gain by four demented patients who may well have had damage to the ventromedial hypothalamus, but hypophagia and weight loss, also presumably due to other forms of neurological damage, appear to be more common in dementia (Morris, Hope, & Fairburn, 1989).

THE NEURAL BASIS OF EATING BEHAVIOR

Although clinical neurology has contributed little to the understanding of binge eating, our growing knowledge of the central nervous system provides the opportunity for an understanding of binge eating. Shortly after World War II, the outlines of the neural structures mediating food intake became apparent. Surprisingly, these structures subsumed not one but two neural systems, one that initiated eating and one that terminated it.

The surprise was not that there are brain areas that initiate eating; such areas had been postulated long before their discovery. The surprise was the discovery of satiety areas that terminate eating. Traditionally, satiety had been viewed as a purely incidental aspect of eating—what happened when the drive to eat ran out of steam. But if satiety were nothing more than such a passive process, it would hardly require dedicated brain structures. Yet satiety structures existed, and their destruction resulted in overeating and obesity. Furthermore, this overeating had some strange and unexpected characteristics.

If rats with impaired satiety systems were allowed free access to food, they overate in an uncontrolled manner. But when any obstruction was placed in their way, their food intake decreased to a level even lower than that of nonobese rats. It made no difference what form the obstruction took—lifting heavy covers to reach the food, solving mazes, pressing levers, withstanding electric shocks, adulterating their food with quinine. In the face of such impediments, obese rats radically reduced their food intake.

These findings led to a major revision of how we view "hunger." Hunger defined by how much food an animal eats may differ dramatically from hunger defined by how hard the animal will work for food. Our understanding of human eating behavior was also affected by these findings. No longer forced to account for all overeating in terms of increased hunger, we could conceive of overeating due to decreased satiety.

A failure of satiety seemed to characterize a pattern of overeating that I had delineated on clinical grounds. This pattern, the "night-eating syndrome" (Stunkard, Grace, & Wolff, 1955), consisted of morning anorexia, evening hyperphagia, and insomnia. It seemed to be precipitated by life stress and to predict the failure of attempts at weight reduction.

A recurring complaint of night eaters was an inability to stop eating once they had started. They rarely spoke of being hungry. Instead, again and again they described how difficult it was to stop eating as long as food were available. Yet if night eaters had no access to food, they rarely developed a strong desire to eat or made any great effort to obtain food. Even when agitated and overeating, it was uncommon for them to leave the house to buy more food.

The heady experience of being able to match a clinical syndrome with clearly specified neural deficits whetted my appetite for more. If there were a clinical analogue of overeating due to failed satiety, might there not also be a clinical analogue of overeating due to an increased hunger? I had begun to ponder this question when a patient strode into my office and described his overeating in precisely this manner.

I will briefly describe this patient to highlight the clinical features of binge eating and to complement the more quantitative aspects of the disorder reviewed in this volume.

A CASE REPORT

Hyman Cohen was a 37-year-old high school teacher referred to me by a mutual friend who told me that Mr. Cohen was a ''compulsive eater'' and described his eating as if it might well be due to an increased hunger drive.

Mr. Cohen had been overweight since childhood and, when I first saw him, weighed 272 lb and was 5 ft 9 in tall. He asked for help in losing weight in order to qualify for the position as principal at the school where he taught.

He assured me that he had no psychological problems and needed help only to control his weight. ''The problem is my obesity and what the hell I am going to do about it. It's completely out of control, I've gained nearly 60 pounds in the last year and I'm eating all the time now.'' He said that since making the appointment to see me, ''I've had this crazy idea. . .Dr. Stunkard is going to take care of me. So I can do anything I want to, because when I get to him everything will be all right.''

I asked how he thought I could help.

''Well, as I see it,'' he began, ''it's all just a matter of will power. I can start a diet any time I want to. And I can lose a hell of a lot of weight when I'm on one. But right now my will power just doesn't seem to be up to it. That's where you come in. It's like hiring a policeman to check on me. If I am going to have to face the scales each week, I'm simply going to have to stop eating so much. It's as simple as that.''

He continued, ''My guilt drives me here, but why do I feel so guilty? Why is it so out of proportion to what I have done? It's not that terrible to overeat and yet I feel it is.''

I asked him if he had any idea why it seemed so terrible. ''I just don't know. I just don't have any idea. It's just that this eating has become an obsession with me. I think about it all the time. It's the first thing I think of when I wake up in the morning and it's the last thing I think of when I go to bed at night.''

I saw Mr. Cohen in psychotherapy once a week and at first could discern no pattern in his eating, which continued in a chaotic manner throughout the day. Almost any kind of frustration, or achievement, could trigger his eating. Nevertheless, he began to feel better, the intense pressure to eat slackened, and, without any special effort, he began to lose weight. Then, 6 weeks after he entered treatment, he described a critical event.

Our appointment began with a long pause. Then Mr. Cohen said, ''I suppose you noticed the weight gain.''

I nodded. His weight, which had fallen to 262 lb in the previous weeks, was back to 272 lb.

After another long pause Mr. Cohen took a deep breath and said, ''Well, I have to begin some time.''

''The day after New Year's day I got my check cashed. I usually eat to celebrate the occasion, so I knew it might happen. On the way to the bank I steeled myself against it. I kept reminding myself of the treatment and about my New Year's resolution about dieting and about having to face you and the scales.''

''Then I got the check cashed. And I kept out a hundred. And everything just seemed to go blank. I don't know what it was. All of my good intentions just seemed to fade away. They just didn't seem to mean anything anymore. I just said, 'What the hell,' and started eating, and what I did then was an absolute sin.''

He described starting in a grocery store where he bought a cake, several pieces of pie, and boxes of cookies. Then he drove through heavy midtown traffic with one hand, pulling food out of the bag with the other hand and eating as fast as he could.

After consuming all of his groceries, he set out on a furtive round of restaurants, staying only a short time in each and eating only small amounts. Although in constant dread of discovery, he had no idea what ''sin'' he felt he was committing. He knew only that it was not pleasurable. ''I didn't enjoy it at all. It just happened. It's like a part of me just blacked out. And when that happened there was nothing there except the food and me, all alone.''

Finally, he went into a delicatessen, bought another $20 worth of food and drove home, eating all the way, ''until my gut ached.''

Mr. Cohen sat looking ahead, a deep frown wrinkling his forehead. ''And that's the whole truth, your honor.''

Once we had identified this pattern of eating, we found that it occurred frequently. Few ''binges'' were as dramatic as this curtain raiser, but once having identified the pattern, it was not difficult to recognize it when it recurred, which it did with disconcerting frequency.

Hyman Cohen not only introduced me to this pattern of eating, but also gave it a name—''binge eating,'' based on its similarity to alcoholic binges. Since then the term has achieved wide currency, and Beglin and Fairburn (1992) have recently assessed the meanings that it has acquired in their paper ''What Is Meant by the Term 'Binge'?'' In view of recent interest in vomiting and other ''inappropriate compensatory behaviors'' to prevent weight gain, it should be noted that Hyman Cohen occasionally vomited. This vomiting, however, was performed to relieve abdominal pain, not to prevent weight gain.

BINGE EATING AND BULIMIA

I described Hyman Cohen and the ''binge-eating syndrome'' in a brief report in 1959 (Stunkard, 1959), amplified the descriptions of binge eaters in 1976 (Stunkard, 1976), and the following year published with colleagues a paper on the binge-eating syndrome and its treatment with the anticonvulsant phenytoin (Wermuth, Davis, Hollister, & Stunkard, 1977). For this study we developed the following criteria for the binge-eating syndrome:

1. Impulsive, episodic, uncontrolled, and rapid ingestion of large quantities of food over a relatively short period of time.
2. Termination of the episode only when a point of physical discomfort has been reached (e.g., abdominal pain and feelings of nausea or distention). Self-induced vomiting supports but is not required for the diagnosis.
3. Subsequent feelings of guilt, remorse, or self-contempt.

The 1977 paper described a modest reduction in the frequency of binge eating. Three years later, in 1980, the third edition of the *Diagnostic and Statistical Manual of Mental Disorders* (DSM-III) of the American Psychiatric Association (1980) adopted these criteria with minor changes and a new name for the disorder—''bulimia.''

The major features of "bulimia" noted in DSM-III were binge eating (the rapid consumption of a large amount of food in a discrete period of time), associated with a fear of loss of control and followed by self-deprecating thoughts. This meaning of bulimia was not inconsistent with the traditional use of the term.

Seven years later, this picture had changed radically. In the revision of DSM-III, DSM-III-R, published in 1987 (APA, 1987), a new diagnosis, "bulimia nervosa," supplanted the earlier diagnosis of "bulimia." Bulimia now came to mean primarily binge-eating that was followed by "purging," usually vomiting, and, in the popular press, bulimia even began to mean the vomiting itself. The restrictiveness of this diagnosis has led to attempts to free binge eating from a necessary connection with subsequent vomiting, and it is true that the diagnosis of bulimia nervosa may include binge eating that is not followed by vomiting. The diagnosis of bulimia nervosa does, however, require that the bingeing be associated with some form of what has come to be called "inappropriate compensatory behavior to prevent weight gain" (letter of July 15, 1992, from B. T. Walsh on behalf of the Eating Disorders Workgroup of the APA). There remained no provision for binge eating that was not followed by such "compensatory behavior." How did this radical change come about?

A DIGRESSION ON BODY SHAPE

The origins of this change in nosology may lie in the development of the valuation of thinness for women and in the dieting and purging utilized to realize it.

Bell (1985) has traced the origins of anorexia nervosa to the extreme fasting practices of medieval (primarily female) saints. Three other authors, however, have argued persuasively that the determinants and manifestations of this fasting, undertaken for religious purposes in medieval times, differ significantly from those of contemporary anorexia nervosa (Brumberg, 1988; Bynum, 1986; Habermas, 1989). Clearly there are similarities between these early "fasting girls" and modern anorexics in the tenacity of their food restriction and in their social status, as members of the well-to-do classes. However, the historical context of these early fasters, particularly their goal of union with the divine, as well as their lessened physical activity, sets them apart from modern anorexics.

Instead of a centuries-long history, there is reason to believe that anorexia nervosa is a new, socially conditioned disorder that first made its appearance in the late 1800s. This position is cogently argued in Brumberg's (1988) scholarly volume on "Fasting Girls: The Emergence of Anorexia Nervosa as a Modern Disease." This argument finds strong support in Heisshunger (voracious appetite) by Habermas (1990), who further considers bulimia nervosa to be an even more recent disorder, dating to the early 1900s. He proposes that both disorders arose in the context of changing societal attitudes toward obesity that were initiated by medical concerns that then became popular beliefs. He describes three key contributions that, over the span of a century, led to the change in attitudes toward obesity—from approbation to concern to societal derogation.

In 1825, Brillat-Savarin (1971) lauded lesser degrees of overweight, even contending that they promoted a longer and happier life. But he was among the first to express concern over the possible dangers of severe obesity. In 1864, Banting (1864) published his letter "Letter on Corpulence," which, according to Habermas (1990), "fell like a bomb in a box of gunpowder." Suddenly, degrees of overweight that had been fully acceptable fell out of favor and weight reduction achieved unprecedented popularity. Soon after the appearance of Banting's treatise, clients were greeted at spas with the question as to whether they dieted, phrased as "Do you Bant?" Mitchell's (1877) popular book on *Blood and Fat* helped to bring these preoccupations to North America. The final contribution was Heckel's (1911) volume on *Les Grandes et les Petites Obésites* that extended medical concerns to even small degrees of overweight. The full impact of social derogation of obesity lagged behind the medical strictures, not appearing until after World War II. But the stage was set for the popular response to the derogation of obesity.

THE APPEARANCE OF ANOREXIA NERVOSA

Habermas (1989) proposes that the first manifestations of pathological responses to social derogation of obesity were the cases of anorexia nervosa described by Lasègue (1873) and Gull (1874). The patients described independently by these authors appear to have manifested anorexia nervosa of the restricting (or nonbulimic) type.

According to Habermas (1989), Charcot was the first to recognize the concerns about body image and the relentless pursuit of thinness in anorexia nervosa. During his examination of an anorexic patient, he discovered a pink ribbon around her waist that she explained as a warning against weight gain, stating, "I prefer dying of hunger to becoming as fat as mama." Charcot's prestige in French medicine led other French physicians, including the influential Janet (1903), to search for (and find) the pursuit of thinness in their anorexic patients, while physicians in other countries failed to look.

For many years descriptions of anorexia nervosa were confined to individual case histories of a disorder that was considered sufficiently rare to warrant reporting. Some of these histories were extensive, such as that of Janet's Nadia in 1903 and a 60-page account by Schnyder in 1912, recently reported by Habermas (1989).

Despite the excellence of occasional case reports, there remained for many years considerable confusion regarding the nature of anorexia nervosa. Simmonds's (1914) report of a lesion in the pituitary gland of an emaciated woman attracted widespread attention and aroused interest in an endocrine basis for weight loss by young women. This interest persisted into the 1940s, delaying clear specification of anorexia nervosa. Another problem was the tendency by other authors to attribute any weight loss of psychological origin to anorexia nervosa. This practice was well exemplified in the 1960 volume on *Anorexia Nervosa* by Bliss and Branch (1960), who considered anorexia nervosa to be any weight loss of at least 25 lb for which an organic basis could not be established.

It was not until the 1960s that a consensus regarding the main features of anorexia nervosa was reached. But this consensus fostered by three leaders in the field, Crisp (1965), Russell (1970), and Bruch (1970, 1973) has persisted to the present time. These authors agreed that the essential feature of anorexia nervosa was a fear of being fat and a resulting "relentless pursuit of thinness." Those features were included in the criteria for anorexia nervosa in DSM-III, and unlike the situation with "bulimia," the diagnosis was retained in DSM-III-R with essentially the same criteria:

> Intense fear of becoming obese
> Disturbance of the body image, e.g., claiming to "feel fat" even when emaciated
> Significant weight loss

BINGEING AND PURGING AMONG PATIENTS WITH ANOREXIA NERVOSA

Some time during the period before World War II, and particularly afterward, anorexia nervosa began to be complicated by distinctive new behaviors—bingeing and purging (usually vomiting).

In 1874, Gull (1874) had mentioned "an occasional voracious appetite" in one of his anorexic patients, and in hindsight it seems possible that the patient also vomited to maintain her lowered body weight. Neither bingeing nor vomiting was, however, reported in the case histories of anorexia nervosa patients until the late 1930s. In 1939, Berkman described binge eating by patients with anorexia nervosa, but it was several years before other such reports appeared. The first description of a series of anorexic patients who binged and vomited appears to have been that of Crisp (1967), who reported binge eating and vomiting in 18% of the anorexic patients. This report was followed by those of Theander (1970) (16%), Bruch (1973) (25%), Casper, Eckert, Halmi, Goldberg, and Davis (1980) (43%), and Garfinkel, Moldofsky, and Garner (1980) (48%).

Findings in the papers by Casper et al. (1980) and Garfinkel et al. (1980) led to the proposal to subtype anorexia nervosa on the basis of the presence or absence of bingeing. Slightly earlier, in 1976, Beumont, Gerye, and Smart (1976) had proposed subtyping anorexia nervosa on the basis of the presence or absence of purging. These two subclassifications have been continued to the present and will be recognized in DSM-IV; anorexia nervosa will be subdivided into a binge-eating/purging type and a restricting type (APA, 1993).* This recognition will be important, for major demographic and psychopathological differences have been discovered between restricting anorexics and those who binge or purge, even though it is not clear whether the bingeing or purging is the more critical behavior (see Garner, Chapter 4, this volume). It is clear that, following World War II, an essentially new syndrome—binge-eating/purging anorexia nervosa—was born. It has rapidly achieved widespread recognition, not the least in the lay press.

BINGEING AND PURGING AMONG PERSONS OF NORMAL WEIGHT—BULIMIA NERVOSA

The recognition accorded to vomiting as a method of weight control in a weight-preoccupied society meant that it would not long be confined to patients with anorexia nervosa. By the early 1970s it was widely practiced by women at prestigious colleges, and I was told at that time by a student that one-fourth of the normal-weight women in her dormitory vomited in an effort to control their weight.

Did bingeing and vomiting occur in persons of normal weight before the 1970s? It seems likely: Briquet (1859) and Abraham (1916) may have described such behaviors, and Wulff (1932) certainly did (Stunkard, 1990). His long paper provided clear and detailed descriptions of normal-weight women who binged and purged. There followed the extensive case re-

---

*The DSM-IV criteria cited in this volume are those that were approved as final by the DSM-IV Eating Disorders Work Group and the Task Force on DSM-IV (APA, 1993). These criteria may be subject to minor editorial revisions before the publication of DSM-IV.

ports of Ellen West by Binswanger (1944) and of Laura by Lindner (1955).

The current era was introduced by the description of Boskind-Lodahl and White (1973) of "bulimarexia"—bingeing and vomiting by persons of normal weight. It was, however, Russell's (1979) landmark paper on "bulimia nervosa" that firmly established this diagnosis. In this paper, Russell described 30 patients of normal weight who, in addition to a fear of becoming fat, binged and purged. Although a majority of these patients had suffered from anorexia nervosa in the past, Russell saw their disorder as "an ominous variant of anorexia nervosa," citing two reasons for this distinction: The patients were of normal weight at the time that they presented for treatment, and they appeared more difficult to treat.

Russell's proposal of the diagnosis of bulimia nervosa was soon followed by attempts to determine the prevalence of this heretofore largely unrecognized disorder. These attempts confirmed that such a disorder did, indeed, exist and early reports suggested that it was relatively common among young women. By 1990, 51 such studies had been reported and a more realistic estimate was possible. In their review Fairburn and Beglin (1990) noted that the more rigorous the study, the lower the prevalence and that the prevalence in these studies was low. Thus, in the four studies in which interviews supplemented self-report questionnaires, even among the college women who are at increased risk of the disorder, the average prevalence was no more than 0.9%. The report by Schotte and Stunkard (1987) is representative of these studies and throws light on the striking difference in the relative frequency of binge eating and vomiting among female college students.

Figure 2.1 shows that, among women, 45% reported bingeing at least once a month; only 3% reported vomiting this often. The distribution depicted in this figure shows an inflection point for both bingeing and vomiting between one and two times per month, with a dramatic fall in the percentages of women who binged and vomited more than once a month. Thus, although a high percentage of women in this high-risk population reported bingeing on an infrequent basis, far fewer vomited this often and very few (0.9%) met the DSM-III criteria for bulimia or the DSM-III-R criteria for bulimia nervosa (1.3%).

Despite this low prevalence, bulimia nervosa was accepted with remarkable rapidity and in 1987 it entered DSM-III-R (APA, 1987) as a formal diagnosis. As we have noted above, the effect on the nosology of eating disorders was dramatic: Bulimia nervosa quickly supplanted the earlier diagnosis of bulimia, leaving no diagnosis for binge eaters who did not also engage in "inappropriate compensatory behaviors," particularly vomiting and laxative abuse. Two eating disorders were now recognized—anorexia nervosa and bulimia nervosa. The resulting nosology had at least three problems:

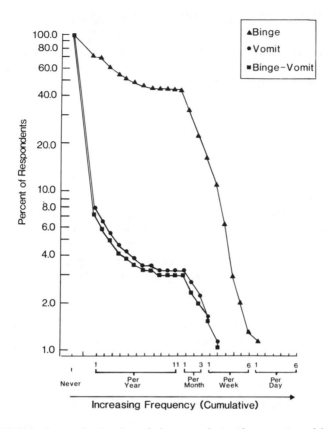

FIGURE 2.1. Logarithmic plot of the cumulative frequencies of binges (triangles), vomiting (circles), and binge-vomit (squares) of female university students. From "Bulimia vs. Bulimic Behaviors on a College Campus" by D. E. Schotte and A. J. Stunkard, 1987, *Journal of the American Medical Association*, *258*, p. 1213. Copyright 1987 by the American Medical Association. Reprinted by permission.

1. A distinction between two behavioral disorders—anorexia nervosa (binge-eating/purging type and bulimia nervosa) based, not on behavioral criteria, but primarily on body weight (Fairburn & Garner, 1986).
2. Strikingly dissimilar behaviors between patients with the same diagnosis. Anorexic patients of the binge-eating/purging type differ significantly from those of the restricting type (see Garner, Chapter 4, this volume).
3. No diagnosis for the large number of primarily obese binge eaters who do not also manifest "inappropriate compensatory behavior."

BINGE EATING AMONG OBESE PERSONS

This chapter is concerned with the third of these problems—persons who binge eat without "compensatory behaviors." The prevalence of such persons is probably high, yet many if not most are excluded from a formal diagnosis. At least four solutions to this problem have been proposed.

The first solution was the effort, notably by Fairburn and Garner (1986), to maintain the diagnosis of bulimia for binge eaters who did not purge. The second effort was that of the Stanford group, which explicitly described "non-purging bulimics" (McCann & Agras, 1990; Telch, Agras, Rossiter, Wilfley, & Kenardy, 1990). A third effort has been to refer to them as "binge-eating obese" persons, on the reasonable assumption that obese persons do not purge (or at least do not purge enough to control their obesity) (Loro & Orleans, 1981; Marcus & Wing, 1988; Marcus et al., 1990). Although these efforts made it possible to diagnose binge eating that was not followed by purging, there remained the requirement that the binge eating be followed by at least some form of "compensatory behavior" if bulimia nervosa were to be diagnosed. In recognition of the large number of (primarily) obese persons who binge eat without such "compensatory behavior" the fourth and most ambitious, effort has been the proposal of a new diagnosis—"binge eating disorder" (Spitzer et al., 1992).

BINGE EATING DISORDER

A group of investigators with experience in the eating disorders has recently developed criteria for this diagnosis that is designed to describe "the many individuals who have problems with recurrent binge-eating, but who do not engage in the compensatory behaviors of bulimia nervosa, vomiting or the use of laxatives" (Spitzer et al., 1992). These criteria are specified in Chapter 1. They consist of:

> Binge eating, which includes both the ingestion of a large amount of food in a short period of time and a sense of loss of control during the binge
> Distress regarding the binge
> Three of five items that include rapid eating, eating until uncomfortably full, and feeling depressed and/or guilty after bingeing

These criteria were refined with the help of a multisite field trial involving 1,984 primarily obese persons. This trial indicated that the diagnosis of binge eating disorder can be made with high reliability and that it is particularly common (30%) among persons attending hospital-affiliated weight control programs.

A number of studies have revealed distinguishing characteristics of obese binge eaters (see Marcus, Chapter 5, this volume). Thus, binge-eating obese persons manifest a far higher prevalence of psychopathology than do obese persons who do not binge (Black, Goldstein, & Mason, 1992; Marcus & Wing, 1988; Marcus et al., 1990). Binge eating increases with increasing adiposity (Telch, Agras, & Rossiter, 1988), and the eating style of binge eaters in the laboratory differs markedly from that of comparably obese non-binge-eaters. An important feature of this disorder is its relationship to the treatment of the large number of obese persons who seek weight reduction programs. At least one study has found that binge eaters drop out of weight control programs and regain their lost weight more rapidly than do comparably obese non-binge-eaters (Marcus & Wing, 1988).

These many distinctive features led to the proposal that binge eating disorder be included as a formal diagnosis in DSM-IV. (This proposal was rejected on the grounds that there were not sufficient data to support the addition of this new diagnostic category. See Fairburn & Wilson, Chapter 1, this volume.) In favor of the inclusion of binge eating disorder was the argument that the diagnosis would recognize a large and distinct group of persons with special problems in treatment. At the present time these patients must be diagnosed as EDNOS—eating disorder not otherwise specified. The arguments against inclusion, articulated by Fairburn, Welch, and Hay (1993) were twofold: Not enough was known about those who binge eat across the weight spectrum, and a formal diagnosis at this stage might hinder further understanding. Regarding the first argument, it is hard to know how much is enough to qualify as a diagnosis and considerably more is already known about binge eating than was known about bulimia nervosa when it was included in DSM-III-R. The complications of including bulimia nervosa as a formal diagnosis in DSM-III-R, which we have noted, may be sufficient to recommend caution before introducing another new diagnosis. The second argument is a caution about attempts to categorize what may be essentially a dimensional construct. The cutting points necessary to convert a dimension into a category may unnecessarily restrict the study of the phenomenon, excluding cases that fail to meet imperfectly designed criteria, and including inappropriate ones that do.

Whatever the eventual outcome of the debate about including binge eating disorder in the next edition of the *Diagnostic and Statistical Manual of Mental Disorders*, there is no doubt that binge eating will be increasingly recognized as a clinical problem and will be the object of ever more research. The present volume represents a major step in this direction.

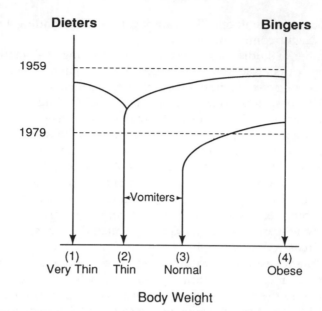

FIGURE 2.2. Origins of four eating patterns differentiated by extent of body weight: (1) anorexia nervosa, restrictor type (or nonbulimic type), (2) anorexia nervosa, bulimic type, (3) bulimia nervosa, (4) "binge eating disorder." Patterns 2 and 3, which involve the introduction of purging in weight control, appear to be of relatively recent origin.

SUMMARY AND CONCLUSIONS

Figure 2.2 depicts a summary of the history of binge eating and of the disorders associated with it. The pattern with the deepest historical roots is that of binge eating, which may go back more than 2 millennia. The second oldest pattern is the uninterrupted dieting that characterizes the restricting type of anorexia nervosa, which has probably existed for more than a century. It appears that these two patterns were the only ones present in 1959 when new descriptions confirmed the status of binge eating (Stunkard, 1959). Bingeing and purging were first reported soon after this time in patients with anorexia nervosa and in persons of normal weight (bulimia nervosa).

The result has been the construction of four disorders, extending from the very thin to the very fat. Arrows labeled 1, 2, and 3 refer to the anorexia nervosa of the restricting and bulimic types and to bulimia nervosa. This chapter has been devoted to the fourth disorder, binge eating, its long history, and its current uncertain diagnostic status.

REFERENCES

Abraham, K. (1916). Untersuchungen ¼uber die fr¼uheste pr¼agenitale Entwicklungsstufe der Libido. In K. Abraham (Ed.), *Psychoanalytische Studien II* (pp. 84-112). Frankfurt: Fischer.

American Psychiatric Association. (1980). *Diagnostic and statistical manual of mental disorders* (3rd ed.). Washington, DC: Author

American Psychiatric Association. (1987). *Diagnostic and statistical manual of mental disorders* (3rd ed. rev.). Washington, DC: Author

American Psychiatric Association. (1993). *DSM-IV draft criteria (3/1/93)*. Washington, DC: Author.

Banting, W. (1864). *Letter on corpulence* (3rd ed.). London: Harrison.

Beglin, S. J., & Fairburn, C. G. (1992). What is meant by the term "binge"? *American Journal of Psychiatry, 149,* 123-124.

Bell, R. (1985). *Holy anorexia.* Chicago: University of Chicago Press.

Beumont, P. J. V. (1991). The history of eating and dieting disorders. *Clinical and Applied Nutrition, 1,* 9-20.

Beumont, P. J. V, Gerye, G. C. W, & Smart, D. E. (1976). Dieters and bingers and purgers in anorexia nervosa. *Psychological Medicine, 6,* 617-622.

Binswanger, L. Der Fall Ellen West. (Ed.). (1944). *Schizophrenie.* Pfuhlingen: Neske.

Blachez, P. F. (1867). Boulimie. *Dictionnaire Encyclopedique des sciences medicales* (vol. 10, pp. 318-325). Paris: Victor Masson et fil.

Black, D. W., Goldstein, R. B., & Mason, E. E. (1992). Prevalence of mental disorder in 88 morbidly obese geriatric clinic patients. *American Journal of Psychiatry, 149,* 227-234.

Bliss, E. L, & Branch, C. H. H. (1960). *Anorexia nervosa: Its history psychology and biology.* New York: Paul Hoeber.

Boskind-Lodahl, M., & White W. C. (1973). The definition and treatment of bulimarexia in college women—a pilot study. *Journal of the American Health Association, 27,* 84-97.

Bouveret, L. (1893). *Traite des maladies de l'estomac.* Paris: Bailliere.

Bray, G. A, & Gallagher, T. F. (1975). Manifestations of hypothalamic obesity in man: A comprehensive investigation of 8 patients and a review of the literature. *Medicine, 54,* 301-330.

Brillat-Savarin, J. A. (1971). *The physiology of taste or meditations on transcendental gastronomy* (trans., M. F. K. Fisher). New York.

Briquet, P. (1859). *Traite de clinique et therapeut de l'hysterie.* Paris: Bailliere.

Bruch, H. (1970). The psychiatric differential diagnosis of anorexia nervosa. In J. E. Meyer & H. Feldman (Eds.), *Anorexia nervosa* (pp. 70-87). Stuttgart: Geroge Thieine Verlag.

Bruch, H. (1973). *Eating disorders: Obesity and anorexia nervosa and the person within.* New York: Basic Books.

Brumberg, J. J. (1988). *Fasting girls: The emergence of anorexia nervosa as a modern disease.* Cambridge, MA: Harvard University Press.

Bynum, C. W. (1986). *Holy feast and holy fast: The religious significance of food to medieval women.* Berkeley: University of California Press.

Casper, R. C. (1983). On the emergence of bulimia nervosa as a syndrome. *International Journal of Eating Disorders, 2,* 3–16.

Casper, R. C., Eckert, E. D., Halmi, K., Goldberg, S. G., & Davis, J. M. (1980). Bulimia: Its incidence and clinical importance in patients with anorexia nervosa. *Archives of General Psychiatry, 37,* 1030–1035.

Crisp, A. H. (1965). Some aspects of the evolution, presentation and follow-up of anorexia nervosa. *Proceedings of the Royal Society of Medicine, 58,* 814–820.

Crisp, A. H. (1967). The possible significance of some behavioral correlates of weight and carbohydrate intake. *Journal of Psychosomatic Research, 11,* 117–131.

Critchley, M. (1962). Periodic hypersomnia and megaphagia in adolescent males. *Brain, 85,* 627– 656.

Descuret, M. (1833). Case of extraordinary congenital bulimia. *Medical Chirurgical Review and Journal of Practical Medicine, 19,* 206–207.

Fairburn, C. G, & Beglin, S. J. (1990). Studies of the epidemiology of bulimia nervosa. *American Journal of Psychiatry, 147,* 401–408.

Fairburn, C. G., & Garner, D. M. (1986). The diagnosis of bulimia nervosa. *International Journal of Eating Disorders, 5,* 403–420.

Fairburn, C. G., Welch, S. L., & Hay, P. J. (1993). The classification of recurrent overeating: The "binge-eating disorder" proposal. *International Journal of Eating Disorders, 13,* 155–160.

Garfinkel, P. E., Moldofsky, H. U., & Garner, D. M. (1980). The heterogeneity of anorexia nervosa. Bulimia as a distinct subgroup. *Archives of General Psychiatry, 37,* 1036–1040.

Gull, W. W. (1874). Anorexia nervosa. *Transactions of the Clinical Society of London, 7,* 22–28.

Habermas, T. (1989). The psychiatric history of anorexia nervosa and bulimia nervosa: Weight concerns and bulimic symptoms in early case reports. *International Journal of Eating Disorders, 3,* 259–273.

Habermas T. (1990). *Heisshunger: Historische Bedingungen der Bulimia Nervosa.* Frankfurt: Fischer.

Heckel, F. (1911). *Les grandes et les petites obesites: Cure radicale.* Paris: Masson.

Hope, R. A., Fairburn, C. G., & Goodwin, G. M. (1989). Increased eating in dementia. *International Journal of Obesity, 8,* 111–115.

James, R. (1743). *A medical dictionary.* London: T. Osborne.

Janet, P. (1903). *Les obsessions et la psychasthenie.* Paris.

Kluver, H., & Bucy, P. C. (1938). An analysis of certain effects of bilateral temporal lobectomy in the rhesus monkey with special reference to psychic blindness. *Journal of Psychology, 5,* 33–54.

Lasegue, E. C. (1873). De l'anorexie hysterique. *Archives of General Medicine, 21,* 385–403.

Liddell, H. G., & Scott, R. (1972). *Greek and English Lexicon.* Oxford: Clarendon Press.

Lilly, R., Cummings, S. L., Beason, F., & Frankel, M. (1983). The human Kluver-Bucy syndrome. *Neurology, 33,* 1141–1145.

Loro, A. J., & Orleans, C. S. (1981). Binge eating in obesity: Preliminary findings and guidelines. *Addictive Behaviors, 6,* 155–166.

Marcus, M. D., Wing, R. R., Ewing, L., Kern, E., Gooding, W., & McDermott, M. (1990). Psychiatric disorders among obese binge eaters. *International Journal of Eating Disorders, 9,* 69–77.

Marcus, M. D., Wing, R. R., & Hopkins, J. (1988). Obese binge eaters: Affect, cognitions and response to behavioral weight control. *Journal of Consulting and Clinical Psychology, 13,* 433–439.

McCann, U. D., & Agras, W. S. (1990). Successful treatment of nonpurging bulimia nervosa with desipramine: A double-blind, placebo-controlled study. *American Journal of Psychiatry, 147,* 1509–1513.

Mitchell, S. W. (1877). *Blood and fat.* Philadelphia: J. B. Lippincott.

Morris, C. H., Hope, R. A., & Fairburn, C. G. (1989). Eating habits in dementia: A descriptive study. *British Journal of Psychiatry 154,* 801–806.

Motherby, G. (1785). *A new medical dictionary: Or a general respiratory of physic.* London: J. Johnson & J. Robinson.

Osler, W. (1892). *Principles and practice of medicine.* Philadelphia: Williams & Wilkins.

Reeves, A. G., & Plum, F. (1969). Hyperphagia, rage and dementia accompanying a ventromedial hypothalamic neoplasm. *Archives Neurology, 20,* 616–624.

Russell, G. F. M. (1970). Anorexia nervosa: Its identity as an illness and its treatment. In J. H. Price (Ed.), *Modern trends in psychological medicine.* London: Butterworths.

Russell, G. F. M. (1979). Bulimia nervosa: An ominous variant of anorexia nervosa. *Psychological Medicine. 9,* 429–448,

Schotte, D. E., & Stunkard, A. J. (1987). Bulimia vs. bulimic behaviors on a college campus. *Journal of American Medical Association, 258,* 1213–1215.

Simmonds, M. (1914). Uber embolische Porogesse en der Hypophyses. *Archif der Pathologichen Anatomie, 217,* 226–239.

Soltmann, O. (1894). Anorexia cerebralis und zentrale Nutritionsneurose. *Jahrbuch der Kinderheilkunde, 38,* 1–13.

Spitzer, R. L., Devlin, M., Walsh, B. T., Hasin, D., Wing, R. R., Marcus, M., Stunkard, A. J., Wadden, T. A., Yanovski, S. Z., Agras, W. S., Mitchell, J., & Nonas, C. (1992). Binge eating disorder: A multisite field trial of the diagnostic criteria. *International Journal of Eating Disorders, 3,* 191–203.

Stein, D. M., & Laakso, W. (1988). Bulimia: A historical perspective. *International Journal of Eating Disorders, 7,* 201–210.

Stunkard, A. J. (1959). Eating patterns and obesity. *Psychiatry Quarterly, 33,* 284–295.

Stunkard, A. J. (1976). *The pain of obesity.* Palo Alto, CA: Bull Publishing Co.

Stunkard, A. J. (1990). A description of eating disorders in 1932. *American Journal of Psychiatry, 147,* 263–268.

Stunkard, A. J., Grace, W. J., & Wolff, H. G. (1955). The night-eating syndrome. A pattern of food intake among certain obese patients. *American Journal of Medicine, 19,* 78–86.

Telch, C. F., Agras, W. S., & Rossiter, E. M. (1988). Binge eating increases with increasing adiposity. *International Journal of Eating Disorders, 7,* 115–119.

Telch, C. F., Agras, W. S., Rossiter, E. M., Wilfley, D., & Kenardy, J. (1990). Group cognitive-behavioral treatment for the nonpurging bulimic: An initial evaluation. *Journal of Consulting and Clinical Psychology, 58,* 629–635.

Theander, S. (1970). Anorexia nervosa: A psychiatric investigation of 94 female patients. *Acta Psychiatrica Scandanavica, 214* (suppl.), 1–194.

Vogel, S. G. (1981). *De polyphago et lithophago Ilfeldae nuper mortuo ac dissecto commentatio historicomedia. Dissertation Gottingen 1771. Historischmedizinische Abhandlung von dem zu Ilfeld versstorbenen und geoffretes Vielfrass und Steinfresser, nebst beigefugten Protokoll und Sektionsberichtes. [Medical-historical contribution on the polyphagic and stone-eating person who died and was dissected at Ilfeld together with the associated protocol and report].* Berlin.

Wermuth, B. M., Davis, K. L., Hollister, L. E., & Stunkard, A. J. (1977). Phenytoin treatment of the binge eating syndrome. *American Journal of Psychiatry, 11,* 1249–1253.

Wulff, M. (1932). Uber einen interessanten oralen Symptomenkomplex und seine Beziehung zur Sucht. *Internationale Zeitshuft fur Psychoanalyse. 18,* 281–302.

Ziolko, H. U., & Schrader, H. C. (1985). Bulimie. *Fortschritte de Neurolojie und Psychiatrie, 53,* 231–258.

CLINICAL CHARACTERISTICS

Binge Eating in Bulimia Nervosa

B. Timothy Walsh

In his landmark paper describing the syndrome of bulimia nervosa, Russell (1979) stated, "Episodes of overeating constitute the most constant feature of the disorder." Thus, overeating was identified as the salient behavioral characteristic of bulimia nervosa. This emphasis on the critical importance of overeating has been followed by the third edition and third revised edition of the American Psychiatric Association's *Diagnostic and Statistical Manual of Mental Disorders* (DSM-III and DSM-III-R), both editions of which required as the first criterion of the diagnosis "recurrent episodes of binge eating (rapid consumption of a large amount of food in a discrete period of time)." DSM-IV is also committed to follow this tradition (American Psychiatric Association, 1993; see Fairburn & Wilson, Chapter 1, this volume). In the DSM-IV criteria for bulimia nervosa, an episode of binge eating is defined on the basis of two criteria:[*]

1. Eating, in a discrete period of time (e.g., within any 2-hour period), an amount of food that is definitely larger than most people would eat during a similar period of time in similar circumstances
2. A sense of lack of control over eating during the episode (e.g., a feeling that one cannot stop eating or control what or how much one is eating)

But what *are* these episodes of overeating? Do such episodes in fact differ from the normal meals of individuals without eating disorders? Do they differ from the occasional overeating of normal individuals? Do

[*]The DSM-IV criteria in this volume are those that were approved as final by the DSM-IV Eating Disorders Work Group and the Task Force on DSM-IV (APA, 1993). These criteria may be subject to minor editorial revisions before the publication of DSM-IV.

patients with bulimia nervosa select specific types of foods during episodes of binge eating? And is the macronutrient composition of the foods consumed during such episodes (i.e., the fraction of calories derived from protein, fat, and carbohydrate) unusual?

This chapter reviews studies that have attempted to address these questions. It shows that the eating behavior of patients with bulimia nervosa has clearly been documented to be abnormal. However, there appears to be substantial overlap between the eating behavior of patients with bulimia nervosa and that of normal individuals. For example, individuals with bulimia nervosa may describe episodes of binge eating that are not objectively different from meals consumed by normal controls, emphasizing the potential importance of distinguishing "objective" from "subjective" bulimic episodes.

In describing the results of studies that have attempted to characterize the eating behavior of patients with bulimia, this chapter describes and uses the definitions adopted by the individual research reports. At the conclusion of this chapter, I return to the question how the eating of individuals with bulimia nervosa is best described in the terms outlined by Fairburn and Wilson (Chapter 1, this volume).

PATIENTS' DESCRIPTIONS OF BINGE EATING

The first reports of binge eating in bulimia nervosa were based on the descriptions provided by patients during clinical assessments. Russell (1979) noted that the "the amounts of food consumed at one sitting could be extraordinarily large," and cited one patient's estimate that she frequently consumed 15,000–20,000 calories in a sitting. Russell also emphasized that patients tend to ingest fattening, carbohydrate-rich foods when binge eating, and tend to abstain from carbohydrate-rich foods when not binge eating.

Mitchell, Pyle, and Eckert (1981) asked 25 outpatients meeting DSM-III criteria for bulimia to report what they consumed during a typical binge-eating episode. The average size was 3,415 kcal, with a range between 1,200 and 11,500 kcal. As was to be documented more rigorously in later studies, Mitchell et al. noted that "a few patients considered a binge-eating episode to be what others might call a large meal."

These initial descriptions were followed by attempts to characterize the patients' eating behavior by requesting them to keep diaries of their food intake.

In one of the first studies using patient diaries, Abraham and Beumont (1982) published information obtained from 32 subjects who presented to an eating disorders clinic complaining of episodes of overeating. In their attempt to characterize binge eating, the investigators did not require that the subjects meet any other criteria. Therefore, while it is probable that most of the participants met criteria for bulimia nervosa, this study probably also includes data from individuals with other eating problems. The patients reported that on a "bad day" of binge eating, they consumed between 3 and 27 times the recommended daily energy allowance of approximately 2,000 kcal. While all patients were requested to provide a record of food eaten during a binge, only ten did so, and no details of the information in these diaries were presented. However, the authors did note that, contrary to the patients' impression that binges had a high carbohydrate content, the records indicated that the binges were just as likely to contain excessive amounts of fat or protein.

In 1986, Rosen, Leitenberg, Fisher, and Khazam (1986) presented a detailed analysis of the eating behavior of 20 patients with bulimia nervosa using data obtained from diaries. All patients met the criteria proposed by Russell for bulimia nervosa, and, in addition, reported binge eating and vomiting a minimum of three times per week. The patients were asked to keep a diary of all food intake for 2 weeks. After the first week, they met with an investigator who reviewed the records and provided additional instructions to improve accuracy. Only data from the second week were analyzed. Patients were not provided with any definition of a binge, so that the data presented reflect the patients' own judgments on what constituted an episode of binge eating.

Data were obtained on 199 binge-eating and 440 non-binge-eating episodes (see Figure 3.1). The average binge contained 1,459 ± 1,172 kcal. However, the range of the calorie content of binge episodes was enormous, with a low of only 45 kcal and a high of 5,138 kilocalories. While 27% of the episodes considered by patients to be binges contained more than 2,000 kcal, 50% contained less than 1,100 kcal and one-third contained less than 600 kcal. The average non-binge-eating episode contained 321 ± 260 kcal with a range of 10 to 1,652 kcal. There was a substantial overlap between the sizes of the binge and the non-binge-eating episodes, so that 65% of the binge-eating episodes fell within the range of the non-binge-eating episodes.

In an attempt to determine what differentiated lower calorie binge episodes from non-binge eating, the authors contrasted non-binge-eating episodes with binge-eating episodes containing 1,652 or fewer kilocalories. They found that in the binge episodes more of the calories were obtained from snack and dessert foods and fewer from fruits and vegetables.

This study has two major findings. First, it provides documentation that during many binge episodes patients with bulimia nervosa do, indeed, consume large amounts of food. However, it also indicates that patients' views of what constitutes a binge episode are strongly influenced

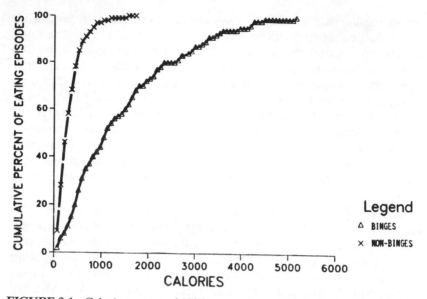

FIGURE 3.1. Caloric content of 199 binge-eating and 440 non-binge-eating episodes. Caloric content was calculated from eating diaries of 20 patients. From "Binge-Eating Episodes in Bulimia Nervosa: The Amount and Type of Food Consumed" by J. C. Rosen, H. Leitenberg, D. Fisher, and C. Khazam, 1986, *International Journal of Eating Disorders, 5,* p. 262. Copyright 1986 by John Wiley & Sons, Inc. Reprinted by permission.

by factors other than the caloric content of the meals, such as whether the foods consumed are viewed as "forbidden."

Woell, Fichter, Pirke, and Wolfram (1989) presented information obtained from 30 women with bulimia. Although the title of this report implies that the patients had bulimia nervosa, explicit diagnostic criteria were not provided. Similarly, although it was indicated that "patients self-monitored their eating by a 24-hour dietary recall for 3 weeks," the methods did not indicate in detail how this was done. Data from the second week of monitoring were presented. In an average binge episode, 1,945 kcal were consumed. However, as in the study of Rosen et al., the range of caloric consumption during binge episodes was very wide; 19 of the 30 patients reported a range of greater than 2,000 kcal between their smallest and largest binge episodes. It appears that all the patients reported at least one episode of binge eating containing more than 1,000 kcal.

Rossiter and Agras (1990) obtained information on the eating behavior of 32 women who met DSM-III-R criteria for bulimia nervosa and used self-induced vomiting following eating binges. Patients recorded all food intake for 1 week in a diary, and data were presented on the

343 episodes that the patients classified as eating binges. The average energy content of a binge episode was 1,173 ± 999 kcal, with a range of 45 to 5,138 kcal. Of these binge episodes, 28% contained less than 500 kcal, 28% contained between 501 and 1000 kcal, 19% contained between 1,001 and 1,500 kcal, 9% were between 1,501 and 2,000 kcal, and 17% contained more than 2,000 kcal.

Data from these self-report studies are quite consistent. They indicate that a significant fraction of what patients with bulimia nervosa describe as binge episodes do, indeed, contain a large number of calories. In the studies of Rosen et al. (1986) and of Rossiter and Agras (1990), between 17% and 27% of the binge episodes contained more than 2,000 kcal. While all these studies are limited by the absence of data from normal subjects, the fact that about one-fourth of the binge episodes contain more calories than most normal individuals consume in 24 hours supports the importance afforded overeating in descriptions of this syndrome. On the other hand, these data also emphasize that many episodes of eating considered by patients to be "binges" do *not* contain an unusually large number of calories. Such episodes of eating appear to be characterized by the consumption of dessert and snack foods that patients with eating disorders believe they should avoid.

LABORATORY STUDIES OF EATING BEHAVIOR

A potentially significant weakness of all the investigations described above is that they are completely dependent on the accuracy of the subjects' reports of their eating behavior (see Wilson, Chapter 11, this volume). Several groups have obtained objective information about the eating behavior of patients with bulimia nervosa by asking them to eat in a laboratory setting where their eating behavior can be monitored. Despite the obvious difficulties associated with asking patients with an eating disorder to engage in their disturbed behavior in a laboratory, a number of studies have successfully employed this technique to explore the nature of binge eating in bulimia nervosa.

Mitchell and Laine (1985) were the first to report on the use of laboratory techniques to examine eating behavior in bulimia. Six women who met DSM-III criteria for bulimia were admitted to the clinical research center of a hospital, and the study was conducted on the second hospital day. They indicated their food preferences and excess amounts were provided; subjects were encouraged to follow their usual patterns of eating, and to signal the nursing staff before and after binge-eating episodes. Under these circumstances, the average binge contained 4,394 ± 2,927 kcal, with a range of 1,436 to 7,178 kcal. On average, 49% of the calories in a binge were derived from carbohydrate, 43% from fat, and 8% from protein.

A similar study was reported by Kaye, Gwirtsman, George, Weiss, and Jimerson (1986). Twelve women meeting DSM-III criteria for bulimia, including one with concurrent anorexia nervosa, were admitted for inpatient treatment of their eating disorder and were studied on their second hospital day. Subjects were alone in a ward bedroom with adjoining toilet facilities, and were offered a tray with 5,000–6,000 kcal of foods they had requested. Patients were instructed to binge and to vomit until whatever effect they desired had been achieved. However, the experimenters terminated the study after the subjects binged and vomited four to five times. The results obtained were similar to those of Mitchell and Laine (1985). On average, binges contained 3,500 $\pm$ 1,338 kcal with 52 $\pm$ 10% derived from carbohydrate, 37 $\pm$ 9% from fat, and 11 $\pm$ 2% from protein.

In collaboration with Kissileff and his colleagues at the Obesity Research Center of St. Luke's/Roosevelt Medical Center, our own group has carried out several laboratory studies of the eating behavior of patients with bulimia nervosa (Kissileff, Walsh, Kral, & Cassidy, 1986; Walsh, Kissileff, Cassidy, & Dantzic, 1989; Hadigan, Kissileff, & Walsh, 1989; LaChaussée, 1992; Walsh, Hadigan, Kissileff, & LaChaussée, 1992). Our studies have differed in several small but important ways from those previously described. First, on some occasions, we have explicitly asked patients to overeat and, on other occasions, to eat normally. Second, we have studied age- and sex-matched controls without eating disorders. The controls have been given the same instructions as the patients with bulimia, including the request to overeat. In this way, we have been able to compare the overeating of patients with eating disorders to the overeating of normal individuals. As have other investigators, in several studies, we have asked subjects to choose their meals from an array of foods. However, all subjects were presented with an identical array of foods from which to make their choices. This eliminates the possibility that, if a difference exists between the food consumption of patients and that of controls, it reflects merely a difference between the groups in their requests for foods.

We recently compiled data from several studies of normal-weight women who met DSM-III criteria for bulimia (prior to 1987) or DSM-III-R criteria for bulimia nervosa (Walsh et al., 1992). These patients all used self-induced vomiting as a primary method of purging. Despite our attempt to elicit both binge-eating and non-binge-eating behavior in response to explicit instructions, examination of data from some individuals suggested that patients did not always follow the instructions. For example, after the non-binge-eating instruction, several patients ate large amounts of food and rated the meal as between ''moderately'' and ''extremely'' typical of a binge. On the other hand, after the instruction to binge eat, some patients ate small amounts of food and rated these meals as only "slightly" or "not at all" typical of a binge. We therefore decided to classify meals eaten by patients on the basis of both the instructions given and the typicality ratings. Specifically, meals consumed following non-binge-eating instructions and rated by the patient as only "slightly" or "not at all" typical of a binge were classified as nonbinge meals. Meals consumed following binge instructions and rated by the patient as between "moderately" and "extremely" typical of a binge were classified as binge meals. From the 36 patients, 25 meals met the criteria for a binge and 26 for a nonbinge meal. However, during one meal classified as a nonbinge, a patient consumed 5,843 kcal more than 12 standard deviations above the mean of the remaining 25 patients' nonbinge meals; data from this meal were omitted. Data from the remaining patient meals were compared to data from the meals of 18 control women. Controls' meals were classified as non-binge or binge meals on the basis of the instructions provided to the subject, as it is not clear what "typical of a binge" means to someone without an eating disorder. In their binge meals, patients with bulimia consumed, on average, 3,583 ± 1,834 kcal, almost three times the amount consumed by controls, who, as indicated above, received identical instructions but consumed only 1,271 ± 373 kcal (see Figure 3.2). Four of the 25 patient binge meals were within the range of the binge meals consumed by controls (434–1,937 kcal). Thus, although the overeating of patients with bulimia nervosa under these conditions is quite different from that of normal individuals, there is still overlap between the size of patients' binge meals and those of controls.

The binge meals of the patients contained much larger absolute amounts of each of the macronutrients than did those of the controls. In other words, compared to the controls, the patients with bulimia nervosa consumed in their binge meals substantially more carbohydrate, fat, and protein. However, when macronutrient composition is calculated on a *relative* basis, as the percentage of calories derived from each macronutrient, the patients' and controls' meals are quite similar. The fraction of calories derived from carbohydrate in the average patient binge meal was 47.0 ± 3.8% compared to 46.1 ± 5.8% in the average control binge meal ($p = .6$). Patients and controls also obtained a similar fraction of calories from fat: 40.1 ± 4.1% versus 38.8 ± 5.4%, respectively ($p = .2$). There was a small but significant difference in the fraction of calories obtained from protein; the mean percentage of calories obtained from protein was 12.1 ± 4.1% in the patients' binge meals compared to 15.0 ± 3.3% in those of the controls ($p = .01$).

Our laboratory studies also suggest that, consistent with clinical impression, patients with bulimia nervosa eat faster and for a longer time

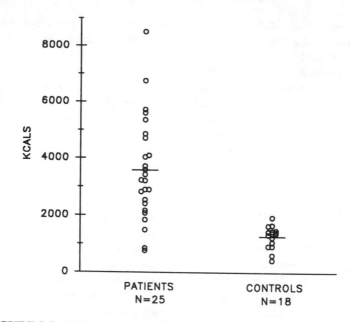

FIGURE 3.2. Caloric content of binge meals consumed in a laboratory by 25 patients and 18 controls. From "Bulimia Nervosa: A Syndrome of Feast and Famine" by B. T. Walsh, C. M. Hadigan, H. R. Kissileff, and J. L. LaChaussée, 1992, in G. H. Anderson and S. H. Kennedy (Eds.), *The Biology of Feast and Famine* (New York: Academic Press), p. 9. Copyright 1992 by the Academic Press. Reprinted by permission.

when binge eating. For example, in a recent analysis of a subgroup of the subjects described above, we found that, during their binge meals, patients, on average, consumed 81.5 kcal per minute for 32.3 minutes, compared to the controls who consumed 38.4 kcal per minute for 28.6 minutes (LaChaussée, Kissileff, Walsh, & Hadigan, 1992).

There were also significant differences between patients and controls in the nonbinge meals. Of particular interest was the observation that patients, on average, consumed *fewer* calories during their nonbinge meal than did controls (469 ± 440 vs. 902 ± 283, $p < .001$; see Figure 3.3). These data are consistent with other reports that individuals with bulimia nervosa, when not binge eating, tend to restrict their caloric intake (Rosen, Leitenberg, Gross, & Wilmuth, 1985; Woell et al., 1989).

The most recent laboratory data regarding the eating behavior of individuals with bulimia nervosa are those of Kaye and colleagues (Weltzin, Hsu, Pollice, & Kaye, 1991; Kaye et al., 1992). This group has constructed a human-feeding laboratory where subjects can reside for days at a time while their eating behavior is monitored. Two computer-

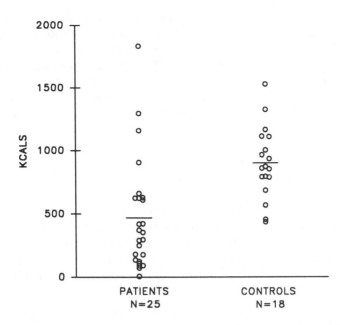

FIGURE 3.3. Caloric content of nonbinge meals consumed in a laboratory by 25 patients and 18 controls. From ''Bulimia Nervosa: A Syndrome of Feast and Famine'' by B. T. Walsh, C. M. Hadigan, H. R. Kissileff, and J. L. LaChaussée, 1992, in G. H. Anderson and S. H. Kennedy (Eds.), *The Biology of Feast and Famine* (New York: Academic Press), p. 11. Copyright 1992 by the Academic Press. Reprinted by permission.

controlled vending machines provide free access to a variety of foods. A private bathroom adjoins the laboratory so that patients may induce vomiting. In one study, the investigators characterized the binge-eating behavior of 21 women of normal body weight with bulimia nervosa who spent 3 days in the human-feeding laboratory. On the second or the third day, the patients were instructed to binge eat; on the other day, they were instructed to eat as they would at home on a day they did not binge. The eating behavior of the patients was compared to that of 11 normal women who were instructed to eat normally on both days.

On the day they were asked to binge eat, the patients consumed a total of 7,101 ± 9,546 kcal, ranging from 206 to 24,691 kcal; controls consumed an average of 1,844 ± 619 kcal/day, with a range of 890 to 3,063 kcal/day. No information is presented on which meals the patients considered typical of their binge eating, and, as in our own laboratory studies, patients in this study did not always eat as requested, presenting difficulties in characterizing ''binge'' meals. Kaye et al. dealt with this problem by examining the meals of 16 patients whose total energy intake on the binge day was more than two standard deviations greater than the mean energy intake of the controls. Most of these patients' meals were within the range of the meals of the controls. However, 28% of the patients' meals contained more than 1,000 kcal and were larger than any meal eaten by a control subject; it was these patient meals that accounted for the increased 24-hour energy consumption in the patient group. Compared to the controls' meals, these patients' meals contained somewhat less carbohydrate (61 $\pm$ 22% vs. 51 $\pm$ 9%, $p < .05$) and more fat (28 $\pm$ 20% vs 38 $\pm$ 8%, $p < .05$). The authors noted a relationship between meal size and macronutrient composition in both patients' and controls' meals: Percentage carbohydrate was inversely and percentage fat was positively related to meal size.

In sum, laboratory studies have provided the most convincing evidence to date that patients with bulimia nervosa engage in overeating that is outside the range of normal eating behavior. However, as found in studies based on patient descriptions, patients often regard as binges those meals falling within the range of meals of normal individuals.

CARBOHYDRATE CRAVING

From the earliest descriptions of the syndrome of bulimia nervosa, the disturbed eating behavior has been described as being characterized by the excessive consumption of carbohydrates. Binge-eating episodes are frequently depicted as being driven by "carbohydrate craving." It is remarkable that the popularity of this phrase persists despite the lack of any evidence to support the excessive consumption of carbohydrates during episodes of binge eating. As indicated above, data from both patient reports and from laboratory studies document that the fraction of calories derived from carbohydrate in binge meals is no greater or even, in the study of Kaye et al. (1992), less than the fraction of calories derived from carbohydrate in the nonbinge meals of patients and controls. What these studies have documented is that, during binge episodes, patients with bulimia nervosa tend to consume an excessive amount of dessert and snack foods (Rosen et al., 1986; Hadigan et al., 1989; Kaye et al., 1992). While it is commonly believed that such foods contain excessive amounts of carbohydrate, they are more accurately viewed as sweet foods with a high fat content. For example, 57% of the calories in Haagen-Dazs vanilla ice cream are from fat and only 36% from carbohydrate; even in devil's food cake, just over half of the calories come from carbohydrate, while 40% are from fat (Bowes, 1989). Furthermore, most normal individuals derive roughly half of their daily caloric intake from carbohydrates, so that a binge meal with a 50% carbohydrate content is not remarkable.

CONCLUSIONS

The information reviewed in this chapter from patient reports and from laboratory studies convincingly documents that individuals with bulimia nervosa consume during some eating episodes amounts of food that are clearly larger than the meals of normal individuals, even when they are overeating. While explicit information is rarely provided, it is highly likely that these episodes of overeating were also associated with a sense of loss of control. (This is a significant omission, given Beglin and Fairburn's [1992] finding that loss of control is central to the lay concept of a binge and the inclusion in the DSM-IV criteria of loss of control in the definition of a binge.) Thus, there is little doubt that such episodes satisfy the DSM-IV criteria for a binge. These data are critically important in establishing with certainty that the diagnosis of bulimia nervosa is associated with the presence of abnormal eating behavior, which meets explicit criteria for an episode of binge eating.

It should be noted that virtually all of the data concerning eating behavior in bulimia nervosa have been obtained from the study of individuals who induce vomiting after binge eating. While vomiting is reported by most patients with bulimia nervosa presenting for treatment at eating disorder clinics, neither vomiting nor any form of purging is required by the DSM-III-R or DSM-IV criteria for bulimia nervosa. Thus, it is unknown whether the eating behavior of patients who binge and abuse laxatives but do not induce vomiting is similar to what has been described in this chapter.

These studies also document the difficulties with the use of the term ''binge'' when it is not further defined. As is well illustrated by the studies of Rosen et al. (1986), Woell et al. (1989), and Rossiter and Agras (1990), a majority of eating episodes considered to be binges by patients contain no more food than do episodes *not* considered to be binges. These small binge episodes appear to be characterized by the consumption of dessert or snack foods that patients generally wish to avoid and therefore are likely to be accompanied by a sense of loss of control. Thus, many episodes of eating viewed by patients as binges are better described as subjective bulimic episodes (see Fairburn & Wilson, Chapter 1, this volume). This distinction can be critical in the treatment of bulimia nervosa. In helping patients reduce objective bulimic episodes, the therapy must provide assistance with the disturbance in behavior. In addressing subjective bulimic episodes, the therapy must address the patient's misconceptions about what constitutes an excessive amount of food.

These studies also suggest that the distinction between objective and subjective bulimic episodes is not a sharp one. There is no indication that what patients refer to as ''binge'' episodes naturally fall into a group of smaller subjective bulimic episodes and another group of distinctly larger objective bulimic episodes. It is possible to set operational, if arbitrary, guidelines for such a distinction. For example, as the largest meal of a control subject contained less than 1,000 kcal, Kaye et al. (1992) chose to view as binge meals those patient meals over 1,000 kcal that occurred on a day the patient had been requested to binge. Such distinctions may be useful in attempting to draw a contrast between clear binge meals and nonbinge meals. However, patients often describe episodes of eating that meet the criteria for an objective bulimic episode, not because they are larger than *any* normal meal, but because they are larger than the meals of normal individuals under similar circumstances. An example might be 800 kcal of ice cream eaten at breakfast time, when accompanied by a sense of loss of control. It is my opinion that the definition of a binge used in DSM-IV is a good one and that it would not be helpful for clinicians to attempt to set a specific minimum number of calories for a binge. However, the data reviewed in this chapter demonstrate that there is enormous variability among the eating episodes of patients with bulimia nervosa and therefore that critical and well-informed clinical judgment is also required to evaluate what constitutes a binge.

ACKNOWLEDGMENTS

I would like to acknowledge the helpful comments of Michael J. Devlin, MD. Work described in this chapter was supported in part by grant MH42206 from the National Institute of Mental Health.

REFERENCES

Abraham, S. F., & Beumont, P. J. V. (1982). How patients describe bulimia or binge eating. *Psychological Medicine, 12*, 625–635.

American Psychiatric Association. (1993). *DSM-IV draft criteria (3/1/93)*. Washington, DC: Author.

Beglin, S. J., & Fairburn, C. G. (1992). What is mean by the term "binge"? *American Journal of Psychiatry, 149*, 123–124.

Bowes, A. D. P. (1989). *Bowes and Church's food values of portions commonly used*. Philadelphia: J. B. Lippincott.

Hadigan, C. M., Kissileff, H. R., & Walsh, B. T. (1989). Patterns of food selection during meals in women with bulimia. *American Journal of Clinical Nutrition, 50*, 759–766.

Kaye, W. H., Gwirtsman, H. E., George, D. T., Weiss, S. R., & Jimerson, D. C. (1986). Relationship of mood alterations to bingeing behavior in bulimia. *British Journal of Psychiatry, 149*, 479–485.

Kaye, W. H., Weltzin, T. E., McKee, M., McConaha, C., Hansen, D., & Hsu, L. K. G. (1992). Laboratory assessment of feeding behavior in bulimia nervosa and healthy women: Methods for developing a human-feeding laboratory. *American Journal of Clinical Nutrition, 55,* 372–380.

Kissileff, H. R., Walsh, B. T., Kral, J. G., & Cassidy, S. M. (1986). Laboratory studies of eating behavior in women with bulimia. *Physiology and Behavior, 38,* 563–570.

LaChaussée, J. L., Kissileff, H. R., Walsh, B. T., & Hadigan, C. M. (1992). The single item meal as a measure of binge-eating behavior in patients with bulimia nervosa. *Physiology and Behavior, 51,* 593–600.

Mitchell, J. E., & Laine, D. C. (1985). Monitored binge-eating behavior in patients with bulimia. *International Journal of Eating Disorders, 4,* 177–183.

Mitchell, J. E., Pyle, R. L., & Eckert, E. D. (1981). Frequency and duration of binge-eating episodes in patients with bulimia. *American Journal of Psychiatry, 138,* 835–836.

Rosen, J. C., Leitenberg, H., Fisher, C., & Khazam, C. (1986). Binge-eating episodes in bulimia nervosa: The amount and type of food consumed. *International Journal of Eating Disorders, 5,* 255–267.

Rosen J. C., Leitenberg H., Gross J., & Willmuth M. (1985). Standardized test meals in the assessment of bulimia nervosa. *Advances in Behaviour Research and Therapy , 7,* 181–197.

Rossiter, E. M., & Agras, W. S. (1990). An empirical test of the DSM-III-R definition of binge. *International Journal of Eating Disorders, 9,* 513–518.

Russell, G. (1979). Bulimia nervosa: An ominous variant of anorexia nervosa. *Psychological Medicine, 9,* 429–448.

Walsh, B. T., Hadigan, C. M., Kissileff, H. R., & LaChaussée, J. L. (1992). Bulimia nervosa: A syndrome of feast and famine. In: G. H. Anderson & S. H. Kennedy (Eds.), *The biology of feast and famine.* New York: Academic Press.

Walsh, B. T., Kissileff, H. R., Cassidy, S. M., & Dantzic, S. (1989). Eating behavior of women with bulimia. *Archives of General Psychiatry, 46,* 54–58.

Weltzin, T. E., Hsu, L. K. G., Pollice, C., & Kaye, W. H. (1991). Feeding patterns in bulimia nervosa. *Biological Psychiatry, 30,* 1093–1110.

Woell, C., Fichter, M. M., Pirke, K. M., & Wolfram, G. (1989). Eating behavior of patients with bulimia nervosa. *International Journal of Eating Disorders, 8,* 557–568.

CHAPTER 4

Binge Eating
in Anorexia Nervosa

David M. Garner

Anorexia nervosa has always been most noted for the symptom of self-imposed starvation; however, episodes of binge eating have been described as common in a subgroup of patients. In his classic paper on anorexia nervosa, Gull (1873) describes occasional bouts of overeating in one patient: "for a day or two the appetite was voracious, but this was rare and exceptional." Binge eating was identified as a symptom in major reports on anorexia nervosa appearing up to 1970 (Berkman 1939; Bliss & Branch, 1960; Bruch, 1962; Crisp, 1967; Dally, 1969; Guiora, 1967; King, 1963; Meyer & Weinroth, 1957; Nemiah, 1950; Russell, 1970; Theander, 1970). Berkman (1939) reported binge eating in two-thirds of his anorexia nervosa patients in response to a sensation of fullness. In later reports, binge eating has been described in approximately one-half of anorexia nervosa patients presenting for treatment (Casper, Eckert, Halmi, Goldberg, & Davis, 1980; Garfinkel, Moldofsky, & Garner, 1980; Hsu, Crisp, & Harding, 1979).

Casper (1983) traced the history of binge eating in anorexia nervosa, highlighting the small number of cases reported in the literature prior to the 20th century. She suggested that the symptom of binge eating has become a more common theme in anorexia nervosa and that this represents a change in the expression of the underlying psychopathology. Russell (1985) considered this change in presentation as reflecting an actual shift over the years in the central psychopathology in anorexia nervosa. In early case reports, there was either an emphasis on starvation as a defense against sexuality or on the theme of asceticism, with food restriction representing such spiritual ideals as self-sacrifice and control over bodily urges (Bell, 1985; Casper, 1983; Rampling, 1985). In the past century, the ascetic motif has become less prominent, replaced by a "drive for thinness" or a "morbid dread of fatness" as the more common motivational themes (Casper, 1983; Russell, 1985).

According to Russell (1985), the increased appearance of binge eating, both in anorexia nervosa and patients who are not emaciated, is the most dramatic evidence for a transformation in the psychopathology of anorexia nervosa. However, the actual extent to which binge eating has become more common in anorexia nervosa is unclear owing to the fact that the symptom may have been identified less reliably in earlier reports. The fact that binge eating is more easily concealed than emaciation may account for underreporting in early writings.

Although there are indications of a metamorphosis in the expression of anorexia nervosa over time, it is also apparent that the conventions used in rendering a diagnosis have changed. Shifts in diagnostic formulations, particularly as they relate to binge eating, have led to changes in the relationship between anorexia nervosa and bulimia nervosa. In the third edition of the *Diagnostic and Statistical Manual of Mental Disorders* (DSM-III) (American Psychiatric Association, [APA], 1980), anorexia nervosa and bulimia nervosa were mutually exclusive. Anorexia nervosa "trumped" bulimia nervosa in the sense that the latter diagnosis could not be made if "bulimic episodes were . . . due to anorexia nervosa." There was no special provision for the anorexia nervosa patient who also engaged in binge eating. In·contrast, DSM-III-R (APA, 1987) permitted the concurrent diagnoses of anorexia nervosa and bulimia nervosa as long as criteria were met for both disorders. The original proposal for the DSM-IV criteria (APA, 1991; DaCosta & Halmi, 1992) returned to the earlier convention of making anorexia nervosa and bulimia nervosa mutually exclusive with the rationale that this avoids the possibly misleading implication that binge eating in anorexia nervosa reflects two independent eating disorders. The DSM-IV (APA, 1993) criteria retain the independence between anorexia nervosa and bulimia nervosa but depart from the earlier convention of subtyping anorexia nervosa exclusively on the basis of binge eating by subdividing the disorder into the restricting and the binge-eating/purging types.* This new subtyping system overcomes many of the arguments against relying upon binge eating as the sole criterion for subtyping (Garner, Shafer, & Rosen, 1992) and it is consistent with recent data indicating that anorexia nervosa patients who *purge* share important clinical and psychometric features, regardless of whether or not they engage in objective episodes of binge eating (Garner, Garner, & Rosen, 1993).

*The DSM-IV criteria cited in this volume are those that were approved as final by the DSM-IV Eating Disorders Work Group and the Task Force on DSM-IV (APA, 1993). These criteria may be subject to minor editorial revisions before the publication of DSM-IV.

There have been other attempts to define the relationship between anorexia nervosa and bulimia nervosa. Russell (1985) suggested that bulimia nervosa should be diagnosed only in those who have experienced a previous episode of anorexia nervosa (including what is referred to as a "cryptic form"). Because the weights of these patients can fluctuate considerably without marked change in clinical presentation, it has also been recommended that the term "bulimia nervosa" be applied to all patients who binge, regardless of weight, reserving the term anorexia nervosa only for emaciated patients who do not binge eat (Fairburn & Garner, 1986, 1988).

Thus, any discussion of the topic of binge eating in anorexia nervosa is complicated by the fact that both the domain of interest and its definitions have been transformed over time. Binge eating is an important clinical feature in many anorexia nervosa patients; however, its definition, measurement, and significance in the disorder remain unresolved.

BULIMIC VERSUS NONBULIMIC SUBTYPES IN ANOREXIA NERVOSA

The original rationale for subtyping anorexia nervosa came from studies in which "bulimic" patients were contrasted with patients who did not engage in binge eating, referred to as a "fasters" (Casper et al., 1980) or "restrictors" (Garfinkel et al., 1980). In a review of 14 studies in which anorexia nervosa patients were subclassified into bulimic and nonbulimic subtypes, DaCosta and Halmi (1992) concluded that differences between these two groups warrant the formal distinction, originally adopted by the DSM-IV workgroup (APA, 1991). Agreement was found across studies indicating that bulimic anorexia nervosa patients were older than the nonbulimic patients at the time of presentation. The duration of illness was consistently longer for bulimic anorexia nervosa patients across the six studies in which these data were reported. This supports earlier observations that bulimic symptoms may relate to chronicity (Casper et al., 1980). Although the results are not consistent across all studies, there is some evidence that bulimic anorexia nervosa patients tend to present at a heavier weight with more frequent premorbid and family obesity than nonbulimic patients (cf. DaCosta & Halmi, 1992).

Perhaps of greatest significance in most studies comparing bulimic and nonbulimic anorexia nervosa patients is the finding that the bulimic subgroup reports greater impulsivity, social involvement, sexual activity, family dysfunction, depression, and generally more conspicuous emotional disturbance (DaCosta & Halmi, 1992; Casper et al., 1980; Garfinkel et al., 1980; Garner, 1991; Garner, Olmsted, & Garfinkel, 1985; Herzog & Norman, 1985; Laessle, Wittchen, Fichter, & Pirke, 1989; Mick-

TABLE 4.1. Impulsivity Measures

Investigator	Stealing	Drug/ alcohol	Suicidality	Self- mutilation	Other impulsivity
Anorexic-restrictors					
Casper et al. (1980)	4%				
Garfinkel et al. (1985)	0%	11.6%/4.8%	7.1%	1.5%	
Garner, Garfinkel, et al. (1989)	9%	19%/34%	12%	10%	19%
Laessle et al. (1989)		4.8%/0%			
Strober (1981)	0%				
Vandereycken & Pierloot (1983)		0%/0%	0%		5%
Anorexic-bulimics					
Casper et al. (1980)	24%				
Garfinkel et al, (1980)	12.1%	28.6%/20.4%	23.1%	9.2%	
Garner, Garfinkel, et al. (1985)	25%	40%/45%	25%	19%	39%
Laessle et al. (1989)		0%/20%			
Strober (1981)	9%				
Vandereycken & Pierloot (1983)		11%	9%		33.3%

Note. Data from DaCosta and Halmi (1992). Copyright 1992 by John Wiley & Sons, Inc. Adapted by permission.

alide & Andersen, 1985; Strober, 1981; Strober, Salkin, Burroughs, & Morrell, 1982; Sunday, Halmi, Werdann, & Levey, 1992; Vandereycken & Pierloot, 1983). Results from studies that compare bulimic and nonbulimic anorexia nervosa patients on parameters of impulsivity are summarized in Table 4.1. It is evident from these findings that the bulimic anorexia nervosa patients have a greater likelihood of reporting these impulse-related behaviors than the nonbulimic group. On the other hand, another way of interpreting these same data is that the vast majority of patients in both the bulimic and nonbulimic groups share the feature of *not* reporting behaviors reflecting impulsivity. Moreover, findings from a number of studies do not indicate meaningful differences between the two subtypes on measures of depression and general psychological distress (e.g., Garner, Garfinkel, & O'Shaughnessy, 1985; Mickalide & Andersen, 1985; Yellowlees, 1985). Thus, there is the danger that the nominal distinction between the bulimic and nonbulimic subtypes could obscure the facts that these two subgroups are more alike than different and that there is extraordinary variability *within* each subgroup on a wide range of demographic, clinical, and psychological variables. Exclusive emphasis on the differences between the two subgroups could reinforce a uniformity myth that would detract from the understanding and management of individual patients.

There are a few instances in which greater psychopathology has been reported for anorexia nervosa restrictors compared to anorexia nervosa bulimics. Compared to anorexia nervosa bulimics, anorexia nervosa restrictors have been found to display greater psychosexual immaturity (Strober, 1981), and to view their world as more unpredictable or uncontrollable (Strauss & Ryan, 1988); however, considering the number of variables on which these groups have been compared, the predominance of psychopathology in the bulimic group is striking.

One explanation for the tendency toward more prominent psychological dysfunction in bulimic anorexia nervosa patients is that the acute emotional distress seen at presentation is a byproduct of chaotic dietary patterns rather than a sign of fundamental psychological deficits. Studies of bulimia nervosa patients indicate that many psychological symptoms ameliorate quickly with the reduction of bingeing–vomiting episodes (Fairburn, Cooper, Kirk, & O'Conner, 1985; Garner et al., 1990; Wilson, Rossiter, Kleifield, & Lindholm, 1986). Eckert, Halmi, Marchi, and Cohen (1987) have indicated that many of the reported differences in overall psychopathology between restricting and bulimic groups disappear with hospital treatment.

In a comprehensive review of four decades of outcome research in anorexia nervosa, Steinhausen, Rauss-Mason, and Seidel (1991) cite eight outcome studies that have specifically examined bulimia as a prognostic factor, and seven of these found that it portends an unfavorable outcome. Only Toner, Garfinkel, and Garner (1986) failed to find meaningful differences in outcome between bulimic and nonbulimic patients (i.e., 5–14 years after initial consultation). However, whether the difference in outcome between bulimic and nonbulimic groups relates to the specific symptom of binge eating or to some associated feature is an important nosological consideration. For example, if binge eating were the key marker for fundamental disturbances in impulse regulation, then it would provide strong support for subtyping on the basis of this symptom. On the other hand, if binge eating were a moderator variable, only incidentally related to prognosis because of its association with other factors such as duration of illness, vomiting, or higher premorbid weight, then the rationale for subtyping cases on the basis of binge eating would be somewhat weaker. Still, a case could be made for differentiating bulimic and nonbulimic subtypes of anorexia nervosa because of the special therapeutic interventions needed to address binge eating (DaCosta & Halmi, 1992). Bingeing is a behavior that patients find particularly distressing and specific strategies designed to bring it under control are germane to a significant subgroup of anorexia nervosa patients.

SUBTYPING ANOREXIA NERVOSA BASED ON PURGING

The system of dividing anorexia nervosa patients into bulimic and restrictor (or faster) subtypes represented in Figure 4.1(a) overlaps with one

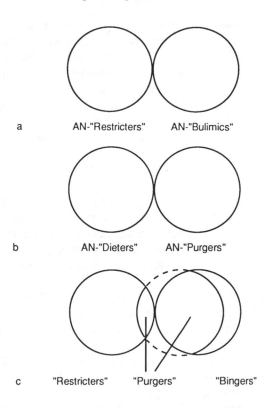

FIGURE 4.1. (a) The anorexia nervosa subtyping systems originally proposed by Casper et al. (1980) and Garfinkel et al. (1980). (b) The subtyping scheme proposed by Beumont et al. (1976). (c) The overlap between subgroups of "restrictors," "bingers," and "purgers." Copyright 1993 by John Wiley & Sons, Inc. Reprinted by permission.

proposed earlier by Beumont and colleagues (Beumont, 1977; Beumont, George, & Smart, 1976) in which patients were classified as either dieters or vomiters and purgers (hereafter referred to simply as purgers,[1] see Figure 4.1[b]). These and subsequent studies using the dieting–purging subtyping system (Bhanji & Mattingly, 1981; Vandereycken & Pierloot,

[1]It appears that Beumont's (1977) intention was to include patients who were "vomiters *and/or* purgers" rather than "vomiters *and* purgers" since only 65% of his vomiting and purging group of patients engaged in "habitual vomiting," 79% engaged in "habitual purgation," and 50% abused diuretics. Because the label "vomiter *and/or* purger" is cumbersome, the convention in the bulimia nervosa literature of referring to patients who engage in self-induced vomiting and/or laxative abuse as "purgers" will be followed (Rossiter, Agras, Telch, & Bruce, 1992; Willmuth, Leitenberg, Rosen, & Cado, 1988).

1983) indicate that purgers are more anxious, depressed, somatizing, hysterical, socially outgoing, sexually experienced, and prone to obesity than dieters. Vandereycken and Pierloot (1983) reported that bulimic anorexia nervosa patients and the overlapping group who purge (in this case, self-induced vomiting, laxative abuse, or diuretic abuse) shared similar clinical features. Both of these groups differed from the anorexia nervosa subgroup who "principally relied on dieting." Compared with the other two groups, dieters were characterized by younger age of onset, shorter duration of illness, less "neurotic disturbance," fewer problems with impulse control, fewer suicide attempts, higher social–educational levels, and lower mortality at follow-up.

Thus, it can be concluded that the findings using the dieter–purger distinction parallel those in which anorexia nervosa patients are subtyped on the basis of the presence or absence of binge eating. Nevertheless, the degree of overlap between these two subtyping strategies as well as their respective theoretical and empirical merits has never really been addressed.

The restricting or fasting groups (Casper et al., 1980; Garfinkel et al., 1980) are not identical to the "dieting" group proposed by Beumont (1977), because self-induced vomiting does not occur in the dieters (by definition) but is present in approximately 20% of patients subtyped as fasters or restrictors (Casper et al., 1980; Garfinkel et al., 1980). Also, although none of the restricting or fasting patients binge eat (by definition), 18% of the dieters report binge-eating episodes (Beumont, 1977). Similarly, the bulimic groups (Casper et al., 1980; Garfinkel et al., 1980) are not equivalent to the purging group (Beumont, 1977). Only a subgroup of the Casper et al. (1980) bulimic sample vomited after meals (57%) or used purgatives (37%); however, it is not clear from this or other reports how many bulimic patients used *either or both* of these compensatory behaviors. Casper et al. (1980) acknowledged the overlap between the two approaches to classifying patients and examined the intercorrelations between self-induced vomiting and clinical symptoms. The results confirmed the Beumont et al. (1976) observations of an association between vomiting and extraversion and poor impulse control, but the rationale for classifying patients on the basis of bingeing rather than purging was not developed. Thus, the relationship between the restrictor–binger and the purger (nonpurger) subtyping systems is represented by Figure 4.1(c). In effect, Beumont's dieters are simply nonpurgers, a term that is somewhat less ambiguous.

A third subtyping system that mixes components of both of the above two schemes was proposed by Halmi (1985) who suggested that restricting anorexia nervosa patients be divided into two types based on the presence or absence of compensatory behavior (i.e., self-induced vomiting or laxative or diuretic abuse). Type I consisted of restrictors who engaged in neither binge eating nor compensatory behaviors. Type II were restrictors who did not binge but who *did* engage in one of these compensatory behaviors. Both of these groups were contrasted with anorexia nervosa patients who engaged in binge eating; they were given the additional diagnosis of bulimia nervosa. All three of these groups can be deduced from Figure 4.1(c) with the appropriate changes in terminology (restrictors who do not purge = Type I; restrictors who do purge = Type II; bingers = anorexia nervosa + bulimia nervosa). The other rationale provided for subtyping the restricting anorexia nervosa patients into two groups based on the presence or absence of compensatory behaviors was the serious physical health consequences and metabolic abnormalities associated with these symptoms (Halmi, 1985). This system has considerable intuitive appeal, because it preserves a relatively homogeneous restrictor group (Type I) by separating it from the subgroup of patients who use potentially dangerous compensatory behaviors. Unfortunately, this classification system has not generated research.

BASIC PROBLEMS WITH THE DEFINITION OF BINGE EATING

Despite the important historical role that binge eating has had in the subtyping of anorexia nervosa, very little is actually known about its nature, frequency, and significance in anorexia nervosa. Although early definitions used in demarcating the "bulimic subtype" specified that binge eating must be recurrent, involve large amounts of food, and occur with the experience of loss of control (Casper et al., 1980; Garfinkel et al., 1980; Strober et al., 1982), there has been little systematic research on the frequency or duration of bulimic episodes, the amount and nature of foods eaten, the temporal parameters of episodes, the factors that precipitate and terminate episodes, or even the actual proportion of episodes that meet the definition of a binge. This is remarkable in light of the conceptual rigor in defining (Cooper & Fairburn, 1987; Fairburn, 1987) and evaluating the properties overeating in bulimia nervosa (Davis, Freeman, & Garner, 1988; Katzman & Wolchik, 1984; Rosen, Leitenberg, Fisher, & Khazam, 1986; Rossiter & Agras, 1990; Rossiter, Agras, Telch, & Bruce, 1992; Walsh, Kissileff, Cassidy, & Dantzic, 1989; Wilson & Eldredge, 1991). Only one extreme form of overeating (i.e., binge eating) has been the subject of research in anorexia nervosa, and the data available on this topic are meager at best. For over a decade, it has been the convention to differentiate subgroups of anorexia nervosa patients on the basis of binge eating, and the term is still central in the subtyping of the disorder according to the DSM-IV (APA, 1993). However, the term "binge eating" is not defined and it is not stated whether these episodes refer to the past or the current symptom picture, and there are no specific guidelines regarding the thresholds for behavior required to meet the definition of binge episodes.

A historical context is provided by a brief review of earlier definitions of "bulimia" used to divide anorexia nervosa patients into bulimic and nonbulimic subgroups. Casper et al. (1980) defined bulimia as the "uncontrollable rapid ingestion of large amounts of food over a short period of time, terminated by physical discomfort, social interruption, or sleep" (p. 1031). Garfinkel et al. (1980) employed a similar definition of bulimia as "an abnormal increase in one's desire to eat, with episodes of excessive ingestion of large quantities of food which the patient viewed as ego-alien and out of her control." Similarly, Strober et al. (1982) designated bulimia as "discrete episodes of unrestricted, rapid ingestion of pathologically excessive amounts of food, followed by marked physical discomfort" (p. 346). Although these definitions are clearly overlapping, the reliability of the methods used in their application has never been fully explored. Casper et al. (1980) obtained the relevant clinical information from a "psychiatric and social history form," and Garfinkel et al. (1980) relied on a "relatively standard" series of questions in a clinical interview. Even less detail is provided by Vandereycken and Pierloot (1983), who divided patients into three subgroups according to "the most prominent and most frequently occurring symptom: dieting . . . bulimia . . . or vomiting and/or purging" (p. 544). Most subsequent reports simply classified anorexia nervosa patients as bulimic or nonbulimic without indicating any rules used for defining subgroups.

As indicated earlier, the DSM-IV (APA, 1993) criteria do not explicitly define "binge eating" for use in subtyping anorexia nervosa. The subtypes are defined as follows:

> *Restricting type:* During the episode of Anorexia Nervosa, the person does not regularly engage in binge eating or purging behavior (i.e., self-induced vomiting or the misuse of laxatives or diuretics).
> *Binge Eating/Purging type:* During the episode of Anorexia Nervosa, the person regularly engages in binge eating or purging behavior (i.e., self-induced vomiting or the misuse of laxatives or diuretics).

Although the term "binge eating" is not defined, the practical problems associated with its use in subtyping anorexia nervosa, are reduced in the DSM-IV diagnostic scheme because most patients who engage in binge eating also purge, and purging presents far fewer definitional problems (Garner et al., 1993). Nevertheless, it is still important to recognize that the DSM-IV subtyping system classifies patients based on the presence or absence of purging *or* binge eating, so the theoretical issues surrounding the definition of binge eating in anorexia nervosa are still relevant.

If it can be presumed that the definition of binge eating for anorexia nervosa is meant to be consistent with that used for bulimia nervosa, then the episodes must be recurrent and must have two additional properties:

> 1) eating, in a discrete period of time (e.g., within any two-hour period), an amount of food that is definitely larger than most people would eat in a similar period of time and under similar circumstances, and,
>
> 2) a sense of lack of control over eating during the episode (e.g., a feeling that one cannot stop eating or control what or how much one is eating). (APA, 1993)

It is further specified, in bulimia nervosa, that binge episodes must have occurred at least twice a week for the past 3 months. Although the definition of binge eating in anorexia nervosa may initially seem quite straightforward, further analysis raises serious questions regarding the conventions that have been applied.

THE PROBLEM OF THRESHOLDS IN DEFINING BINGE EATING IN ANOREXIA NERVOSA

Although the definition of what constitutes a binge episode is no less complicated for anorexia nervosa than for bulimia nervosa, establishing *thresholds* for duration, frequency, size of a binge, and associated states (e.g., experience of loss of control) presents a different set of conceptual and diagnostic dilemmas for anorexia nervosa (Garner et al., 1992). Whereas the diagnostic rules with respect to binge eating for bulimia nervosa are primarily aimed at *excluding* cases that might be considered less severe, the goal in anorexia nervosa has always been to make a *qualitative* distinction between separate subtypes.

Thus, it remains ambiguous whether the thresholds for size, frequency, duration, and associated loss of control for binge eating for anorexia nervosa should be the same as those applied for bulimia nervosa. How should patients be classified who have engaged in clear episodes of binge eating (without purging), but who do not meet these *frequency* or *duration* thresholds? Answers to these questions govern the relative heterogeneity or homogeneity of the two subtypes, both in terms of eating behavior and psychopathology that may be associated with the eating behavior.

FREQUENCY OF BINGE EPISODES

Very little is known about the frequency of binge episodes in anorexia nervosa. Although the methodology for gathering frequency data was not well validated, early studies did provide estimates. Garfinkel et al. (1980) reported on the frequency of bulimic episodes in a sample of 68 anorexia nervosa patients who experienced the symptom of bulimia at the time of initial consultation. Based on a clinical interview, it was determined that 25 (37%) of these patients experienced episodes at least daily, 28 (41%) reported episodes one to five times a week, and 15 (22%) one to three times a month. In the Casper et al. (1980) sample, 16% of the bulimic patients reported binge episodes at least daily, 27% several times a week, 24% about once a week, and 33% less than once a week.

Given these data, there are obvious problems in using the frequency criterion applied to bulimia nervosa as the guideline for subtyping anorexia nervosa. A significant proportion of anorexia nervosa patients classified as ''bulimic'' in the earlier studies would not have met the ''two episodes a week'' criterion (Casper et al., 1980; Garfinkel et al., 1980). In earlier studies, should these patients have been moved to the ''restricting'' or ''fasting'' subgroups and, in the absence of purging, what is their status under the DSM-IV? A detailed analysis of patients reporting infrequent bulimic episodes would be worthwhile because it is not clear whether these individuals more closely resemble patients for whom binge episodes are a dominant clinical feature. *However, to propose a subtyping system for anorexia nervosa that requires a threshold for frequency of binge eating that is similar to that recommended for bulimia nervosa is premature because it is based on insufficient published data.*

ONSET OF BINGE EATING
IN ANOREXIA NERVOSA

Beumont, Booth, Abraham, Griffiths, and Turner (1983) reported considerable variability in the time-frame for the appearance of binge eating, self-induced vomiting, and purgative abuse in a sample of 25 anorexia nervosa patients. In one of the most detailed descriptions of binge eating, Abraham and Beumont (1982) conducted detailed interviews with 32 consecutive patients who presented at an eating disorder clinic with the complaint of binge eating. Although only a minority of these patients ($n = 14$) had achieved a body weight that would have qualified for anorexia nervosa (nine had actually been treated for the disorder), and just three were below 85% of standard body weight at the time of presentation, it seemed from the patients' reports that binge eating often developed early in the course of anorexia nervosa, frequently antedating the first episode of emaciation. In all cases, the episodes of binge eating followed a period of "increased concern about body weight, manifested by the intention to diet" (p. 628).

This observation is in contrast to other studies that have linked binge eating to chronicity. Hsu (1988) indicated that restricting anorexics develop bulimia about twice as often as bulimic anorexics move to a restricting subtype. Kreipe, Churchill, and Strauss (1989) reported that although only 6 of 49 adolescent anorexia nervosa patients (13%) had a history of binge eating before hospitalization, 22 (45%) initiated the symptom during the mean 6.5-year follow-up period.

PAST VERSUS CURRENT BINGE EATING

Early studies that distinguished patients on the basis of binge eating employed different temporal parameters in defining the symptom. Casper et al. (1980) assigned patients to the bulimic subgroup if they currently *or ever* experienced binge eating, whereas for Garfinkel et al. (1980) the bulimic subtype "experienced bulimia *at the time* of initial consultation" (p. 1037). There has been considerable ambiguity in subsequent research regarding which of these criteria were used. The degree of overlap between different subtyping schemes and the relative merits of each have not been the subject of empirical investigation. This is particularly important because patients may move between bulimic and nonbulimic phases of their eating disorder and because classification based on historical versus current eating patterns may lead to very different conclusions. The DSM-IV criteria (APA, 1993) ignore this issue by simply stating that the person must "regularly" engage in binge eating without any guidance regarding the meaning of this term. On intuitive grounds alone, there would seem to be little merit in assigning patients to the binge-eating/purging subtype of anorexia nervosa in the absence of *current* binge eating unless there are compelling data to indicate that a history of this behavior denotes unique and enduring features.

DISCRETE PERIOD OF TIME

Although it is probably not the most critical factor in the definition of binge eating in anorexia nervosa, the theoretical or empirical justification for requiring that episodes occur in a discrete period of time (e.g., within any 2-hour period), as with bulimia nervosa, may be questioned. The original DSM-III criteria for bulimia nervosa required a time frame of usually less than 2 hours, but this was dropped because the DSM-III-R committee was not convinced that there should be any specific time limit to a binge episode (Pope, Hudson, Spitzer, & Williams, 1988). The reintroduction of this requirement in the DSM-IV criteria for bulimia nervosa is problematic, because it could conceivably exclude a patient who meets all other elements for binge eating but who binges and vomits more or less without interruption for prolonged periods. In these cases, it is often virtually impossible for either the patient or the trained interviewer to determine when one episode stops and another begins. During these chaotic periods, the entire experience may be clouded by intense affect and mental stupor. Although this issue may not present major practical problems in subtyping cases of anorexia nervosa, it has never been made clear why this aspect of the definition of binge eating is necessary.

SIZE OF BINGE EPISODES

The term "binge eating" has not universally denoted large amounts of food either in the mind of patients or of researchers (Beglin & Fairburn, 1992). Although the DSM-IV criteria for anorexia nervosa (binge-eating/purging type) do not explicitly state that patients must consume an *objectively* large amount of food, again assuming continuity with the definition used for bulimia nervosa, binge eating requires the consumption of an amount of food that is "definitely larger than most people would eat during a similar period of time and under similar circumstances." It is now well established that many of the episodes of overeating described as binge episodes by bulimia nervosa patients do not meet the "definitely larger" criterion (Davis et al., 1988; Rosen et al., 1986; Rossiter & Agras, 1990; also see Walsh, Chapter 3, this volume). There are no comparable data for anorexia nervosa patients, but it is reasonable to expect that the same would apply for this group. Although some definitions of the bulimic subtype of anorexia nervosa have required that the quantity of food consumed must be large (Casper et al., 1980; Garfinkel et al., 1980; Strober, 1981), "large" has not been operationally defined and it is not clear how rigorously the size requirement has been enforced. Commenting on an earlier study, Beumont (1988) concludes that "binge-eating was a symptom in 76% of the anorexia nervosa patients and, although the actual amount of food consumed during such episodes may not have been massive, eating at these times was subjectively experienced as uncontrolled" (p. 172). For earlier studies that divided anorexia nervosa patients into bulimic and non-bulimic subtypes (cf. DaCosta & Halmi, 1992), this raises the question of how patients should have been classified if they primarily or exclusively engaged in *subjective* bulimic episodes followed by self-induced vomiting or laxative abuse? (See Fairburn & Wilson, Chapter 1, this volume, for definition of subjective and objective bulimic episodes) Did individuals who primarily engaged in *subjective* bulimic episodes followed by purging more closely resemble their objectively bulimic or their nonbulimic counterparts? Did the amount eaten, the sense of loss of control surrounding this behavior, the compensatory behaviors (vomiting or laxative abuse), or some combination of these markers define the most homogeneous or the most meaningful subgroup of patients? Obviously, anorexia nervosa patients who engage in *subjective* bulimic episodes (i.e., loss of control but the amount of food eaten is small) may also have *objective* bulimic episodes at other times; however, there has been no systematic research on the proportion of bulimic episodes that qualify as subjective or objective in these patients.

Because some anorexia nervosa patients engage in compensatory behaviors after eating small amounts of food, subtyping them exclusively on the basis of the amount eaten introduced both practical and theoretical problems in earlier studies (DaCosta & Halmi, 1992). First, on a practical level, it is difficult to determine exactly how much patients have eaten prior to vomiting. Recent data for bulimia nervosa patients indicate that although there is a high correlation between recalled and actual food intake, patients' recall of the size of binge meals may be greater than actual size of binge meals (Hadigan, LaChaussée, Walsh, & Kissileff, 1992).

Second, although theoretical questions can be raised about the merit of defining binge episodes in terms of the amount eaten in bulimia nervosa, the issue becomes even more debatable with anorexia nervosa. In contrast to bulimia nervosa, eating relatively large amounts of food is one of the therapeutic objectives in anorexia nervosa! Particularly within the context of inpatient treatment, anorexia nervosa patients are encouraged to repeatedly consume objectively large amounts of food during a discrete period of time and they routinely experience this as a loss of control. This would technically conform to the definition of binge eating. As part of treatment, anorexia nervosa patients are encouraged to eat larger amounts of food but to reinterpret these quantities as appropriate (Garner, 1986; Garner & Bemis, 1982, 1985). Thus, relying on the amount of food eaten as a basis for subtyping anorexia nervosa, without taking possible therapeutic issues into consideration, adds yet another impediment to defining binge eating in objective terms. Nevertheless, defining binge eating in strictly subjective terms is also confusing because it means that identical amounts of food can be defined differently for different individuals or for the same individual over time. In sum, to use the size of binge episodes as a basis for defining subgroups of anorexia nervosa patients, in the absence of convincing data showing that this feature is meaningfully related to etiology or response to treatment, is completely unwarranted.

LOSS OF CONTROL DURING BINGE EPISODES

One of the other key elements in defining binge eating has been that it occurs within the context of a "sense of lack of control over eating during the episode (e.g., a feeling that one cannot stop eating or control what or how much one is eating)" (APA, 1993). This is consistent with the definition of binge episodes in early studies of bulimic anorexia nervosa patients (Casper et al., 1980; Garfinkel et al., 1980); however, it is not explicitly required in the DSM-IV criteria for subtyping anorexia nervosa. Again, although the significance of loss of control is still the subject of debate with respect to bulimia nervosa, the decision to require this attribute in order to satisfy the definition of binge eating has different diagnostic consequences for anorexia nervosa and bulimia nervosa. For bulimia nervosa, not satisfying this criterion would lead to exclusion; however, this is really not applicable in subtyping anorexia nervosa. If planned episodes of prodigious eating, followed by self-induced vomiting, were not defined as "binge episodes," it is conceivable that this could have led to the irrational decision in earlier studies to relegate such patients to the restrictor subtype (cf. DaCosta & Halmi, 1992). Although this possibility is less likely with the shift to the restricting versus binge-eating/purging subtyping system (APA, 1993), it is still theoretically possible for patients to be classified as restrictors if they engage in planned binge episodes. Although the majority of anorexia nervosa patients who engage in binge eating may report that they experience a lack of control over this behavior, individual differences in the meaning of this construct are not well understood. Sometimes the "planned" nature of eating binges is a function of chronicity in that these patients admit that they once felt a lack of control over their behavior, but now it is predictable and even pleasurable (Beumont, 1988). Intuitively, it could be argued that patients who view their aberrant behavior as under control or even desirable might have a worse prognosis than those for whom the same behavior is as ego-dystonic. Although we know very little about the number of patients (if any) that might fall into such a category, the definition of binge eating, if it is to be used for subtyping, should explicitly address the possibility.

TARGETING VOMITING AND/OR LAXATIVE ABUSE FOR SUBTYPING

The practical problems of defining binge episodes in an unambiguous manner (i.e., size, frequency, temporal parameters, associated features) and the resulting implications for subthreshold cases (Garner, Shafer, & Rosen, 1992; Garner, Garner, & Rosen, 1993) has provided justification for the DSM-IV scheme for targeting vomiting and/or laxative abuse as key symptoms in subtyping anorexia nervosa. Vomiting and laxative abuse are discrete behaviors with distinct terminations; thus, their use avoids many of the qualitative measurement problems associated with binge eating. The other rationale for subtyping the anorexia nervosa patients based on the presence or absence of compensatory behaviors is the serious physical health consequences and metabolic abnormalities associated with these symptoms (Beumont, 1988; Halmi, 1985).

The original DSM-IV proposal for subtyping anorexia nervosa (APA, 1991; DaCosta & Halmi, 1992) conformed to the earlier traditions of using the presence or absence of binge eating as the *sole criterion* for determining subgroup membership. This prompted Garner et al. (1993) to examine a dataset that overlapped with the one used in our earlier studies (Garfinkel et al., 1980; Garfinkel & Garner, 1982; Garner, Garfinkel, & O'Shaughnessy, 1985; Garner, Olmsted, & Garfinkel, 1985). The major research question was whether restrictors who purge were more similar to pure restrictors (i.e., restrictors who neither binged nor purged) and should remain as part of the restrictor group for subtyping purposes, or whether they were really more similar to the subgroup of anorexia nervosa who engage in binge eating. A large group of anorexia nervosa patients ($n = 190$), who would have been considered restrictors according to the earlier convention, were divided into two subgroups. The first group consisted of pure restrictors (AN-R $n = 116$) who reported no bingeing, vomiting, or laxative abuse in the last month. The second group of restrictors ($n = 74$) consisted of patients who did not binge, but who reported vomiting and/or laxatives abuse at least monthly (i.e., anorexia nervosa restrictor–purgers, AN-RP). There were no restrictors who used diuretics but did not engage in self-induced vomiting or laxative abuse. Thus, of the 190 patients who would have been classified as restrictors in earlier studies, 39% currently engaged in vomiting *and/or* laxative abuse in this analysis. Of the AN-RP group, 39% vomited exclusively, 46% abused laxatives exclusively, and 15% engaged in both of these compensatory behaviors. This is in contrast to the AN-B group in which 38% vomited only, 9% abused laxatives only, and 41% exhibited both of these behaviors (12% of this group neither vomited nor abused laxatives). Both

TABLE 4.2. Analysis of Variance Comparisons Between Anorexia Nervosa Subgroups (Restricting Nonpurgers, Restricting Purgers, and Bulimic Anorexics)

Item	Restricting nonpurgers (AN-R, $n = 116$) Mean (SD)		Restricting purgers (AN-RP, $n = 74$) Mean (SD)		Bulimic anorexics (AN-B, $n = 190$) Mean (SD)		F	p value
Age	21.0^{ab}	(6.0)	23.9^{a}	(6.2)	23.8^{b}	(5.8)	9.17	.0001
Age at onset	18.3	(4.7)	18.8	(4.8)	19.0	(4.6)	0.97	n.s.
Duration of illness (years)	2.8^{ab}	(3.8)	5.1^{a}	(6.4)	4.8^{b}	(4.6)	7.64	.0006
Weight (% MPMW)	67.2^{a}	(8.5)	70.4^{b}	(10.2)	74.7^{ab}	(8.5)	26.88	.00001
Maximum adult weight (% MPMW)	93.7^{ab}	(16.2)	99.3^{a}	(17.4)	101.5^{b}	(13.7)	9.67	.0001
Minimum adult weight (% MPMW)	62.9^{a}	(10.1)	64.4	(12.9)	67.7^{a}	(8.9)	8.85	.0002

Note. Shared superscripts indicated significant group differences at $p < .05$. From Garner, Garner, and Rosen (1993). Copyright 1993 by John Wiley & Sons, Inc. Adapted by permission.

of the restrictor groups (AN-R and AN-RP) were compared to each other and to the anorexia nervosa bulimics (AN-B, $n = 190$) who were defined in a manner similar to earlier studies (Garfinkel et al., 1980; Garner, Garfinkel, & O'Shaughnessy, 1985).

In our analysis, the only departure from earlier studies was that all patients were required to have a current weight at or below 85% of matched population mean weight. The three groups were compared on a wide range of clinical and psychometric variables. Although all three groups displayed similar levels of psychological disturbance on many variables, the overall pattern of findings indicated that the purging groups (i.e., AN-RP and AN-B) resembled each other, and both were different from the pure restricters (AN-R) on many clinical and psychometric dimensions. As indicated in Table 4.2, although all three groups had a similar age of onset, the AN-RP and AN-B groups were both older and had been ill about twice as long, on average, compared to the AN-R group. This finding is particularly important in light of the association between outcome and duration of illness in anorexia nervosa (Hall, Slim, Hawker, & Salmond, 1984; Hsu et al., 1979).

On measures of psychopathology, the findings for the AN-RP group were striking. The AN-RP group displayed significantly more psychopathology than the AN-R group on most measures where group differences were found, and their profile of disturbance was very similar to that observed with the AN-B group. In addition, the AN-RP group had significantly higher total scores than the AN-R group on the Eating Attitudes Test (EAT-26), the Dieting scale and the Bulimia and Food Preoccupation scale of the EAT-26 (Garner, Olmsted, Bohr, & Garfinkel, 1982). Although all three groups were similar on most Eating Disorders Inventory (EDI) subscales (Garner, 1991; Garner, Olmsted, & Polivy, 1983), the AN-B group scored significantly higher than the AN-R group on the Drive for Thinness and Interoceptive Awareness subscales (not shown on table) and higher than both other groups in the Bulimia subscale. Similarly, the AN-RP group displayed significantly more psychological distress than the AN-R group on the Hopkins Symptom Checklist (HSCL) (Derogatis, Lipman, Rickels, Uhlenhuth, & Covi., 1974). The AN-RP group had higher scores on the Total HSCL as well as on the Somatization, Obsessive-Compulsive, and Depression subscales. Similarly, they had higher scores on the Beck Depression Inventory (BDI) (Beck, Ward, Mendelson, Mock, & Erbaugh, 1961).

The proportions of patients reporting suicide attempts were significantly greater in the AN-RP (23%) and AN-B (22%) groups compared to the AN-R (3%) group. This is important because suicide is a major contributor to the mortality observed in anorexia nervosa (Theander, 1985). Clearly, the AN-RP group is suffering from severe emotional distress with little evidence that it is distinctive from the AN-B on any meaningful dimension other than binge eating. The failure to find differences between AN-R and AN-B groups on important variables such as depression in our earlier studies (e.g., Garner, Garfinkel, & O'Shaughnessy, 1985) can be explained by the inclusion of the more symptomatic AN-RP patients in the original AN-R group. In other words, removing the AN-RPs from the original AN-R group, makes the pure restrictors a much more homogeneous and less symptomatic group. Although these results are of interest, it should be emphasized that they are based on data derived from a clinical interview using definitions of bingeing and vomiting that are less rigorous than those in use today. However, these results support the DSM-IV subtyping system in which patients formerly considered as restrictors (but who also purged), are now shifted to the binge-eating/purging subtype.

As mentioned earlier, another compelling reason for the recent changes reflected in the DSM-IV criteria for subtyping anorexia nervosa is the serious physical health consequences associated with vomiting and laxative abuse (Comerci, 1990; Mitchell & Boutacoff, 1986; Halmi, 1985; Mitchell, Pomeroy, & Huber, 1988). In questioning the validity of bulimia nervosa as a diagnostic entity, Beumont (1988) has emphasized the need for diagnostic formulations to highlight these potentially dangerous compensatory behaviors.

Thus, to the degree that subtyping anorexia nervosa is intended to connote meaningful subgroup differences in terms of medical risks, chronicity, emotional distress, impulsivity, and suicidal risk, the symptom profile of the AN-RPs in the Garner et al. (1993) study provides support for the DSM-IV criteria because they now rely heavily on the presence or absence of purging behaviors in defining diagnostic subgroups. Although this deviates from earlier conventions relying on binge episodes as the defining characteristic in subtyping anorexia nervosa (cf. APA, 1991; Casper et al., 1980; DaCosta & Halmi, 1992; Garfinkel et al., 1980), there really has never been compelling evidence that bingeing is the prime marker or locus of pathology for best demarcating meaningful subgroups. Nevertheless, the DSM-IV system still fails to address the fact that *binge eating* plays a central role in the formula for subtyping anorexia nervosa in the absence of data where this symptom has been systematically defined and evaluated.

In light of this, it is reasonable to question whether the DSM-IV should have opted to subtype anorexia nervosa exclusively on the basis of the presence or absence of compensatory behaviors rather than binge eating. The data from the Garner et al. (1993) study were reanalyzed to address this question by dividing all anorexia nervosa patients into either purgers or nonpurgers, irrespective of whether they engaged in binge eating. Practically speaking, dividing patients into purgers and nonpurgers involved a relatively minor redistribution of patients from the three-group analyses. The AN-RP group was combined with 88% of the AN-B group (those who purged) to form the purging group ($n = 241$). The nonpurgers ($n = 139$) consisted of all of the AN-Rs plus the 12% of the former AN-B patients who did not purge. Results on clinical and psychometric variables closely paralleled the three group analyses, with the purgers displaying significantly greater psychopathology on most measures. In fact, the means for the nonpurging group changed very little from those of the AN-R means in the earlier analyses. Thus, an argument could be made for combining the AN-R patients with the small number of nonpurging bulimic anorexia nervosa patients to form a nonpurging anorexia nervosa subgroup. This would eliminate many of the formidable problems associated with the definition of binge eating mentioned earlier. Perhaps the best argument against this scheme, and in favor of the current DSM-IV criteria for subtyping anorexia nervosa, is that it would compromise the homogeneity of the pure restrictor subgroup.

Historically, binge eating has assumed a prominent role as the target symptom in subtyping anorexia nervosa; however, it may be that the *absence of binge eating*, within the context of severe undernutrition, deserves greater notice. The more that is known about the biology of weight regulation, and its implications for binge eating as a *normative response* to extreme weight suppression all along the weight spectrum (cf. Garner & Wooley, 1991), the more difficult it becomes to conceptualize the binge-eating anorexic as exhibiting a bizarre loss of control in the face of starvation. Far more perplexing is the relatively small proportion of eating disorder patients, the pure restrictors, who can tolerate their cravings for food for protracted periods without the expected loss of control. These patients may be thought of as the "aristocrats" of eating disorder patients because of their steadfast *unnatural* control over biological urges (Garner et al., 1993). The factors that permit sustained abstinence from binge eating in the face of severe restrictive dieting and weight suppression remain unknown. These may relate to primary biological dysfunction of hypothalamic–pituitary origin (Russell, 1970), or to the development of well-refined cognitive controls over biological urges (Garner & Bemis, 1982, 1985), or some combination of these and other factors implicated in the pathogenesis of anorexia nervosa (cf. Garner, 1993). Nevertheless, the anomalous control displayed by restricting patients tends to break down over time, and many of these patients eventually succumb to purging within the context of eating various amounts of food.

As if this entire diagnostic question were not confusing enough at this point, an issue needs to be raised that is rarely considered with regard

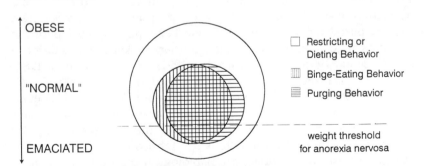

FIGURE 4.2. The relationship between bingeing, purging, and restricting in eating disorder patients at different body weights showing that all of these behaviors characterize subgroups of patients at different points along the weight spectrum. Adapted from Garner, Garner, and Rosen (1993), *International Journal of Eating Disorders, 13,* 171–185. Copyright 1993 by John Wiley & Sons, Inc. Reprinted by permission.

to the subtyping systems that have been used for anorexia nervosa. Denoting anorexia nervosa subtypes as "restrictors," "fasters," or "dieters" fails to adequately acknowledge that *all anorexia nervosa patients restrict their food intake, diet, and probably fast for abnormally long periods of time.* Some do this in association with binge eating, some with purging, some with both of these symptoms, and some with neither. Similarly, the vast majority of other nonemaciated eating disorder patients engage in restrictive dieting. Again, some binge eat, some purge, some do both, and some do neither. These symptoms occur at body weights falling all along the weight continuum. At the risk of reaching well beyond the readers' tolerance for Venn diagrams, Figure 4.2 provides an illustration of the relationship between the meaningful subgroups of patients who binge and/or purge at different body weights and highlights the fact that all eating disorder patients restrict their food intake.

SIGNIFICANCE OF BINGE EATING

Understanding the significance of binge eating would greatly facilitate answering many of the questions raised thus far in this chapter. Since the introduction of the term "bulimia nervosa" in Russell's (1979) classic paper the significance of binge eating remains controversial. It has been viewed either as a marker for a distinct syndrome of either psychological (Johnson & Connors, 1987) or biological origin (Pope & Hudson, 1988). It has been conceptualized as a compulsive or addictive behavior; however, in a thoughtful and comprehensive review, Wilson (1991) dispels the credibility of this model. (Also see Wilson, Chapter 7, this volume.) Binge eating has also been conceptualized as one of a constellation of symptoms resulting when external cultural imperatives to diet are pitted against internal biological systems responsible for the homeostatic regulation of body weight (Garner, Rockert, Olmsted, Johnson, & Coscina, 1985; Garner & Wooley, 1991; Polivy & Herman, 1985; Russell, 1979; Wardle, 1980; see also Polivy & Herman, Chapter 10, this volume; Blundell & Hill, Chapter 11, this volume.) The clinical observation that bingeing may play a role in numbing or modulating unpleasant emotions was described by Casper et al. (1980) and has become popular in other psychodynamic formulations (cf. Johnson & Connors, 1987). Although exclusively psychological or biological theories are inconsistent with what is known about the multiform expression of eating disorders, the unqualified attribution of bingeing to dieting must be tempered by the observation that binge eating is not a universal response to dieting, the quintessential example being anorexia nervosa restrictors. Although it has been argued that binge eating reflects fundamental problems of impulse control (cf. DaCosta & Halmi, 1992), many of the characteristics previously thought to distinguish bulimic anorexia nervosa patients also apply to patients who do not experience objective episodes of binge eating, but who control their weight, at least in part, through purging (Garner et al., 1993).

Finally, the shortcomings raised in using binge eating in the subtyping anorexia nervosa are not meant to diminish in any way the value of continued attempts to understand the nature and the significance of binge eating in this disorder. For many anorexia nervosa patients, binge eating is a central feature in their clinical presentation. For those for whom binge eating is not yet manifested, the threat of its emergence is usually a source of profound dread.

SUMMARY

The symptom of binge eating has been identified in anorexia nervosa for many years, and it is associated with certain deficits in psychosocial functioning. However, very little is actually known about the frequency or duration of bulimic episodes, the amount and nature of food eaten, the temporal parameters of episodes, the factors that precipitate and terminate episodes, or even the actual proportion of episodes that meet the definition of binge eating. Moreover, there are serious questions about the reliability of methods actually used in earlier studies that classified anorexia nervosa patients as bulimic. Although it has been hypothesized that binge eating is related to fundamental problems with impulse control or other underlying psychopathology, the precise relationship between these variables remains unclear.

Despite these unanswered questions, the DSM-IV system for subtyping anorexia nervosa relies, at least in part, on determining the presence or absence of binge eating. However, the term "binge eating" has not been defined, and there are no specific guidelines regarding the thresholds for binge eating necessary to qualify for membership in the binge-eating/purging group, in the absence of compensatory behaviors. Given how little is known about the nature and significance of binge eating in anorexia nervosa, and the ambiguities regarding its definition, it would seem to be premature to use binge eating as the basis for formally subtyping anorexia nervosa. Arguments made for targeting compensatory behaviors in the diagnosis of anorexia nervosa are supported by recent data indicating that anorexia nervosa patients who purge, regardless of whether or not they report objective bulimic episodes, may be meaningfully distinguished from pure restrictor anorexic patients in terms of important clinical and psychometric features. Although the nature and the significance of binge eating in anorexia nervosa is not clear at this time, it remains an important area for future research.

ACKNOWLEDGMENTS

I would like to thank Maureen Garner, PhD, and Lionel Rosen, MD, for their comments on an earlier draft of this manuscript.

REFERENCES

Abraham, S. F., & Beumont, P. J. V. (1982). How patients describe bulimia or binge eating. *Psychological Medicine, 12,* 625–635.

American Psychiatric Association. (1980). *Diagnostic and statistical manual of mental disorders* (3rd ed.). Washington, DC: Author.

American Psychiatric Association. (1987). *Diagnostic and statistical manual of mental disorders* (3rd ed., rev.). Washington, DC: Author.

American Psychiatric Association, Task Force of the DSM-IV. (1991). *DSM-IV options book: Work in progress 9/1/91.* Washington, DC: Author.

American Psychiatric Association. (1993). *DSM-IV draft criteria (3/1/93).* Washington, DC: Author.

Beck, A. T., Ward, C. H., Mendelson, M., Mock, J., & Erbaugh, J. (1961). An inventory for measuring depression. *Archives of General Psychiatry, 4,* 561–571.

Beglin, S. J., & Fairburn, C. G. (1992). What is meant by the term ''binge''? *American Journal of Psychiatry, 149,* 123–124.

Bell, R. (1985). *Holy anorexia.* Chicago: University of Chicago Press.

Berkman, J. M. (1939). Functional anorexia and functional vomiting. *Medical Clinics of North America, 23,* 901–912.

Beumont, P. J. V. (1977). Further categorization of patients with anorexia nervosa. *Australian and New Zealand Journal of Psychiatry, 11,* 123–126.

Beumont, P. J. V. (1988). Bulimia: It is an illness entity? *International Journal of Eating Disorders, 7,* 167–176.

Beumont, P. J. V., Booth, A. L., Abraham, S. F., Griffiths, D. A., & Turner, T. R. (1983). A temporal sequence of symptoms in patients with anorexia nervosa: A preliminary report. In P. L. Darby, P. E. Garfinkel, D. M. Garner, & D. V. Coscina (Eds.), *Anorexia nervosa: Recent developments in research* (pp. 129–136). New York: Alan R. Liss.

Beumont, P. J. V., George, G. G., & Smart, D. E. (1976). ''Dieters'' and ''vomiters and purgers'' in anorexia nervosa. *Psychological Medicine, 6,* 617–622.

Bhanji, S., & Mattingly, D. (1981). Anorexia nervosa: some observations on ''dieters'' and ''vomiters,'' cholesterol and carotene. *British Journal of Psychiatry, 139,* 238–241.

Bliss, E. L., & Branch, C. H. H. (1960). *Anorexia nervosa: Its history, psychology, and biology.* New York: Paul Hoever.

Bruch, H. (1962). Perceptual and conceptual disturbances in anorexia nervosa. *Psychosomatic Medicine, 24,* 187–194.

Bruch, H. (1973). *Eating disorders: Obesity, anorexia nervosa and the person within.* New York: Basic Books.

Casper, R. C. (1983). On the emergence of bulimia nervosa as a syndrome: A historical view. *International Journal of Eating Disorders, 2,* 3–16.

Casper, R. C., Eckert, E. D., Halmi, K. A., Goldberg, S. C., & Davis, J. M. (1980). Bulimia: Its incidence and clinical importance in patients with anorexia nervosa. *Archives of General Psychiatry, 37,* 1030–1034.

Cooper, Z., & Fairburn, C. G. (1987). The Eating Disorder Examination: A semi-structured interview for the assessment of the specific psychopathology of eating disorders. *International Journal of Eating Disorders, 6,* 1–8.

Comerci, G. D. (1990). Medical complications of anorexia nervosa and bulimia nervosa. *Medical Clinics of North America, 74,* 1293–1310.

Crisp, A. H. (1967). The possible significance of some behavioral correlates of weight and carbohydrate intake. *Journal of Psychosomatic Research, 11,* 117–131.

DaCosta, M., & Halmi, K. A. (1992). Classification of anorexia nervosa: Question of subtypes. *International Journal of Eating Disorders, 11,* 305–313.

Dally, P. J. (1969). *Anorexia nervosa.* New York: Grune & Stratton.

Davis, R., Freeman, R. J., & Garner, D. M. (1988). A naturalistic investigation of eating behavior in bulimia nervosa. *Journal of Consulting and Clinical Psychology, 56,* 273–279.

Derogatis, L., Lipman, R., Rickels, K., Uhlenhuth, E. H., & Covi, L. (1974). The Hopkins Symptom Checklist (HSCL): A self-report symptom inventory. *Behavioral Science, 19,* 1–15.

Eckert, E. D., Halmi, K. A., Marchi, P., & Cohen, J. (1987). Comparison of bulimic and non-bulimic anorexia nervosa patients during treatment. *Psychological Medicine, 17,* 891–898.

Fairburn, C. G. (1987). The definition of bulimia nervosa: Guidelines for clinicians and research workers. *Annals of Behavioral Medicine, 9,* 3–7.

Fairburn, C. G., Cooper, P. J., Kirk, J., & O'Connor, M. (1985). The significance of the neurotic symptoms of bulimia nervosa. *Journal of Psychiatric Research, 19,* 135–140.

Fairburn, C. G., & Garner, D. M. (1986). The diagnosis of bulimia nervosa. *International Journal of Eating Disorders, 5,* 403–419.

Fairburn, C. G., & Garner, D. M. (1988). Diagnostic criteria for anorexia nervosa and bulimia nervosa: The importance of attitudes to shape and weight. In D. M. Garner & P. E. Garfinkel (Eds.), *Diagnostic issues in anorexia nervosa and bulimia nervosa* (pp. 36–55). Monograph Series. New York: Brunner/Mazel.

Garfinkel, P. E., & Garner, D. M. (1982). *Anorexia nervosa: A multidimensional perspective.* New York: Brunner/Mazel.

Garfinkel, P. E., Moldofsky, H., & Garner, D. M. (1980). The heterogeneity of anorexia nervosa. *Archives of General Psychiatry, 37,* 1036–1040.

Garner, D. M. (1986). Cognitive therapy for anorexia nervosa. In K. D. Brownell & J. P. Foreyt (Eds.), *Handbook of eating disorders: Physiology, psychology, and treatment of obesity, anorexia, and bulimia* (pp. 301–327). New York: Basic Books.

Garner, D. M. (1991). *The Eating Disorder Inventory-2 Professional Manual.* Odessa, FL: Psychological Assessment Resources.

Garner, D. M. (1993). Pathogenesis of anorexia nervosa. *Lancet, 341,* 1631–1635.

Garner, D. M., & Bemis, K. M. (1982). A cognitive-behavioral approach to anorexia nervosa. *Cognitive Therapy and Research, 6,* 123–150.

Garner, D. M., & Bemis, K. M. (1985). Cognitive therapy for anorexia nervosa. In D. M. Garner & P. E. Garfinkel (Eds.), *Handbook of psychotherapy for anorexia nervosa and bulimia* (pp. 107–146). New York: Guilford Press.

Garner, D. M., Garfinkel, P. E., & O'Shaughnessy, M. (1985). The validity of the distinction between bulimia with and without anorexia nervosa. *American Journal of Psychiatry, 142,* 581–587.

Garner, D. M., Garner, M. V., & Rosen, L. W. (1993). Anorexia nervosa "restricters" who purge: Implications for subtyping anorexia nervosa. *International Journal of Eating Disorders, 13,* 171–185.

Garner, D. M., Olmsted, M. P., Bohr, Y., & Garfinkel, P. E. (1982). The Eating Attitudes Test: Psychometric features and clinical correlates. *Psychological Medicine, 12,* 871–878.

Garner, D. M., Olmsted, M. P., Davis, R., Rockert, W., Goldbloom, D., & Eagle, M. (1990). The association between bulimic symptoms and reported psychopathology. *International Journal of Eating Disorders, 9,* 1–15.

Garner, D. M., Olmsted, M. P., & Garfinkel, P. E. (1985). Similarities among bulimic groups selected by different weights and weight histories. *Journal of Psychiatric Research, 19,* 129–134.

Garner, D. M., Olmsted, M. P., & Polivy, J. (1983). Development and validation of a multidimensional Eating Disorder Inventory for anorexia nervosa and bulimia. *International Journal of Eating Disorders, 2,* 15–34.

Garner, D. M., Rockert, W., Olmsted, M. P., Johnson, C. L., & Coscina, D. V. (1985). Psychoeducational principles in the treatment of bulimia and anorexia nervosa. In D. M. Garner & P. E. Garfinkel (Eds.), *Handbook of psychotherapy for anorexia nervosa and bulimia* (pp. 513–572). New York: Guilford Press.

Garner, D. M., Shafer, C. L., & Rosen, L. W. (1992). Critical appraisal of the DSM-III-R diagnostic criteria for eating disorders. In S. R. Hooper, G. W. Hynd, & R. E. Mattison (Eds.), *Child psychopathology: diagnostic criteria and clinical assessment.* Hillsdale, NJ: Erlbaum.

Guiora, A. Z. (1967). Dysorexia: A psychopathological study of anorexia nervosa and bulimia. *American Journal of Psychiatry, 124,* 391–393.

Gull, W. W. (1873). Anorexia hysterica (apepsia hysteria). *British Medical Journal, 2,* 527.

Hadigan, C. M., LaChaussée, J. L., Walsh, B. T., & Kissileff, H. R. (1992). 24-hour dietary recall in patients with bulimia nervosa. *International Journal of Eating Disorders, 22,* 107–111.

Hall, A., Slim, E., Hawker, F., & Salmond, C. (1984). Anorexia nervosa: Long-term outcome in 50 female patients. *British Journal of Psychiatry, 145,* 407–413.

Halmi, K. A. (1985). Classification of the eating disorders. *Journal of Psychiatric Research, 19,* 113–119.

Herzog, D. B., & Norman, D. K. (1985). Subtyping eating disorders. *Comprehensive Psychiatry, 26,* 375–380.

Hsu, L. K. G. (1988). The outcome of anorexia nervosa: A reappraisal. *Psychological Medicine, 18,* 807–812.

Hsu, L. K. G., Crisp, A. H., & Harding, B. (1979). Outcome in anorexia nervosa. *Lancet, i,* 61–65.

Johnson, C., & Connors, M. E. (1987). *The etiology and treatment of bulimia nervosa*. New York: Basic Books.

Katzman, M. A., & Wolchik, S. A. (1984). Bulimia and binge eating in college women: A comparison of personality and behavioral characteristics. *Journal of Consulting and Clinical Psychology, 52*, 423–428.

King, A. (1963). Primary and secondary anorexia nervosa syndromes. *British Journal of Psychiatry, 109*, 470–479.

Kreipe, R. E., Churchill, B. H., & Strauss, J. (1989). Long-term outcome of adolescents with anorexia nervosa. *American Journal of Diseases of Children, 143*, 1322–1327.

Laessle, R. G., Wittchen, H. U., Fichter, M. M., & Pirke, K. M. (1989). The significance of subgroups of bulimia and anorexia nervosa: Lifetime frequency of psychiatric disorders. *International Journal of Eating Disorders, 8*, 569–574.

Meyer, B. C., & Weinroth, L. A. (1957). Observations on psychological aspects of anorexia nervosa. *Psychosomatic Medicine, 19*, 389–398.

Mickalide, A. D., & Anderson, A. E. (1985). Subgroups of anorexia nervosa and bulimia: Validity and utility. *Journal of Psychiatric Research, 19*, 121–128.

Mitchell, J. E., & Boutacoff, M. A. (1986). Laxative abuse complicating bulimia: Medical and treatment implications. *International Journal of Eating Disorders, 5*, 325–334.

Mitchell, J. E., Pomeroy, C., & Huber, M. (1988). A clinician's guide to the eating disorders medicine cabinet. *International Journal of Eating Disorders, 7*, 211–233.

Nemiah, J. C. (1950). Anorexia nervosa: a clinical psychiatric study. *Medicine, 29*, 225–268.

Polivy, J., & Herman, C. P. (1985). Dieting and bingeing: A causal analysis. *American Psychologist, 40*, 193–201.

Pope, H. G., & Hudson, J. I. (1988). Is bulimia nervosa a heterogeneous disorder? Lessons from the history of medicine. *International Journal of Eating Disorders, 7*, 155–166.

Pope, H. G., Hudson, J. I., Spitzer, R. L., & Williams, J. B. W. (1988). Revisions in the DSM-III criteria for bulimia nervosa. In D. M. Garner & P. E. Garfinkel (Eds.), *Diagnostic issues in anorexia nervosa and bulimia nervosa* (pp. 26–35). New York: Brunner-Mazel.

Rampling, D. (1985). Ascetic ideals and anorexia nervosa. *Journal of Psychiatric Research, 19*, 89–94.

Rosen, J. C., Leitenberg, H., Fisher, C., & Khazam, C. (1986). Binge-eating episodes in bulimia nervosa: The amount and type of food consumed. *International Journal of Eating Disorders, 5*, 255–267.

Rossiter, E. M., & Agras, W. S. (1990). An empirical test of DSM-III-R definition of binge. *International Journal of Eating Disorders, 9*, 513–518.

Rossiter, E. M., Agras, W. S., Telch, C. F., & Bruce, B. (1992). The eating patterns of non-purging bulimic subjects. *International Journal of Eating Disorders, 11*, 111–120.

Russell, G. F. M. (1970). Anorexia nervosa: Its identity as an illness and its treatment. In J. H. Price (Ed.), *Modern trends in psychological medicine* (Vol. 2, pp. 131–164). London: Butterworths.

Russell, G. F. M. (1979). Bulimia nervosa: An ominous variant of anorexia nervosa. *Psychological Medicine, 9,* 429–448.

Russell, G. F. M. (1985). The changing nature of anorexia nervosa: An introduction to the conference. *Journal of Psychiatric Research, 19,* 101–109.

Steinhausen, C. H., Rauss-Mason, C., & Seidel, R. (1991). Follow-up studies of anorexia nervosa: A review of four decades of outcome research. *Psychological Medicine, 21,* 447–454.

Strauss, J., & Ryan, R. M. (1988). Cognitive dysfunction in eating disorders. *International Journal of Eating Disorders, 7,* 19–27.

Strober, M. (1981). A comparative analysis of personality organization in juvenile anorexia nervosa. *Journal of Youth and Adolescence, 10,* 285–295.

Strober, M., Salkin, B., Burroughs, J., & Morrell, W. (1982). Validity of the bulimia–restrictor distinction in anorexia nervosa: Parental personality characteristics and family psychiatric morbidity. *Journal of Nervous and Mental Disease, 170,* 345–351.

Sunday, S. R., Halmi, K. A., Werdann, L., & Levey, C. (1992). Comparison of body size estimation and eating disorder inventory scores in anorexia and bulimia patients with obese, and restrained and unrestrained controls. *International Journal of Eating Disorders, 11,* 133–149.

Theander, S. (1970). Anorexia nervosa: A psychiatric investigation of 94 female patients. *Acta Psychiatrica Scandinavica* (suppl. 214).

Theander, S. (1985). Outcome and prognosis in anorexia nervosa and bulimia: Some results of previous investigations, compared with those of a Swedish long-term study. *Journal of Psychiatric Research, 19,* 493–508.

Toner, B. B., Garfinkel, P. E., & Garner, D. M. (1986). Long-term follow-up of anorexia nervosa. *Psychosomatic Medicine, 48,* 520–529.

Vandereycken, W., & Pierloot, R. (1983). The significance of subclassification in anorexia nervosa: A comparative study of clinical features in 141 patients. *Psychological Medicine, 13,* 543–549.

Walsh, B. T., Kissileff, H. R., Cassidy, S. M., & Dantzic, S. (1989). Eating behavior of women with bulimia. *Archives of General Psychiatry, 46,* 54–58.

Wardle, J. (1980). Dietary restraint and binge eating. *Behavior Analysis and Modification, 4,* 201–209.

Willmuth, M. E., Leitenberg, H., Rosen, J. C., & Cado, S. (1988). A comparison of purging and nonpurging normal weight bulimics. *International Journal of Eating Disorders, 7,* 825–835.

Wilson, G. T. (1991). The addiction model of eating disorders: A critical analysis. *Advances in Behaviour Research and Therapy, 13,* 27–72.

Wilson, G. T., & Eldredge, K. L. (1991). Frequency of binge eating in bulimic patients: Diagnostic validity. *International Journal of Eating Disorders, 10,* 557–561.

Wilson, G. T., Rossiter, E., Kleifield, E. I., & Lindholm, L. (1986). Cognitive-behavioral treatment of bulimia nervosa: A controlled evaluation. *Behaviour Research and Therapy, 24,* 277–288.

Yellowlees, A. J. (1985). Anorexia and bulimia in anorexia nervosa: A study of psychosocial functioning and associated psychiatric symptomatology. *British Journal of Psychiatry, 146,* 648–652.

Binge Eating
in Obesity

Marsha D. Marcus

Although Stunkard (1959) identified binge eating as a distinct eating pattern in some obese individuals, this phenomenon received little systematic attention until the mid-1980s. It is now widely recognized that there is a subgroup of obese individuals with significantly disordered eating characterized by binge eating and psychosocial impairment. However, research on disordered eating behavior among overweight individuals is in its infancy and many questions remain to be answered. In this chapter, findings related to binge eating in obese individuals are reviewed and unresolved issues are emphasized.

It should be noted at the outset that few of the studies of binge eating in obesity have utilized the definition of binge episodes adopted in this volume, i.e., the consumption of an objectively large amount of food given the circumstances with loss of control. Therefore, care will be taken to specify the criteria used in each of the background investigations discussed as well as to highlight the studies that have used the currently acceptable definition of a binge.

PREVALENCE OF BINGE EATING
IN OBESE INDIVIDUALS

The prevalence of binge eating among obese individuals is not known, but clinically significant binge problems are common among those seeking treatment for obesity. Defining a binge episode as the consumption of large or enormous amounts of food in short periods of time, Loro and Orleans (1981) found that 28.6% of obese patients who sought obesity treatment self-reported binge eating two or more times per week. Gormally, Black, Daston, and Rardin (1982), using a semistructured interview based on the third edition of the *Diagnostic and Statistical Manual of Mental Disorders* (DSM-III) criteria for bulimia (American Psychiatric Association, 1980), observed that 23% of overweight individuals applying for treatment had serious binge-eating problems. This finding was replicated by Keefe, Wyshogrod, Weinberger, and Agras (1984), who also found that, on interview, 23% of a group of obese individuals who had participated in a behavioral weight control program met DSM-III criteria for bulimia. Thus, available data indicate that more than 20% of overweight individuals seeking obesity treatment report significant problems with binge eating. However, none of these investigations used strictly defined criteria for binge eating, and those seeking treatment are not likely to be representative of obese individuals in general.

A recent study by Spitzer et al. (1992) defined a binge as the consumption of a large amount of food with an associated loss of control, a definition that resembles that adopted in this volume. The study was conducted as part of a multisite field trial of the proposed criteria for binge eating disorder (BED). This syndrome is characterized by regular binge eating without the regular compensatory purge or diet behaviors of bulimia nervosa (see Fairburn & Wilson, Chapter 1, this volume). Using a self-report questionnaire, these investigators found that 30.1% of a group of patients currently enrolled in weight control programs met diagnostic criteria for BED, compared to only 2% of subjects in the community samples. The 30.1% prevalence rate of BED observed in weight control patients is comparable to that observed in the previously described studies of obese individuals seeking treatment. However, further research is needed to clarify the rate of binge-eating problems among obese individuals in the community, since most of the community individuals surveyed in the Spitzer et al. (1992) study were in the normal weight range.

Epidemiological studies of binge-eating behavior among obese individuals are also needed to clarify other relevant characteristics of this group. For example, Spitzer et al. (1992) found that BED was likelier to occur in women than in men in both the treatment and community groups, but, as already noted, the community sample in the study was predominantly of normal weight. Similarly, data from obese individuals in treatment studies indicate that serious binge-eating problems are associated with increased adiposity (Telch, Agras, & Rossiter, 1988), and younger age (Marcus, Wing, & Lamparski, 1985), but we do not know if these findings would hold true in community groups of obese individuals. Finally, the individuals in previous studies have been predominantly middle-class Caucasians aged 30–45. Thus, community-based investigations using interview methodology are critical to enhance our understanding of this problem in individuals who differ in socioeconomic status, age, and ethnic backgrounds.

BINGE-EATING BEHAVIOR IN OBESE SUBJECTS

Anecdotal and descriptive studies have indicated that obese binge eaters closely resemble normal-weight bulimia nervosa patients with the notable exception that obese individuals do not report regular purge behaviors (Marcus & Wing, 1987). More recent research suggests both similarities and differences in the profiles of obese binge eaters and normal-weight bulimia nervosa patients. However, prior to discussion of these findings a conceptual note is in order.

Diagnostic Considerations

Studies providing data on obese binge eaters have used varying inclusion criteria. The adoption of differing definitions of the problem to be studied makes across-study comparisons difficult and may hinder the clarification of variables that may prove to have significant implications. Two such variables are weight (obese or nonobese) and purge behaviors (presence or absence).

For example, many recent studies have focused on "nonpurging bulimia" rather than on binge eating in obesity per se (e.g., McCann, Rossiter, King, & Agras, 1991; Rossiter, Agras, Telch, & Bruce, 1992; Telch, Agras, Rossiter, Wilfley, & Kenardy, 1990) Thus, obese and nonobese individuals were included in these investigations, but individuals who reported current or past purge behaviors (self-induced vomiting or abuse of laxatives or diuretics) were excluded. On average, the individuals in studies of nonpurging bulimia were significantly overweight as evidenced by the fact that the body mass index (BMI) of participants in these investigations was over 30 [BMI is calculated by weight(kg)/height(M)^2] and individuals with a BMI over 27 are considered to be obese (Pi-Sunyer, 1991). However, not *all* subjects in these studies were obese. For example, the range of weights of subjects in the Telch et al. (1990) study was 64.4 to 112.5 kg.

In the Spitzer et al. (1992) field trial of BED, as in the studies of nonpurging bulimia, both normal weight and obese individuals were studied. The diagnosis of BED was clearly associated with higher BMI, but a significant proportion of the small number of BED cases identified in the community sample ($n = 19$) had never been obese ($n = 8$). However, in contrast to the studies of nonpurging bulimia, the BED criteria in DSM-IV include individuals who purge at a frequency that falls short of that required for a diagnosis of bulimia nervosa. Finally, a third group of investigators have focused specifically on binge eating in obese individuals (Marcus, Wing, & Hopkins, 1988; Marcus, Smith, Santelli, & Kaye, 1992). In these studies, individuals of normal weight were excluded, but subjects reporting infrequent or intermittent purge behaviors were included.

In summary, it is clear that there are both obese and normal-weight individuals who report clinically significant problems with binge eating, but who do not regularly purge. However, it may be that normal-weight binge eaters differ from obese binge eaters in ways that have not as yet been identified. For example, obese and nonobese binge eaters may differ in the use of strict dieting or fasting between binge episodes to compensate for the effects of binge eating. Similarly, some obese individuals with binge-eating problems do report purge behaviors (Marcus et al., 1988), although not often at frequency levels required for a diagnosis of bulimia nervosa. However, it is not known whether purge behavior is associated with differing clinical characteristics or treatment outcome in obese binge eaters. Future research is needed to resolve these issues.

Binge Behavior

Several recent studies have shed light on binge-eating behavior in obese individuals, although methodological differences among them render overall conclusions equivocal. Rossiter et al. (1992) studied 22 women (average BMI = 33, SD = 5.7) who were seeking treatment for binge eating and who reported an average of at least two binge eating episodes (perceived ingestion of a large amount of food in a short time period) for the previous 6 months, loss of control during episodes, persistent concerns with shape and weight, and no current or past purge behavior. All subjects completed 7-day food records and noted binge episodes in their records. The food records yielded 225 self-described binge episodes that were analyzed for calorie and macronutrient intake and duration of episodes.

According to the food records, subjects averaged 5 binge days and 10.6 binge episodes during the 7-day assessment period. There was considerable variability in calorie intake and duration of episodes. The average calorie consumption was 602 kcal (SD = 634), only half that (1,200 kcal) previously observed by the authors in bulimia nervosa patients (Rossiter & Agras, 1990). The average duration of episodes was 38.5 minutes, with a range of 1 to 880 minutes. As would be expected, overall calorie intake was significantly higher on binge days (M = 2,357 kcal) than on nonbinge-eating days (M = 1,528 kcal). Finally, when macronutrient intake during binge episodes and nonbinge days was compared, there were no differences in the percentage of calorie intake in fat or carbohydrate, but intake of protein and fiber was higher on nonbinge days.

This investigation is significant as an initial attempt to learn about the binge behavior of nonpurging patients who binge eat, but the generalizability of findings is limited due to the lack of a control group of nonbinge-eating subjects. Further, the use of 7-day food records is problematic. Recent research has shown that energy intake reported in 7-day food records in free-living volunteers is significantly lower than actual intake independently assessed by sophisticated methodology (Livingstone et al., 1990; Mertz et al., 1991). The use of food records may be even more problematic with eating-disorder patients when shame and/or denial may affect perceptions and reports of eating behavior.

In another recent study (Marcus et al., 1992), the investigators utilized the Eating Disorder Examination (EDE) (Cooper & Fairburn, 1987; Fairburn & Cooper, Chapter 15, this volume), a semistructured interview designed to assess the complete range of psychopathology and behaviors specific to eating disorders, to evaluate 17 obese women seeking treatment for binge-eating problems. The EDE focuses on eating behaviors during the previous 28 days and yields five subscale scores, Restraint, Overeating, Shape Concern, Weight Concern, and Eating Concern. The EDE appears preferable to either food records or 7-day calendar recall methods in the assessment of binge eating, since it includes a thorough examination of subjects' eating habits. Further, the use of a 28-day time frame is probably more reliable for obese subjects whose eating behavior in a given week may not accurately reflect the binge-eating problem; for example, it is not uncommon for obese individuals to have a binge-free week while dieting (see Wilson, Chapter 11, this volume, for a discussion of assessment issues).

Objective bulimic episodes on the EDE are defined as episodes of eating that involve eating an unusually large amount of food given the circumstances *and* loss of control at the time. Subjective bulimic episodes are defined as episodes of eating where there is loss of control, but although the subject perceives the food intake as large, the amount is not actually large given the circumstances. The decision about what constitutes a large amount of food is made by the interviewer. When there is any doubt, the interviewer is directed not to classify the intake as large, and a subjective bulimic episode is coded.

The obese binge eaters in the Marcus et al. (1992) study reported significant difficulties with binge eating. On average, subjects reported objective bulimic episodes on 6.4 days and subjective episodes on 7.4 days during the previous 4 weeks. (The number of reported episodes was slightly higher, 7.0 objective episodes and 9.1 subjective episodes.) In contrast, a recent investigation using the EDE with normal-weight bulimia nervosa patients (Fairburn et al., 1991) reported an average of 23.7 objective bulimic episodes for these individuals, suggesting that bulimia nervosa patients have significantly higher frequencies of binge eating. However, conclusions about the relative severity of binge eating in bulimia nervosa patients compared to obese binge eaters are premature, since duration of episodes may vary between these groups of patients.

The subjects in the Marcus et al. (1992) study tended to report episodes of long duration (nearly 24% of episodes lasted the entire day) with food intake spread over the duration of the binge. Thus, total intakes were "borderline" large in many instances, and coded conservatively as subjective episodes. In contrast, as noted by Rossiter et al. (1992), the overeating episodes of normal-weight bulimia nervosa patients are more discrete and are punctuated by purging.

In summary, evidence from the Rossiter et al. (1992) and Marcus et al. (1992) studies indicates that obese binge eaters report binge eating on 3–5 days per week. However, since a significant number of binge episodes in obese patients are of day-long duration (Marcus et al., 1992) and because there are potential difficulties in the recall and demarcation of specific episodes (Rossiter et al., 1992), it appears warranted to follow the recommendation of Rossiter et al. (1992) to focus on number of binge days rather than episodes in the assessment of these patients.

Finally, two recent investigations have included both nonpurging bulimia patients (most of whom were obese) and purging bulimia nervosa patients. McCann et al. (1991) observed an average of 3.7 binge episodes per week in nonpurging patients compared to an average of 14.9 episodes per week in purging patients. However, no information about calorie intake or duration of episodes was collected, precluding fine-grained analyses of potential similarities and differences in binge behaviors between purging and nonpurging subjects. In contrast, Williamson, Prather, McKenzie, and Blouin (1990) observed a comparable frequency of binge episodes per week in purging (7.9 episodes) and nonpurging subjects (8.4 episodes). Again, it is difficult to reconcile the conflicting findings, but the study populations may have differed (e.g. nonpurging subjects averaged 34 years of age in the Williamson et al., 1990, study and 44.9 years in the McCann et al., 1991, study), or different definitions of binge eating may have been used. Additional investigations that compare the eating behavior of obese binge eaters and bulimia nervosa patients are needed to clarify similarities and differences in the eating behavior of these groups.

Purge Behaviors

As previously noted, studies of obese nonpurging bulimic subjects have, by definition, excluded individuals with current or past purge behaviors, but purge behaviors are not unknown in obese individuals. In fact, some obese individuals report *regular* purge behaviors and thus may meet

DSM-III-R criteria for bulimia nervosa, although obese patients appear to be uncommon among patients presenting for bulimia nervosa treatment. For example, Mitchell, Pyle, Eckert, Hatsukami, and Soll (1990) identified only 25 subjects who weighed 30% or more over ideal body weight in a series of 591 patients treated for bulimia nervosa. These investigators found that obese bulimia nervosa patients were likelier than normal-weight patients to abuse laxatives. It is not known whether normal-weight and obese bulimia nervosa patients differ in treatment outcome.

Purge behaviors are also reported among binge eaters seeking obesity treatment. Marcus et al. (1988) reported that approximately 13% of a group of obese binge eaters used self-induced vomiting at least occasionally and 26% misused laxatives. More recently, Marcus et al. (1992) found that 6.7% of obese binge eaters reported an episode of vomiting during the previous 28 days and 6.7% reported the use of laxatives. Finally, Hudson et al. (1988) reported that among a group of obese individuals who met DSM-III criteria for bulimia, 9% reported self-induced vomiting, 17% reported laxative misuse, and 39% reported the use of diuretics.

In summary, it appears that a subgroup of obese binge eaters do report purge behaviors, but in many cases they do not occur with sufficient frequency to be considered ''regular.'' However, it is apparent that purge behaviors are not rare among obese binge eaters, and thus it may be important to more clearly operationalize the term ''regular'' as it applies to purge behavior in bulimia nervosa, since an infrequent but consistent pattern of purging (e.g., once a month) could be considered regular. Moreover, future studies are needed to determine whether obese ''occasional purgers'' differ from nonpurgers on any relevant clinical parameters or in treatment outcome.

Dieting, Shape, and Weight Concerns

Although questions remain about the binge and purge behaviors of obese binge eaters, available data indicate that, with the important exception of dietary restraint, obese binge eaters report levels of eating disorder psychopathology comparable to those of a group of previously described normal-weight bulimia nervosa patients. Marcus et al. (1992) reported that there were no significant differences between obese binge eaters and a previously described group of bulimia nervosa patients (Wilson & Smith, 1989) on four of five EDE subscales, Overeating, Eating Concern, Shape Concern, and Weight Concern; however, bulimia nervosa patients had significantly higher levels on the Restraint Subscale (Figure 5.1).

Obese binge eaters tended to note intense preoccupation with shape

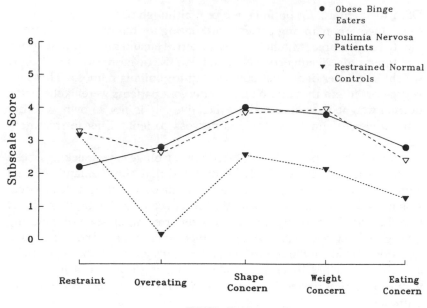

FIGURE 5.1. EDE scoring profiles of obese binge eaters, normal-weight bulimia nervosa patients and normal-weight restrained eaters. From "Characterization of Eating Disordered Behavior in Obese Binge Eaters" by M. D. Marcus, D. Smith, R. Antelli, and W. Kaye, 1992, *International Journal of Eating Disorders*, *12*, p. 252. Copyright 1992 by John Wiley & Sons, Inc. Reprinted by permission.

and weight and to report that shape and/or weight played an important role in self-evaluation. However, future research directly comparing obese binge eaters with bulimia nervosa patients is needed to clarify potential differences and similarities between these groups in shape and weight concerns. For example, few of the obese women desired an ideal body weight that would be considered unrealistically slim. Thus, although the level of shape and weight preoccupation in obese women appears to be intense, in contrast to bulimia nervosa patients obese binge eaters do not seem to overvalue an extremely thin body size.

There was one significant difference between the obese binge eaters and bulimia nervosa patients in the Marcus et al. (1992) study. The obese subjects reported levels on the Restraint Subscale the EDE that were significantly lower than those reported for normal-weight bulimia nervosa patients (Wilson & Smith, 1989). Obese binge eaters frequently reported strict dieting standards but did not necessarily obey the rules during the 28-day assessment period. In addition, several subjects also reported that they were overwhelmed by repeated failures and so had given up all efforts to diet. Future studies are required to clarify the role of dieting in the development and maintenance of binge-eating problems in obese individuals.

The relationship among binge eating, dieting, and obesity is unclear. Dieting usually precedes the onset of binge eating in normal-weight individuals, but there are few systematic data relating to obese binge eaters. Available information indicates that these patients tend to report juvenile onset of obesity (Marcus et al., 1992), strong family histories of obesity, and frequent bouts of dieting and weight loss (Spitzer et al., 1992). However, one study (Wilson, Nonas, & Rosenblum, 1993) found that approximately two-thirds of a sample of obese binge eaters reported binge eating prior to the development of obesity. Thus, additional studies are needed to clarify the relationships among binge eating, dieting, and the development and maintenance of obesity.

COMPARISONS OF OBESE BINGE EATERS AND NON-BINGE-EATERS

There are a growing number of studies that have examined differences between obese binge eaters and obese individuals without binge-eating problems. These studies have added to our understanding of disordered eating and underscored the heterogeneity of obesity.

Dietary Attitudes and Behavior

Although obese binge eaters may not show the same level of dieting behavior as normal-weight bulimia nervosa patients, they clearly differ from obese non-binge-eaters in dieting attitudes and eating behavior. For example, Gormally et al. (1982) reported that obese binge eaters were characterized by a continual struggle to avoid binge episodes and perfectionistic standards for dieting. In contrast, obese non-binge-eaters did not report problems controlling urges to eat or rigid standards for dieting. Wilson et al. (1993) used a self-report version of the Eating Disorder Examination to classify 170 obese individuals seeking treatment as either binge eaters (minimum frequency of one episode per week) or non-binge-eaters. When compared to non-binge-eaters ($n = 129$), obese binge eaters of similar weight ($n = 31$) reported significantly less perceived control over eating, more fear of weight gain, more dissatisfaction with weight, and more food and weight preoccupation.

Differences between bingers' and non-binge-eaters' specific dieting practices are less clear. Marcus et al. (1985) asked obese 66 applicants to a behavioral weight control program to complete the Binge Eating Scale (Gormally et al., 1982), a measure designed to assess binge-eating severity in obese individuals, and the Eating Inventory (Stunkard & Messick, 1985), a measure of habitual dieting behavior. The Eating Inventory consists of three subscales, Cognitive Restraint (deliberate use of dieting strategies such as calorie counting and portion control), Disinhibition (overeating in response to emotional or cognitive cues), and Hunger. Severity of binge eating was significantly associated with two of the three factors of the Eating Inventory, Disinhibition and Hunger ($p < .001$). These findings were recently replicated by Lowe and Caputo (1991), who also found significant associations between binge severity and the Disinhibition and Hunger subscales of the Eating Inventory. However, in contrast to Marcus et al. (1985), who did not observe a relationship between binge severity and the Cognitive Restraint subscale, Lowe and Caputo (1991) found that Cognitive Restraint was negatively associated with binge severity in obese individuals. That is, binge eaters were less likely than non-binge-eaters to use strategies such as portion control, calorie counting, or eating slowly to moderate intake. A third report has corroborated that binge eaters and non-binge-eaters do not appear to differ on specific diet-related behaviors. Wilson et al. (1993) found no differences between binge eaters and non-binge-eaters in food restriction, avoidance of specific foods or adherence to specific dietary rules. These data suggest that obese binge eaters, in contrast to non-binge-eaters, are more preoccupied by thoughts of food and impulses to overeat, but appear to be no likelier than obese nonbingers to utilize specific strategies to control their weight.

Eating Behavior

Recently, differences between obese binge eaters and non-binge-eaters have been studied in the laboratory (Goldfein, Walsh, Devlin, LaChaussee, & Kissileff, 1992; Yanovski et al., 1992). Goldfein et al. (1992) sought to determine whether obese women meeting criteria for binge eating disorder differed from obese non-binge-eaters in eating behavior. On separate occasions subjects were asked to consume a binge meal of ice cream and a binge meal chosen from an array of foods. There were no between-group differences in the calorie intake of the ice cream meal, but binge eaters consumed significantly more calories over a longer duration when presented with an array of items. No differences in macronutrient intake were observed.

In the Yanovski et al. (1992) study, 10 obese women who met criteria for binge eating disorder and 9 non-binge-eating control subjects participated in three laboratory meals. All subjects attended an adaptation session where they were presented with a high-fat yogurt shake. Subsequently, all subjects returned for two experimental sessions where they were provided a meal comprised of items such as chicken, rice, and salad as well as typical binge items including ice cream, cake, and potato chips. At experimental sessions subjects were given tape-recorded instructions to eat as much as they would in a normal meal or to let themselves go and to eat as much as they could. The two instructional sets were presented across subjects in a counterbalanced order. When subjects were directed to eat normally, binge eaters consumed an average of 2,343 kcal in comparison to an average of 1,640 kcal for non-binge-eaters, $p < .02$; the groups did not differ in macronutrient intake. When subjects were instructed to eat as much as they could, binge eaters again consumed significantly more than non-binge-eaters (2,963 vs. 2,017, $p < .005$). In addition, binge eaters ingested a significantly greater percentage of calories as fat and less as protein. (It is interesting to note that the calorie intake of binge eaters during a single episode in this laboratory study was greater than the whole day intake self-reported in the Rossiter et al. [1992] study described earlier, again suggesting that food records are of questionable validity in assessing binge behavior.)

In summary, initial laboratory investigations indicate that binge eaters ingest significantly more than non-binge-eaters of comparable weight in regular meals as well as during episodes of overeating. It also appears that binge eaters may consume more fat during binge episodes. This finding is consistent with recent findings on the eating behavior of normal-weight bulimia nervosa patients. Weltzin, Hsu, Pollice, and Kay (1991) reported that the percentage of fats, but not carbohydrates, increased in bulimia nervosa patients as meal size and overall 24-hour calorie intake increased. Thus, available evidence suggests that both normal-weight and overweight binge eaters eat high-fat foods during overeating episodes.

Psychiatric Status

Numerous questionnaire studies have confirmed that there are robust differences between obese binge eaters and non-binge-eaters in severity of depressive symptoms (Marcus et al., 1988; Prather & Williamson, 1988), symptoms of personality disorder (Fitzgibbon & Kirschenbaum, 1990), and psychiatric symptomatology, in general (Kolotkin, Revis, Kirkley, & Janick, 1987; Marcus et al., 1988). Moreover, at least one questionnaire study has found that obese binge eaters and non-binge-eaters report differences in alcohol abuse and histories of physical or sexual victimization. Kanter, Williams, and Cummings (1992) identified 164 self-reported binge eaters on the basis of modified DSM-III-R criteria for bulimia nervosa (APA, 1987) and 114 individuals who denied binge-eating problems among a group of 336 adults seeking treatment for obesity. Subjects completed questionnaires documenting personal history of alcohol use, parental alcohol abuse, and history of physical and sexual abuse. Results indicated that the binge eaters, when compared to non-binge-eaters, reported significantly more personal and parental abuse of alcohol and higher overall rates of physical or sexual victimization. In summary, data from questionnaire studies indicate profound differences between obese binge eaters and non-binge-eaters in psychiatric status. However, findings based on self-report must be treated cautiously because clinical interviews are required to establish clearly psychiatric diagnoses and histories.

Studies that have utilized structured psychiatric interviews have also documented differences between binge eaters and non-binge-eaters in lifetime prevalence rates of diagnosable psychiatric disorders. Hudson et al. (1988) compared 23 obese women who met DSM-III criteria for bulimia to 47 obese women who did not meet criteria for bulimia. The obese bulimic subjects reported significantly higher lifetime prevalence rates of major affective disorders than the obese nonbulimic subjects. Marcus et al. (1990a) utilized the Diagnostic Interview Survey, a highly structured psychiatric interview, to compare lifetime prevalence rates of DSM-III psychiatric disorders in 25 obese binge eaters and 25 non-binge-eaters of similar age and weight. Sixty percent of binge eaters met criteria for one or more psychiatric disorder compared to 28% of non-binge-eaters, $p < 0.05$. There were also significant differences between binge eaters and non-binge-eaters in the lifetime prevalence rate of affective disorders, 32% versus 8%, $p < 0.05$, respectively. Episodes of major depression in binge eaters were all characterized by weight gain, suggesting that weight changes during depressive episodes may contribute to obesity in these subjects and/or that binge eating may be exacerbated during periods of depression.

In a third study (Yanovski, Nelson, Dubbert, & Spitzer, in press) the Structured Clinical Interview for DSM-III-R was used to assess both Axis I and Axis II disorders in 43 obese individuals who met criteria for binge eating disorder and 85 control subjects. As in the above investigations, there were significantly higher lifetime rates of mood disorders among individuals meeting criteria for binge eating disorder. Binge eaters compared to non-binge-eaters also reported a higher lifetime prevalence rates of panic disorder. The Yanovski et al. (in press) study is of particular interest because interview methodology was also used to assess rates of personality disorders. Results indicated that binge eaters were likelier than non-binge-eaters to meet criteria for any personality disorder as well as the specific diagnoses of borderline and avoidant personality disorder.

In summary, interview studies have found consistently that obese binge eaters have higher lifetime prevalence rates of mood disorders than obese non-binge-eaters. Although the Yanovski et al. (in press) study found higher rates of panic disorder among obese binge eaters, neither the Marcus et al. (1990a) study nor the Hudson et al. (1988) investigations observed significant differences between binge eaters and non-binge-eaters in rates of other specific psychiatric disorders. However, the sample sizes in both investigations were too small to detect differences in disorders that are less prevalent than depression. For example, Marcus et al. (1990a) found that more binge eaters (16%) than non-binge-eaters (4%) reported a lifetime history of social phobia, but this difference was not significant. Similarly, Hudson et al. reported nonsignificant differences between obese binge eaters and non-binge-eaters in alcohol abuse or dependence (22% vs. 9%, respectively). Potential differences between binge eaters and non-binge-eaters in alcohol abuse are especially relevant, since bulimia nervosa and alcohol abuse commonly co-occur (see Wilson, Chapter 6, this volume), and these patients may require alternative treatments (Mitchell, Pyle, Eckert, & Hatsukami, 1990). Thus, studies of larger groups of binge eaters and non-binge-eaters are needed to allow for meaningful comparisons of disorders other than depression.

Only one study (Yanovski et al., in press) to date has used interview methodology to compare obese patients with and without binge-eating problems in rates of personality disorders. Since personality pathology is believed to complicate treatment of bulimia nervosa (Johnson, Tobin, & Enright, 1989) and has been shown to negatively affect treatment outcome of disorders including major depression and panic disorder (Reich & Green, 1991), additional studies of Axis II diagnoses among obese binge eaters are warranted.

Studies comparing rates of psychiatric comorbidity in obese binge eaters and normal-weight bulimia nervosa patients may also shed light on the spectrum of eating disorder patients, since extant studies have yielded conflicting data. For example, McCann et al. (1991) found that purging bulimics when compared to nonpurging bulimics had higher rates of major depression, panic disorder, and past anorexia nervosa as well as more narcissistic, self-defeating, and borderline features. Similarly, Prather and Williamson (1988) found that bulimia nervosa patients self-reported more psychiatric symptomatology than overweight binge eaters. In contrast, Shisslak, Pazda, and Crago (1990) found that overweight bulimics reported more psychopathology than normal-weight bulimics, but less than underweight bulimic patients on the Minnesota Multiphasic Personality Inventory (MMPI).

Response to Treatment

Clinical observers (Meyer, 1973; Wilson, 1976) have consistently suggested that binge eating is negatively associated with treatment outcome in weight control programs and initial empirical work also has indicated poorer weight losses in binge eaters. Gormally, Rardin, and Black (1980) found that a history of repeated weight loss coupled with frequent binge eating was associated with good short-term weight loss but poor maintenance in a behavioral program. Keefe et al. (1984) retrospectively assessed patients who had completed a nine-session behavioral weight control program. Patients who met DSM-III criteria for bulimia lost significantly less weight than nonbulimics both at posttreatment and 6-month follow-up.

In a prospective investigation, Marcus et al. (1988) identified a group of obese women who met DSM-III criteria for bulimia and a group of similar age and weight who reported few or no problems with binge eating. Patients were randomized to a standard or modified behavioral weight control program, and all patients attended weekly meetings for 10 weeks with follow-up assessments at 6 and 12 months. The standard behavioral weight control program emphasized self-monitoring of calories, stimulus control techniques, self-reinforcement, planning ahead, goal setting, techniques to deal with negative emotions, and cognitions and relapse prevention. The modified program included these components and added strategies recommended for normal-weight binge eaters that could be readily integrated into the behavior weight control program. These included the use of a structured meal plan of three meals per day, instruction on the use of exercise as an alternative to overeating, and training in the use of positive self-statements to counteract negative thinking about dieting and coping with urges to overeat. However, the focus of the modified treatment condition continued to be weight loss. Subjects in both standard and modified conditions were instructed to consume 1,000–1,200 cal/day, to self-monitor caloric intake (not binges), and because binge eaters and non-binge-eaters were treated together in groups, there was no discussion of binge eating or the attitudes and behaviors associated with it.

The results of this study confirmed marked differences between binge eaters and non-binge-eaters in treatment outcome. Contrary to hypothesis, however, *no* significant differences between the standard and modified treatment conditions were observed on any outcome measure. Collapsing data across treatment conditions, binge eaters and non-binge-eaters did not differ significantly in the amount of weight lost during active treatment (10.1 and 11.4 lb, respectively). However, non-binge-eaters maintained a significantly greater weight loss than binge eaters

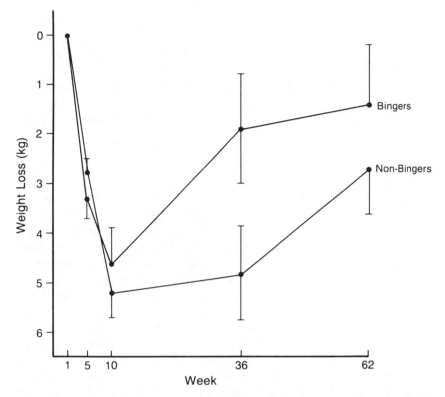

FIGURE 5.2. Weight change (*M* ± SEM) as a function of binge status. From "Obese Binge Eaters: Affect, Cognitions, and Response to Behavioral Weight Control" by M. D. Marcus, R. R. Wing, and J. Hopkins, 1988, *Journal of Consulting and Clinical Psychology, 56,* p. 437. Copyright 1988 by the American Psychological Association. Reprinted by permission.

at the 6-month follow-up. Weight loss from pretreatment to 6-month follow-up was 4.1 lb for binge-eaters compared to 10.6 lb for non-binge-eaters, $p < 0.02$. The difference in weight loss between binge eaters and non-binge-eaters was not significant at 1-year follow-up (3.6 vs. 6.4 lb, respectively) (see Figure 5.2). Self-reported mood improved for all subjects during the course of treatment, replicating previous findings about mood and participation in behavioral weight control programs (Wing, Marcus, Epstein, & Kupfer, 1983). However, binge eaters reported more distress than non-binge-eaters at all assessment points. Similarly, binge eaters continued to report significantly more maladaptive eating behavior than non-binge-eaters throughout the period of study. Thus, the pattern of maladaptive eating behavior and associated dysphoria of binge eaters was not ameliorated by behavioral obesity treatment.

In summary, findings from the weight control literature suggest that standard or modified behavioral weight control programs are not adequate to address the binge-eating problems of obese women and that these patients require programs that specifically target their bulimic behaviors.

Recent investigations have sought to determine whether treatments that focus on disordered eating rather than weight loss would be effective in the treatment of obese binge eaters. Two studies (Smith, Marcus, & Kaye, 1992; Telch et al., 1990) have found that short-term group cognitive-behavioral therapy is effective in reducing binge eating in overweight patients, indicating that this treatment may be effective in addressing the specific problems of these patients. Moreover, two other investigations (Marcus et al., 1990b; McCann & Agras, 1990b) have indicated that another modality used to treat bulimia nervosa, antidepressant medication, may also be useful in treating obese binge eaters.

Despite the promising results of the studies of cognitive-behavioral therapy and antidepressants, important questions about the treatment of obese binge eaters remain. First, the effects of treatment have been modest. For example, only 50% of the patients in the Smith et al. (1992) cognitive-behavioral therapy study and 60% of patients in the McCann & Agras (1990b) antidepressant study were abstinent from binge eating at posttreatment. Second, it is not known how patients treated with either modality fare over longer term follow-up. Significant relapse was observed in the Telch et al. (1990) study of cognitive-behavioral therapy; 79% of patients were abstinent from binge eating at posttreatment, but only 46% of patients remained abstinent at 10-week follow-up. Binge eating also tended to return to baseline levels after antidepressant drug withdrawal in the McCann and Agras (1990b) investigation. These data suggest that obese binge eaters may require more intensive treatments and that to evaluate treatment longer term follow-up is essential.

Finally, neither the Telch et al. (1990) or Smith et al. (1992) studies observed weight loss in obese binge eaters over the short term. Although it is possible that weight loss would occur over time as the result of successful treatment of disordered eating, the long-term effect on weight of cognitive-behavioral treatment of binge eating is not known.

We believe that it is necessary to address both the disordered eating and obesity in these patients. Obesity is associated with increased risk of a variety of health problems including hypertension, diabetes, certain cancers, and cardiovascular disease. The health risks of obesity are significant at a body mass index greater than 27 and increase with the severity of obesity (Pi-Sunyer, 1991). Obese binge eaters are vulnerable to significant morbidity associated with eating disorders *and* obesity, and thus the successful treatment of these patients must lead to both normalization of eating and at least moderate weight loss. Additional research to determine the long-term effects of cognitive-behavioral therapy on both binge eating and weight is needed. Further, research on the long-term effects of behavioral weight control programs is required, since previous work showing poor treatment outcome of binge eaters in behavioral weight control programs (Keefe et al., 1984; Marcus et al., 1988) was conducted utilizing treatments that were considerably briefer (9–10 sessions) and less comprehensive than those in current use.

Our research group at the University of Pittsburgh is currently conducting a study designed to test the long-term effectiveness of a 24-week cognitive-behavioral treatment program developed specifically for obese binge eaters. This program is an adaptation of Fairburn's cognitive-behavioral approach that has been used successfully with bulimia nervosa patients (see Fairburn, 1985; Fairburn, Marcus, & Wilson, Chapter 16, this volume for a description of these adaptations). Moreover, we will compare the outcome of this treatment to that achieved with an intensive behavioral weight control program. Investigations such as this, and others that are in progress, are likely to greatly enhance our understanding of obese binge eaters in the next several years.

REFERENCES

American Psychiatric Association. (1980). *Diagnostic and statistical manual of mental disorders* (3rd ed.). Washington, DC: Author.

American Psychiatric Association. (1987). *Diagnostic and statistical manual of mental disorders* (3rd ed., rev.). Washington, DC: Author.

Cooper, Z., & Fairburn, C. (1987). The Eating Disorder Examination: A semistructured interview for the assessment of the specific psychopathology of eating disorders. *International Journal of Eating Disorders, 6,* 1–8.

Fairburn, C. G. (1985). A cognitive-behavioral treatment for bulimia. In D. M. Garner & P. E. Garfinkel (Eds.), *Handbook of psychotherapy for anorexia nervosa and bulimia* (pp. 160–192). New York: Guilford Press.

Fairburn, C. G., Jones, R., Peveler, R. C., Carr, S. J., Solomon, R. A., O'Connor, M. E., Burton, J., & Hope, R. A. (1991). Three psychological treatments for bulimia nervosa: A comparative trial. *Archives of General Psychiatry, 48,* 463–469.

Fitzgibbon, M. L., & Kirschenbaum, D. S. (1990). Heterogeneity of clinical presentation among obese individuals seeking treatment. *Addictive Behaviors, 15,* 291–295.

Goldfein, J., Walsh, B. T., Devlin, M. J., LaChaussee, J., & Kissileff, H. (1992, April). *Eating behavior in binge eating disorder.* Paper presented at the fifth International Conference on Eating Disorders, New York.

Gormally, J., Black, S., Daston, S., & Rardin, D. (1982). The assessment of binge eating severity among obese persons. *Addictive Behaviors, 7,* 47–55.

Gormally, J., Rardin, D., & Black, S. (1980). Correlates of successful response to a behavioral weight control clinic. *Journal of Counseling Psychology, 27,* 179–191.

Hudson, J. I., Pope, H. G., Jr., Wurtman, J., Yurgelun-Todd, D., Mark, S., & Rosenthal, N. E. (1988). Bulimia in obese individuals: Relationship to normal weight bulimia. *Journal of Nervous and Mental Disease, 176,* 144–152.

Johnson, C., Tobin, D., & Enright, A. (1989). Prevalence and clinical characteristics of borderline patients in an eating-disordered population. *Journal of Clinical Psychiatry, 50,* 9–15.

Kanter, R. A., Williams, B. E., & Cummings, C. (1992). Personal and parental alcohol abuse, and victimization in obese binge eaters and non-bingeing obese. *Addictive Behaviors, 17,* 439–445.

Keefe, P. H., Wyshogrod, D., Weinberger, E., & Agras, W. S. (1984). Binge eating and outcome of behavioral treatment of obesity: A preliminary report. *Behaviour Research and Therapy, 22,* 319–321.

Kolotkin, R. L., Revis, E. S., Kirkley, B., & Janick, L. (1987). Binge eating in obesity: Associated MMPI characteristics. *Journal of Consulting and Clinical Psychology, 55,* 872–876.

Livingstone, M. B. E., Prentice, A. M., Strain, J. J., Coward, W. A., Black, A. E., Barker, M. E., McKenna, P. G., & Whitehead, R. G. (1990). Accuracy of weighed dietary records in studies of diet and health. *British Medical Journal, 300,* 708–712.

Lowe, M. R., & Caputo, G. C. (1991). Binge eating in obesity: Toward the specification of predictors. *International Journal of Eating Disorders, 10,* 49–55.

Marcus, M. D., Smith, D., Santelli, R., & Kaye, W. (1992). Characterization of eating disordered behavior in obese binge eaters. *International Journal of Eating Disorders, 12,* 249–256.

Marcus, M. D., & Wing, R. R. (1987). Binge eating among the obese. *Annals of Behavioral Medicine, 9,* 23–27.

Marcus, M. D., Wing, R. R., Ewing, L., Kern, E., Gooding, W., & McDermott, M. (1990a). Psychiatric disorders among obese binge eaters. *International Journal of Eating Disorders, 9,* 69–77.

Marcus, M. D., Wing, R. R., Ewing, L., Kern, E., McDermott, M., & Gooding, W. (1990b). A double-blind, placebo-controlled trial of fluoxetine in the treatment of obese binge eaters and non-binge eaters. *American Journal of Psychiatry, 147,* 876–881.

Marcus, M. D., Wing, R. R., & Hopkins, J. (1988). Obese binge eaters: Affect, cognitions and response to behavioral weight control. *Journal of Consulting and Clinical Psychology, 56,* 433–439.

Marcus, M. D., Wing, R. R., & Lamparski, D. (1985). Binge eating and dietary restraint in obese patients. *Addictive Behaviors, 10,* 163–168.

McCann, U. D., & Agras, W. S. (1990a). Non-purging bulimia nervosa and binge eating disorder. *American Journal of Psychiatry, 147,* 1509–1513.

McCann, U. D., & Agras, W. S. (1990b). Successful treatment of non-purging bulimia nervosa with desipramine: A double-blind, placebo-controlled study. *American Journal of Psychiatry, 147,* 1509–1513.

McCann, U. D., Rossiter, E. M., King, R. J., & Agras, W. S. (1991). Non-purging bulimia: A distinct subtype of bulimia nervosa. *International Journal of Eating Disorders, 10,* 679–687.

Mertz, W., Tsui, J. C., Judd, J. T., Reiser, S., Hallfrisch, J., Morris, E. R., Steele, P. D., & Lashley, E. (1991). What are people really eating? The relation between energy intake derived from estimated diet records and intake determined to maintain body weight. *American Journal of Clinical Nutrition, 54,* 291–295.

Meyer, R. G. (1973). Delay therapy: Two case reports. *Behavior Therapy, 4,* 709–711.

Mitchell, J. E., Pyle, R., Eckert, E. D., & Hatsukami, D. (1990). The influence of prior alcohol and drug abuse problems on bulimia nervosa treatment outcome. *Addictive Behaviors, 15,* 169–173.

Mitchell, J. E., Pyle, R. L., Eckert, E. D., Hatsukami, D., & Soll, E. (1990). Bulimia nervosa in overweight individuals. *The Journal of Nervous and Mental Disease, 178,* 324–327.

Pi-Sunyer, F. X. (1991). Health implications of obesity. *American Journal of Clinical Nutrition, 53,* 1595–1603.

Prather, R. C., & Williamson, D. A. (1988). Psychopathology associated with bulimia, binge eating, and obesity. *International Journal of Eating Disorders, 7,* 177–184.

Reich, J. H., & Green, A. I. (1991). Effects of personality disorders on outcome of treatment. *Journal of Nervous and Mental Disease, 179,* 74–82.

Rossiter, E. M., & Agras, W. S. (1990). An empirical test of the DSM-III-R definition of binge. *International Journal of Eating Disorders, 9,* 513–518.

Rossiter, E. M., Agras, W. S., Telch, C. F., & Bruce, B. (1992). The eating patterns of non-purging bulimic subjects. *International Journal of Eating Disorders, 10,* 656–666.

Shisslak, C. M., Pazda, S. L., & Crago, M. (1990). Body weight and bulimia as discriminators of psychological characteristics among anorexic, bulimic, and obese women. *Journal of Abnormal Psychology, 99,* 380–384.

Smith, D. E., Marcus, M. D., & Kaye, W. (1992). Cognitive-behavioral treatment of obese binge eaters. *International Journal of Eating Disorders, 12,* 257–262.

Spitzer, R. L., Devlin, M., Walsh, B. T., Hasin, D., Wing, R. R., Marcus, M. D., Stunkard, A., Wadden, T., Yanovski, S., Agras, S., Mitchell, J., & Nonas, C. (1992). Binge eating disorder: A multisite field trial of the diagnostic criteria. *International Journal of Eating Disorders, 11,* 191–203.

Stunkard, A. J. (1959). Eating patterns and obesity. *Psychiatric Quarterly, 33,* 284–292.

Stunkard, A. J., & Messick, S. (1985). The three-factor eating questionnaire to measure dietary restraint, disinhibition and hunger. *Journal of Psychosomatic Research, 29,* 71–83.

Telch, C. F., Agras, W. S., & Rossiter, E. M. (1988). Binge eating increases with increasing adiposity. *International Journal of Eating Disorders, 7,* 115–119.

Telch, C. F., Agras, W. S., Rossiter, E. M., Wilfley, D., & Kenardy, J. (1990). Group cognitive-behavioral treatment for the non-purging bulimic: An initial evaluation. *Journal of Consulting and Clinical Psychology, 58,* 629–635.

Weltzin, T. E., Hsu, L. K. G., Pollice, C., & Kaye, W. H. (1991). Feeding patterns in bulimia nervosa. *Biological Psychiatry, 30,* 1093–1110.

Williamson, D. A., Prather, R. C., McKenzie, S. J., & Blouin, D. C. (1990). Behavioral assessment procedures can differentiate bulimia nervosa, compulsive overeaters, obese, and normal subjects. *Behavioral Assessment, 12,* 239–252.

Wilson, G. T. (1976). Obesity, binge eating, and behavior therapy: Some clinical observations. *Behavior Therapy, 7,* 700–701.

Wilson, G. T., Nonas, C. A., & Rosenblum, G. D. (1993). Assessment of binge-eating in obese patients. *International Journal of Eating Disorders, 13,* 25–34.

Wilson, G. T., & Smith, D. (1989). Assessment of bulimia nervosa: An evaluation of the eating disorder examination. *International Journal of Eating Disorders, 8,* 173–179.

Wing, R. R., Marcus, M. D., Epstein, L. H., & Kupfer, D. (1983). Mood and weight loss in a behavioral treatment program. *Journal of Consulting and Clinical Psychology, 51,* 153–155.

Yanovski, S. Z., Leet, M., Yanovski, J. A., Flood, M., Gold, P. W., Kissileff, H. R., & Walsh, B. T. (1992). Food selection and intake of obese women with binge eating disorder. *American Journal of Clinical Nutrition, 56,* 975–980.

Yanovski, S. Z., Nelson, J. E., Dubbert, B. K., & Spitzer, R. L. (in press) Psychiatric co-morbidity in obese binge eaters. *American Journal of Psychiatry.*

CHAPTER 6

Binge Eating and Addictive Disorders

G. Terence Wilson

Binge eating is commonly regarded as an addictive behavior that is largely indistinguishable from alcohol or drug abuse. This addiction model of binge eating is exemplified by the treatment philosophy of so-called 12-Step programs for "overeaters" (Elizabeth L., 1988), such as Overeaters Anonymous (Yeary, 1987). Adoption of such an addiction model of binge eating has profound consequences for the treatment of binge eaters. Furthermore, beyond the practical ramifications, this notion raises a number of critically important theoretical issues regarding commonalities among different forms of substance use and abuse, including food.

SIMILARITIES BETWEEN BINGE EATING AND ADDICTIVE DISORDERS

The apparent similarities between binge eating and addictive behavior or psychoactive substance abuse are obvious. Both alcoholics and binge eaters refer to "craving" and "loss of control" in trying to make sense of their problems. Both become preoccupied with the substance, and they make repeated attempts to stop. Both disorders impair the individual's physical and social functioning, and both may involve denial and secrecy. Binge eating is often used to regulate emotions and cope with stress in a manner similar to alcohol or drugs (Johnson & Connors, 1987; Krahn, 1991; Wooley & Wooley, 1981). But this functional similarity does not make binge eating an addictive disorder. These are only superficial commonalities, as Bemis (1989), Vandereycken (1990), and Wardle (1987) have argued. Tiffany (1990) has detailed behavior characteristic of psychoactive substance abusers that closely resembles the behavior of patients with eating disorders; namely, actions that are "relatively fast and efficient, . . . stimulus bound, difficult to impede in the presence of the triggering stimuli, effortless, and enacted in the absence of awareness'' (p. 154). The point is that these behavioral characteristics exemplify what he calls automatic action schemata in general. There is nothing uniquely relevant to substance abuse in these behaviors.

The problem with inferring identity of clinical disorder from these similarities is one of reasoning by analogy. As Vandereycken (1990) points out, one hazard of reasoning by analogy is what he calls ''selective reduction,'' whereby certain resemblances are emphasized and differences ignored. The resemblance between the two disorders, however superficial, is both salient and familiar. The analogue is readily ''available'' to us and biases our judgment (Nisbett & Ross, 1980).

Defining Addiction

The concept of addiction has been debased by promiscuous and imprecise usage to describe virtually any form of repetitive behavior (Peele, 1989; Wilson, 1991). Nevertheless, it is the notion of addiction-as-a-disease (AAD) that is typically extended to binge eating. According to this thinking, some individuals are biologically vulnerable to certain foods (e.g., sugar or white flour, defined as toxic chemicals) that can cause dependence, that the disorder is a progressive illness that can never be eliminated but only managed as a lifelong problem, that treatment must begin by interrupting (detoxifying) the abuse of food, and that since the etiologies of chemical dependence and eating disorders are similar, treatment for eating disorders should not differ fundamentally from that of alcohol or drug dependence. It follows logically from these premises that the recommended treatment is a 12-step program—Overeaters Anonymous (OA)—that is modeled after Alcoholics Anonymous (AA) (Yeary, 1987). Bemis (1985) has referred to this AAD model as the abstinence model of eating disorders. As applied to a psychoactive substance use disorder such as alcoholism, the defining clinical features of the AAD notion are tolerance, physical dependence, loss of control over use, and/or craving (Gordis, 1990; Jonas, 1990). Does binge eating show these clinical features?

Tolerance

Tolerance is a concept drawn from the drug literature, referring to the fact that a drug has progressively less physiological impact as a function of repeated administrations. *Behavioral tolerance* is a particular form of this phenomenon. It refers to the well-established finding that after the organism becomes used to receiving a drug in a particular situation, it comes to anticipate future drug administration in that situation by making compensatory responses that attenuate the effects of the drug. Siegel (1983) has detailed the classical conditioning process whereby specific internal and external (environmental) cues (CSs), which are reliably associated with drug ingestion (the UCS), come to elicit conditioned responses (CRs) that are opposite in direction to the unconditioned response (UCR). These are known as anticipatory conditioned compensatory responses (CCRs), and represent the body's attempt to maintain equilibrium by counteracting the drug's primary effects. The greater the number of pairings of drug-related CSs with the UCS, the stronger the CCR, and hence the weaker the actual drug effect. Behavioral tolerance occurs similarly with food intake (Woods, 1991). Food intake in the presence of predictable environmental stimuli leads to the classical conditioning of cephalic phase responses (CPRs) (e.g., insulin secretion to balance anticipated meal-associated increase in blood glucose). The sight, smell, taste, and even the thought of food can become CSs eliciting a conditioned insulin release (Jansen, 1990). Affect that is associated with food intake can also serve as a CS (Booth, 1988).

Both Jansen (1990) and Woods and Brief (1988) have extended this concept of conditioned behavioral tolerance to the analysis of binge eating. According to this view, the strength of the classically conditioned, compensatory responses will be a function of the person's learning history. A disorganized or chaotic eating pattern, which is characteristic of an individual with eating disorders, will increase the likelihood of a strong conditioned insulin response. Consistent with this view, intermittent dieters have increased cephalic insulin responses (Jansen, 1990). The anticipatory secretion of insulin lowers blood sugar level and produces a conditioned compensatory response of hypoglycemia. The stronger this conditioned compensatory hypoglycemic response becomes, the more it dilutes the effects of specific foods. In this sense tolerance to food can occur. But the implications of this hypothesis for overcoming tolerance to food are very different from the AAD model of alcohol or other psychoactive substances.

Physical Dependence and Withdrawal

In the classical conditioning model of behavioral tolerance, CCRs are experienced as craving or withdrawal from the drug (Siegel, 1983). In the case of the alternating cycles of successful and unsuccessful dieting that are associated with binge eating, the occurrence of hyperinsulinemia triggers an exaggerated hypoglycemic reaction that is experienced as hunger or craving for specific foods (Jansen, 1990; Woods, 1991). The way to cope with tolerance and withdrawal symptoms with psychoactive substance abuse is abstinence. The opposite implication follows for food intake in bulimia nervosa. Here the goal of intervention would be to establish regular and predictable meals, without rigid abstention from particular foods, to avoid the compensatory hypoglycemia that allegedly drives craving and withdrawal (Woods & Brief, 1988). The goal would be to break the contingency or predictive relationship between specific food-related cues and CPRs by systematic exposure to these cues without the UCS (binge), along with eating previously avoided foods under conditions unrelated to binge eating (not predictive of a binge). Such a goal is at odds with the philosophy of the AAD or abstinence model of binge eating.

The third edition, revised, of the *Diagnostic and Statistical Manual of Mental Disorders* (DSM-III-R) (American Psychiatric Association [APA], 1987) does not use the term "addiction," but refers instead to "dependence" and "abuse of psychoactive substances." DSM-III (APA, 1980) had used the class name of "substance use disorders." The term "substance" was changed to "psychoactive substance" in DSM-III-R because it was too broad and could have been misinterpreted to include food (Rounsaville, Spitzer, & Williams, 1986). Nevertheless, Goodrick and Foreyt (1991) have recently characterized obese binge eaters as "food dependent" in terms of DSM-III-R criteria for psychoactive substance abuse. They assert that "two-thirds of all obese persons may be carbohydrate cravers who eat not only to relieve hunger but to combat tension, anxiety, mental fatigue, and depression" (p. 1245). Such an assertion is highly questionable. As discussed below and by Walsh (Chapter 3, this volume), normal-weight bulimia nervosa patients do not appear to be "carbohydrate cravers." Obese binge eaters similarly show no preferential consumption of carbohydrates (Goldfein, Walsh, Devlin, LaChaussee, & Kissileff, 1992; Yanovski et al., 1992).

Ironically, the treatment prescriptions Goodrick and Foreyt (1991) derive from their food-dependence formulation of binge eating in the obese do not conform to what one would expect from such a conceptualization. In contrast to treatments of dependence on psychoactive substances, they recommend against abstinence from any particular foodstuffs. Rather, they advocate flexible but healthy eating with the major focus of treatment not on diet, but on dysfunctional cognitions, emotional states, and the need for social support. These guidelines are more representative of a cognitive–behavioral approach to the treatment of binge eating than any addiction model (Bemis, 1985; Wilson, 1991).

Loss of Control

The concept of loss of control is the defining feature of the classical disease theory of alcoholism (Jellinek, 1960). The notion was that the ingestion of alcohol triggers an uncontrollable biochemical reaction to continue drinking that overrides all reason or choice. Alcoholics cannot stop drinking even though they recognize its destructive consequences. Hence the phrase "One drink away from a drunk." Eating-disorder patients who are binge eaters often speak of being "one bite away from a binge," and in DSM-IV a necessary criterion for an episode of binge eating is that it involve loss of control (see Fairburn & Wilson, Chapter 1, this volume).

Although the assumption is commonplace that ingestion of any small amount of an addictive substance will trigger inevitable, involuntary loss of consummatory control in "addicted" individuals, experimental research has indicated otherwise. In alcohol dependence it is clear that self-regulation of alcohol consumption is critically influenced by a range of social-learning processes, including operative reinforcement contingencies and the alcoholic's expectations regarding its effects (Marlatt & Gordon, 1985). Although severity of physical dependence might interact with psychosocial contingencies in regulating drinking, alcohol in the bloodstream alone does not trigger uncontrollable drinking (Wilson, 1988).

Experimental research on loss of control in binge eating is sparse. Duchmann, Williamson, and Stricker (1989) adapted a commonly used laboratory method for analyzing loss of control over consumption in a study of bulimic patients. Patients with bulimia nervosa and overweight, nonpurging binge eaters ate a serving of chocolate pudding, after which they were asked to make taste ratings of two types of ice cream. The amount of ice cream they consumed during this taste test, assessed surreptitiously, was the main dependent measure. The patients were told that they would be required to remain in the laboratory for 90 minutes following the experimental procedures, the intent being to convince bulimia nervosa patients that they could not vomit after eating the pudding and ice cream. The overweight binge eaters consumed significantly more ice cream than either the bulimia nervosa patients or a control group of normal subjects. The behavior of the overweight binge eaters was consistent with that of normal-weight, nonbulimic dieters in similar laboratory studies in which they ate more food following a high-calorie preload than in the absence of a preload. This phenomenon is known as counterregulation and has been put forward as a model of binge eating (Polivy & Herman, 1985).[1] What is noteworthy in the present context is that the bulimia nervosa patients appear not to have counterregulated. The bulimia nervosa patients did not differ from the normal controls. Compared with the overweight binge eaters, they showed no loss of control following the consumption of a forbidden food, presumably because they knew they could not purge.

The results of the Duchmann et al. (1989) study indicate that bulimia nervosa patients do not necessarily lose control despite violating their dietary restraint by ingesting a high-sugar/high-fat food. A second study similarly showed that bulimia nervosa patients do not necessarily lose control and binge despite eating small amounts of forbidden foods such as a candy bar (Rosen, Leitenberg, Fondacaro, Gross, & Willmuth, 1985). These findings are consistent with data from studies of alcoholics and run counter to the AAD notion of loss of control over eating. They also reveal differences between normal-weight bulimia nervosa patients (those who purged) and obese binge eaters (those who did not purge). McCann, Perri, Nezu, and Lowe (1992) have similarly shown that obese patients who were binge eaters, but not obese non-binge-eaters, counterregulated in the standard laboratory situation. Collectively, these studies indicate that analyses of the similarity of binge eating to addictive disorders must take into account potential differences among groups of binge eaters rather than lumping them together as is often the case (e.g., Yeary, 1987).

Craving

The concept of craving has been an elusive and controversial one in the substance abuse disorders. If taken to mean an irresistible desire, as it is defined in the disease theory of alcoholism, the concept is without convincing empirical support. As with the concept of loss of control, evidence exists showing that craving is heavily influenced by the psychological and environmental conditions in which it is assessed (Fingarette, 1988; Jansen, 1990). There is no evidence that people with eating disorders experience craving as a direct biochemical result of consuming a particular "toxic" nutrient to which they are sometimes said to be "allergic"[2] (Bemis, 1985; Wardle, 1987). In their review of the literature, Rodin and Reed (1987) concluded that there was "no clear body of literature showing a systematic relationship between response to sweetness and eating disorders" (p. 198). Nor did these authors find consistent differences in responses to sugar in obese individuals, or patients with bulimia or anorexia nervosa.

A subset of obese people are said to crave carbohydrates and snack selectively on carbohydrate-rich foods (Wurtman, 1988). Carbohydrates increase tryptophan, which, in turn, enhances the release of serotonin in the brain. However, the relevance of this research for binge eating has yet to be demonstrated. Turner, Foggo, Bennie, Carroll, Dick, and Goodwin (1991) conducted an experimental analysis of the psychological and biological effects of a simulated carbohydrate binge in bulimia nervosa patients and matched controls. Each group consumed a 500-ml drink consisting of either 1,200 kcal of carbohydrates or an inactive placebo mixture "of negligible calorific value" on two consecutive mornings following a fast. Overall, the results showed little carbohydrate-specific effect on subjective responses. What effects there were tended to be negative and nonsupportive of the notion that binge eating is mediated by carbohydrate craving. In the control subjects, ratings of hunger were significantly decreased during the 2 hours following consumption of both drinks, although the effect was greater for the carbohydrate challenge. In the bulimia nervosa patients hunger ratings were depressed before and after consumption, with no significant difference between the carbohydrate and placebo drinks. The patients also reported greater increases in nausea after carbohydrate consumption. Ratings of mood were not improved by the consumption of the carbohydrate drink. In fact, the rating for "good mood" was lower in the patients following carbohydrate consumption. Measures of prolactin, growth hormone, and cortisol failed to indicate any carbohydrate-mediated stimulation in either group.

There is no evidence that patients with bulimia nervosa crave sugar or even preferentially consume sugar and other carbohydrates during binge eating (see Walsh, Chapter 3, this volume). When the binge eating and other eating of bulimia nervosa patients and the eating of normal controls are studied directly in the laboratory, macronutrient selection is similar for both groups. The most striking difference between the binge and nonbinge meals of bulimic patients is the amount of food consumed, not its macronutrient composition. This suggests that the essential appetitive abnormality in bulimia nervosa is in the control of amount of food consumed, not in the craving for a specific macronutrient (Walsh, Kissileff, Cassidy, & Dantzic, 1989). The same holds true for obese binge eaters (Goldfein et al., 1992; Yanovski et al., 1992).

Conclusion

By these traditional criteria of tolerance, physical dependence, loss of control, and craving, then, binge eating does not fit the AAD model. Of course, there are other ways of conceptualizing addictive behavior. The cognitive-behavioral model of addictive behaviors differs from classical disease theory in many fundamental respects (Donovan, 1988; Marlatt & Gordon, 1985; Wilson, 1988). Briefly put, addictive behavior is seen as an interactive product of biological, psychological, and sociological influences. Both addictive and nonaddictive behaviors are regulated by the same social cognitive variables and laws of learning. There is no inevitable loss of control over behavior, and no inexorable progression to a final disease state. The cognitive-behavioral model of addictive behaviors provides a state-of-the-art analysis of the psychological processes and procedures that are responsible for successful or unsuccessful self-regulation of behavior. As such, as Wardle (1987) points out, the model is useful in suggesting specific therapeutic strategies for binge eating that were developed in the treatment of alcohol abuse. Self-control techniques and relapse prevention, now integral components of cognitive-behavioral treatment (CBT) programs for bulimia nervosa (Fairburn & Cooper, 1989; Fairburn, Marcus, & Wilson, Chapter 16, this volume), are obvious examples. The problem even with the cognitive–behavioral model of addiction is that although it differs fundamentally from the disease model, the emphasis is nonetheless on curbing or controlling consumption. This approach conflicts sharply with the therapeutic implications that may be drawn from what is known about the development and maintenance of binge eating (see Wilson, 1991).

COMORBIDITY BETWEEN BINGE EATING AND PSYCHOACTIVE SUBSTANCE ABUSE

The Prevalence of Psychoactive Substance Abuse in Individuals with Binge Eating

Clinical Samples

Lifetime history of comorbidity of binge eating and psychoactive substance abuse varies across the weight spectrum and differs widely among different studies. In anorexia nervosa the reported co-occurrence has ranged from 6.7% (Eckert, Goldberg, Halmi, Casper, & Davis, 1979) to 23% (Cantwell, Sturzenberger, Burroughs, Salkin, & Green, 1977). In the largest study of its kind, Eckert et al. (1979) found that 7 of 105 female patients (6.7%) with anorexia nervosa reported alcohol problems. The patients with alcohol problems had significantly higher rates of stealing, binge eating, and purging. The lifetime prevalence of alcohol abuse in women in the United States has been estimated to be 1.7%, and 3.0% for alcohol dependence (Helzer et al., 1990). These data suggest that the rate of alcohol problems among anorexia nervosa patients is higher than would be expected. The Eckert et al. (1979) study found a lower comorbidity rate of alcohol problems than that reported in much smaller studies of anorexia nervosa patients (Crisp & Toms, 1972). More recently, Halmi et al. (1991) reported a rate of 8.1% in a sample of 62 anorexia nervosa patients, which did not differ from that of normal controls.

In patients with bulimia nervosa, lifetime history of comorbidity of binge eating and psychoactive substance abuse ranges from 9% to 55% (Schwalberg, Barlow, Alger, & Howard, 1992; Walsh, Roose, Glassman, Gladis, & Sadik, 1985). In Germany, Laessle, Wittchen, Fichter, and Pirke (1989) compared four subgroups of patients with eating disorders meeting DSM-III criteria: anorexia nervosa, restricting subtype; anorexia nervosa, bulimic subtype; bulimics with a history of anorexia nervosa; and bulimics without a history of anorexia nervosa. All three bulimic groups had significantly higher lifetime frequency of substance abuse disorders than the anorexic restrictors. The percentages for alcohol abuse or dependence were 0%, 20%, 13%, and 18.5% for the four subgroups, numbers that are significantly higher than the lifetime prevalence of only 6.1% for substance abuse disorders in the general West German population (Laessle et al., 1989). It is of note that co-occurrence of anxiety disorders and affective disorders with eating disorders was far higher than that of substance abuse disorders and eating disorders.

In the United States, Kassett et al. (1989) found that 55% of a sample of 40 patients with bulimia nervosa had a substance abuse disorder. In a study of 275 patients with bulimia (DSM-III criteria), Mitchell, Hatsukami, Eckert, and Pyle (1985) found that 34.4% reported a history of problems with alcohol and other drugs. Of these, 17.7% reported a prior history of treatment for chemical dependence.

Evidence of an association between binge eating and psychoactive substance abuse in obese patients is mixed. Hudson et al.'s (1988) comparison of samples of obese binge eaters and non-binge-eaters revealed no difference in rates of substance abuse disorder (21% and 15%, respectively). Both had lower rates than normal-weight patients with bulimia nervosa. The absence of a significant difference in rates of psychoactive substance abuse between obese patients with and without binge eating has been replicated in five other studies with widely varying methodologies (Brody, Devlin, & Walsh, 1992; Goldfein et al., 1992; Marcus et al., 1990; Specker, de Zwaan, Pyle, Raymond, & Mitchell, 1992; Wilson, Nonas, & Rosenblum, 1993).

In contrast to Hudson et al.'s (1988) finding of a difference between normal-weight and obese binge eaters, both Schwalberg et al. (1992) and Mitchell, Pyle, Eckert, Hatsukami, and Soll (1990) found no difference between normal weight bulimia nervosa patients and obese binge eaters. In the latter study there was no difference in alcohol abuse between normal weight bulimia nervosa patients (37.5%) and obese binge eaters (44.0%) even though the two groups differed in terms of other psychiatric disorders. Muddying the water still further are results from McCann, Rossiter, King, and Agras's (1991) comparison of patients with bulimia nervosa and patients with what they term ''non-purging bulimia'' (those who met all of the DSM-III-R criteria for bulimia nervosa except purging). None of the purging bulimia nervosa patients, but 23% of the non-purging patients, reported a lifetime history of substance abuse on the SCID.

CONCLUSION

The interpretation of these studies must take into account a number of methodological limitations. One problem is diagnosis and classification. The diagnostic criteria employed in the different studies vary for both eating and psychoactive substance abuse disorders. Ideally, patterns of co-occurrence should be assessed using both categorical and dimensional data on disordered eating and psychoactive substance use and abuse. For the most part, only diagnostic categories are reported. The focus on diagnostic categories might miss specific associations between certain features of an eating disorder and psychoactive substance abuse. For example, it could be argued that binge eating per se is the behavior most likely to be linked to other excessive substance use or abuse. Testing this hypothesis would require specific—and reliable—measurement of binge eating and its association with psychoactive substance use. This hypothesized relationship would also need to be assessed across the weight spectrum, from anorexia nervosa to obesity. Alternatively, it might be that other features of eating disorders, such as purging, are differentially linked to psychoactive substance abuse.

A second problem is that of measurement. Assessment methods for measuring the attitudes and behavior that define eating disorders and psychoactive substance abuse are of varying, and in some instances, questionable validity.

With these limitations in mind, it appears that alcohol problems are more common in clinical samples of patients with bulimia nervosa than in people without psychological problems. In the absence of studies using general psychiatric control groups, in addition to normal controls, this difference cannot be interpreted as indicating a specific association between eating disorders and substance abuse disorders.

Community Samples

A limitation of interpreting the results from clinical samples is that even if there is high co-occurrence between eating disorders and alcohol problems, it may only reflect what Helzer and Pryzbeck (1988) call Berkson's bias, i.e., ''an increased tendency for persons with multiple diagnoses to seek and receive treatment and thus fall into study populations drawn from treatment sources'' (p. 219). There is evidence that only a minority of individuals with an eating disorder enter treatment (Fairburn, 1992, personal communication), and it is not unlikely that those with additional disorders, such as depression or a substance abuse disorder, are more likely to present for treatment and therefore be represented in clinical samples. Representative, community samples need to be studied. At present there have been few studies of this type. One of note is Helzer and Pryzbeck's (1988) investigation of the comorbidity of alcoholism and other psychiatric disorders using the Epidemiological Catchment Area (ECA) samples. They found no association between alcoholism and anorexia nervosa. Unfortunately, the prevalence of bulimia was not assessed. Nevertheless, the DSM-III diagnosis of anorexia nervosa included the bulimic subtype of this disorder who, on the basis of clinical reports, appear to abuse alcohol and drugs significantly more than the nonbulimic patients (DaCosta & Halmi, 1992).

A second study was conducted on 2,163 female twins from the Virginia population-based twin register using structured psychiatric interviews to establish DSM-III-R diagnoses (Kendler et al., 1991). Of the 123 subjects with bulimia nervosa, 15.5% had a lifetime diagnosis of alcoholism. The statistically significant odds ratio was 3.23, which was second only to that for anorexia nervosa.

The Prevalence of Binge Eating in Individuals with Substance Abuse

If eating disorders and substance abuse do covary, there should be a complementary higher prevalence of eating disorders in people with substance abuse disorders. This relationship has received little research attention. Four studies in England have found a high rate of eating problems in alcoholics. Beary, Lacey, and Merry (1986) found that of 20 consecutive patients admitted to an inpatient alcoholism treatment unit, 35% reported a prior eating disorder. Lacey and Moureli (1986) found that 40% of a series of hospitalized alcoholic women reported a past or present eating disorder. Similar results were obtained in a third study of 31 women between the ages of 17 and 40 who had been hospitalized for alcoholism (Peveler & Fairburn, 1990). Binge eating and eating disorders were assessed using a self-report version of the Eating Disorder Examination (EDE). Twenty-six percent of the women met diagnostic criteria (DSM-III-R) for a current eating disorder, and 19% reported a history of anorexia nervosa. As many as 36% reported the symptom of binge eating. Other studies have shown a higher-than-expected rate of binge eating in patients with cocaine abuse (e.g., Jonas, Gold, Sweeney, & Pottash, 1987).

A fourth study improved on the methodology of the preceding investigations by assessing 52 women attending an Alcohol Treatment Unit with the EDE, a standardized and validated investigator-based interview that measures the behavior and attitudes characteristic of clinical eating disorders (Taylor, Peveler, Hibbert, & Fairburn, in press). In comparison with a sample of women drawn from a community-based study of the prevalence of eating disorders, the alcohol clinic patients reported significantly more binge eating, self-induced vomiting, and laxative abuse. Of the patients, 11.5% had a history of anorexia nervosa compared with only 1.7% of the community sample. The parallel figures for a lifetime history of bulimia nervosa were 17.3% versus 7.0%. Alcohol clinic patients with a past or present eating disorder were younger than those with an alcohol problem alone, and reported an earlier onset of their drinking problem. Fewer than half of the cases of a past or present eating disorder had been detected by the clinic.

A fifth study in the United States similarly found unusually high rates of eating-disorder symptoms in female alcoholics (Striegel-Moore, Cronan, Goebel, Pena, & Scheibe, 1992). Assessment with the EDE showed that 2% of 45 inpatients met criteria for current bulimia nervosa, with 16% reporting a history of the disorder. As many 18% were classified as currently meeting criteria for eating disorders not otherwise specified (EDNOS). Patients with a current diagnosis of an eating disorder reported significantly more symptoms associated with Axis I and Axis II disorders. Replicating the Taylor et al. (in press) data, Striegel-Moore et al. (1992) found that the patients with eating disorders were significantly younger than the others. Moreover, in all but one case the treatment clinical staff were unaware of patients' past or present eating disorder.

Conclusion

The evidence suggests that the rate of eating disorders in patients with alcohol or cocaine abuse is significantly higher than in the population at large. Despite the different assessment methods and varying diagnostic criteria, the consistency of this finding suggests an association between eating disorders and psychoactive substance abuse disorders. What cannot be determined from these studies is whether this association is specific. It may be that the rate of eating disorders is comparable in other psychiatric disorders, such as anxiety disorders.

FAMILY STUDIES OF THE CO-OCCURRENCE OF EATING DISORDERS AND PSYCHOACTIVE SUBSTANCE ABUSE DISORDERS

A number of studies have reported significantly higher-than-expected rates of alcohol and drug problems among the relatives of probands with anorexia nervosa or bulimia nervosa. The lifetime prevalence among first-degree relatives has ranged from 21.9% (Kassett et al., 1989) to 60.0%

(Bulik, 1987). (Since these studies have been focused on eating disorders rather than binge eating per se, the specific association with the latter cannot be directly assessed.) Yet it would be premature to conclude that there is a specific familial association between alcohol and eating disorders. Studies including a psychiatric control group have not found such an association: The prevalence of alcohol problems in the families of patients with eating disorders seems to be no higher than in other psychiatric disorders, such as anxiety disorders (Kushner, Sher, & Beitman, 1990; Schwalberg et al., 1992).

The methodological problems with studies of comorbidity apply to the family studies. Assessment of eating disorders and alcohol abuse has been less than optimal. Family histories of alcohol abuse have been based mainly on self-report by the proband with an eating disorder. Direct interview of the relatives using standardized diagnostic criteria is needed. Moreover, none of the studies to date has assessed the influence of comorbid disorders among family members with alcohol abuse. Alcoholism is a heterogeneous disorder that is frequently associated with other psychiatric disorders (e.g., antisocial disorder, anxiety disorders, and depression). The impact of these comorbid disorders must be taken into account in family studies of the link between eating and alcohol problems. Finally, the family studies to date have included as probands eating-disordered patients seeking treatment. Studies of probands drawn from the community are needed.

MECHANISMS LINKING BINGE EATING AND PSYCHOACTIVE SUBSTANCE ABUSE

Several hypotheses have been put forward to explain the putative association between binge eating and psychoactive substance abuse disorders.

Common Genetic/Biological Diathesis

A common speculation is that binge eating and psychoactive substance abuse are both expressions of the same underlying biological vulnerability (Jonas, 1990). One version of this view is that the high rates of eating disorders in women and alcohol abuse in men are sex-specific expressions of an underlying "addictive" predisposition. It is argued that societal constraints on excessive drinking by women make eating a more culturally available form of substance use and abuse (Bulik, 1987).

The nature of the underlying biological vulnerability has been a matter for speculation. For example, Reid (1990) has proposed that alcohol and eating disorders might be explained by a common opioidergic mechanism. There is evidence showing that endogenous opioids play a role in the regulation of alcohol consumption as well as appetite. For example, Volpicelli, O'Brien, Alterman, and Hayashida (1990) have shown that naltrexone (an opioid antagonist) can reduce craving for alcohol and decrease drinking in alcohol-dependent patients, results they interpret as support for their hypothesis that alcohol is reinforcing because of its effects on opioidergic systems. Uncontrolled studies also suggest that naloxone or naltrexone reduces binge eating in bulimia nervosa patients (Jonas, 1990). One double-blind, placebo-controlled study of naloxone, however, showed only modest effects in decreasing binge eating (Mitchell, Laine, Morley, & Levine, 1986), and another showed no effect at all, although the sample size was small (Alger, Schwalberg, Bigaouette, Michalek, & Howard, 1991).

A Common Addictive Personality

Psychometric findings from the assessment of the personalities of patients with eating disorders and those with substance use disorders offer little support for the view that the problems are functionally equivalent. For example, Leon, Kolotkin, and Kogeski (1979) found that neither bulimic nor restricting anorexics scored in the addictive range on the MacAndrew Addiction Scale (MAC) (MacAndrew, 1965), nor did they differ from normal controls. Other largely negative findings have been reported by Butterfield and LeClair (1988). In contrast, De Silva and Eysenck (1987) found that patients with bulimia nervosa resembled the personality profile of drug-dependent patients on the Addiction Scale of the Eysenck Personality Questionnaire (EPQ). Moreover, the bulimic patients differed significantly from both restricting anorexics and normal controls. A closer look at the items that identified bulimics as addicts shows that they involve feelings of anxiety and depression (Gossop & Eysenck, 1980). An alternative interpretation of the data is that they simply indicate that the bulimics were more disturbed along dimensions of psychopathology not unique to psychoactive substance use disorders.

Binge Eating Leads to Substance Abuse

Another hypothesis is that eating disorders lead to psychoactive substance abuse (Krahn, 1991). In animals, food deprivation reliably increases the self-administration of drugs such as alcohol (Carroll & Meisch, 1984). There is evidence of a change in the central reward mechanisms, in addition to specific effects on operant behavior. Humans, too, may increase their drug intake when food deprived (Franklin, Schiele, Brozek, & Keys, 1948). Both anorexic patients who are binge eaters and bulimia nervosa patients significantly restrict their caloric intake between binges. In terms of the reciprocal reinforcement analysis of consummatory behavior, this self-imposed dietary restriction could have two major effects: (1) It might increase the reward value of highly palatable, high-fat, "binge" foods and prompt binge eating; and (2) it might increase the reward value of alternative reinforcers such as psychoactive substances leading to abuse (Krahn, 1991).

There are problems with this analysis, however. It does not explain why it is predominantly the bulimic and not the restrictor anorexia nervosa patients who abuse alcohol or drugs. Both groups of patients severely restrict food intake, but only one turns to alternative consummatory reinforcers. Hence, something more than dietary restriction is required to explain comorbid psychoactive substance abuse. Since non-bulimic-restrained eaters often restrict their food intake as much as bulimia nervosa patients, they should abuse other substances as much as binge eaters. Whether highly restrained eaters as a whole use or abuse psychoactive substances more than unrestrained eaters remains to be assessed.

If eating disorders lead to psychoactive substance abuse, they should have an earlier onset. Unfortunately, few studies address the issue of order of onset, and they all rely upon retrospective patient reports of unknown validity. Jones, Cheshire, and Moorhouse (1985) reported that all 27 of their alcoholic patients reported an earlier onset of eating disorders, with the time interval ranging from less than 5 years to more than 10. Beary et al. (1986) and Lacey and Moureli (1986) similarly reported that eating disorders preceded alcohol problems in their samples. They also found that problem drinking occurred at a significantly earlier age in those women with a history of eating disorders than those with no such history. Beary et al. (1986) go as far as to suggest that eating disorders are a risk factor for alcohol problems. Katzman and Marcus Strauss (1988) found that virtually all their female cocaine abuse patients reported that the onset of the eating disorder preceded drug abuse or developed at the same time. Studies of alcohol problems in samples of individuals with eating disorders have not addressed the question of temporal patterning.

The reciprocal reinforcement hypothesis predicts that successful elimination of binge eating in bulimia nervosa patients, together with significantly reduced dietary restraint, would undermine the use of psychoactive substances. The broad-based and lasting effects of successful CBT treatment, showing no symptom substitution, are consistent with this view. It might be that patients who cease to binge, but who continue to restrain their eating severely, would be most likely to increase their use/abuse of psychoactive drugs following treatment.

THERAPEUTIC IMPLICATIONS OF TREATING BINGE EATING AS AN ADDICTIVE DISORDER

The AAD or abstinence model prescribes increased and endless dietary restraint, featuring absolute avoidance of particular foods (e.g., sugar), highly structured eating patterns (Yeary, 1987), and as Bemis (1989) points out, a sense of powerlessness and reinforcement of a dichotomous thinking pattern. These prescriptions conflict with much of what is now known about the development, maintenance, and modification of binge eating (see Wilson, 1991).

In stark contrast, cognitive-behavioral treatment is designed to reduce dietary restraint and alter abnormal attitudes about the importance of body weight and shape (Wilson & Fairburn, in press). Whereas most bulimia nervosa patients complain that they have no control over eating and eat too much, the data show that they eat too little outside their bulimic episodes (see Walsh, Chapter 3, this volume). Both the physiological sequelae of caloric deprivation and the psychological costs of self-denial must be remedied by the establishment of regular, nutritionally balanced meals and the introduction of previously avoided foods into a more flexible diet (Fairburn, 1989; Wardle, 1987). The theoretical analyses of the development of the twin processes of tolerance and withdrawal effects with regard to food by Woods and Brief (1988) and Jansen (1990) dictate the same strategies. Thus, the therapeutic objectives of the AAD approach are viewed in CBT as processes that are likely to maintain binge eating.

The evidence from controlled clinical trials consistently shows that CBT produces broad and lasting reductions in binge eating and the other hallmark symptoms of bulimia nervosa. Moreover, CBT results in generalized therapeutic improvement, reliably reducing associated psychopathology (e.g., depression) (Fairburn, Agras, & Wilson, 1992). Preliminary findings on the treatment of obese binge eaters are also encouraging (Telch, Agras, Rossiter, Wilfley, & Kenardy, 1990; Smith, Marcus, & Kaye, 1992). There has been no hint of symptom substitution and no indication that any other form of substance abuse supplants binge eating in controlled studies—at least at follow-ups of up to 4 years, which are the longest to date (Fairburn, 1992, personal communication).

There are no data showing the effectiveness of therapy based on the AAD model (Malenbaum, Herzog, Eisenthal, & Wyshak, 1988). The well-documented effectiveness of CBT disconfirms seminal predictions of the AAD model of binge eating and raises serious questions about the use of treatment methods based on this addiction model. Empirical evaluation of the key tenets of a 12-step program is a pressing need.

Lacey and Evans (1986) have argued for the existence of a "multi-impulsive form of bulimia'' in which binge eating is interchangeable with other impulsive behaviors including psychoactive substance abuse. These patients are said to have a fundamental personality disorder with ''protean manifestations'' of impulsivity. Limiting treatment to a single expression, such as binge eating, would either be ineffective or result in some form of symptom substitution. In the absence of controlled research, these largely anecdotal observations remain speculative.

Another implication of the AAD model is that treatment must focus directly on the restructuring of eating habits, and this must include abstinence from designated toxic foodstuffs. Psychological therapy is not encouraged other than to address other related personal issues. Yeary and Heck (1989) bluntly state, ''It is as fruitless to attempt psychotherapy with a still-symptomatic bulimic as it is with an intoxicated alcoholic'' (p. 244). In their study of 40 members of OA who met DSM-III criteria for bulimia, Malenbaum et al. (1988) found that 39 endorsed the statement ''Until a person deals with her eating behavior she cannot deal with her psychological problems.'' This dismissal of the role of psychological therapy is refuted by the success of interpersonal psychotherapy (IPT) in the treatment of bulimia nervosa. In IPT there is no focus whatsoever on the patient's eating habits or weight, only on past and present interpersonal issues in the person's life. Yet IPT has been shown to be as effective as CBT in reducing binge eating in normal-weight bulimia nervosa patients (Fairburn et al., 1991; Fairburn, Jones, Peveler, Hope, & O'Connor, in press), and a group adaptation of IPT has been shown effective with obese binge eaters (Wilfley et al., in press).

Treatment of Patients with Dual Diagnoses of Eating and Psychoactive Substance Abuse Disorders

Although the available evidence does not establish an inherent link between binge eating and psychoactive substance abuse, the clinical reality is that patients seeking treatment often have both disorders. Accordingly, clinicians who treat these two patient populations must be alert to the likelihood of comorbidity and routinely look for their presence.

Two studies have examined the impact of a prior history of psychoactive substance abuse on the psychological treatment of bulimia nervosa patients. Contrary to their prediction, Mitchell et al. (1990) reported no difference between patients with and without a prior history of substance abuse. Strasser, Pike, and Walsh (1992) assessed the influence of a past history of substance abuse (based on DSM-III-R criteria) on the treatment of bulimia nervosa patients with antidepressant treatment (desipramine). Consistent with Mitchell et al.'s (1990) findings, they found no difference between the two groups in terms of binge eating at the end of treatment. (Other measures of bulimia nervosa indicated that the patients with a positive past history of substance abuse actually fared better than those without such a history.)

No empirical data exist showing how best to treat the patient with co-occurring eating and psychoactive substance abuse disorders. Alcohol and drug abuse is typically an exclusionary criterion for selecting subjects for controlled outcome studies of eating disorders. The presence of eating disorders in treatment studies of alcoholics has been completely ignored. Clinical observations about treatment of co-occurring disorders are influenced, not surprisingly, by the clinician's theoretical framework. The ADD model calls for integrated treatment of what is seen as a common underlying addictive disease process. Patients with either eating or substance abuse disorders are viewed as indistinguishable and may even be treated together in the same way. A 12-step program, incorporating the principles of Alcoholics Anonymous and Overeaters Anonymous, is regarded as the treatment of choice for these dually addicted patients (Yeary & Heck, 1989).

In my opinion, if the alcohol or drug abuse is severe, it should be treated first. There are compelling clinical reasons for tackling psychoactive substance abuse as quickly as possible. Moreover, a systematic and sustained focus on binge eating or other aspects of the eating disorder is impossible under these circumstances. Once the psychoactive substance abuse problem is under control, attention can then be directed to the binge eating. On the other hand, if the alcohol or drug abuse is not severe, the disorders may be treated simultaneously. If both disorders are to be treated with a cognitive-behavioral approach, there need be little concern about patients being confronted with contradictory and hence confusing concepts and treatment goals. Alternatively, if the psychoactive substance abuse disorder is treated with a 12-step approach based on the AAD model and the eating disorders treated with CBT, then the similarities and dissimilarities between the two disorders and their respective treatments need to be made clear to the patient.

ACKNOWLEDGMENTS

Portions of this chapter are drawn from Wilson (1991). Preparation of this chapter was facilitated by support from the John D. and Catherine T. MacArthur Foundation Network on Health and Behavior.

NOTES

1. The nature of counterregulation and its relevance for understanding eating disorders have been challenged, however (Charnock, 1989).

2. The broader area of food allergies and sensitivity is a controversial and uncertain one. In a recent landmark double-blind controlled study, Jewett, Fein, and Greenberg (1990) have shown that many people who appear to be allergic to specific foods (i.e., food sensitive) are responding to psychological factors such as suggestion rather than the biochemical effect of food substances.

REFERENCES

Alger, S. A., Schwalberg, M. D., Bigaouette, J. M., Michalek, A. V., & Howard, L. J. (1991). Effect of tricyclic antidepressant and opiate antagonist on binge eating behavior in normoweight bulimic and obese, binge-eating subjects. *American Journal of Clinical Nutrition, 53*, 865–871.

American Psychiatric Association. (1980). *Diagnostic and statistical manual of mental disorders.* Washington, DC: Author.

American Psychiatric Association. (1987). *Diagnostic and statistical manual of mental disorders* (3rd ed., rev.). Washington, DC: Author.

Beary, M. D., Lacey, J. H., & Merry, J. (1986). Alcoholism and eating disorders in women of fertile age. *British Journal of Addiction, 81*, 685–689.

Bemis, K. M. (1985). Abstinence and nonabstinence models for the treatment of bulimia. *International Journal of Eating Disorders, 4*, 407–437.

Bemis, K. M. (1989). *Phobia, obsession, or addiction: What underlies the eating disorders?* Paper presented at the National Conference on the Eating Disorders, Columbus, OH.

Booth, D. A. (1988). Culturally corralled into food abuse: The eating disorders as physiologically reinforced excessive appetites. In K. M. Pirke, W. Vandereycken, & D. Ploog (Eds.), *Psychobiology of bulimia nervosa* (pp. 18–32). Berlin: Springer-Verlag.

Brody, M., Devlin, M. J., & Walsh, B. T. (1992, April 24–26). *Reliability and validity of binge eating disorder.* Paper presented at fifth International Conference in Eating Disorders, New York.

Bulik, C. M. (1987). Drug and alcohol abuse by bulimic women and their families. *American Journal of Psychiatry, 144*, 1604–1606.

Butterfield, P. S., & LeClair, S. (1988). Cognitive characteristics of bulimic and drug-abusing women. *Addictive Behaviors, 13*, 131–138.

Cantwell, D. P., Sturzenberger, S., Burroughs, J., Salkin, B., & Green, J. K. (1977). Anorexia nervosa—an affective disorder. *Archives of General Psychiatry, 34*, 1087–1093.

Carroll, M. E., & Meisch, R. A. (1984). Increased drug-reinforced behavior due to food deprivation. In M. E. Carroll & R. A. Meisch (Eds.), *Advances in behavioral pharmacology* (Vol. 4, pp. 47–88). New York: Academic Press.

Charnock, D. J. K. (1989). A comment on the role of dietary restraint in the development of bulimia nervosa. *British Journal of Clinical Psychology, 28*, 329–340.

Crisp, A. H., & Toms, D. A. (1972). Primary anorexia nervosa or weight phobia in the male: Report on 13 cases. *British Medical Journal, 1*, 334–338.

DaCosta, M. D., & Halmi, K. A. (1992). Classification of anorexia nervosa: The question of subtypes. *International Journal of Eating Disorders, 11*, 305–310.

De Silva, P., & Eysenck, S. (1987). *Personality and Individual differences, 8*, 749–751.

Donovan, D. M. (1988). Assessment of addictive behaviors: Implications of an emerging biopsychosocial model. In D. M. Donovan & G. A. Marlatt (Eds.), *Assessment of addictive behaviors* (pp. 3–50). New York: Guilford Press.

Duchmann, E. G., Williamson, D. A., & Stricker, P. M. (1989). Bulimia, dietary restraint, and concern for dieting. *Journal of Psychopathology and Behavioral Assessment, 11*, 1–13.

Eckert, E. D., Goldberg S. C., Halmi, K. A., Casper, R. C., & Davis, J. M. (1979). Alcoholism in anorexia nervosa. In R. W. Pickens & L. L. Heston, (Eds.), *Psychiatric factors in drug abuse* (pp. 267–283). New York: Grune & Strattan.

Elizabeth, L. (1988). *Twelve steps for overeaters.* New York: Harper & Row.

Fairburn, C. G., Agras, W. S., & Wilson, G. T. (1992). The research on the treatment of bulimia nervosa: Practical and theoretical implications. In G. H. Anderson & S. H. Kennedy (Eds.), *The biology of feast and famine: Relevance to eating disorders* (pp. 317–340). New York: Academic Press.

Fairburn, C. G., & Cooper, P. J. (1989). Eating disorders. In K. Hawton, P. M. Salkovskis, J. Kirk, & D. M. Clark (Eds.), *Cognitive behaviour therapy for psychiatric problems* (pp. 277–314). New York: Oxford University Press.

Fairburn, C. G., Jones, R., Peveler, R. C., Carr, S. J., Solomon, R. A., O'Connor, M. E., Burton, J., & Hope, R. A. (1991). Three psychological treatments for bulimia nervosa: A comparative trial. *Archive of General Psychiatry, 48*, 463–469.

Fairburn, C. G., Jones, R., Peveler, R. C., Hope, R. A., & O'Connor, M. (in press). Psychotherapy and bulimia nervosa: The longer-term effects of interpersonal psychotherapy, behaviour therapy and cognitive behaviour therapy. *Archives of General Psychiatry.*

Fingarette, H. (1988). *Heavy drinking: The myth of alcoholism as a disease.* Berkeley: University of California Press.

Franklin, J. C., Schiele, B. C., Brozek, J., & Keys, A. (1948). Observations on human behavior in experimental semistarvation and rehabilitation. *Journal of Clinical Psychology,* 428–445.

Goldfein, J., Walsh, B. T., Devlin, M. J., LaChaussée, J., & Kissileff, H. (1992, April, 24). *Eating behavior in binge eating disorder.* Paper presented at the Fifth International Conference on Eating Disorders, New York.

Goodrick, G. K., & Foreyt, J. P. (1991). Why treatments for obesity don't last. *Journal of the American Dietetic Association, 91*, 1243–1247.

Gordis, E. (1990). Introduction. In *Alcohol and health.* Washington, DC: U.S. Department of Health and Human Services.

Gossop, M. R., & Eysenck, S. B. G. (1980). A further investigation into the personality of drug addicts in treatment. *British Journal of Addiction, 75*, 305–311.

Halmi, K. A., Eckert, E., Marchi, P., Sampugnaro, V., Apple, R., & Cohen, J. (1991). Comorbidity of psychiatric diagnoses in anorexia nervosa. *Archives of General Psychiatry, 48*, 712–718.

Helzer, J. E., Canino, G. J., Yeh, E. K., Bland, R C., Lee, C. K., Hwu, H. G., & Newman, S. (1990). Alcoholism—North America and Asia. *Archives of General Psychiatry, 47,* 313–319.

Helzer, J. E., & Pryzbeck, T. R. (1988). The co-occurrence of alcoholism with other psychiatric disorders in the general population and its impact on treatment. *Journal of Studies on Alcohol, 49,* 219–224.

Hudson, J. I., Pope, H. G., Wurtman, J., Yurgelun-Todd, D., Mark, S., & Rosenthal, N. E. (1988). Bulimia in obese individuals. Relationship to normal-weight bulimia. *Journal of Nervous and Mental Disease, 176,* 144–152.

Jansen, A. (1990). *Binge eating: Notes and data.* Unpublished manuscript, University of Limburg, Maastricht, the Netherlands.

Jellinek, E. M. (1960). *The disease concept of alcoholism.* New Brunswick, NJ: Hillhouse Press.

Jewett, D. L., Fein, G., & Greenberg, M. (1990). A double-blind study of provocation to determine food sensitivity. *New England Journal of Medicine, 323,* 429–433.

Jonas, J. M. (1990). Do substance-abuse, including alcoholism, and bulimia covary? In L. D. Reid (Ed.), *Opioids, bulimia, and alcohol abuse and alcoholism* (pp. 247–258). New York: Springer-Verlag.

Jonas, J. M., Gold M. S., Sweeney, D., & Pottash, A. L. C. (1987). Eating disorders and cocaine abuse: A survey of 259 cocaine abusers. *Journal of Clinical Psychiatry, 48,* 47–50.

Jones, D. A., Cheshire, M., & Moorhouse, H. (1985). Anorexia nervosa, bulimia and alcoholism—association of eating disorder and alcohol. *Journal of Psychiatric Research, 19,* 377–380.

Johnson, C. L., & Connors, M. E. (1987). *The etiology and treatment of bulimia nervosa.* New York: Basic Books.

Kassett, J. A., Gershon, E. S., Maxwell, M. E., Guroff, J. J., Kazuba, D. M., Smith, A. L., Brandt, H. A., & Jimerson, D. C. (1989). Psychiatric disorders in the first-degree relatives of probands with bulimia nervosa. *American Journal of Psychiatry, 146,* 1468–1471.

Katzman, M. A., & Marcus Strauss, I. D. (1988). *Eating disorders and substance abuse: Dual addictions and gender.* Paper presented at the 22nd Annual Association for Advancement of Behavior Therapy Convention, New York.

Kendler, K. S., MacLean, C., Neale, M., Kessler, R., Heath, A., & Eaves, L. (1991). The genetic epidemiology of bulimia nervosa. *American Journal of Psychiatry, 148,* 1627–1637.

Krahn, D. D. (1991). The relationship of eating disorders and substance abuse. *Journal of Substance Abuse, 3,* 239–254.

Kushner, M., Sher, K. J., & Beitman, B. (1990). The relation between alcohol problems and the anxiety disorders. *American Journal of Psychiatry, 147,* 685–695.

Lacey, J. H., & Evans, C. D. H. (1986). The impulsivist: A multi-impulsive personality disorder. *British Journal of Addiction, 81,* 641–649.

Lacey, J. H., & Moureli, E. (1986). Bulimic alcoholics: Some features of a clinical sub-group. *British Journal of Addiction, 81,* 389–393.

Laessle, R. G., Wittchen, H. U., Fichter, M. M., & Pirke, K. M. (1989). The significance of subgroups of bulimia and anorexia nervosa: Lifetime frequency of psychiatric disorders. *International Journal of Eating Disorders, 8*, 569–574.

Leon, G. R., Kolotkin, R., & Kogeski, G. (1979). MacAndrew Addiction Scale and other MMPI characteristics associated with obesity, anorexia and smoking behavior. *Addictive Behaviors, 4*, 401–407.

MacAndrew, C. (1965). The differentiation of male alcoholic outpatients from nonalcoholic psychiatric outpatients by means of the MMPI. *Quarterly Journal of Studies on Alcohol, 26*, 238–246.

Malenbaum, R., Herzog, D., Eisenthal, S., & Wyshak, G. (1988). Overeaters anonymous: Impact on bulimia. *International Journal of Eating Disorders, 7*, 139–143.

Marcus, M. D., Wing, R. R., Ewing, L., Kern, E., Gooding, W., & McDermott, M. (1990). Psychiatric disorders among obese binge eaters. *International Journal of Eating Disorders, 9*, 69–77.

Marlatt, G. A., & Gordon, J. R. (Eds.). (1985). *Relapse prevention: Maintenance strategies in the treatment of addictive behaviors.* New York: Guilford Press.

McCann, K. L., Perri, M. G., Nezu, A. M., & Lowe, M. R. (1992). An investigation of counterregulatory eating in obese clinic attenders. *International Journal of Eating Disorders, 12*, 161–170.

McCann, U. D., Rossiter, E. M., King, R. J., & Agras, W. S. (1991). Nonpurging bulimia: A distinct subtype of bulimia nervosa. *International Journal of Eating Disorders, 10*, 679–688.

Mitchell, J. E., Hatsukami, D., Eckert, E. D., & Pyle, R. L. (1985). Characteristics of 275 patients with bulimia. *American Journal of Psychiatry, 142*, 482–485.

Mitchell, J. E., Laine, D. E., Morley, J. E., & Levine, A. S. (1986). Naloxone but not CCK-8 may attentuate binge-eating behavior in patients with the bulimia syndrome. *Biological Psychiatry, 21*, 1399–1406.

Mitchell, J. E., Pyle, R., Eckert, E. D., & Hatsukami, D., & Soll, E. (1990). The influence of prior alcohol and drug abuse problems on bulimia nervosa treatment outcome. *Addictive Behaviors, 15*, 169–173.

Nisbett, R., & Ross, L. (1980). *Human inference.* Englewood Cliffs, NJ: Prentice Hall.

Peele, S. (1989). *Diseasing of America: Addiction treatment out of control.* Lexington, MA: Lexington Books.

Peveler, R. C., & Fairburn, C. G. (1991). Eating disorders in women who abuse alcohol. *British Journal of Addiction, 85*, 1633–1638.

Polivy, J., & Herman, C. P. (1985). Dieting and bingeing: A causal analysis. *American Psychologist, 40*, 193–201.

Reid, L. D. (1990). *Opioids, bulimia, and alcohol abuse and alcoholism.* New York: Springer-Verlag.

Rodin, J., & Reed, D. (1987). Sweetness and eating disorders. In J. Dobbing (Ed.), *Sweetness* (pp. 193–204). Springer-Verlag.

Rosen, J. C., Leitenberg, H., Fondacaro, K. M., Gross, J., & Willmuth, M. E. (1985). Standardized test meals in assessment of eating behavior in bulimia nervosa: Consumption of feared foods when vomiting is prevented. *International Journal of Eating Disorders, 4*, 59–70.

Rounsaville, B. J., Spitzer, R. L., & Williams, J. B. W. (1986). Proposed changes in DSM-III substance use disorders: Description and rationale. *American Journal of Psychiatry, 143,* 463-468.

Schwalberg, M. D., Barlow, D. H., Alger, S. A., & Howard, L. J. (1992). A comparison of bulimics, obese binge eaters, social phobics, and individuals with panic disorder on comorbidity across DSM-III-R anxiety disorders. *Journal of Abnormal Psychology, 101,* 675-681.

Siegel, S. (1983). Classical conditioning, drug tolerance, and drug dependence. In R. Smart, F. Glaser, Y. Israel, H. Kalant, R. Popham, & W. Schmidt (Eds.), *Research advances in alcohol and drug problems* (Vol. 7, pp. 207-246). New York: Plenum Press.

Smith, D. E., Marcus, M. D., & Kaye, W. (1992). Cognitive-behavioral treatment of obese binge eaters. *International Journal of Eating Disorders, 12,* 249-256.

Specker, S., de Zwaan, M., Pyle, R., Raymond, N., & Mitchell, J. (1992, April 24). *Psychiatric disorders among obese patients with binge eating disorder (BED).* Paper presented at Fifth International Conference on Eating Disorders, New York.

Strasser, T. J., Pike, K. M., & Walsh, B. T. (1992). The impact of prior substance abuse on treatment outcome for bulimia nervosa. *Addictive Behavior, 17,* 387-396.

Striegel-Moore, R. H., Cronan, S., Goebel, A., Pena, L., & Scheibe, K. (1992, April, 24). *Disordered eating in female in-patients with psychoactive substance abuse disorder.* Paper presented at the Fifth International Conference on Eating Disorders, New York.

Taylor, A. V., Peveler, R. C., Hibbert, G. A., & Fairburn, C. G. (in press). Eating disorders among women receiving treatment for an alcohol problem. *International Journal of Eating Disorders*

Telch, C. F., Agras, W. S., Rossiter, E., Wilfley, D., & Kenardy, J. (1990). Group cognitive-behavioral treatment for the non-purging bulimic: An initial evaluation. *Journal of Consulting and Clinical Psychology, 58,* 629-635.

Tiffany, S. T. (1990). A cognitive model of drug urges and drug-use behavior: Role of automatic and nonautomatic processes. *Psychological Review, 97,* 147-168.

Turner, M. St J., Foggo, M., Bennie, J., Carroll, S., Dick, H., & Goodwin, G. M. (1991). Psychological, hormonal and biochemical changes following carbohydrate bingeing: A placebo controlled study in bulimia nervosa and matched controls. *Psychological Medicine, 21,* 123-133.

Vandereycken, W. (1990). The addiction model in eating disorders: Some critical remarks and a selected bibliography. *International Journal of Eating Disorders, 9,* 95-101.

Volpicelli, J. R., O'Brien, C. P., Alterman, A. I., & Hayashida, M. (1990). Naltrexone and the treatment of alcohol-dependence: Initial observations. In L. D. Reid (Ed.), *Opioids, bulimia, and alcohol abuse and alcoholism.* New York: Springer-Verlag.

Walsh, B. T., Kissileff, H. R., Cassidy, S. M., & Dantzic, S. (1989). Eating behavior of women with bulimia. *Archives of General Psychiatry, 46,* 54-58.

Walsh, B. T., Roose, S. P., Glassman, A. H., Gladis, M., & Sadik, C. (1985). Bulimia and depression. *Psychosomatic Medicine, 47,* 123-131.

Wardle, J. (1987). Compulsive eating and dietary restraint. *British Journal of Clinical Psychology, 26,* 47–55.

Wilfley, D. E., Agras, W. S., Telch, C. F., Rossiter, E. M., Schneider, J. A., Cole, A. G., Sifford, L., & Raeburn, S. D. (in press). Group CBT and group interpersonal psychotherapy for non-binging bulimics: A controlled comparison. *Journal of Consulting and Clinical Psychology.*

Wilson, G. T. (1988). Alcohol use and abuse: A social learning analysis. In D. Chaudron & A. Wilkinson (Eds.), *Theories of alcoholism* (pp. 239–288). Toronto: Addiction Research Foundation.

Wilson, G. T. (1991). The addiction model of eating disorders: A critical analysis. *Advances in Behaviour Research and Therapy, 13,* 27-72.

Wilson, G. T., & Fairburn, C. G. (in press). Cognitive treatments for eating disorders. *Journal of Consulting and Clinical Psychology.*

Wilson, G. T., Nonas, K. A., & Rosenblum, G. D. (1993). Assessment of binge-eating in obese patients. *International Journal of Eating Disorders, 13,* 25–34.

Woods, S., & Brief, D. J. (1988). Physiological factors. In D. M. Donovan & G. A. Marlatt (Eds.), *Assessment of addictive behaviors* (pp. 296–322). New York: Guilford Press.

Woods, S. C. (1991). The eating paradox: How we tolerate food. *Psychological Review, 98,* 488–505.

Wooley, S. C., & Wooley, O. W. (1981). Overeating as substance abuse. In N. Mello (Ed.), *Advances in substance abuse* (Vol. 2, pp. 41–68). Greenwich, CT: JAI Press.

Wurtman, J. (1988). Carbohydrate craving, mood changes, and obesity. *Journal of Clinical Psychiatry, 49,* 37–39.

Yanovski, S. Z., Leet, M., Yanovski, J. A., Flood, M., Gold, P. W., Kissileff, H. J., & Walsh, B. T. (1992). Food selection and intake of obese women with binge eating disorder. *American Journal of Clinical Nutrition, 56,* 975–980.

Yeary, J. (1987). The use of overeaters anonymous in the treatment of eating disorders. *Journal of Psychoactive Drugs, 19,* 303-309.

Yeary, J. R., & Heck, C. L. (1989). Dual diagnosis: Eating–disorders and psychoactive substance dependence. *Journal of Psychoactive Drugs, 21,* 239-249.

EPIDEMIOLOGY AND ETIOLOGY

Binge Eating and Bulimia Nervosa: Distribution and Determinants

Christopher G. Fairburn
Phillipa J. Hay
Sarah L. Welch

This chapter is concerned with the epidemiological research on binge eating and bulimia nervosa, epidemiology being the study of the distribution and determinants of disease in populations. It will review the findings of the research to date, taking particular account of methodological issues, and it will consider ways in which epidemiological studies might answer broader questions than those simply concerning prevalence and incidence.

THE DISTRIBUTION OF BULIMIA NERVOSA AND BINGE EATING

Bulimia Nervosa

Since the early 1980s there has been intense interest in the prevalence of the eating disorder bulimia nervosa. This has been stimulated by the recent unexplained emergence of the disorder. Prior to the mid-1970s bulimia nervosa was rarely seen in clinical practice and had received little attention. Ten years later it was the eating disorder most commonly encountered by clinicians. Figure 7.1 shows the rates of referral to a major eating disorder center in Canada (Garner & Fairburn, 1988). It can be seen that between 1975 and 1986 the referral rates for anorexia nervosa

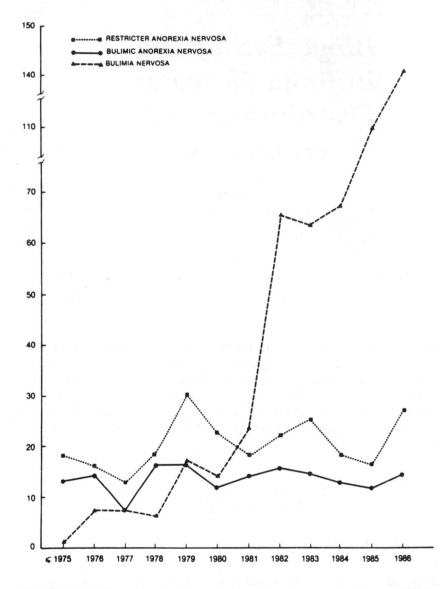

FIGURE 7.1. Rates of referral to an eating disorder center in Canada (Clarke Institute of Psychiatry and the Toronto General Hospital). From "Relationship between Anorexia Nervosa and Bulimia Nervosa: Diagnostic Implications" (p. 60) by D. M. Garner and C. G. Fairburn, 1988, in *Diagnostic Issues in Anorexia Nervosa and Bulimia Nervosa*, edited by D. M. Garner and P. E. Garfinkel, New York, Brunner/Mazel. Copyright 1988 by Brunner/Mazel, Inc. Reprinted by permission.

were relatively stable, whereas there was a remarkable upsurge in the rates of referral for bulimia nervosa. Equivalent findings have been reported from Wellington in New Zealand, where the annual referral rate for bulimia nervosa increased between 1977 and 1986 from 6 to 44 per 100,000 females aged 15 to 29 years, while those for anorexia nervosa did not change (Hall & Hay, 1991). A similar trend was observed in London with annual referral rates for bulimia nervosa increasing between 1980 and 1989 from 2.8 to 10.1 per 10,000 females aged 15 to 40 years (Lacey, 1992). At the same time, the findings of surveys in Great Britain suggested that bulimia nervosa was largely undetected; for example, of 499 cases detected in a 1980 media survey, only 2.5% were in treatment (Fairburn & Cooper, 1982).

By 1989 over 50 studies of the prevalence of bulimia nervosa had been published,[1] and these were the subject of a review by Fairburn and Beglin (1990). Four major points were made in this review.

1. *Study samples.* The samples studied were not ideal since half consisted of college students, often those enrolled in psychology classes at prestigious private universities. Since the findings of the early media-based surveys suggested that students formed only a minority of those with bulimia nervosa (Fairburn & Cooper, 1982; Fairburn & Cooper, 1984), there was a clear need to move the focus of research away from students toward women in the general population.

2. *Method of assessment.* Studies should not rely exclusively upon self-report questionnaires to detect cases. Instead, clinical interviews are required to make diagnoses, although self-report questionnaires may be used to identify cases for interview. The significance of this point is evident from Table 7.1, which summarizes the findings of the prevalence studies, subdividing them on the basis of their method of case detection. It can be seen that the prevalence rates obtained from studies that rely exclusively upon self-report questionnaires to make diagnoses are variable and higher than those derived from interview-based studies. In contrast, the prevalence rates generated by the latter studies are remarkably consistent.

3. *Response bias.* Consistency should not be confused with accuracy. The fact that the interview-based studies obtained consistent findings does not mean that they are accurate. The studies could be subject to equivalent sources of error. It was pointed out, for example, that there was some evidence suggesting that eating disorders are overrepresented among those who choose not to take part in prevalence studies. It was therefore possible that even the prevalence figures derived from the better interview-based studies might be underestimates of the true rates.

4. *Clinical significance.* The clinical significance of the findings of the

TABLE 7.1. Prevalence of Bulimia Nervosa as Determined by Studies That Used Three Different Methods of Case Detection

	Diagnosis			
	DSM-III bulimia	DSM-III bulimia with weekly binge eating	DSM-III bulimia with weekly binge eating and purging	Bulimia nervosa: Russell (1979) or DSM-III-R criteria
Self-Report Questionnaires				
Prevalence (%)				
Mean (SD)	9.0 (4.3)	3.6 (2.0)	2.8 (2.8)	2.6 (1.0)
Range	3–19	0–7	1–10	2–4
Number of studies	20	13	11	4
Interview—Preliminary Studies				
Prevalence (%)				
Mean (SD)	1.9 (1.9)	—	—	1.6 (—)
Range	0–5	—	—	—
Number of studies	4	0	0	1
Interview—More Sophisticated Studies				
Prevalence (%)				
Mean (SD)	1.5 (1.0)	—	1.0 (—)	0.9 (0.3)
Range	1–3	—	—	0–1
Number of studies	4	—	1	4

Note: Data from Fairburn and Beglin (1990). Copyright 1990 by the American Psychiatric Assocation. Adapted by permission.

prevalence studies was difficult to assess, since no comparisons had been made between community-based and clinic-based cases. There was an assumption that the cases detected in community surveys were as severe as those seen in clinical practice, but this assumption was not warranted. Indeed, the finding that few community-based cases were in treatment suggested that those detected in community surveys might be a less disturbed group.

Recent Interview-Based Studies of General Population Samples

Since the Fairburn and Beglin (1990) review was written, work has continued to be published on the prevalence of bulimia nervosa. This work will now be reviewed, taking particular account of the above points, starting with the studies of general population samples and then considering those of special subgroups.

　　With regard to research methods, recent findings have reinforced the concern about the use of self-report instruments to make the diagnosis of bulimia nervosa. For example, Beglin and Fairburn (1992c) found that the widely used practice of directly translating diagnostic criteria into items on a self-report questionnaire resulted in the production of an inefficient case-finding instrument. While interviews are to be preferred to self-report questionnaires when identifying cases of bulimia nervosa, not all interviews would be expected to perform equally well. Respondent-based interviews are likely to share many of the limitations of self-report questionnaires, since they are in essence verbally ad-ministered self-report questionnaires. (See Fairburn & Cooper, Chapter 15, this volume, for a description of the difference between respondent-based and investigator-based interviews.) It is therefore of note that Bush-nell, Wells, Hornblow, Oakley-Browne, and Joyce (1990) found a signifi-cant discrepancy between the diagnoses of bulimia nervosa made on the basis of the Diagnostic Interview Schedule (DIS), a respondent-based interview, and those made by clinicians. In their study the lifetime preva-lence of bulimia—using the criteria of the third edition of the *Diagnostic and Statistical Manual of Mental Disorders* (DSM-III) (Amer-ican Psychiatric Association [APA], 1980)—based on clinician's assess-ment was about two-thirds the rate based on the DIS (using DSM-III criteria).

The prevalence studies of most significance are five interview-based studies of general population samples. The study by Rand and Kuldau (1992), also reported by Langer, Warheit, and Zimmerman (1991), is of least interest, since it used the DSM-III (APA, 1980) criteria rather than the preferred DSM-III-R criteria, and since the sample was mostly aged 55 years or over. Among women aged 18 to 30 years ($n = 242$), the point prevalence of DSM-III bulimia was 4.1%. No cases were identified among the men in this age group. The study from New Zealand by Bushnell et al. (1990) was more sophisticated in that assessment was by interviewers using the DIS, and by clinicians, and various different diagnostic sys-tems were applied. As in the previous study, bulimia nervosa was found to be uncommon in men: It was mainly concentrated among young wom-en. The point prevalence of draft DSM-III-R bulimia nervosa among women aged 18 to 44 years ($n = 777$) was 0.5% (based upon clinician's ratings) and the lifetime prevalence was 1.6%. This difference between the rates of current and lifetime disorder suggests that bulimia nervosa does not tend to run a chronic course. Another interesting finding was that of a strong cohort effect with a higher lifetime prevalence among young women: The lifetime prevalence of DSM-III bulimia among women aged 18 to 24 years was 4.5%; among women aged 25 to 44 years it was 2.0%; and among women 45 to 64 years it was 0.4%.

There have been two interview-based studies of general population samples of adolescents. The first was by Johnson-Sabine, Wood, Patton, Mann, and Wakeling (1988). Using a two-stage design, 1,010 girls from state schools in London were studied. They were aged 14 to 16 years. The point prevalence of bulimia nervosa was 1.0%.[2] No cases of anorexia nervosa were detected, but it was known that there were two cases among those individuals who declined to take part. The second study focused on a large sample (n = 5,596) of New Jersey adolescents (Whitaker et al., 1990). DSM-III diagnostic criteria were used, and only lifetime prevalence rates are given. The lifetime prevalence rate among the girls was 0.5% for anorexia nervosa and 4.0% for DSM-III bulimia (excluding those with current or past anorexia nervosa). The equivalent figures for the boys were lower, at 0.0% and 0.2%, respectively. The other finding of note was that while the majority of cases of anorexia nervosa had previously come to medical attention, this was not true of the bulimia nervosa cases, few of whom had ever discussed their problems with a professional despite high levels of functional impairment. Indeed, bulimia nervosa was associated with the lowest rate of service contact of any of the disorders studied (major depression, dysthymic disorder, panic disorder, generalized anxiety disorder, and obsessive–compulsive disorder).

The fifth study of note was of female same-sex twins from the Virginia population-based register (Kendler et al., 1991). DSM-III-R criteria were used and 2,163 twins were interviewed. The lifetime prevalence of bulimia nervosa was 2.8%, and the lifetime risk was 4.2% (that is, the proportion of individuals who would be expected to receive the diagnosis if they completed their age at risk, defined as age 50). As in the Bushnell study, there was evidence of a marked cohort effect. When the sample was divided into three birth cohorts (before 1950, mean age = 42.3 years; 1950–59, mean age = 33.0 years; and from 1960 onward, mean age = 23.6 years), it was found that the more recent the birth cohort, the higher the risk for bulimia nervosa and the earlier the age at onset (see Figure 7.2). As Kendler and colleagues point out, while these findings are consistent with a cohort effect for bulimia nervosa, it is conceivable that they were due to either a cohort effect for awareness of bulimia nervosa as a disorder or time-dependent forgetting. Both these explanations seem improbable. Awareness of the syndrome bulimia nervosa seems unlikely to have influenced subjects' responses to questions concerning their prior experience of key features of the disorder, such as uncontrolled overeating and compensatory self-induced vomiting. It also seems implausible that age-dependent forgetting would account for the large differences in risk between subjects who are young and close in age.

The importance of taking account of the potential biasing influence of nonparticipants has received further support from the findings of a

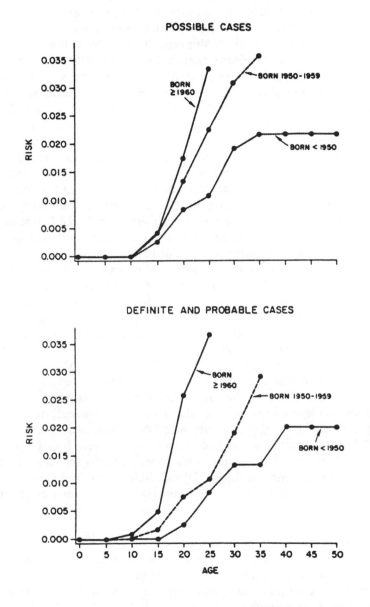

FIGURE 7.2. Lifetime cumulative risk for bulimia nervosa among female twins from three birth cohorts. From ''The Genetic Epidemiology of Bulimia Nervosa'' by K. S. Kendler, C. MacLean, M. Neale, R. Kessler, A. Heath, and L. Eaves, 1991, *American Journal of Psychiatry, 148*, p. 1631. Copyright 1991 by the American Psychiatric Association. Reprinted by permission.

study of those who chose not to take part in a survey on eating disorders (Beglin & Fairburn, 1992b). A high rate of eating problems was found, suggesting that such problems may be overrepresented among those who elect not to take part in surveys of this type. It seems likely that estimates of the prevalence of eating disorders are indeed underestimates and that, as Fairburn and Beglin (1990) suggested, it may never be possible to get accurate figures for the rates of eating disorders in community samples.

The clinical significance of the epidemiological findings is still difficult to assess. We are making a detailed comparison of the clinical features of patients referred for treatment with those of cases detected in the community, the great majority of whom are not in treatment. Preliminary findings indicate that although the clinic group show a greater level of behavioral disturbance, as indicated by their rates of overeating and self-induced vomiting on the investigator-based interview, the Eating Disorder Examination (EDE) (Cooper & Fairburn, 1987; see Fairburn & Cooper, Chapter 15, this volume), they are equivalent in other respects. Their levels of dietary restraint and concern about shape and weight appear to be no different, and their degree of general psychiatric disturbance does not differ (Welch & Fairburn, 1992b). The report of Whitaker et al. (1990) of a high level of functional impairment found among adolescents with bulimia nervosa is consistent with our findings. Taking these results together, it seems that the cases detected in community surveys are a significantly disturbed group.

To evaluate further the significance of the findings of the prevalence studies, more needs to be known about the course of the cases detected in community surveys (i.e., the natural history of the disorder) and how it compares with that of clinic referrals. To date very few well-diagnosed (i.e., by clinical interview) community-based cases have been followed-up. King (1991) recontacted five out of seven cases at 2-year follow-up and found that three (3/5, 60%) still met diagnostic criteria for bulimia nervosa, and Patton, Johnson-Sabine, Wood, Mann, and Wakeling (1990) followed-up four cases for 1 year and found that two still met diagnostic criteria (2/4, 50%).

Recent Interview-Based Studies of Special Subgroups

In the Fairburn and Beglin (1990) review it was noted that the studies of this type had been of a lower standard than the mainstream prevalence studies. Since then, methods have improved and certain important findings have emerged.

PEOPLE WITH DIABETES MELLITUS

Since 1990 there have been three controlled interview-based studies of the prevalence of eating disorders among adolescents and young adults with diabetes mellitus. All three have used the EDE (Fairburn, Peveler, Davies, Mann, & Mayou, 1991; Peveler, Fairburn, Boller, & Dunger, 1992; Striegel-Moore, Nicholson, & Tamborlane, 1992). In each case the EDE was adapted to distinguish features characteristic of eating disorders from similar features resulting directly from having diabetes and the influence of treatment. The findings have been consistent in disconfirming the impression arising from the earlier less sophisticated studies that eating disorders are overrepresented among patients with diabetes mellitus.

PEOPLE WITH PSYCHIATRIC DISORDERS

At the time of the Fairburn and Beglin review there had been three studies of the prevalence of bulimia nervosa among psychiatric inpatients, and their results were inconsistent. One study found a high prevalence (Kutcher, Whitehouse, & Freeman, 1985); one found a prevalence equivalent to that of a college sample, although the rates of vomiting and laxative misuse were higher (Esman, Dechillo, & Moughan, 1986); and one found no cases at all (Whitehouse, Adams, & Marche, 1989). Since then, Hay and Hall (1991) have reported finding that 7 out of 59 (11.9%) recently admitted female psychiatric inpatients met DSM-III-R diagnostic criteria for bulimia nervosa. None of the cases had previously been detected. There were no cases of anorexia nervosa. Lower rates were found in a study of 143 attenders at a psychiatric emergency clinic (Johnson & Hillard, 1990). Four cases of DSM-III-R bulimia nervosa were found, two female (3.0%) and two male (2.6%).

The studies of the prevalence of bulimia nervosa among those with alcohol problems are reviewed by Wilson (Chapter 6, this volume).

In the absence of studies of the rates of eating disorder features among community samples of those with psychiatric disorders, it is not possible to say whether eating disorders are genuinely overrepresented among those with psychiatric disorder or whether these findings are an expression of referral bias.

GENERAL PRACTICE ATTENDERS

In a large study of general-practice attenders in London, King (1989) showed that eating disorders often go unrecognized by family doctors. This finding has recently been confirmed by Whitehouse, Cooper, Vize, Hill, and Vogel (1992). Using a two-stage design and a brief version of the EDE, 540 consecutive female attenders (aged 16 to 35 years) were assessed. Eight cases of bulimia nervosa were detected, four of whom were not known to their doctor.

PEOPLE FROM DEVELOPING COUNTRIES

There have been very few studies of the prevalence of eating disorders among those from developing countries. They are thought to be rare. Using a two-stage design, Mumford, Whitehouse, and Choudry (1992) studied 369 schoolgirls at three leading English-medium schools in Lahore. One-year DSM-III-R prevalence rates were reported. One case of bulimia nervosa was detected. In contrast, the same group found a 1-year prevalence rate of 3.4% (7/204) among Asian schoolgirls living in Bradford in England (Mumford, Whitehouse, & Platts, 1991). The latter finding is striking, since Lacey and Dolan (1988) have reported that Asians and black women are markedly underrepresented among those who present for treatment.

Binge Eating

At first sight it may seem curious that less is known about the prevalence of binge eating than that of bulimia nervosa. There are several explanations for this apparent anomaly. One is that the recent two-stage surveys designed to detect cases of bulimia nervosa do not generate figures for the prevalence of binge eating. Therefore, with one noteworthy exception, the published data come from the early surveys that relied exclusively upon self-report questionnaires, some of which simply asked people whether they had episodes of binge eating. This practice is problematic, since the term has no specific meaning. For example, Beglin and Fairburn (1992a) showed that there are discrepancies between the lay and technical uses of the term, with young women appearing to place great emphasis on loss of control over eating and less on the amount actually eaten, whereas not until DSM-IV was loss of control part of the technical definition of a binge (see Fairburn & Wilson, Chapter 1, this volume).*

Even if the term "binge" is avoided in self-report questionnaires, such instruments are still not accurate at assessing binge eating when compared with clinical assessments. In a related study Fairburn and Beglin (1992) showed that there was relatively poor agreement between a self-report version of the EDE and the EDE interview itself when assessing binge eating, whereas there was good agreement for behavior such as self-induced vomiting, which does not pose problems of definition. Similarly, Bushnell et al. (1990) found that one of the sources of the disagreement between clinicians' diagnoses of bulimia nervosa and

*The DSM-IV criteria cited in this volume are those that were approved as final by the DSM-IV Eating Disorders Work Group and the Task Force on DSM-IV (APA, 1993). These criteria may be subject to minor editorial revisions before the publication of DSM-IV.

TABLE 7.2. Prevalence of Key Features of Bulimia Nervosa Determined by Studies Using Self-Report Questionnaires

	Prevalence (%)			Number of studies
	Mean	*SD*	Range	
Binge eating				
Current	35.8	21.4	7–79	16
At least weekly	15.7	9.4	5–39	11
Current strict dieting or				
fasting	29.0	15.0	7–55	8
Self-induced vomiting				
Current	8.0	5.1	2–21	14
At least weekly	2.4	1.4	0–4	8
Laxative misuse				
Current	5.8	3.3	2–12	11
At least weekly	2.7	1.6	1–5	5

Note. Data from Fairburn and Beglin (1990). Copyright 1990 by the American Psychiatric Association. Adapted by permission.

those made using the DIS was that clinicians used a narrower definition of binge eating. Given these problems of definition and assessment, it is not surprising that Fairburn and Beglin (1990) in their review found great variability in the figures available on the prevalence of binge eating (see Table 7.2).

Recently there has been renewed interest in the prevalence of binge eating, stimulated by the proposal by Spitzer and colleagues that a new category of eating disorder be established to recognize those who have recurrent episodes of binge eating yet do not meet diagnostic criteria for bulimia nervosa (Devlin, Walsh, Spitzer, & Hasin, 1992; see Fairburn & Wilson, Chapter 1, this volume). This proposal led to a large study designed to evaluate possible diagnostic criteria for so-called binge eating disorder (Spitzer et al., 1992). Unfortunately, the great majority of the methodological shortcomings mentioned earlier apply to this study, in particular, reliance upon an unvalidated self-report questionnaire to assess binge eating and associated features, lack of a satisfactory general population sample,[3] and a poor response rate in some groups. As a result it is not possible to place confidence in the prevalence rates obtained either for binge eating itself or for binge eating disorder. For information, the rates for binge eating were 45.9% in the weight control samples, 6.3% in the community samples, and 83.3% in the Overeaters Anonymous samples. These rates are for both sexes combined. The equivalent rates for binge eating disorder were 30.1% in the weight control samples (31.9% for females and 20.8% for males), 2.0%

in the community samples (2.5% for females and 1.1% for males), and 71.2% in the Overeaters Anonymous samples (sex ratio not given).

No data have been published on the prevalence of binge eating as defined in DSM-IV. Most studies have not required the presence of loss of control when identifying binges, and the study by Spitzer et al. (1992) did not use a contextual definition of "large" (i.e., their definition did not require an "amount of food that is definitely larger than most people would eat during a similar period of time *in similar circumstances*" [APA, 1993], emphasis added). We therefore report data of relevance from a recent Oxford study (Fairburn, Beglin, & Davies, 1992).

The subjects comprised a general population sample of women, aged 16 to 35 years, identified from the case registers of two general practices in Oxfordshire, one rural and one suburban. Two hundred eighty five women selected at random from these registers were contacted by letter and asked if they would take part in a study of women's eating habits and weight. Those who did not reply were sent a second letter. If there was no response, they were contacted by telephone or visited at home, and the study was explained to them. Subjects who agreed to participate (n = 243, 85.3%) were interviewed using the EDE. (See Wilson, Chapter 11, this volume, for an assessment of the EDE, and Fairburn & Cooper, Chapter 15, this volume, for a copy of the interview schedule). The mean age of the subjects was 26.6 years (SD = 5.5). Twenty-one (8.6%) reported at least one DSM-IV binge (objective bulimic episodes in EDE terminology) over the past month; 10 (4.1%) reported at least four such episodes (i.e., an average rate of weekly), and four (1.7%) reported at least eight episodes (i.e., an average of at least twice weekly, the rate required to make a DSM-IV diagnosis of bulimia nervosa or binge eating disorder). With respect to the previous 3 months, 9.6% reported at least 1 episode, 3.3% reported at least 12 such episodes (i.e., an average rate of once weekly), and 2.5% reported at least 24 episodes (i.e., an average of at least twice weekly). Thus, binge eating, as defined in DSM-IV, does not appear to be a common behavior even among the group thought to be most at risk (i.e., young women).

Sixty-nine of the subjects (28.4%) in this study were overweight (a body mass index [BMI] of 25 or more[4]), of whom 11 (15.9%) reported at least one episode of binge eating and 4 (5.8%) at least weekly episodes. The corresponding figures for those with a BMI below 25 were 6.3% and 1.7%, respectively. Fourteen subjects (5.8%) were significantly overweight (a BMI of 30 or more), of whom 3 (21.4%) reported at least one episode of binge eating and 2 (14.3%) at least weekly episodes. Thus, DSM-IV binges appear to be more common among those who are overweight than those of a healthy weight. (See Marcus, Chapter 5, this volume, for an account of binge eating in obesity.)

Conclusions

1. Research methods have improved and therefore more confidence may be placed in the findings of the prevalence studies.
2. The best studies of the point prevalence of bulimia nervosa among adolescent and young adult women yield figures between 0.5% and 1.0%. These may be underestimates of the true rates in the general population given the overrepresentation of eating disorders among those who choose not to take part in surveys on the topic.
3. Bulimia nervosa is uncommon among men.
4. There appears to be a cohort effect with young women today being at greater risk of developing bulimia nervosa than were their counterparts a decade or more ago.
5. The cases identified in community surveys appear to have levels of morbidity comparable to those of patients seeking treatment.
6. Only a small proportion of cases of bulimia nervosa are in treatment. Both general practitioners and psychiatrists often fail to detect the disorder.
7. Little is known about the prevalence of binge eating.

THE DETERMINANTS OF BINGE EATING AND BULIMIA NERVOSA

A number of factors have been implicated in the etiology of eating disorders. Many of these factors have emerged from studies of the etiology of anorexia nervosa, from which generalizations concerning the etiology of bulimia nervosa are sometimes made. Studies focusing on the etiology of bulimia nervosa are comparatively scarce, and there has been almost no research on the etiology of binge eating itself.

The main factors implicated in the etiology of bulimia nervosa are having a family history of an eating disorder, affective disorder, substance abuse, or obesity; and a personal history of affective disorder, obesity, diabetes mellitus, or sexual abuse. Further factors include certain personality traits, disturbed family relationships and parenting, and parental overconcern with dieting and body shape or weight (Hsu, 1990). The research that has implicated these factors has had certain shortcomings. Four problems are of particular note.

The first problem is that samples representative of all those with bulimia nervosa have not been studied: Almost all the work has been based on patient samples, yet as already indicated there is good evidence that most of those with bulimia nervosa do not come to medical attention. The research findings may therefore be distorted by selection bias.

This limitation applies to all the putative etiological factors.

A second problem is that most studies, with the exception of that by Kendler et al. (1991),[5] have been narrow in perspective with their focus being on a limited range of putative etiological factors (or even, more commonly, on a single factor). As a result almost nothing is known about the relative contributions of different classes of factors or how they interact. This limitation applies even to the more methodologically sophisticated investigations such as the family genetic studies (e.g., Kassett et al., 1989). Such studies are of obvious value in identifying familial aggregation of disorders, but their findings need to be supplemented by studies that examine family factors alongside others.

Third, since general psychiatric control groups have rarely been included, it has not been possible to determine whether the etiological factors implicated are specific to eating disorders or whether they are common to psychiatric disorder in general. Indeed, some studies have not included control groups at all. The research regarding sexual abuse provides an example of this problem (Pope & Hudson, 1992). While several studies have found high rates of sexual abuse among those with bulimia nervosa, none have included adequate control groups. It is therefore unclear whether the rate is higher than among the general population. We have recently addressed this issue in the context of our community-based case-control study (see below). The findings indicate that there is an increased risk of psychiatric disorder conferred by sexual abuse, but it is not specific to bulimia nervosa (Welch & Fairburn, 1992a).

Lastly, little attention has been paid to the timing and mode of operation of putative etiological factors, for example, whether they increase the risk of developing an eating disorder, whether they contribute to its maintenance once it has developed, or whether they do both. Studies relating to personality traits as putative etiological factors are particularly vulnerable to this criticism, since most have limited themselves to assessment of personality in subjects with active eating disorder symptomatology. The etiological significance of the findings of such studies cannot be interpreted, since the factors implicated may be predisposing factors, maintaining factors, or even consequences of the disorder. Timing is of obvious importance in the study of all factors whose mode of operation is thought to be environmental rather than constitutional.

THE POTENTIAL OF EPIDEMIOLOGICAL METHODS FOR STUDYING THE ETIOLOGY OF BINGE EATING AND BULIMIA NERVOSA

Epidemiological studies may generate information of relevance to etiology. Descriptive studies provide data on the rates of occurrence of disorder in various different groups and, if the rates differ, the findings may have implications for etiology. To date, much of the research on eating disorders has been of this type. Analytic studies are designed to test etiological hypotheses about why certain groups are at increased or decreased risk of developing the disorder in question, in other words, to identify risk and protective factors. They fall into two groups, case-control studies and cohort studies. In the former, those with the disorder are compared with those who are free from it and their exposure to putative etiological factors is compared. This design can be executed relatively quickly and is efficient in its use of cases. In the latter, those exposed to a putative etiological factor are compared with those not exposed with respect to their rate of development of the disorder. This design is not well suited to the simultaneous study of several putative risk factors, and usually requires a very long period of study. To date there have been few case-control studies and, apart from the small study by Patton et al. (1990), no cohort studies. The third type of study is experimental in character and tests etiological hypotheses by determining whether the rates of disorder are changed by altering exposure to a suspected cause. This type of study has limited applications in this specific area.

With these considerations in mind, we will now describe in outline three ongoing studies, with the hope that others might embark upon equivalent or complementary studies, and to illustrate the point that epidemiological research methods can address questions other than those concerning prevalence and incidence.

A Case–Control Study of the Development of Bulimia Nervosa

Given the limited current knowledge of the etiology of bulimia nervosa and binge eating, we believe that the epidemiological research design likely to be most fruitful is the case-control design, since it is both practicable, unlike cohort and experimental studies, and allows the simultaneous testing of multiple etiological hypotheses. If designed with attention to the four points mentioned earlier, case-control studies should yield findings of value.

We are currently engaged in a case-control study designed to identify specific risk factors for the development of bulimia nervosa. Subjects with DSM-III-R bulimia nervosa are being compared with two other groups, those with no eating disorder and those with other psychiatric disorders but no eating disorder. There is individual matching with respect to age and parental social class. The three groups are being compared with respect to their exposure (prior to the age of onset of eating disorder of the index case) to the main factors implicated in the etiology of eating disorders. Assessment is by research clinical interview using standardized measures where available. The subjects are recruited from the community by administering a self-report case-finding questionnaire to 16- to 35-year-old women identified from general-practice case registers. This is a good way of obtaining a general population sample in Great Britain, since the great majority (about 98%) of the population are registered with a general practitioner.

This study will show which of the putative risk factors for bulimia nervosa are risk factors for the development of the disorder; it will assess their relative contributions; and it will indicate whether they are specific to bulimia nervosa or common to psychiatric disorder in general in young adult women. It will be free from the biases that come from studying patient samples.

A Study of the Maintenance of Bulimia Nervosa

Little is known about the natural history of bulimia nervosa, yet in the absence of such information it is impossible to assess the impact of treatment on the course of the disorder. Knowledge of the factors and processes that influence the course of eating disorders is central to the rational development of more effective treatments. Strictly speaking, only longitudinal studies that have investigated samples not exposed to treatment provide information on natural history. To date there have been two such studies (which have used interview methods) (Patton et al. 1990; King, 1991), but because of design limitations they have recruited very few cases.

To describe the natural history of bulimia nervosa, we are reassessing at annual intervals the cases of bulimia nervosa detected in the course of the case-control study outlined above, and to investigate the factors and processes that influence this course, we are relating change in the eating disorder to background variables (i.e., family and personal history variables), properties of the disorder itself (e.g., severity of concerns about shape and weight, thereby testing the cognitive view of the disorder [Fairburn, Cooper, & Cooper, 1986]), and the occurrence of intervening life events.

Prospective studies of this type may also be used to examine the relationships between disorders. The relationship between bulimia nervosa and certain other disorders is the subject of debate with three conditions attracting particular interest, affective disorder (Levy, Dixon, & Stern, 1989), substance abuse (see Wilson, Chapter 6, this volume), and obesity (Garner & Fairburn, 1988). To examine the relationship between bulimia nervosa and these three disorders we are exploring how they covary over time. Few studies in this field have used this approach, and all have relied on patient samples, which are likely to be biased with respect to comorbidity.

A Study of the Classification of those Eating Disorders Characterized by Recurrent Overeating

Controversy surrounds the current scheme for classifying those eating disorders characterized by recurrent episodes of overeating (see Fairburn & Wilson, Chapter 1, this volume). For example, Spitzer et al. (1992) argued that a new diagnostic category, binge eating disorder, should be included in DSM-IV. This disorder is characterized by recurrent overeating in the absence of extreme weight control behavior of the type required to make a diagnosis of bulimia nervosa. We believe that too little is known about those with recurrent overeating to justify introducing this new eating disorder (Fairburn, Welch, & Hay, 1993). In a compromise between these two positions, DSM-IV has included binge eating disorder as an instance of EDNOS.

Epidemiological research of the type outlined should generate the kind of information needed to derive and evaluate diagnostic schemes for eating disorders. Using the same procedure as we are using to recruit cases of bulimia nervosa for the case-control study, we are recruiting a community-based sample of people with recurrent episodes of overeating. We plan to identify clinically meaningful subgroups among these individuals on the basis of their ratings on the EDE. The resulting subgroups will be compared with respect to their current clinical features, the history of their eating disorder, the presence of putative risk factors for eating disorders, and their course, to examine their descriptive, construct, and predictive validity.

Conclusions

1. There has been little research on the etiology of bulimia nervosa and almost none on binge eating.
2. The main factors implicated in the etiology of bulimia nervosa are a family history of an eating disorder, affective disorder, substance abuse, or obesity; and a personal history of affective disorder, obesity, diabetes mellitus, or sexual abuse.
3. The majority of studies have had four major shortcomings: They have used patient samples, which may be biased; they have been narrow in perspective; general psychiatric control groups have rarely been used; and little attention has been paid to the timing of operation of etiological factors.
4. Recent studies with improved methods have failed to confirm certain earlier findings, for example, the studies of diabetes mellitus and sexual abuse as risk factors. Therefore the etiological factors presently implicated must be regarded as putative rather than definite.

5. Epidemiological research methods may be used to address etiological questions. While the resulting findings with respect to causation will inevitably be incomplete, they should inform future work on treatment and prevention.

ACKNOWLEDGMENTS

Our research on the etiology and classification of eating disorders is supported by a program grant from the Wellcome Trust and by project grants from the MacArthur Foundation and the Johann Jacobs Foundation. Two of us (CGF and SLW) are supported by the Wellcome Trust, and the other (PJH) holds a Nuffield Research Fellowship. The data on the prevalence of DSM-IV binge eating were collected jointly with Sarah Beglin (with support from the Wellcome Trust). We are grateful to Zafra Cooper for her comments on an earlier version of the chapter.

NOTES

1. Many of the earlier prevalence studies were concerned with the DSM-III syndrome "bulimia," the forerunner of the DSM-III-R and DSM-IV syndromes bulimia nervosa.

2. The narrow diagnostic criteria of Russell (1979) were used. These are equivalent to those for the purging subtype of DSM-IV bulimia nervosa. See Fairburn and Wilson (Chapter 1, this volume) for a description of the evolution of diagnostic schemes for bulimia nervosa.

3. The community samples comprised students attending health education classes (n = 121), new employees at a medical center (n = 446), and subjects selected randomly from the Staten Island, New York, telephone book (n = 464). While the participation rate was high for the first two samples, approximately three out of every seven telephone respondents refused to take part.

4. BMI = weight in kg/(height in m)^2. Mild obesity may be defined as a BMI between 25.0 and 29.9, and moderate obesity as a BMI between 30.0 and 39.9. A BMI of 40.0 or more is indicative of severe obesity (Garrow, 1988).

5. The study by Kendler et al. (1991) is of female twins from the Virginia population-based twin register. Its findings suggest that about 50% of the variance in liability to bulimia nervosa is due to additive gene action and about 50% to individual-specific environment. However, as the authors note, given the modest number of affected twins, the results from model fitting have to be interpreted with caution.

REFERENCES

American Psychiatric Association. (1980). *Diagnostic and statistical manual of mental disorders* (3rd ed.). Washington, DC: Author.

American Psychiatric Association. (1987). *Diagnostic and statistical manual of mental disorders* (3rd ed., rev.). Washington, DC: Author.

American Psychiatric Association. (1993). *DSM-IV draft criteria (3/1/93)*. Washington, DC: Author.

Beglin, S. J., & Fairburn, C. G. (1992a). What is meant by the term "binge"? *American Journal of Psychiatry, 149*, 123–124.

Beglin, S. J., & Fairburn, C. G. (1992b). Women who choose not to participate in surveys on eating disorders. *International Journal of Eating Disorders, 12*, 113-116.

Beglin, S. J., & Fairburn, C. G. (1992c). The evaluation of a new instrument for detecting eating disorders in community samples. *Psychiatry Research, 44*, 191–201.

Bushnell, J. A., Wells, J. E., Hornblow, A. R., Oakley-Browne, M. A., & Joyce, P. (1990). Prevalence of three bulimia syndromes in the general population. *Psychological Medicine, 20*, 671–680.

Cooper, Z., & Fairburn, C. G. (1987). The Eating Disorder Examination: A semi-structured interview for the assessment of the specific psychopathology of eating disorders. *International Journal of Eating Disorders, 6*, 1–8.

Devlin, M. J., Walsh, B. T., Spitzer, R. L., & Hasin, D. (1992). Is there another binge eating disorder? A review of the literature on overeating in the absence of bulimia nervosa. *International Journal of Eating Disorders, 11*, 333–340.

Esman, A. H., Dechillo, N., & Moughan, V. (1986). "Hidden" eating disorders in female patients. *American Journal of Psychiatry, 143*, 803.

Fairburn, C. G., & Beglin, S. J. (1990). Studies of the epidemiology of bulimia nervosa. *American Journal of Psychiatry, 147*, 401–408.

Fairburn, C. G., & Beglin, S. J. (1992). *The assessment of eating disorders: Interview or self-report questionnaire?* Manuscript submitted for publication.

Fairburn, C. G., Beglin, S. J., & Davies, B. (1992). *Eating habits and disorders amongst young adult women: An interview-based study.* Unpublished manuscript.

Fairburn, C. G., & Cooper, P. J. (1982). Self-induced vomiting and bulimia nervosa: An undetected problem. *British Medical Journal, 284*, 1153–1155.

Fairburn, C. G., & Cooper, P. J. (1984). Binge-eating, self-induced vomiting and laxative abuse: A community study. *Psychological Medicine, 14*, 401–410.

Fairburn, C. G., Cooper, Z., & Cooper, P. J. (1986). The clinical features and maintenance of bulimia nervosa. In K. D. Brownell & J. P. Foreyt (Eds.), *Handbook of eating disorders: Physiology, psychology and treatment of obesity, anorexia and bulimia.* (pp. 389–404). New York: Basic Books.

Fairburn, C. G., Peveler, R. C., Davies, B. A., Mann, J. I., & Mayou, R. A. (1991). Eating disorders in young adults with insulin dependent diabetes: A controlled study. *British Medical Journal, 303*, 17–20.

Fairburn, C. G., Welch, S. L., & Hay, P. J. (1993). The classification of recurrent overeating: The "Binge Eating Disorder" proposal. *International Journal of Eating Disorders, 13*, 155–160.

Garner, D. M., & Fairburn, C. G. (1988). Relationship between anorexia nervosa and bulimia nervosa: Diagnostic implications. In D. M. Garner & P. E. Garfinkel (Eds.), *Diagnostic issues in anorexia nervosa and bulimia nervosa* (pp. 56–79). New York: Brunner/Mazel.

Garrow, J. S. (1988). *Obesity and related diseases*. Edinburgh: Churchill Livingstone.

Hall, A., & Hay, P. J. (1991). Eating disorder patient referrals from a population region 1977–1986. *Psychological Medicine, 21*, 697–701.

Hay, P. J., & Hall, A. (1991). The prevalence of eating disorders in recently admitted psychiatric in-patients. *British Journal of Psychiatry, 159*, 562–565.

Hsu, L. K. G. (1990). *Eating disorders*. New York: Guilford Press.

Johnson, A. S., & Hillard, J. R. (1990). Prevalence of eating disorders in the psychiatric emergency room. *Psychosomatics, 31*, 337–341.

Johnson-Sabine, E., Wood, K., Patton, G., Mann, A., & Wakeling, A. (1988). Abnormal eating attitudes in London schoolgirls—a prospective epidemiological study: Factors associated with abnormal response on screening questionnaires. *Psychological Medicine, 18*, 615–622.

Kassett, J. A., Gershon, E. S., Maxwell, M. E., Guroff, J. J., Kazuba, D. M., Smith, A. L., Brandt, H. A., & Jimerson, D. C. (1989). Psychiatric disorders in the first-degree relatives of probands with bulimia nervosa. *American Journal of Psychiatry, 146*, 1468–1471.

Kendler, K. S., MacLean, C., Neale, M., Kessler, R., Heath, A., & Eaves, L. (1991). The genetic epidemiology of bulimia nervosa. *American Journal of Psychiatry, 148*, 1627–1637.

King, M. B. (1989). Eating disorders in a general practice population: Prevalence, characteristics and follow-up at 12 to 18 months. *Psychological Medicine* (suppl. 14).

King, M. B. (1991). The natural history of eating pathology in attenders to primary medical care. *International Journal of Eating Disorders, 10*, 379–387.

Kutcher, S. P., Whitehouse, A. M., & Freeman, C. P. L. (1985). ''Hidden'' eating disorders in Scottish psychiatric inpatients. *American Journal of Psychiatry, 142*, 1475–1478.

Lacey, J. H. (1992). The treatment demand for bulimia: A catchment area report of referral rates and demography. *Psychiatric Bulletin, 16*, 203–205.

Lacey, J. H., & Dolan, B. M. (1988). Bulimia in British blacks and Asians: A catchment area study. *British Journal of Psychiatry, 152*, 73–79.

Langer, L. M., Warheit, G. J., & Zimmerman, R. S. (1991). Epidemiological study of problem eating behaviors and related attitudes in the general population. *Addictive Behaviors, 16*, 167–173.

Levy, A. B., Dixon, K. N., & Stern, S. L. (1989). How are depression and bulimia related? *American Journal of Psychiatry, 146*, 162–169.

Mumford, D. B., Whitehouse, A. M., & Choudry, I. Y. (1992). Survey of eating disorders in English-medium schools in Lahore, Pakistan. *International Journal of Eating Disorders, 11*, 173–184.

Mumford, D. B., Whitehouse, A. M., & Platts, M. (1991). Sociocultural correlates of eating disorders among Asian schoolgirls in Bradford. *British Journal of Psychiatry, 158*, 222–228.

Patton, G. C., Johnson-Sabine, E., Wood, K., Mann, A. H., & Wakeling, A. (1990). Abnormal eating attitudes in London schoolgirls—a prospective epidemiological study: Outcome at twelve month follow-up. *Psychological Medicine, 20*, 383–394.

Peveler, R. C., Fairburn, C. G., Boller, I., & Dunger, D. (1992). Eating disorders in adolescents with insulin-dependent diabetes mellitus: a controlled study. *Diabetes Care, 15,* 1356–1360.

Pope, H. G., & Hudson, J. I. (1992). Is childhood sexual abuse a risk factor for bulimia nervosa? *American Journal of Psychiatry, 149,* 455–463.

Rand, C. S. W., & Kuldau, J. M. (1992). Epidemiology of bulimia and symptoms in a general population: Sex, age, race and socioeconomic status. *International Journal of Eating Disorders, 11,* 37–44.

Russell, G. F. M. (1979). Bulimia nervosa: An ominous variant of anorexia nervosa. *Psychological Medicine, 9,* 429–448.

Spitzer, R. L., Devlin, M., Walsh, B. T., Hasin, D., Wing, R., Marcus, M., Stunkard, A., Wadden, T., Yanovski, S., Agras, S., Mitchell, J., & Nonas, C. (1992). Binge Eating Disorder: A multisite field trial of the diagnostic criteria. *International Journal of Eating Disorders, 11,* 191–203.

Striegel-Moore, R. H., Nicholson, T. J., & Tamborlane, W. V. (1992). Prevalence of eating disorder symptoms in preadolescent and adolescent girls with IDDM. *Diabetes Care, 15,* 1361–1368.

Welch, S. L., & Fairburn, C. G. (1992a). Sexual abuse and bulimia nervosa: Three integrated case-control comparisons. Submitted for publication.

Welch, S. L., & Fairburn, C. G. (1992b, April). *Bias and bulimia nervosa.* Paper presented at the Fifth International Conference on Eating Disorders, New York.

Whitaker, A., Johnson, J., Shaffer, D., Rapoport, J. L., Kalikow, K., Walsh, B. T., Davies, M., Braiman, S., & Dolinsky, A. (1990). Uncommon troubles in young people: Prevalence estimates of selected psychiatric disorders in a nonreferred adolescent population. *Archives of General Psychiatry, 47,* 487–496.

Whitehouse, A. M., Adams, R., & Marche, J. (1989). Are there hidden eating disorders among psychiatric inpatients? *International Journal of Eating Disorders, 8,* 235–238.

Whitehouse, A. M., Cooper, P. J., Vize, C. V., Hill, C., & Vogel, L. (1992). Prevalence of eating disorders in three Cambridge general practices: Hidden and conspicuous morbidity. *British Journal of General Practice, 42,* 57–60.

Etiology of Binge Eating: A Developmental Perspective

Ruth H. Striegel-Moore

Epidemiological studies have shown striking gender-related differences in prevalence rates for the behavior of binge eating, and more especially for those psychiatric disorders where binge eating is a defining feature (i.e., bulimia nervosa) or a prominent associated feature (i.e., anorexia nervosa) (Fairburn & Beglin, 1990; Fairburn, Hay, & Welch, Chapter 7, this volume). Preliminary results of field trials for the newly formulated binge eating disorder (for definition, see Fairburn & Wilson, Chapter 1, this volume) also find a greater prevalence of women among individuals who meet criteria for this disorder (Bruce & Agras, 1992; Spitzer et al., 1992; Wilson, Nonas, & Rosenblum, 1993). This gender-related difference prompts the question of why women are at such disproportionate risk for the development of binge eating (Striegel-Moore, Silberstein, & Rodin, 1986). Only a minority of girls or women engage in binge eating, however, necessitating that we ask which girls or women in particular will develop this symptom. With remarkable consistency, binge eating has been found to typically emerge during late adolescence: In clinical samples, the modal age of onset is 18 years (Kassett, Gwirtsman, Kaye, Brandt, & Jimerson, 1988; Mitchell, Hatsukami, Eckert, & Pyle, 1985; Mitchell, Pyle, Eckert, Pomeroy, & Hatsukami, 1988; Pyle, 1985; Remschmidt & Herpertz-Dahlmann, 1990; Shore & Porter, 1990; Turnbull, Freeman, Barry, & Henderson, 1989; Woodside & Garfinkel, 1992); in nonclinical samples, the symptom appears a few years later (e.g., Kendler et al., 1991). What is it about girls' passage through adolescence and into adulthood, we need to ask, that renders them vulnerable to developing binge eating?

In a majority of cases, binge eating appears to be the consequence of prolonged restrictive weight control efforts (typically dieting), which in turn are initiated by profound feelings of weight dissatisfaction. The relationship between dieting and binge eating is explored in detail by Polivy and Herman (Chapter 9, this volume) and by Blundell and Hill (Chapter 10, this volume). The hierarchical ordering of symptoms from weight dissatisfaction to dieting to binge eating suggests that efforts to understand binge eating need to encompass investigations of the origins of body image dissatisfaction and of dieting to control shape or weight.

Although there is some empirical support for the "restraint model" (for review, see Heatherton & Polivy, 1992; Polivy & Herman, Chapter 9, this volume), there are patients in whose life dieting plays a minor role, yet who exhibit severe binge eating. For example, the restraint model may be insufficient for an understanding of the high prevalence of binge eating among lesbian women, many of whom rarely diet to lose weight (Bradford & Ryan, 1987). A large number of binge eaters identified in a study by Wilson and his colleagues (Wilson et al., 1993) denied that dieting preceded onset of their binge eating. Alternative views to the restraint model emphasize the role of emotions in precipitating binge eating, describing the behavior as an attempt to escape awareness of unpleasant emotional states (Heatherton & Baumeister, 1991; Shulman, 1991), or as a form of stress-induced eating (for reviews, see Cattanach & Rodin, 1988; Ganley, 1989; Slochower, 1983). Together, these models suggest a pathway into binge eating that does not require a history of dieting. It is plausible that different risk factors may be associated with the different pathways. Whenever possible, throughout this chapter, I will attempt to explain women's heightened risk for binge eating considering both pathways.

In this chapter, I will address the two overarching questions of "Why women?" and "Why young women?" within the framework of developmental psychopathology. This perspective suggests that the answers to these questions can be uncovered by focusing on the emergence of binge eating within the broader context of female development, by exploring the particular developmental tasks and processes that may promote binge eating, and by examining individual characteristics and familial or social relationships that put a girl at risk.

In the first part of this chapter, I will explore the links between female identity and binge eating, seeking to answer the question of "Why women?" I will argue that normal female sex-role socialization renders girls and women vulnerable both to the excessive pursuit of thinness, a salient factor in the restraint model, and to the experience of aversive self-relevant awareness, a salient factor in the emotional eating models. The second part of the chapter is devoted to the question of "Why young women?" and offers a detailed analysis of the specific developmental challenges and psychosocial tasks of adolescence implicated in the etiology of binge eating. I will attempt to show that increased risk results from the particular nature of these tasks as well as from contextual factors such as timing of puberty. In each of these two parts, I will only briefly comment on individual vulnerability factors, as the question of "Which women in particular?" was addressed by Fairburn, Hay, and Welch (Chapter 7, this volume).

FEMININITY AND BINGE EATING

Although several prominent feminist therapists have emphasized the role of femininity in the development of disordered eating (Boskind-Lodahl, 1976; Chernin, 1985; Orbach, 1978; Steiner-Adair, 1986), femininity has received relatively little attention in the empirical literature, possibly due to confusion over the concept. As a stimulus variable, femininity refers to the degree to which an individual possesses characteristics associated with the female sex-role stereotype (i.e., the culturally determined conceptions of appropriate and desirable behaviors of females; Bem, 1974; Spence & Helmreich, 1978). The more a woman is perceived to exhibit sex-role-appropriate characteristics, the more feminine she will be perceived to be. As a subject variable, femininity refers to a woman's gender identity, to her phenomenological sense of femaleness (Spence, 1985). A central component of identity, gender identity develops early in childhood and it is inextricably linked with a culture's sex-role expectations. The more a woman experiences herself as possessing traits characteristic of her cultures' female sex-role stereotype, the more feminine she will perceive herself to be. Two components of contemporary Western cultures' female sex-role stereotype are critical to an understanding of women's increased risk for the development of binge eating: Women are expected to be more interpersonally oriented than men, and beauty is a central aspect of femininity.

The Relational Self

Women have been described as different from men in their needs, emotions, and behaviors pertaining to interpersonal relationships. Women are more likely than men to include in their self-definitions relevant relationships and social ties (McGuire & McGuire, 1982), and they are said to care more than men about others' feelings and welfare (Dusek & Flaherty, 1981; Eisenberg, Miller, Shell, McNalley, & Shea, 1991). Women appear to be more interested than men in gaining social approval and in avoiding disapproval (Simmons & Rosenberg, 1975). Women seem to be more prone than men to experience self-presentationally relevant emotions such as shame and embarrassment (Lewis, 1987; Silberstein, Striegel-Moore, & Rodin, 1987). A metaanalysis of research on gender-related differences in nonverbal behavior led DePaulo (1992) to conclude that women's nonverbal behavior in interpersonal situations is exceptionally well suited to conveying the impression of being sociable, likable, and interested in the other person.

Some have argued that these gender-related differences are the result of fundamental differences in male and female developmental patterns and reflect basic differences in male and female identity. Whether these gender-related differences are simply due to differences in socialization experiences or are the result of biological sex differences remains a matter of considerable debate (e.g., Deaux & Major, 1987). According to Miller (1976), connection with others provides a primary context for growth across a woman's life span. For women, unlike for men, the task of identity development does not culminate in separation–individuation, but in rather relationship-differentiation (Kaplan & Surrey, 1984). The differentiated self is aware of its own unique properties, yet is achieved and articulated within the context of important relationships. A woman's basic sense of self-worth is said to be closely tied to her ability to establish mutually empathic and reciprocally empowering relationships. Within this framework, women are described to be highly vulnerable to others' opinions of them and behaviors toward them. A woman's failed effort to find mutuality and understanding in a relationship represents a fundamental challenge to her identity and results in aversive emotional states such as self-blame and low self-esteem (Kaplan, 1986).

In our culture, physical attractiveness contributes significantly to success in the social domain. Two recent metaanalyses of studies on beliefs about, correlates of, and outcomes of attractiveness have concluded that the attractiveness stereotype (''What is beautiful is good''; Dion, Berscheid, & Walster, 1972) applies most strongly to traits and skills related to social competence (Eagly, Ashmore, Makhijani, & Longo, 1991; Feingold, 1992). Both attractive male and female individuals are perceived to be more sociable and more socially skilled than unattractive individuals (Feingold, 1992). Correlational studies examining the question of whether this stereotype is based on true differences suggest that attractive individuals are less socially anxious, more popular, and more socially skilled than unattractive individuals (Feingold, 1992). Finally, there is ample evidence that beauty is associated with preferential treatment by others (for review, see Hatfield & Sprecher, 1985). Although both men and women benefit from being attractive, beauty matters especially in the lives of women (Banner, 1983; Feingold, 1990, 1991; Hatfield & Sprecher, 1985; Rodin, Silberstein, & Striegel-Moore, 1985). Gender-related differences in the preferential treatment of attractive individuals are particularly pronounced in heterosexual relationships. For instance, physical attractiveness is more strongly associated with opposite-sex popularity for women than for men (Feingold, 1990, 1991). Compared to women, men place greater emphasis on the physical appearance of their romantic partners (S. Davis, 1990; Nevid, 1984; Sprecher, 1989), and thinness is an important component of how attractive and desirable a woman is perceived to be (Smith, Walfdorf & Trembath, 1990; Tiggermann & Rothblum, 1988).

Given the greater importance of a woman's physical appearance in achieving interpersonal success, and given that women seem to care more about other's opinions and approval, it is not surprising that women make appearance and weight high priorities in their lives (Pliner, Chaiken, & Flett, 1990). As I will describe next, women's body image concerns further derive from the link between femininity and beauty.

The Role of Beauty in Female Identity

Being concerned with one's appearance and making efforts to enhance and preserve one's beauty are central features of the female sex-role stereotype (Brownmiller, 1984; Rodin et al., 1985). The association of beauty (thinness) and femininity is reflected and amplified by the mass media. For instance, even though the mass media portray women in an increasing range of social roles, with very few exceptions, these roles are represented by young, thin, highly attractive women (Atkin, Moorman, & Lin, 1991; Betterton, 1987; Bretl & Cantor, 1988, D. Davis, 1990; Downs & Harrison, 1985; Ferguson, Kreshel, & Tinkham, 1990; Signorielli, 1989; Sullivan & O'Connor, 1988). Women who challenge traditional views of femininity, because of their political orientation (e.g., feminist) or because of their sexual orientation (e.g., lesbians) are often stereotyped as physically unattractive (Brown, 1985; Goldberg, Gottesdiener, & Abramson, 1975; Klentz, Beaman, Mapelli, & Ullrich, 1987).

Physically attractive women are perceived as more feminine and unattractive women as more masculine (Cash, Gillen, & Burns, 1977; Cash, Dawson, Bowen, Davis, & Galumbeck, 1989; Cox & Glick, 1986; Gillen, 1981; Heilman & Saruwatori, 1979). Given the current ideal of female beauty, it is not surprising to find that thin women are rated more feminine than heavier women (Guy, Rankin, & Norvell, 1980). Furthermore, research suggests a relationship between women's eating behavior and perceived femininity (for review, see Rolls, Fedoroff, & Guthrie, 1991). For example, one study found that women who were described to research subjects as eating small meals were rated significantly more feminine, less masculine, more concerned with their appearance, and more attractive than women who reportedly had eaten large meals. Manipulation of meal size descriptions had no effect on ratings of male targets (Chaiken & Pliner, 1987). Another study grouped subjects into same-sex or mixed-sex pairs. Each pair was asked to work on a task independently but in the same room, while being offered the opportunity to snack on crackers. The more a female subject ate, the less feminine she was rated by her male or female partner. In contrast, the number of crackers eaten by male subjects was unrelated to how feminine (or masculine) they were perceived by their male or female partners (Pliner & Chaiken, 1990, Study 1).

Research further suggest that women adjust their eating behavior to project a favorable impression. Two studies found that women ate less of a snack that was provided during a get-acquainted session when they interacted with a desirable male confederate than when they interacted with an undesirable male, a desirable female, or an undesirable female confederate (Mori, Chaiken, & Pliner, 1987; Pliner & Chaiken, 1990). To further support the interpretation that women use their eating behavior to create a favorable impression, Pliner and Chaiken (1990, Study 2) surveyed male and female students regarding their eating behavior in relation to social motives. Women indicated that they would eat less to project an image of femininity and of desirability than they would eat under circumstances where being perceived as desirable or feminine was less salient. Interestingly, women also reported that they would restrict their eating in the presence of other women if they were motivated to show superiority over or to compete with these women. Hence, in a culture that equates beauty and its pursuit with femininity, a woman who is engaged in efforts to enhance or preserve her beauty serves to affirm others' perceptions of her as feminine (i.e., as possessing gender-congruent attributes).

Beyond impression management, however, pursuit of beauty and thinness serves another, perhaps even more important, function: affirmation of a woman's own sense of femininity. Popular writing on women's issues has offered rich descriptions of women's pursuit of beauty as an important strategy of identity affirmation (e.g., Brownmiller, 1984; Freedman, 1984), a theme that has received little empirical attention. As Spence (1985) proposed, gender identity is developed and continuously affirmed by adoption and display of sex-role congruent behaviors. Furthermore, identity crises are resolved by engaging in behaviors that affirm central aspects of one's identity. Young girls' initial use of cosmetics has been portrayed as a rite of passage into womanhood, as a "sex-role specific behavior in the service of *feminine identity development*" (Cash, Rissi, & Chapman, 1985, p. 248, emphasis added). I believe the same can be said for dieting among adolescents. Clinically, I have observed that for many women the salience of their weight increases when they feel challenged in their femininity (e.g., after a romantic disappointment).

I have sketched out a picture of female identity that is characterized by a strong emphasis on both connection and beauty. It is now time to ask which mechanisms might account for the fact that only some but not all women develop binge eating.

Femininity and Binge Eating: Hypotheses about Risk

In light of the discussion above, one might argue simply that the more feminine a girl or woman is or, put differently, the more she defines herself based on her physical appearance and based on her relationships with others, the more vulnerable she will be to develop binge eating. Even though a growing number of studies have attempted to show that femininity and disordered eating are correlated (e.g., Brown, Cross, & Nelson, 1990), significant methodological problems characterize this literature. Most notably, these studies apply femininity scales that are both outdated and too narrow in scope (for review, see Timko, Striegel-Moore, Silberstein, & Rodin, 1987). Standard femininity scales essentially measure expressiveness but do not assess importance of appearance to a woman's sense of self, nor do they tap interpersonal vulnerability involving desire for intense closeness, fear of abandonment, and definition of the self through connection (Leadbeater, Blatt, & Quinlan, 1992). Furthermore, these scales were standardized almost 20 years ago and do not reflect changes in the female sex-role stereotype over the past 2 decades. Given these limitations, I would argue that research to date has not tested properly the hypothesized link between femininity and binge eating.

Why would some women be more feminine than others? Girls differ in the degree to which they are exposed to and experience pressure to conform with the female sex-role stereotype. Socialization of concern with beauty and thinness occurs in virtually every social context (e.g., Dietz, 1990; Pierce, 1990; Purcell & Stewart, 1990). However, research on sex-role socialization has not yet focused specifically on how girls internalize the mandate for beauty. For example, research is needed to assess the impact of exposure to mass media on girls' self-image. A few studies have begun to explore the role of parental influence (primarily maternal influence) and peer pressure on girls' body esteem and eating behavior. For example, girls whose mothers were more critical of their daughters' weight reported elevated scores on measures of disordered eating compared to girls whose mothers were accepting of their daughter's appearance (Pike & Rodin, 1991). Mothers who diet are significantly more likely to have daughters who diet as well (Attie & Brooks-Gunn, 1989; Pike & Rodin, 1991). However, fathers should not be overlooked as a potentially important source of social pressure. A recent study found that parents on a diet, regardless of sex, were significantly more likely to encourage their child to lose weight than parents who did not diet to lose weight (Striegel-Moore & Kearney-Cooke, in press). Initial research suggests that a relationship between weight-related teasing and poor body esteem and dieting in adolescent girls (Fabian & Thompson, 1989). Certain social contexts such as ballet schools or gymnastic teams have been shown to foster weight dissatisfaction, dieting, and binge eating (e.g., Brownell, Rodin, & Wilmore, 1992). Hence, social pressure to be thin likely promotes poor body image, which in turn may prompt dieting efforts.

While some girls may internalize sociocultural messages about femininity because they are exposed to particularly intense social pressures, other girls may accept the "tyranny of being nice" (Steiner-Adair, 1986) because they are more susceptible to social influences. An extensive clinical and theoretical literature describes identity deficits as central to the development of disordered eating in women (see, for example, Tobin, Chapter 14, this volume), yet this literature rarely explores how femininity, as a key component of female identity, is implicated in the development of disordered eating. Girls who feel insecure about their identity, especially about how they are valued by others, may focus on physical appearance because such a focus provides a concrete way to construct an identity. As object relation theorists have argued, women who are unable to experience a "true self" become hypervigilant about how they appear to others, often resulting in amplified attention to physical appearance (Johnson & Connors, 1987; Jones, 1985; Strober, 1991). Consistent with this view, research has found relationships between public self-consciousness and concern with physical appearance (Miller & Cox, 1982; Solomon & Schopfler, 1982), and between social self-deficits and disordered eating (Striegel-Moore, Silberstein, & Rodin, in press). For most girls, the contemporary beauty ideal is biologically unattainable. Efforts to create an adequate self by pursuing an adequate physical self are doomed to failure and are likely to result in a vicious cycle: Self-deficits may intensify appearance-related concerns; perceived deficits in one's attractiveness in turn may be a potent source of social anxiety, hence contributing further to social self-dysfunction.

Although an extensive psychoanalytic literature has examined the

origins of self-deficits, typically placing much of the blame on inadequate parenting (e.g., Miller, 1981), traumatic life events may be particularly relevant for understanding the identity deficits observed in many
patients with disordered eating. Specifically, the role of sexual abuse as
a causal factor in the etiology of identity deficits and, as a consequence,
in the etiology of binge eating has been considered only fairly recently
(for review, see Pope & Hudson, 1992). Girls are at risk of being sexually
abused at a much higher rate than boys, and studies have consistently
shown an association between sexual abuse and symptoms related to
identity and self-regulation (e.g., dissociation, poor body esteem, poor
self-esteem, affective instability) (e.g., Cutler & Nolen-Hoeksema, 1991;
Pribor & Dinwiddie, 1992). Whether sexual abuse constitutes a specific
risk factor for the development of binge eating remains a matter of considerable debate. While it may not be a specific risk factor, sexual abuse
may explain differential risk.

Lastly, during developmental transitions that render salient questions
about identity, women may focus on appearance in an effort to affirm
their own identity. Given that body-image dissatisfaction, dieting, and
binge eating typically emerge during adolescence, this particular developmental period has received increasing attention among researchers interested in the etiology of binge eating. This literature will be described
in the following section.

THE CHALLENGES OF FEMALE
ADOLESCENT DEVELOPMENT

Published research to date suggests that with few exceptions, binge eating is rarely seen in children. Several reasons may explain the low prevalence of the symptom in prepubertal children. Children may not have
access to large amounts of food. Children who do overeat may not yet
experience or think of their behavior as out of control, because they may
not yet have developed a desire to control their food intake. Children
may express emotional distress in other ways and may not yet require
eating as a socially more accepted way of self-soothing. Perhaps most
importantly, however, the precipitating factors of feeling fat and of dieting are also relatively uncommon among children. Even though weight
is already a salient issue for many girls before reaching puberty (for
review, see Thelen, Lawrence, & Powell, 1992), prepubertal girls primarily worry about *becoming* fat, but do not yet *feel* fat (e.g., Striegel-Moore,
Nicholson, Tamborlane, 1992). For example, in a random sample of 600
white and black girls ages 9 years and 10 years, 35% were "very afraid
of gaining weight," but only half of these girls indicated that they were

unhappy about their present weight (Striegel-Moore, Pike, Wilfley, Schreiber, & Rodin, 1992). The predictive value of fear of fatness needs to be tested prospectively. Perhaps girls who fear becoming fat the most are at greatest risk for engaging in rigid, prolonged dieting once they experience pubertal weight gain, thus raising their risk for binge eating. Based on concurrent correlations, a significant relationship between fear of fatness and bulimic symptoms have been found in high school students (Bennett, Spoth, & Borgen, 1991). Once girls have reached puberty, weight-dissatisfaction dieting and binge eating emerge among a sizable number of girls. What is it about this developmental period that raises risk for these symptoms? Perhaps it is the particular nature of the psychosocial tasks for adolescence—which each raise questions about a girl's sense of self—that explain the increased risk for the development of binge eating during this period. Additionally, risk may be elevated during adolescence because of the degree of stress experienced as a result of the sizable number of normative life changes involved. This stress perspective suggests a relationship between the number of changes adolescents have to cope with and the risk for binge eating. Lastly, timing of development may be a crucial factor in determining risk.

The Psychosocial Tasks of Adolescence

Normal adolescent development involves major challenges, which include adjusting to the biological changes of puberty, establishing heterosexual relationships, coping with increased achievement expectations and setting goals for one's future, moving toward autonomous functioning; and, encompassing all of the other tasks, establishing a cohesive and positive sense of self.

Adjusting to the Biological Changes of Puberty

In the context of contemporary cultural norms of female beauty, the fat spurt associated with puberty (Tanner, 1978) poses a particular challenge to young girls. Whereas physical maturation brings boys closer to the masculine beauty ideal of a well-developed, muscular body, for girls maturation involves a development away from what is currently considered beautiful.

Following puberty, girls' body-image satisfaction decreases dramatically and feeling fat leads the list of adolescent girls' concerns about their physical appearance (Gralen, Levine, Smolak, & Murnen, 1990; Rosen, Silberg, & Gross, 1988; Shore & Porter, 1990). Cross-sectional studies suggest that body-image dissatisfaction remains pervasive among girls throughout late adolescence (Story et al., 1991). The rise and eventual plateau of weight dissatisfaction are paralleled by a rise in dieting and related weight control behaviors (Bennett et al., 1991; Leichner, Arnett, Rallo, Srikameswaran, & Vulcano, 1986; Shore & Porter, 1990; Story et al., 1991; Rosen et al., 1988). Adolescent girls who diet are significantly more likely to report binge eating. In a sample of more than 34,000 public school students ages 12 to 18 years, chronic dieters (defined as students who had been on a diet more than 10 times during the past year, or were always dieting during the past year) were four times (female students) to six times (male students) more likely to acknowledge ever having had an episode of binge eating (Story et al., 1991). Whether this concurrent relationship between dieting and binge eating supports the restraint model of binge eating needs to be confirmed in prospective studies. While causal models have focused on the progression from weight dissatisfaction to dieting to binge eating, we need to consider also the possibility that some women initiate dieting to counteract weight gain resulting from binge eating.

Consistently, underweight girls have been found to be most satisfied with their weight and least likely to diet, compared to girls of average weight and those who are overweight (George & Krondl, 1983; Simmons & Blyth, 1987; Story et al., 1991). Hence, being underweight appears to be an important protective factor regarding the initiation of dieting. Whether being underweight protects against the development of binge eating remains to be explored. Perhaps the physiological consequences of starvation are the same as (or even more pronounced) for slender girls as for heavier girls.

Clearly, binge eating is more common among dieters; however, dieters who report binge eating are by far outnumbered by dieters who do not engage in episodes of binge eating. For example, referring to the past 28 days, 38% of high school students reported that they restricted their food intake regularly to control their weight, whereas only 3% acknowledged regular binge-eating episodes (Striegel-Moore & Huydic, in press). The question arises whether a minimal duration of restrictive dieting or a minimal number of repeated dieting efforts is required before the symptom of binge eating emerges. Furthermore, research is needed to determine more carefully what adolescents mean when they report that they are "dieting to lose weight." Possibly, a relationship between restrictiveness of the diet (nutritional content, range of permissible foods) and binge eating will be found. Moreover, girls who eventually begin binge eating may hold more dysfunctional beliefs about food and eating than girls who diet but do not binge eat. Lastly, biological differences in the physiological sequelae of dieting may account for differential risk (see Blundell & Hill, Chapter 10, this volume).

Given that weight dissatisfaction and dieting emerge in response to puberty, the potential role of sex hormones in the development of disordered eating has also been considered. Menstrual abnormalities are more common in girls and women with disordered eating than in healthy women (e.g., Kreipe, Strauss, Hodgman, & Ryan, 1989), and in some patients menstrual abnormalities appeared to predate the onset of the eating disorder (for review, see Newman & Halmi, 1988). Because even modest calorie restriction results in endocrine changes involving the hypothalamic-pituitary-gonadal axis (e.g., Pirke & Ploog, 1987), these abnormalities are likely the result and not the cause of dieting. Importantly, however, dieting appears to have more of a differential effect on endocrine function in women compared to men, a gender-related difference that may explain in part why women are at greater risk for developing binge eating (e.g., Goodwin, Fairburn, & Cowen, 1987). Research is needed to elucidate the role of biological variables in the progression from dieting to binge eating. Perhaps some women are more vulnerable than others to adverse effects in response to food deprivation, including metabolic changes requiring increasing food restriction for successful weight control (e.g., Pirke et al., 1990) and secondary depression (e.g., Laessle, Schweiger, & Pirke, 1988). Moreover, the normative hormonal changes during adolescence may heighten adverse physiological consequences of dieting.

Hormonal changes during puberty may increase risk for binge eating beyond their influence on body weight or on appetite regulation. Although there is a growing literature on the role of hormones in adolescent mood and behavior (for a recent review, see Buchanan, Eccles, & Becker, 1992), much of this research is based on cross-sectional data. Utilization of this literature for the delineation of risk factors for binge eating is therefore conjectural. Some studies suggest that pubertal development is accompanied by an increase in moodiness (Larsen, Csikszentmihalyi, & Graef, 1980), irritability (Buchanan, 1991; Dorn, Crockett, & Peterson 1988), and depression (Brooks-Gunn & Warren, 1989; Paikoff, Brooks-Gunn, & Warren, 1991). In as much as negative affect and labile mood contribute to binge eating, the hormonal changes associated with puberty may contribute to an increased risk for binge eating, particularly in girls who with a temperamental predisposition to negative affectivity and deficits in affect regulation.

Establishing Heterosexual Relationships

Most girls begin dating during early adolescence. Initial research suggests a relationship between interest in dating and dieting during early adolescence, possibly due to the salience of attractiveness for girls interested in dating (Gralen et al., 1990). Furthermore, adolescent girls experience dating as more stressful than boys (Bush & Simmons, 1987), perhaps because girls emphasize intimacy more than boys (e.g., Moore & Boldero, 1991) and are more likely to attribute failure of relationships to an inadequate self (Kaplan, 1986). Adolescence is also associated with the initiation of adult sexual behaviors. A major social trend over the past few decades has involved changes in the sexual behavior of teenagers, especially girls. Specifically, adolescent girls have become sexually active at increasingly younger ages (e.g., Boxer, Levinson, & Petersen, 1989; Brooks-Gunn & Furstenberg, 1989). Some girls feel ill prepared for adult sexuality and describe experiencing considerable peer pressure to be sexually active. For example, a survey of adolescent girls found that of those girls who were sexually active, 61% indicated that they initiated intercourse in response to peer pressure rather than because they wanted to (Udry & Billy, 1987). Many parents do not feel prepared for their children, especially their daughters, to become sexually active and find it difficult to discuss sexual matters with them (Boxer et al., 1989; Hayes, 1987). Parental unavailability to talk openly with their daughters may interfere with girls' decision making and, increase girls' anxiety about sexuality (e.g., Biglan et al., 1990).

The clinical literature on eating disorders includes numerous references to the role of psychosexual development in the etiology of anorexia nervosa and bulimia nervosa. Self-starvation is described as the adolescent girl's response to her fear of adult sexuality (Bruch, 1978; Crisp, 1980; Selvini-Palazzoli, 1971). Studies of adolescent patients confirm that anorexic patients (restrictors and bingers alike) report negative attitudes about sexuality (for review, see Coovert, Kinder, & Thompson, 1989; Leon, 1989), though typically these studies do not include appropriate comparison groups. Whether fear of and negative attitudes about sexuality play a role in the etiology of binge eating has not yet been established empirically. Perhaps sexual anxieties and conflict do in fact promote dieting and, in turn, binge eating. Alternatively, sexual anxieties may promote binge eating as a way of coping with the aversive emotional state.

In Pursuit of Superwoman

The transition from elementary school to junior high school is a normative life event with far-reaching implications, involving entry into a large, more complex setting that places greater academic demands on its pupils and disrupts existing friendship networks (for review, see Eccles & Midgley, 1989). For many students, this transition results in a drop in academic performance, a decline in extracurricular activities, and a marked decrease in self-esteem (e.g., Simmons Burgeson, Carlton-Ford, & Blyth,

1987). Developmentally, this school change coincides with a greater emphasis on evaluation and social comparison among students (e.g., Feldlaufer, Midgley, & Eccles, 1988); an intensification of gender-related socialization by parents, teachers, and peers; and an increase in sex-role stereotyped conceptions of self and others (for reviews, see Harter, 1990; Hill & Lynch, 1983). Although many students appear to recover their self-confidence once they have become familiar with their new school environment, qualitative research is needed to explore how students cope with this transition. I would conjecture that girls who focus on their appearance in an effort to boost their self-image and to gain peer acceptance may be at greater risk for binge eating than girls who can utilize non-appearance-related strategies.

Middle adolescence is associated with an intensification of achievement concerns, as career planning becomes an increasingly salient issue. Over the past few decades, a new female sex-role stereotype has emerged, characterized by a proliferation of expectations for women, essentially demanding that women be "both beautiful and smart" (Selvini-Palazzoli, 1971). The current cultural myth of the superwoman embodies the view that a woman can extend her responsibilities from wife and mother to career woman without compromising quality of performance in any of her roles or extolling undue personal sacrifice. These unrealistic expectations have been implicated in the rise of eating disorders, particularly bulimia nervosa (Levine & Smolak, 1992; Steiner-Adair, 1986; Striegel-Moore et al., 1986; Timko et al., 1987). For example, a study of adolescent girls found that they shared a common notion of the superwoman ideal as a woman who has it all: career, family, beauty. Interestingly, those girls who seemed to have internalized most strongly the superwoman ideal scored significantly higher on the Eating Attitudes Test (EAT) (Garner, Olmsted, Bohr, & Garfinkel, 1982), than girls who set a more realistic goal for themselves (Steiner-Adair, 1986). Similarly, female college students who considered many roles central to their sense of self obtained significantly higher EAT scores than students who were more selective in their choice of roles (Thornton, Leo & Alberg, 1991; Timko et al., 1987).

Why would pursuit of the superwoman ideal increase risk for binge eating? Some have argued that the superwoman ideal is inherently conflictual by requiring women to assume incompatible traits (Steiner-Adair, 1986; Barnett, 1986) and that it generates stress by involving a multitude of role demands (Spade & Reese, 1991; Timko et al., 1987). Binge eating may be seen as a stress-related symptom, a woman's effort to soothe herself without making demands on others. Additionally, I would suggest that embracing the exaggerated ideal of superwoman reflects a more fundamental disturbance of identity, where a girl is unable to prioritize roles and thus tries to live up to whatever ideal is currently in style. As discussed earlier, a focus on appearance provides a concrete task resulting in visible accomplishments that are typically met with social approval.

Achieving Autonomy

Some clinicians have assigned particular importance to the task of achieving autonomy in the development of binge eating. Noting that bingeing emerges at the time when a young woman confronts the task of leaving home, the symptom of bingeing is seen as an expression of a girl's conflict over separating from her family of origin (Wooley & Wooley, 1985). However, research has not yet explored the specific processes that might link autonomy and binge eating. To facilitate such research, the complex construct of autonomy needs to be broken down into meaningful dimensions. Autonomous functioning encompasses self-control over affect and behavior, being able to take responsibility for self and others, decision making and moral reasoning based on internal standards, and changing one's familial relationships (especially the parent–child relationship) from dependency and asymmetry to mutuality.

Focusing on the parent–child relationship, Frank and colleagues (Frank, Avery, & Laman, 1988) empirically derived three dimensions of autonomy: connection/separation (empathy, concern, closeness), competence (independence, decision making), and emotional autonomy (personal control, self-assertion). Gender comparisons revealed a mixed pattern of gender-related differences: Young adult women scored higher on measures of connection, lower on measures of emotional autonomy, and no different from young men on measures of competence. During adolescence, both adolescent boys and girls experience normative changes in the parent–child relationship, including an increase in parent–child conflict during early adolescence, a decrease in time spent with parents, a decline in yielding to parental authority, and a decrease in emotional closeness (for review, see Paikoff & Brooks-Gunn, 1991). Because girls are more emotionally involved with their parents than boys, girls may be more negatively affected by discord with their parents. Compared to boys, adolescent girls have been found to report more interpersonal stresses related to the parent–child relationship (Windle, 1992). A longitudinal study of adolescents found that low levels of family support (assessed with items that seem to tap connection) were predictive of problem behaviors in girls but not boys (Windle, 1992). Windle (1992) argued that given girls' greater socialization toward the interpersonal world, lower level of family support may, in and of itself, be perceived as stressful because lack of connection is gender-role inconsistent. Correlational studies have described the families of bulimic patients as disconnected and low in emotional support (for review, see Strober & Humphrey, 1987). Similarly, a study of high school girls reported that mothers' ratings of family cohesion were significantly related with their daughters' scores on the Eating Disorder Inventory (EDI) (Pike & Rodin, 1991). Finally, maternal ratings of the family as incohesive, disorganized, and low in emotional support were predictive of an increase in daughters' disordered eating at a 2-year follow-up (Attie & Brooks-Gunn, 1989). Together, these studies suggest that of the various dimensions of autonomy, connection may be particularly useful to pursue in further research on the etiology of binge eating.

Self-regulation of affect and behavior is another dimension of autonomy relevant to our discussion. The temperamental characteristics of affective instability and poor impulse control have been considered risk factors for the development of binge eating (e.g., Johnson & Wonderlich, 1992), and some have argued for a typology of binge eaters based on the role of binge eating in affect regulation (Steinberg, Tobin, & Johnson, 1990). These temperamental dispositions may render a child ill prepared for the task of achieving autonomy. Prospective studies are needed to ascertain whether temperamental characteristics such as affective instability play a role in the etiology of binge eating.

Achieving a Coherent, Positive Sense of Self

Identity formation, involving beliefs about the nature, consistency, and value of the self, appears to be more difficult for girls than boys, as reflected in girls' greater identity instability, higher self-consciousness, greater concerns about popularity, lower body esteem, and lower self-esteem (Hill & Lynch, 1983; Simmons, Blyth, & McKinney, 1983). Although self-esteem generally improves from middle to late adolescence (Wigfield, Eccles, Iver, Reuman, & Midgley, 1991), poor body esteem remains a major source of self-devaluation for adolescent girls (e.g., Allgood-Merten, Lewinsohn, & Hops, 1990).

During adolescence, self-awareness and self-reflection increase noticeably, whereby much of this heightened self-awareness is interpersonally focused, and social comparison of self with peers are common (e.g., de Armas & Kelly, 1989; Grotevant & Cooper, 1985). Adolescent girls are more self-conscious (including social anxiety, private self-consciousness, and public self-consciousness) than adolescent boys (Allgood-Merten et al., 1990), and self-consciousness has been found associated with greater self-criticism (Fenigstein, 1979), social withdrawal (Carver, Blaney, & Scheier, 1979), increased vulnerability to depression (Lewinsohn, Hoberman, Teri, & Hautzinger, 1985), and poor self-esteem and disordered eating (e.g., Striegel-Moore et al., in press).

Low self-esteem has been widely discussed as a likely risk factor for the development of binge eating. Several mechanisms may explain the association between low self-esteem and dieting and binge eating. Low self-esteem may prompt a girl to improve her physical appearance. A prospective study of adolescent girls found poor self-esteem to be predictive of high EAT scores (Attie & Brooks-Gunn, 1989). The relationship between dieting and self-esteem may be more complicated however. Girls who diet to improve their self-esteem may experience a further decrease in self-esteem if their diet efforts fail. For example, Rosen, Gross, and Vara (1987) reported that girls who were trying to lose weight had significantly lower self-esteem than girls who made no effort to change their weight. Importantly, two-thirds of the girls who dieted to lose weight reported normal body weights. For these girls, weight loss may have been particularly difficult to achieve, adding to their sense of ineffectiveness. Furthermore, low self-esteem may affect how dieters respond to caloric deprivation and cognitive restraint. In a standard restraint experiment, self-esteem was found to mediate the eating behavior of restrained subjects: Only dieters who had low self-esteem showed a counterregulatory pattern of overeating in response to a preload (Polivy, Heatherton, & Herman, 1988). Based on these findings, one might conjecture that prolonged dieting results in binge eating only if the dieter experiences low self-esteem. Finally, and not yet explored empirically, one might argue that low self-esteem promotes binge eating as a palliative strategy.

Psychosocial Tasks of Adolescence: Mechanism of Risk

The qualitative exploration of the psychological tasks of adolescence may be well suited to explain symptom choice (why bingeing?) yet may not explain fully differential risk for binge eating. Two hypotheses may be postulated to account for the fact that only some girls develop binge eating in response to these challenges of adolescence. The additive stress hypothesis predicts that risk is related to the number of challenges encountered simultaneously (or near simultaneously). Several studies have shown that the more life changes a girl encounters within a short time period, the more distressed she will be (e.g., Compas, 1987; Compas, Howell, Phares, Williams, & Guinta, 1989; Petersen & Hamburg, 1986; Siegel & Brown, 1988; Simmons et al. 1987). Only few studies thus far have applied this framework to symptomatic eating. Levine and Smolak (1992) found elevated EAT scores in a nonclinical sample of girls for whom onset of dating coincided with onset of menarche, whereas either event alone was unrelated with scores on the EAT. Based on retrospective interviews of anorexic patients, Strober (1984) reported that as a group, bulimic anorexics reported significantly more life changes 8 months prior to onset of the eating disorder. Moreover, degree of life stress was significantly correlated with severity of binge eating. Among a sample of female students, worsening of disordered eating during the first year of college was significantly correlated with perceived stress (Striegel-Moore, Silberstein, Frensch, & Rodin, 1989). In a laboratory study of binge eaters, stress of an interpersonal nature was found to be particularly likely to induce the desire to binge (Cattanach, Malley, & Rodin, 1988).

A second hypothesis concerns the timing of maturation. The early-timing hypothesis predicts that girls whose pubertal timing is accelerated relative to their peers will be at greater risk for developing binge eating than their on-time or late-maturing peers. A growing literature suggests that early-maturing girls are particularly vulnerable to a wide range of adjustment difficulties in adolescence, and that these difficulties are not transient phenomena but persist into adulthood (for review, see Stattin & Magnusson, 1990). Early timing may represent a risk factor for the etiology of binge eating for several reasons. Early-maturing girls are typically shorter and fatter than their on-time or late-maturing peers, and these differences in body build remain once all girls have completed maturation (Simmons et al., 1983). Early-maturing girls are particularly dissatisfied with their weight; in fact, Brooks-Gunn (1988) has concluded that body image is the psychological variable most affected by early maturation. Hence, early timing may increase risk for binge eating because of the hypothesized causal link between dieting and binge eating. Furthermore, one may speculate that early maturation increases risk for emotional eating because early-maturing girls may experience greater stress than their peers. Early maturation is associated with increased daughter–parent conflict (Stattin & Magnusson, 1990). Early-maturing girls are perceived by others as more mature, are more apt to request and be granted greater freedom from their parents, and associate more with older friends (Stattin & Magnusson, 1990). This acceleration of development may require early-maturing girls to cope with experiences for which they have not yet developed adequate cognitive or emotional levels of maturity. For example, early-maturing girls begin dating at a younger age than on-time girls (Gargiulo, Attie, Brooks-Gunn, & Warren; 1987). Interestingly, one study found that female students with a history of binge eating reported initiating heterosexual activities at a significantly younger age than students who had no history of binge eating (Dykens & Gerrard, 1986). Both hypotheses need to be tested more fully. Likely, potentiating and moderating factors such as life events, personal vulnerabilities, and familial factors need to be included to achieve accurate predictions of differential risk for binge eating (e.g., Fairburn, Hay, & Welch, Chapter 7, this volume; Levine, 1987; Striegel-Moore et al., 1986).

IMPLICATIONS FOR TREATMENT AND PREVENTION

This chapter has emphasized the central contribution of female sex-role socialization in the etiology of binge eating. The relational focus of female identity renders women interpersonally vulnerable. Furthermore, the central role of beauty in female identity and in women's interpersonal relationships serves to channel women's identity concerns into preoccupation with shape and weight.

This conceptualization suggests that identity affirmation is an important treatment goal. An exploration of contextual factors and their role in the etiology and maintenance of binge eating offers the promise of empowering the client by being able to differentiate between societal and social factors that influence their lives from those problems that are under their own control and for which clients can accept responsibility for change. Given the importance of the social context, therapists need to realize that positive treatment outcome may involve not only changes in clients' behavior but also changes in their social context. For example, some clients may find it necessary to establish new friendship networks with individuals who are less exploitative of the client needs for connection. The success of interpersonal psychotherapy in the treatment of bulimic women illustrates that a focus on clients' interpersonal relationships results in significant behavioral improvement (Fairburn, Jones, Peveler, Hope, & O'Connor, in press). As a next step, research needs to explore the role of the therapeutic relationship in treatment outcome.

Given the central role of sociocultural factors in the etiology of binge eating, primary prevention needs to encompass interventions at multiple levels: societal, institutional, familial, and individual (Striegel-Moore, 1992). A majority of current primary prevention programs target individuals. These programs focus extensively on increasing girls' acceptance of diverse body shapes and on discouraging young women from dieting (e.g., Levine, & Hill, 1991); hence, they address primarily the restraint pathway to binge eating. In contrast, interventions addressing the emotional eating pathway are less well developed. To date, no controlled prevention outcome trial has been reported. The analysis of binge eating presented here suggests that in the absence of significant changes in women's social context, preventive interventions aimed solely at the individual level will be of limited success.

REFERENCES

Allgood-Merten, B., Lewinsohn, P. M., & Hops, H. (1990). Sex differences and adolescent depression. *Journal of Abnormal Psychology, 99,* 55–63.

Atkin, D. J., Moorman, J., & Lin, C. A. (1991). Ready for prime time: Network series devoted to working women in the 1980's. *Sex Roles, 25,* 677–685.

Attie, J., & Brooks-Gunn, F. (1989). Development of eating problems in adolescent girls: A longitudinal study. *Developmental Psychology, 25*, 70–79.

Banner, L. (1983). *American beauty.* New York: Knopf.

Barnett, L. R. (1986). Bulimarexia as symptom of sex-role strain in professional women. *Psychotherapy, 23*, 311–315.

Bem, S. L. (1974). The measurement of psychological androgyny. *Journal of Consulting and Clinical Psychology, 42*, 155–162.

Bennett, N. A. M., Spoth, R. L., & Borgen, F. H. (1991). Bulimic symptoms in high school females: Prevalence and relationship with multiple measures of psychological health. *Journal of Community Psychology, 19*, 13–28.

Betterton, R. (Ed.). (1987). *Looking on: Images of femininity in the visual arts and media.* London: Pandora.

Biglan, A., Metzler, C. W., Wirt, R., Ary, D., Noell, J., Ochs, L., French, C., & Hood, D. (1990). Social and behavioral factors associated with high-risk sexual behavior among adolescents. *Journal of Behavioral Medicine, 13*, 245–261.

Boskind-Lodahl, M. (1976). Cinderella's stepsisters: A feminist perspective on anorexia nervosa and bulimia. *Signs, 2*, 342–356.

Boxer, A., Levinson, R. A., & Petersen, A. C. (1989). Adolescent sexuality in the lifespan: An introduction. In J. Worrell & F. Danner (Eds.), *The adolescent as decision-maker* (pp. 209–243). New York: Academic Press.

Bradford, J., & Ryan, C. (1987). *The national lesbian health care survey.* Washington, DC: National Lesbian and Gay Foundation.

Bretl, D. J., & Cantor, J. (1988). The portrayal of men and women in U.S. television commercials: A recent content analysis and trends over 15 years. *Sex Roles, 18*, 595–609.

Brooks-Gunn, J. (1988). Antecedents and consequences of girls' maturational timing. *Journal of Adolescent Health Care, 9*, 365–373.

Brooks-Gunn, J., & Furstenberg, F. (1989). Adolescent sexual behavior. Special issue: Children and their development: Knowledge base, research agenda, and social policy application. *American Psychologist, 44*, 249–257.

Brooks-Gunn, J., & Warren, M. P. (1989). Biological and social contributions to negative affect in young adolescent girls. *Child Development, 60*, 40–55.

Brown, J. A., Cross, H. J., & Nelson, J. M. (1990). Sex-role identity and sex-role ideology in college women with bulimic behavior. *International Journal of Eating Disorders, 9*, 571–575.

Brown, L. (1985). Women, weight, and power: Feminist theoretical and therapeutic issues. *Women and Therapy, 4*, 61–72.

Brownell, K. D., Rodin, J., & Wilmore, J. H. (1992). *Eating, body weight, and performance in athletes: Disorders of modern society.* Philadelphia: Lea & Febiger.

Brownmiller, S. (1984). *Femininity.* New York: Simon & Schuster.

Bruce, B., & Agras, W. S. (1992). Binge eating in females: A population-based investigation. *International Journal of Eating Disorders, 12*, 365–374.

Bruch, H. (1978). *The golden cage: The enigma of anorexia nervosa.* Cambridge, MA: Harvard University Press.

Buchanan, C. M. (1991). Pubertal status in early-adolescent girls: Relations to mood, energy, and restlessness. *Journal of Early Adolescence, 11,* 185–200.

Buchanan, C. M., Eccles, J. S., & Becker, J. B. (1992). Are adolescents the victims of raging hormones: Evidence for activational effects of hormones on mood and behavior at adolescence. *Psychological Bulletin, 111,* 62–107.

Bush, D. M., & Simmons, R. G. (1987). Gender and coping with entry into early adolescence. In R. C. Barnett, L. Biener, & G. K. Baruch (Eds.), *Gender and stress* (pp. 185–217). New York: Free Press.

Carver, C., Blaney, P., & Scheier, M. (1979). Focus of attention, chronic expectancy, and responses to a feared stimulus. *Journal of Personality and Social Psychology, 37,* 1186–1195.

Cash, T. F., Dawson, K., Bowen, M., Davis, P., & Galumbeck, C. (1989). Effects of cosmetics use on the physical attractiveness and body image of American college women. *Journal of Social Psychology, 129,* 349–355.

Cash, T. F., Gillen, B., & Burns, (1977). Sexism and "beautism" in personnel consultant decision making. *Journal of Applied Psychology, 62,* 301–310.

Cash, T. F., Rissi, J., & Chapman, R. (1985). Not just another pretty face: Sex roles, locus of control, and cosmetics use. *Personality and Social Psychology Bulletin, 11,* 246–257.

Cattanach, L., Malley, R., & Rodin, J. (1988). Psychologic and physiologic reactivity to stressors in eating disordered individuals. *Psychosomatic Medicine, 50,* 591–599.

Cattanach, L., & Rodin, J. (1988). Psychosocial components of the stress process in bulimia. *International Journal of Eating Disorders, 7,* 75–88.

Chaiken, S., & Pliner, P. (1987). Women but not men are what they eat: The effect of meal size and gender on perceived femininity and masculinity. *Personality and Social Psychology Bulletin, 13,* 166–176.

Chernin, K. (1985). *The hungry self: Women, eating, and identity.* New York: Harper & Row.

Compas, B. E. (1987). Stress and life events during childhood and adolescence. *Clinical Psychology Review, 7,* 275–302.

Compas, B. E., Howell, D. C., Phares, V., Williams, R. A., & Guinta, C. T. (1989). Risk factors for emotional/behavioral problems in young adolescents: A prospective analysis of adolescent and parental stress and symptoms. *Journal of Consulting and Clinical Psychology, 57,* 732–740.

Coovert, D. L., Kinder, B. N., & Thompson, J. K. (1989). The psychosexual aspects of anorexia nervosa and bulimia nervosa: A review of the literature. *Clinical Psychology Review, 9,* 169–180.

Cox, C. L., & Glick, W. H. (1986). Resume evaluations and cosmetics use: When more is not better. *Sex Roles, 14,* 51–58.

Crisp, A. H. (1980). *Anorexia nervosa: Let me be.* London: Academic Press.

Cutler, S. E., & Nolen-Hoeksema, S. (1991). Accounting for sex differences in depression through female victimization: Childhood sexual abuse. *Sex Roles, 24,* 425–437.

Davis, D. M. (1990). Portrayals of women in prime-time network television: Some demographic characteristics. *Sex Roles, 23,* 325–332.

Davis, S. (1990). Men as success objects and women as sex objects: A study of personal advertisements. *Sex Roles, 23*, 43–50.

de Armas, A., & Kelly, J. A. (1989). Social relationships in adolescence: Skill development and training. In J. Worrell & F. Danner (Eds.), *The adolescent as decision-maker* (pp. 59–79). New York: Academic Press.

Deaux, K., & Major, B. (1987). Putting gender into context: An interactive model of gender-related behavior. *Psychological Review, 94*, 369–389.

DePaulo, B. M. (1992). Nonverbal behavior and self-presentation. *Psychological Bulletin, 111*, 203–243.

Dietz, W. H. (1990). You are what you eat—what you eat is what you are. *Journal of Adolescent Health Care, 11*, 76–81.

Dion, K. K., Berscheid, E., & Walster, E. (1972). What is beautiful is good. *Journal of Personality and Social Psychology, 24*, 285–290.

Dorn, L. D., Crockett, L. J., & Peterson, A. C. (1988). The relationship of pubertal status to intrapersonal changes in young adolescents. *Journal of Early Adolescence, 8*, 405–419.

Downs, A. C., & Harrison, S. K. (1985). Embarrassing age spots or just plain ugly? Physical attractiveness stereotyping as an instrument of sexism on American television commercials. *Sex Roles, 13*, 9–19.

Dusek, J. B., & Flaherty, J. F. (1981). The development of the self-concept during the adolescent years. *Monographs of the Society for Research in Child Development, 46*, 67.

Dykens, E. M., & Gerrard, M. (1986). Psychological profiles of purging bulimics, repeat dieters, and controls. *Journal of Consulting and Clinical Psychology, 54*, 283–288.

Eagly, A. H., Ashmore, R. D., Makhijani, M. G., & Longo, L. C. (1991). What is beautiful is good, but. . . : A meta-analytic review of research on the physical attractiveness stereotype. *Psychological Bulletin, 110*, 109–128.

Eccles, J. S., & Midgley, C. (1989). Stage/environment fit: Developmentally appropriate classrooms for early adolescents. In R. Ames & C. Ames (Eds.), *Research on motivation in education* (Vol. 3, pp. 139–181). San Diego, CA: Academic Press.

Eisenberg, N., Miller, P., Shell, R., McNalley, S., & Shea, C. (1991). Prosocial development in adolescence: A longitudinal study. *Developmental Psychology, 27*, 849–857.

Fabian, L. J., & Thompson, J. K. (1989). Body image and eating disturbances in young females. *International Journal of Eating Disorders, 8*, 63–74.

Fairburn, C. G., & Beglin, S. J. (1990). Studies of the epidemiology of bulimia nervosa. *American Journal of Psychiatry, 147*, 401–408.

Fairburn, C. G., Jones, R., Peveler, R. C., Hope, R. A., & O'Connor, M. (in press). Psychotherapy and bulimia nervosa: The longer-term effects of interpersonal psychotherapy, behaviour therapy, and cognitive behaviour therapy. *Archives of General Psychiatry*.

Feingold, A. (1990). Gender differences in effects of physical attractiveness on romantic attraction: A comparison across five research paradigms. *Journal of Personality and Social Psychology, 59*, 981–993.

Feingold, A. (1991). Sex differences in the effects of similarity and physical attractiveness on opposite-sex attraction. *Basic and Applied Social Psychology, 12,* 981–993.

Feingold, A. (1992). Good-looking people are not what we think. *Psychological Bulletin, 111,* 304–341.

Feldlaufer, H., Midgley, C., & Eccles, J. S. (1988). Student, teacher, and observer perceptions of the classroom environment before and after the transition to junior high school. *Journal of Early Adolescence, 8,* 133–156.

Fenigstein, A. (1979). Self-consciousness, self attention, and social interaction. *Journal of Personality and Social Psychology, 37,* 75–86.

Ferguson, J. H., Kreshel, P. J., & Tinkham, S. F. (1990). In the pages of *Ms*: Sex role portrayals of women in advertising. *Journal of Advertising, 19,* 40–51.

Frank, S. J., Avery, C. B., & Laman, M. S. (1988). Young adult's perceptions of their relationships with their parents: Individual differences in connectedness, competence, and emotional autonomy. *Developmental Psychology, 24,* 729–737.

Freedman, R. J. (1984). Reflections on beauty as it relates to health in adolescent females. *Women and Health, 9,* 29–45.

Ganley, R. M. (1989). Emotion and eating in obesity: A review of the literature. *International Journal of Eating Disorders, 8,* 343–361.

Gargiulo, J., Attie, I., Brooks-Gunn, J., & Warren, M. P. (1987). Girls' dating behavior as a function of social context and maturation. *Developmental Psychology, 23,* 730–737.

Garner, D. M., Olmsted, M. P., Bohr, Y., & Garfinkel, P. E. (1982). The Eating Attitudes Test: Psychometric features and clinical correlates. *Psychological Medicine, 12,* 871–878.

George, R. S., & Krondl, M. (1983). Perceptions and food use of adolescent boys and girls. *Nutrition and Behavior, 1,* 115–125.

Gillen, B. (1981). Physical attractiveness: A determinant of two types of goodness. *Personality and Social Psychology Bulletin, 7,* 277–281.

Goldberg, P. A., Gottesdiener, M., & Abramson, P. R. (1975). Another put-down of women? Perceived attractiveness as a function of support for the feminist movement. *Journal of Personality and Social Psychology, 32,* 113–115.

Goodwin, G. M., Fairburn, C. G., & Cowen, P. J. (1987). Dieting changes serotonergic function in women, not men: Implications for the etiology of anorexia nervosa. *Psychological Medicine, 17,* 839–842.

Gralen, S. J., Levine, M. P., Smolak, L., & Murnen, S. K. (1990). Dieting and disordered eating during early and middle adolescence: Do the influences remain the same? *International Journal of Eating Disorders, 9,* 501–512.

Grotevant, H. D., & Cooper, C. R. (1985). Patterns of interaction in family relationships and the development of identity exploration in adolescence. Special Issue: Family development. *Child Development, 56,* 415–428.

Guy, R. F., Rankin, B. A., & Norvell, M. J. (1980). The relation of sex role stereotyping to body image. *Journal of Psychology, 105,* 167–173.

Harter, S. (1990). Self and identity development. In S. S. Feldman & G. R. Elliot (Eds.), *At the threshold: The developing adolescent* (pp. 352–387). Cambridge, MA: Harvard University Press.

Hatfield, E., & Sprecher, S. (1985). *Mirror mirror: The importance of looks in everyday life*. New York: State University of New York.

Hayes, C. D. (1987). *Risking the future: Adolescent sexuality, pregnancy, and child bearing*. Washington, DC: National Academy Press.

Heatherton, T. F., & Baumeister, R. F. (1991). Binge-eating as escape from self-awareness. *Psychological Bulletin, 110,* 86–108.

Heatherton, T. F., & Polivy, J. (1992). Chronic dieting and eating disorders: A spiral model. In J. H. Crowther, D. L. Tennenbaum, S. E. Hobfoll, & M. A. P. Stephens (Eds.), *The etiology of bulimia nervosa* (pp. 133–155). Washington, DC: Hemisphere.

Heilman, M. E., & Saruwatori, L. R. (1979). When beauty is beastly: The effects of appearance and sex on evaluations of job applicants for managerial and non-managerial jobs. *Organizational Behavior and Human Performance, 23,* 360–372.

Hill, J. P., & Lynch, M. E. (1983). The intensification of gender-related role expectations during early adolescence. In J. Brooks-Gunn & A. C. Peterson (Eds.), *Girls at puberty: Biological and psychological perspectives* (pp. 201–228). New York: Plenum Press.

Johnson, C., & Connors, M. (1987). *The etiology and treatment of bulimia nervosa: A biosocial perspective*. New York: Basic Books.

Johnson, C., & Wonderlich, S. (1992). Personality characteristics as a risk factor in the development of eating disorders. In J. H. Crowther, D. L. Tennenbaum, S. E. Hobfoll, & M. A. P. Stephens (Eds.), *The etiology of bulimia nervosa: The individual and familial context* (pp. 179–198). Washington, DC: Hemisphere.

Jones, D. M. (1985). Bulimia: A false identity. *Clinical Social Work Journal, 13,* 305–316.

Kaplan, A. G. (1986). The "self-in-relation": Implications for depression in women. *Psychotherapy: Theory, Research and Practice, 23,* 234–242.

Kaplan, A. G., & Surrey, J. L. (1984). The relational self in women: Developmental theory and public policy. In L. Walker (Ed.), *Women and mental health policy* (pp. 79–94). Beverly Hills, CA: Sage.

Kassett, J. A., Gwirtsman, H. E., Kaye, W. H., Brandt, H. A., & Jimerson, D. C. (1988). Pattern of onset of bulimic symptoms in anorexia nervosa. *American Journal of Psychiatry, 145,* 1287–1288.

Kendler, K. S., MacLean, C., Neale, M., Kessler, R., Heath, A., & Eaves, L. (1991). The genetic epidemiology of bulimia nervosa. *American Journal of Psychiatry, 148,* 1627–1637.

Klentz, B., Beaman, A. L., Mapelli, S. D., & Ullrich, J. R. (1987). Perceived physical attractiveness of supporters and nonsupporters of the women's movement: An attitude-similarity-mediated error. *Personality and Social Psychology Bulletin, 13,* 513–523.

Kreipe, R. E., Strauss, J., Hodgman, C. H., & Ryan, R. M. (1989). Menstrual cycle abnormalities and subclinical eating disorders: A preliminary report. *Psychosomatic Medicine, 51,* 81–86.

Laessle, R. G., Schweiger, U., & Pirke, K. M. (1988). Depression as a correlate of starvation in patients with eating disorders? *Biological Psychiatry, 23,* 16–23.

Larsen, R., Csikszentmihalyi, M., & Graef, R. (1980). Mood variability and the psychosocial adjustment of adolescents. *Journal of Youth and Adolescence*, 9, 469–490.

Leadbeater, B. J., Blatt, S. J., & Quinlan, D. M. (1992). *Depression and problem behaviors in adolescents: Gender-linked pathways in the development of psychopathology*. Manuscript under review.

Leichner, P., Arnett, J., Rallo, J. S., Srikameswaran, S., & Vulcano, B. (1986). An epidemiologic study of maladaptive eating attitudes in a Canadian school age population. *International Journal of Eating Disorders*, 5, 969–982.

Leon, G. (1989). Diagnostic and psychopathological issues in bulimia nervosa. In W. G. Johnson (Ed.), *Advances in eating disorders* (pp. 157–174). Greenwich, CT: JAI Press.

Levine, M. P. (1987). *Student eating disorders: Anorexia nervosa and bulimia*. Washington, DC: National Education Association.

Levine, M. P., & Hill, L. (1991). *A five day lesson plan on eating disorders: Grades 7–12*. Columbus, OH: National Anorexic Aid Society of Harding Hospital.

Levine, M. P., & Smolak, L. (1992). Toward a model of the developmental psychopathology of eating disorders: The example of early adolescence. In J. Crowther, D. Tennenbaum, S. Hobfoll, & M. A. P. Stephens (Eds.), *The etiology of bulimia nervosa* (pp. 59–80). Washington, DC: Hemisphere.

Lewinsohn, P., Hoberman, H., Teri, L., & Hautzinger, M. (1985). In S. Reiss & R. Bootzin (Eds.), *Theoretical issues in behavior therapy* (pp. 331–359). New York: Academic Press.

Lewis, H. B. (1987). Shame—the "sleeper" in psychopathology. In H. B. Lewis (Ed.), *The role of shame in symptom formation* (pp. 1–28). Hillsdale, NJ: Erlbaum.

McGuire, W. J., & McGuire, C. V. (1982). Significant others in self-space: Sex differences and developmental trends in the social self. In J. Suls (Ed.), *Social psychological perspectives on the self* (pp. 71–96). Hillsdale, NJ: Erlbaum.

Miller, A. (1981). *Prisoners of childhood: The drama of the gifted child and the search for the true self*. New York: Basic Books.

Miller, J. B. (1976). *Toward a new psychology of women*. Boston: Beacon Press.

Miller, L. C., & Cox, C. L. (1982). For appearances' sake: Public self-consciousness and makeup use. *Personality and Social Psychology Bulletin*, 8, 748–751.

Mitchell, J. E., Hatsukami, D., Eckert, E. D., & Pyle, R. L. (1985). Characteristics of 275 patients with bulimia. *American Journal of Psychiatry*, 142, 482–485.

Mitchell, J. E., Pyle, R., Eckert, E., Pomeroy, C., & Hatsukami, D. (1988). Patients versus symptomatic volunteers in bulimia nervosa research. *International Journal of Eating Disorders*, 7, 837–843.

Moore, S., & Boldero, J. (1991). Psychosocial development and friendship functions in adolescence. *Sex Roles*, 25, 521–536.

Mori, D., Chaiken, S., & Pliner, P. (1987). "Eating lightly" and the self-presentation of femininity. *Journal of Personality and Social Psychology*, 53, 693–702.

Nevid, J. S. (1984). Sex differences in factors of romantic attraction. *Sex Roles*, 11, 401–411.

Newman, M. M., & Halmi, K. A. (1988). The endocrinology of anorexia nervosa and bulimia nervosa. *Neurologic Clinics, 6,* 195–211.

Orbach, S. (1978). *Fat is feminist issue.* New York: Berkeley Press.

Paikoff, R. L., & Brooks-Gunn, J. (1991). Do parent–child relationships change during puberty? *Psychological Bulletin, 100,* 47–66.

Paikoff, R. L., Brooks-Gunn, J., & Warren, M. P. (1991). Predictive effects of hormonal change on affective expression in adolescent females over the course of one year. *Journal of Youth and Adolescence, 20,* 191–214.

Petersen, A. C., & Hamburg, B. A. (1986). Adolescence: A developmental approach to problems and psychopathology. *Behavior Therapy, 17,* 480–499.

Pierce, K. (1990). A feminist theoretical perspective on the socialization of teenage girls through *Seventeen* magazine. *Sex Roles, 23,* 491–500.

Pike, K. M., & Rodin, J. (1991). Mothers, daughters, and disordered eating. *Journal of Abnormal Psychology, 100,* 198–204.

Pirke, K. M., & Ploog, D. (1987). Biology of human starvation. In P. J. V. Beumont, G. D., Burrows, & R. C. Casper (Eds.), *Handbook of eating disorders* (pp. 79–102). Amsterdam: Elsevier.

Pirke, K. M., Tuschl, R. J., Spyra, B., Laessle, R. G., Schweiger, U., Broocks, A., Sambauer, S., & Zitzelsberger, G. (1990). Endocrine findings in restrained eaters. *Physiology and Behavior, 47,* 903–906.

Pliner, P., & Chaiken, S. (1990). Eating, social motives, and self-presentation in women and men. *Journal of Experimental Social Psychology, 26,* 240–254.

Pliner, P., Chaiken, S., & Flett, G. (1990). Gender differences in concern with body weight and physical appearance over the life span. *Personality and Social Psychology Bulletin, 16,* 263–273.

Polivy, J., Heatherton, T. F., & Herman, C. P. (1988). Self-esteem, restraint, and eating behavior. *Journal of Abnormal Psychology, 97,* 354–356.

Pope, H. G., & Hudson, J. I. (1992). Is childhood sexual abuse a risk factor for bulimia nervosa? *American Journal of Psychiatry, 149,* 455–463.

Pribor, E. F., & Dinwiddie, S. H. (1992). Psychiatric correlates of incest in childhood. *American Journal of Psychiatry, 149,* 52–56.

Purcell, P., & Stewart, L. (1990). Dick and Jane in 1989. *Sex Roles, 22,* 177–185.

Pyle, R. L. (1985). The epidemiology of eating disorders. *Pediatrician, 12,* 102–109.

Remschmidt, H., & Herpertz-Dahlmann, B. (1990). Bulimia in children and adolescents. In M. Fichter (Ed.). *Bulimia nervosa: Basic research, diagnosis and therapy* (pp. 84–98). New York: Wiley.

Rodin, J., Silberstein, L. R., & Striegel-Moore, R. H. (1985). Women and weight: A normative discontent. In T. B. Sonderegger (Ed.), *Nebraska symposium on Motivation* (pp. 267–308). Lincoln: University of Nebraska Press.

Rolls, B. J., Fedoroff, I. C., & Guthrie, J. F. (1991). Gender differences in eating behavior and body weight regulation. *Health Psychology, 102,* 133–142.

Rosen, J. C., Gross, J., & Vara, L. (1987). Psychological adjustment of adolescents attempting to lose or gain weight. *Journal of Consulting and Clinical Psychology, 55,* 742–747.

Rosen, J. C., Silberg, N. T., & Gross, J. (1988). Eating Attitudes Test and Eating Disorders Inventory: Norms for adolescent girls and boys. *Journal of Consulting and Clinical Psychology, 56,* 305–308.

Selvini-Palazzoli, M. (1971). Anorexia nervosa. In S. Arieti (Ed.), *World biennial of psychiatry and psychotherapy* (Vol. 1, pp. 197–218). New York: Basic Books.

Shore, R. A., & Porter, J. E. (1990). Normative and reliability data for 11 to 18 year olds on the Eating Disorders Inventory. *International Journal of Eating Disorders, 9,* 201–207.

Shulman, D. (1991). A multitiered view of bulimia. *International Journal of Eating Disorders, 10,* 333–344.

Siegel, J. M., & Brown, J. D. (1988). A prospective study of stressful circumstances, illness symptoms, and depressed mood among adolescents. *Developmental Psychology, 24,* 715–721.

Signorielli, N. (1989). Television and conception about sex roles: Maintaining conventionality and the status quo. *Sex Roles, 21,* 341–360.

Silberstein, L. R., Striegel-Moore, R. H., & Rodin, J. (1987). Feeling fat: A woman's shame. In H. B. Lewis (Ed.), *The role of shame in symptom formation* (pp. 89–108). Hillsdale, NJ: Erlbaum.

Simmons, R. G., & Blyth, D. A. (1987). *Moving into adolescence: The impact of pubertal change and school context.* New York: Aldine Press.

Simmons, R. G., Blyth, D. A., & McKinney, K. L. (1983). The social and psychological effects of puberty on white females. In J. Brooks-Gunn & A. C. Petersen (Eds.), *Girls at puberty: Biological and psychological perspectives* (pp. 229–272). New York: Plenum Press.

Simmons, R. C., Burgeson, R., Carlton-Ford, S., & Blyth, D. A. (1987). The impact of cumulative change in early adolescence. *Child Development, 58,* 1220–1234.

Simmons, R. G., & Rosenberg, F. (1975). Sex, sex roles, and self-image. *Journal of Youth and Adolescence, 4,* 229–258.

Slochower, J. A. (1983). *Excessive eating.* New York: Human Sciences Press.

Smith, J. E., Waldorf, V. A., & Trembath, D. L. (1990). "Single white male looking for thin, very attractive. . ." *Sex Roles, 23,* 675–685.

Solomon, M. R., & Schopfler, J. (1982). Self-consciousness and clothing. *Personality and Social Psychology Bulletin, 8,* 508–514.

Spade, J. Z., & Reese, C. A. (1991). We've come a long way, maybe: College student's plans for work and family. *Sex Roles, 24,* 309–321.

Spence, J. T. (1985). Gender identity and its implications for the concept of masculinity and femininity. In T. B. Sonderegger (Ed.), *Nebraska symposium on motivation* (pp. 59–96). Lincoln: University of Nebraska Press.

Spence, J. T., & Helmreich, R. L. (1978). Gender, sex roles, and the psychological dimensions of masculinity and femininity. In J. T. Spence & R. L. Helmreich (Eds.), *Masculinity and femininity* (pp. 3–18). Austin: University of Texas Press.

Spitzer, R. L., Devlin, S., Walsh, B. T., Hasin, D., Wing, R. Marcus, M., Stunkard, A., Wadden, T., Yanovski, S. Agras, S., Mitchell, J., & Nonas, C. (1992). Binge eating disorder: A multisite field trial of the diagnostic criteria. *International Journal of Eating Disorders, 11,* 191–203.

Sprecher, S. (1989). The importance to males and females of physical attractiveness, earning potential, and expressiveness in initial attraction. *Sex Roles, 21,* 591–607.

Stattin, H., & Magnusson, D. (1990). *Pubertal maturation in female development.* Hillsdale, NJ: Erlbaum.

Steinberg, S., Tobin, D., & Johnson, C. (1990). The role of bulimic behaviors in affect regulation: Different functions for different patient subgroups. *International Journal of Eating Disorders, 9,* 51–55.

Steiner-Adair, K. (1986). The body politic: Normal female adolescent development and the development of eating disorders. *Journal of the American Academy of Psychoanalysis, 14,* 95–114.

Story, M., Rosenwinkel, K., Himes, J. H., Resnick, M., Harris, L. J., & Blum, R. W. (1991). Demographic and risk factors associated with chronic dieting in adolescents. *American Journal of Diseases of Children, 145,* 994–998.

Striegel-Moore, R. H. (1992). Prevention of bulimia nervosa: Questions and challenges. In J. H. Crowther, D. L. Tennenbaum, S. E. Hobfoll, & M. A. P. Stephens (Eds.), *The etiology of bulimia nervosa* (pp. 203–223). Washington, DC: Hemisphere.

Striegel-Moore, R. H., & Huydic, E. (in press). Disordered eating and substance abuse in female high school students: Comorbidity or coincidence? *International Journal of Eating Disorders.*

Striegel-Moore, R. H., & Kearney-Cooke, A. (in press). Exploring determinants and consequences of parents' attitudes about their children's physical appearance. *International Journal of Eating Disorders.*

Striegel-Moore, R. H., Nicholson, T. J., & Tamborlane, W. V. (1992). Prevalence of eating disorder symptoms in preadolescent and adolescent girls with IDDM. *Diabetes Care, 15,* 1361–1368.

Striegel-Moore, R. H., Pike, K. M., Wilfley, D. E., Schreiber, G., & Rodin, R. (1992). *Drive for thinness in black and white preadolescent girls: The NHLBI growth and health study.* Manuscript submitted for publication.

Striegel-Moore, R. H., Silberstein, L. R., Frensch, P., & Rodin, J. (1989). A prospective study of disordered eating among college students. *International Journal of Eating Disorders, 8,* 499–509.

Striegel-Moore, R. H., Silberstein, L. R., & Rodin, J. (1986). Toward an understanding of risk factors for bulimia. *American Psychologist, 41,* 246–263.

Striegel-Moore, R. H., Silberstein, L. R., & Rodin, J. (in press). The social self in bulimia nervosa: Public self-consciousness, social anxiety, and perceived fraudulence. *Journal of Abnormal Psychology.*

Strober, M. (1984). Stressful life events associated with bulimia in anorexia nervosa: Empirical findings and theoretical speculations. *International Journal of Eating Disorders, 3,* 3–17.

Strober, M. (1991). Disorders of the self in anorexia nervosa: An organismic-developmental paradigm. In C. L. Johnson (Ed.), *Psychodynamic treatment of anorexia nervosa and bulimia* (pp. 354–373). New York: Guilford Press.

Strober, M., & Humphrey, L. L. (1987). Familial contributions to the etiology and course of anorexia nervosa and bulimia. *Journal of Consulting and Clinical Psychology, 55,* 654–659.

Sullivan, G. L., & O'Connor, P. J. (1988). Women's role portrayals in magazine advertising. *Sex Roles, 18,* 181–188.

Tanner, J. M. (1978). *Foetus into man: Physical growth from conception to maturity.* Cambridge, MA: Harvard University Press.

Thelen, M. H., Lawrence, C. M., & Powell, A. L. (1992). Body image, weight control, and eating disorders among children. In J. Crowther & S. Hobfoll (Eds.), *The etiology of bulimia nervosa: The individual and familial context* (pp. 81–101). Washington, DC: Hemisphere.

Thornton, B., Leo, R., & Alberg, K. (1991). Gender role typing, the superwoman ideal, and the potential for eating disorders. *Sex Roles, 25,* 469–484.

Tiggermann, M., & Rothblum, E. D. (1988). Gender differences in social consequences of perceived overweight in the United States and Australia. *Sex Roles, 18,* 75–86.

Timko, C., Striegel-Moore, R. H., Silberstein, L. R., & Rodin, J. (1987). Femininity/masculinity and disordered eating in women: How are they related? *International Journal of Eating Disorders, 6,* 701–712.

Turnbull, J., Freeman, C. P. L., Barry, F., & Henderson, A. (1989). The clinical characteristics of bulimic women. *International Journal of Eating Disorders, 8,* 399–409.

Udry, J. R., & Billy, J. O. G. (1987). Initiation of coitus in early adolescence. *American Sociological Review, 52,* 841–855.

Wigfield, A., Eccles, J. S., Iver, D. M., Reuman, D. A., & Midgley, C. (1991). Transitions during early adolescence: Changes in children's domain-specific self-perceptions and general self-esteem across the transition to junior high school. *Developmental Psychology, 27,* 552–565.

Wilson, G. T., Nonas, C. A., & Rosenblum, G. D. (1993). Assessment of binge-eating in obese patients. *International Journal of Eating Disorders, 13,* 25–34.

Windle, M. (1992). A longitudinal study of stress buffering for adolescent problem behaviors. *Developmental Psychology, 28,* 522–530.

Woodside, D. B., & Garfinkel, P. E. (1992). Age of onset in eating disorders. *International Journal of Eating Disorders, 12,* 31–36.

Wooley, S. C., & Wooley, O. W. (1985). Intensive outpatient and residential treatment for bulimia. In D. M. Garner & P. E. Garfinkel (Eds.), *Handbook of psychotherapy for anorexia nervosa and bulimia* (pp. 391–430). New York: Guilford Press.

Etiology of Binge Eating: Psychological Mechanisms

Janet Polivy
C. Peter Herman

The etiology of binge eating has been the subject of abundant speculation but little consensus. Various etiological mechanisms have been proposed for the behavior of binge eating, as well as for the various eating disorder syndromes of which binge eating forms a part. Psychological factors play a prominent role in many of these proposals. Indeed, the standard definition of binge eating includes a psychological feature, a sense of lack of control over one's eating.

Specifying the etiology of binge eating has proven to be a difficult task, as is evident in the aforementioned lack of consensus. Among the complicating factors is the absence of a guarantee that binge eating and the various associated eating disorders all stem from the same cause. Even more troublesome is the constraining assumption that binge eating has a cause (an etiology) in the same sense that a disease has a cause. Binge eating is a complex behavioral pattern; accounting for it by reference to a single cause is likely to be futile and misleading. If psychological factors contribute to binge eating—and they do—we would do well to look for such influences at various stages of the binge. We should also expect to find that different psychological factors might operate at different phases of the binge-eating episode.

Several phases of binge eating can be identified, each of which can be analyzed in terms of determining influences, including psychological influences. While others have discussed two stages—antecedents and consequences (e.g., Lingswiler, Crowther, & Stephens, 1989a, 1989b; Orleans & Barnett, 1984; Schlundt & Johnson, 1990)—we will divide the binge episode into five phases for the purposes of this chapter. We will examine the impact of psychological mechanisms at each of these stages, and then evaluate the various models that have been proposed to explain binge eating in terms of how they recognize and explain the operation of these psychological mechanisms at each phase.

We will refer to the first stage of binge eating as the prebinge phase. We will discuss here the preconditions for an eating binge, including sociocultural influences (such as the diet culture), personality variables (such as low self-esteem), and chronic behavioral patterns (such as dieting and excessive exercising), that have developed in response to cultural and individual predispositions. The second phase consists of the triggering, or eliciting, of binge-eating behavior. Distal preconditions and proximate triggers of binges are both frequently identified as antecedents to binges (e.g., Lingswiler et al., 1989a; Orleans & Barnett, 1984; Schlundt & Johnson, 1990); indeed, failure to discriminate a chronic precondition from an acute trigger is part of the reason that discussions of etiology have been so unproductive. Factors maintaining the binge to its completion will be discussed as the third stage of binge eating. At the fourth phase, termination, or ending the binge episode, we find that binges may stop for reasons other than the removal of the initial cause of the binge. The fifth and final phase in our analysis is the postbinge phase, wherein we encounter the consequences of a binge, some of which may serve as exacerbating preconditions for future binges.

PRECONDITIONS FOR BINGE EATING

Much has been written about the current cultural pressures on women to be thin, and the impact this has had on the prevalence of eating disorders (e.g., Polivy, Garner, & Garfinkel, 1986; Silverstein, Peterson, & Perdue, 1986; Striegel-Moore, Silberstein, & Rodin, 1986). Since the 1960s, Western society has placed increasing demands on women to be slim, idealizing thin bodies and denigrating overweight. This emphasis on slimness has coincided with a dramatic increase in the incidence of eating disorders, particularly anorexia nervosa and bulimia nervosa. The derogation of fatness and idealization of thinness have also been accompanied by a high degree of body-image dissatisfaction in females, especially adolescent and young women (e.g., Cash & Brown, 1987; Garfinkel et al., 1992; Garner, Garfinkel, & Bonato, 1987; Hawkins & Clement, 1980; Hawkins, Turell, & Jackson, 1983; Miller, Coffman, & Linke, 1980; Polivy, Herman, & Pliner, 1990; Rosen, Gross, & Vara, 1987; Ruderman

& Grace, 1988). Bulimia nervosa patients have been shown to be especially dissatisfied with their bodies (Fairburn & Garner, 1986; Garfinkel et al., 1992). Moreover, body-image dissatisfaction—and, more specifically, wanting to be thinner—seems to predict which (normal) female subjects are dieting to lose weight on any given day (e.g., Miller et al., 1980; Rosen et al., 1987); body-size or shape dissatisfaction may not be a perfect predictor of dieting, but it is one of the best predictors available.

The pressure on women to be thin in order to be attractive has thus contributed to the current soaring prevalence of dieting in young women (e.g., Herman & Polivy, 1980; Jakobovits, Halstead, Kelley, Roe, & Young, 1977; Miller et al., 1980; Polivy & Herman, 1985, 1987; Rosen & Gross, 1987; Silverstein & Perdue, 1988). (It is tempting, and probably correct, to assume that the desire for thinness corresponds to a desire for attractiveness; but we should remember that thinness is associated with other positive attributes as well, including perceived competence and health. Many dieters pursue all three of these allegedly correlated objectives.) Chronic dieting, in turn, has often been cited as a contributing factor in the development of binge eating (e.g., Abraham & Beumont, 1982; Garner, Rockert, Olmsted, Johnson, & Coscina, 1985; Hsu, 1990; Lingswiler et al., 1989a; Orleans & Barnett, 1984; Polivy & Herman, 1985, 1987; Pyle, Mitchell, & Eckert, 1981; Schlundt & Johnson, 1990), with more stringent diets being more likely to provoke binge eating (Orleans & Barnett, 1984).

Recently, excessive exercising has also been implicated as a cause of binge eating (Yates, Leehey, & Shisslak, 1983). The statistical association of excessive exercising and binge eating does not clarify matters much. Excessive exercise is also associated with dieting, body dissatisfaction, and some other preconditions of binge eating to be discussed below. Whether excessive exercise will ultimately be seen as having an independent causal role, though, will depend on how clearly researchers can discriminate the separate influences of highly intercorrelated variables.

One precondition for binge eating thus seems to be the desire to be thinner, as expressed through restricted caloric input (dieting) or increased caloric output (exercise). The pursuit of thinness presumably promotes feelings of deprivation and deservingness. (Whether chronic dieters are actually calorically deprived is debatable; the evidence suggests that chronic dieters [or restrained eaters] may ordinarily eat less than nondieters [e.g., Klesges, Klem, & Bene, 1989; Tuschl, Laessle, Kotthaus, & Pirke, 1989; Tuschl, Platte, Laessle, Stichler, & Pirke, 1990], more than nondieters [Wardle & Beales, 1988], or more variably than nondieters [Herman & Polivy, 1988b].) Dieters' deprivation—whether real or imagined—has been identified as a contributor to overeating and eating binges (e.g., Abraham & Beumont, 1982; Davis, Freeman, & Garner, 1988; Hawkins & Clement, 1980; Herman & Polivy, 1988b; Johnson & Connors, 1987; Lingswiler et al., 1989a; Orleans & Barnett, 1984; Polivy & Herman, 1985, 1987; Pyle et al., 1981; Rosen, Tacy, & Howell, 1990). Deprivation may operate in a straightforward fashion, by instigating a drive toward repletion; another, not incompatible possibility is that deprivation alters one's perceptual reactivity to attractive food cues, making them more irresistible. Similarly, attempted deprivation may make dieters more prone to feel distress over their dietary failures, or more aroused and emotionally labile. Whether the eating is pulled by attraction to forbidden foods or pushed by internal needs is at present unclear, but there is abundant evidence that restraining one's intake is a precondition for bouts of overeating.

Another characteristic associated with body-image dissatisfaction, dieting, and binge eating is low self-esteem (e.g., Herman & Polivy, 1988a; Johnson, Connors, & Tobin, 1987; Johnson, Steinberg, & Lewis, 1988). Both bulimia nervosa patients and dieters appear to have lower than average self-esteem (e.g., Dykens & Gerrard, 1986; Eldredge, Wilson, & Whaley, 1990; Garfinkel & Garner, 1982; Herman & Polivy, 1988a; Mayhew & Edelmann, 1989; Polivy, Heatherton, & Herman, 1988; Ruderman & Grace, 1988). It may well be that having a low opinion of oneself makes individuals vulnerable to the pressures to be thin and thus more likely to diet. This would explain the negative correlation between self-esteem and chronic dieting status, and between self-esteem and body dissatisfaction (Heatherton & Polivy, 1992). It may also be, however, that those who decide to diet and then find themselves subsequently losing control of their eating and engaging in eating binges may feel worse and worse about themselves, lowering their self-esteem with each dieting failure (Orleans & Barnett, 1984). Thus, lowered self-esteem could be a precondition or cause for dieting, or it could be an outcome of unsuccessful dieting and binge eating. The current correlational nature of the data on dieting, binge eating, and self-esteem does not allow us to discriminate between these alternatives. In either case, binge eating seems to occur more in those with lower self-esteem (Johnson et al., 1987; Polivy et al., 1988; Rosen & Leitenberg, 1985).

Other personality factors that characterize binge eaters might also be seen as preconditions for binge eating. Patients with bulimia and dieters have both been characterized as more anxiety prone, dysphoric, and emotionally unstable (e.g., Edwards & Nagelberg, 1986; Eldredge et al., 1990; Hawkins & Clement, 1980; Herman & Polivy, 1980; Johnson & Larson, 1982; Pyle et al., 1981; Ruderman, 1986; Ruderman & Grace, 1987; Ruderman & Grace, 1988; Willmuth, Leitenberg, Rosen, & Cado, 1988). Again, such descriptions are based upon correlational data, so we cannot conclude anything about causality. Dieting and binge eating could be caused by a neurotic personality structure; dieting and binge eating could cause individuals to become more distressed and score higher on measures of emotional instability; or a third factor (such as body dissatisfaction) could cause both.

One prospective study of dieting and self-reported distress (Rosen et al., 1990) did indicate that dieting increases distress, rather than the reverse. Moreover, such elevated distress may be associated with an increase in eating disorder symptomatology over time (Striegel-Moore, Silberstein, Frensch, & Rodin, 1989) (although in this study it was distress at the end of the year that was associated with increased eating pathology at that time; distress was not measured at the initial assessment). However they get that way, those who diet and binge appear to be more neurotic or unstable than normal, and this becomes part of the background personality that contributes to further binges. Moreover, as we shall see in the next section, emotional distress has also been implicated as a direct cause or trigger for eating binges. People who are chronically distressed are, not surprisingly, more likely to become distressed on a particular occasion.

Binge eaters have been described as having an irrational, dichotomous thinking style, which leads in turn to a dichotomous eating style in which they either starve or stuff themselves (e.g., Garner & Bemis, 1985; Johnson & Connors, 1987; Johnson et al., 1987; Kales, 1990; King, Herman, & Polivy, 1987; Lingswiler et al., 1989a; Mizes, 1988; Orleans & Barnett, 1984; Zotter & Crowther, 1991). They tend to see situations as black or white, and use faulty reasoning and cognitive distortions to judge themselves in an irrational manner. When eating, they have more negative thoughts about food and eating (Willmuth et al., 1988). Even normal dieters seem prone to irrational thinking (Ruderman, 1985b), especially about eating and food (King et al., 1987; Knight & Boland, 1989). This makes dieters especially prone to disinhibited eating or binges when they think they have broken their diets.

A conditioning model of binge eating (Booth, 1988; Booth, Lewis, & Blair, 1990) posits that dieters have become conditioned to binge eat in response to fattening snack foods. This conditioning occurs when a dieter decides to go off her diet and eats (often as not, fattening snack foods) on an empty stomach; nutritional reinforcers condition a larger appetite for those foods whenever dieting is being abandoned (i.e., under similar circumstances). This process may lead ultimately to an excessive appetite for snack foods, and even to binges.

The nutritional consequences of a binge may be aversive, but purging often relieves negative affect, thereby reinforcing a binge–purge cycle. If continued eating on a full stomach gets reinforced in this manner (nutritionally or affectively), one may start to experience cravings even when sated, a "conditioned de-satiation for the favourite bingeing foods" (Booth, 1988, p. 23). This leads to what Booth calls "belly bulimia" due to instigating conditioned stimuli from the gut. One's prior dieting and eating behavior thus set up the preconditions for future binge-eating episodes.

Heatherton and Baumeister (1991) have proposed that bingers are susceptible to external food cues when they are in a state of distress brought on by self-perceptions of inadequacy or failure. In an attempt to escape their distress, binge eaters narrow their attention to the immediate stimulus environment and avoid broadly meaningful thought. This narrowing of cognitive focus onto specific cues (such as food) disengages their normal inhibitions against eating, which are part of the broad self-improvement agenda that is jettisoned under distress. If attractive food is available, the "escape from higher meanings" will lead directly to mindless immersion in eating.

In addition to societal and individual characteristics that predispose the individual toward binge eating, family conditions may play an important role (Strober & Humphrey, 1987). For example, Humphrey (1986, 1987) has posited (and found) that parents of bulimia nervosa patients are insufficiently nurturing and empathic to their daughters. This emotional shortfall is reciprocated by the patients themselves. Since these data were collected on patients who already had bulimia nervosa, it is impossible to determine whether the disturbed familial interaction patterns contributed to the binge eating or whether the bulimia caused disturbed familial interactions. The most we can conclude from these data is that having less empathic, nurturing parents may be a precondition for binge eating in bulimia nervosa.

Other studies have uncovered further deficits in such families, including lack of parental affection; negative, hostile, and disengaged interactions within the family; parental impulsivity; and familial alcoholism and obesity (Strober & Humphrey, 1987). Bulimia nervosa patients, and to some extent their parents as well, see their families as more conflictual and disengaged and less cohesive and nurturing than do normal control subjects. Laboratory studies of family interactions in these families show enmeshed, intrusive, hostile patterns, and negating of the child's emotional needs (Strober & Humphrey, 1987). It is not clear how this potentiates or activates weight concerns, nor is it clear that such patterns are unique to bulimic families, but since such familial pathology has in some studies been demonstrated to precede the appearance of the daughter's eating disorder, faulty family interaction patterns must be considered a likely precondition for binge eating.

To summarize, the suggested preconditions for binge eating include societal preference for thin physiques, which imparts a desire to be thinner and dissatisfaction with one's current body shape. This internalized pressure impels young women to attempt to become thinner by dieting. Dieting has been shown to be associated with, and precede (Polivy & Herman, 1985), binge eating. Both dieting and binge eating have been linked to lower self-esteem, although it is not clear whether low self-esteem is a precondition or outcome of dieting, binge eating, or both. A personality feature of dieters and binge eaters that may be more directly associated with their binge eating is emotional instability or dysphoria. Another hypothesized psychological precondition for binge eating is a learning or conditioning history that predisposes one to overreact to particular food cues by overeating or even binge eating. A similar hypersensitivity to food cues, driven by a desire to escape the broader implications of one's actions by responding almost mindlessly to immediate perceptual cues, has been proposed as a common reaction when individuals are distressed with themselves. There may also be a contribution from disturbed family interaction patterns, though this is not yet conclusively demonstrated to be an actual or exclusive precondition of binge eating.

Because preconditions are by their very nature chronic, it is difficult if not impossible to create them for experimental purposes; because for the most part these preconditions are unpleasant and/or dangerous, it would be unethical to create them even if we could. The inability to create or manipulate these preconditions, however, means that research on preconditions is inevitably correlational in nature, often taking the form of regression or risk factor approach. This approach is unsatisfying in at least two respects. First and foremost, it is usually difficult if not impossible to establish causality from correlational data. Path-analytic strategies are often unconvincing, and longitudinal or cross-lagged panel data are onerous to collect and in correspondingly short supply. Another problem with the risk factor approach is that most of the alleged risk factors for binge eating are highly intercorrelated with one another. What appears to be a reliable risk factor may not be an independent risk factor at all but merely a strong correlate of a real risk factor. Statistical adjustments to partial out the relative effects of correlated variables are, like the related technique of path analysis, generally unsatisfying and inconclusive. It seems likely then, that the analysis of preconditions may never attain the precision possible in the analysis of other phases of binge eating.

PSYCHOLOGICAL TRIGGERING MECHANISMS

The most frequently cited instigator of a binge episode is stress or negative affect (Abraham & Beumont, 1982; Baucom & Aiken, 1981; Davis et al., 1988; Elmore & De Castro, 1990; Frost, Goolkasian, Ely, & Blanchard, 1982; Heatherton & Baumeister, 1991; Herman & Polivy, 1975; Herman, Polivy, Lank, & Heatherton, 1987; Johnson & Larson, 1982; Johnson, Steinberg, & Lewis, 1988; Kaye, Gwirtzman, George, Weiss, & Jimerson, 1986; Lingswiler et al., 1989a; Polivy & Herman, 1976a; Pyle, Mitchell, & Eckert, 1981; Rosen & Leitenberg, 1985; Ruderman, 1985a; Schotte, Cools, & McNally, 1990; Wilson, 1984). Experimentally induced dysphoria causes restrained eaters (Heatherton, Herman, & Polivy, 1991; Herman & Polivy, 1975; Herman et al., 1987; Ruderman, 1985a; Schotte et al., 1990) or dieters (Baucom & Aiken, 1981) to eat more than similarly distressed unrestrained eaters or nondieters; distressed dieters also eat more than do nondistressed dieters. Interestingly, distressed dieters' overeating seems to be connected specifically to threats to self-image such as failure, rather than to mere physical fear (Heatherton, Herman, & Polivy, 1991). Similarly, depressed outpatients who are not dieters eat less as a result of their depression and lose weight, but restrained depressives eat more and gain weight (Polivy & Herman, 1976a). Finally, although experimental studies on bulimia nervosa patients are rare, these patients frequently report that their binges are triggered by some sort of emotional distress (Abraham & Beumont, 1982; Davis et al., 1988; Elmore & De Castro, 1990; Johnson & Larson, 1982; Lingswiler et al., 1989a; Pyle et al., 1981).

Various explanations for how distress triggers binge eating have been offered. Heatherton and Baumeister (1991) argue that negative self-focused affect causes painful self-awareness, which the individual seeks to escape by narrowing her cognitive focus from more abstract levels (including self-evaluation) to concrete, immediate environmental stimuli (such as food). The binge results from the loss of higher level cognitions, including those that ordinarily maintain inhibited eating in the service of abstract goals such as weight loss or not losing control of one's eating.

Herman, Polivy, and Heatherton (1991; Heatherton, Polivy, & Herman, 1991) present an analysis derived both from the Heatherton and Baumeister argument above and from Slochower's (1983) earlier claim that distress causes fat people (potential binge eaters) to become more external or responsive to the stimulus properties of food. Heatherton et al. argue that distress makes people more externally focused, and thus more sensitive and/or responsive to external cues. Because dieters tend to be out of touch with their internal states, they do not react to physiological, distress-induced hunger suppression signals (as nondieters do). Since the experiments upon which this analysis is based all provided food to the distressed subjects, and little else in the way of external cues to which they might respond, the dieters' externality makes the food all the more salient, rendering its allure more powerful than their dietary resolve. In the face of such powerful cues to eat, and with the negative affect providing an excuse to seek comfort by eating, dieters abandon their diets, ignore satiety cues, and overeat.

A similar view of the operation of stress on binge eating is offered by Davis et al. (1988), who have proposed that stress reduces the perceived importance or feasibility of dietary self-control, which is then abandoned for a binge episode.

Another way of thinking about the role of distress as a trigger for binge eating involves affect self-regulation. Johnson (Johnson & Connors, 1987; Johnson & Larson, 1982; Johnson et al., 1988; Steinberg, Tobin, & Johnson, 1989) posits that binge eating in bulimia nervosa enables the patient to reorganize herself when she feels overwhelmed or threatened with disintegration. Several authors have noted that bingeing appears to relieve anxiety (e.g., Beumont, 1988; Elmore & De Castro, 1990; Hsu, 1990; Kaye et al., 1986; Orleans & Barnett, 1984; Schlundt & Johnson, 1990; Wilson, 1984), possibly through distraction from one's problems (e.g., Fairburn & Cooper, 1987; Hawkins & Clement, 1984), or by displacing feelings of distress from other, more threatening issues onto the seemingly more manageable problem of overeating (Hawkins & Clement, 1984; Herman & Polivy, 1988a; Johnson et al., 1988; Schlundt & Johnson, 1990; Thompson, Berg, & Shatford, 1987). "The young woman may then make the logical error of redefining her problem as being the uncontrolled overeating itself, or the overweight appearance, rather than the original interpersonal or academic difficulty" (Hawkins & Clement, 1984, p. 248). The binge may be comforting simply because it feels good and because it is relaxing to eat, especially if one has been restraining one's eating (e.g., Hawkins & Clement, 1984; Orleans & Barnett, 1984; Schlundt & Johnson, 1990). Rosen and Leitenberg (e.g., Leitenberg, Rosen, Gross, Nudelman, & Vara, 1988; Rosen & Leitenberg, 1982, 1985, 1988b) argue that while binge eating may initially provide relief, eventually it becomes the purging following the binge that relieves stress and negative affect. Even without purging, though, binge eating has been shown to be anxiety reducing in bulimia nervosa patients (Elmore & De Castro, 1990; Kaye et al., 1986). This relief is temporary, of course, and is followed by feelings of guilt, self-deprecation, being out of control (Abraham & Beumont, 1982; Elmore & De Castro, 1990; Hawkins & Clement, 1984; Lingswiler et al., 1989b; Wilson, 1984), or depression (Abraham & Beumont, 1982; Elmore & De Castro, 1990).

It is worth examining the similarities and differences between the two general views of distress as a trigger of binge eating presented so far. In both cases, distress is likely to induce binge eating (in those who are predisposed). In the first case, however, the eating is disinhibited by distress (i.e., the normal reasons for not eating are overridden), and eating appears to come under the control of the available food stimuli. This analysis is essentially one of stimulus control of eating, with distress altering the controlling stimuli. In the affect regulation model, distress induces eating not by altering the controlling stimuli, but by altering the dieter's purpose. She is trying to cope with the distress, which eating may, in one way or another, alleviate.

Regardless of whether a binge represents a coping attempt, some form of affect regulation, or simply a loss of motivation to restrict one's eating any further, stress seems to be a reliable triggering mechanism for binge eating.

Another frequently cited trigger for binge eating is the presence of attractive, fattening food cues (Johnson et al., 1987) or hunger/food cravings (Mitchell, Hatsukami, Eckert, & Pyle, 1985; Orleans & Barnett, 1984; Pyle et al., 1981). As was suggested above, the presence of attractive food cues may interact with distress to set off a binge, but it appears that external food cues and/or internal hunger/craving cues can occasionally provoke a binge even in the absence of distress. Dieters are particularly likely to binge following the ingestion of some quantity of forbidden food (e.g., Abraham & Beumont, 1982; Herman & Mack, 1975; Herman & Polivy, 1988b; Kales, 1989; Orleans & Barnett, 1984; Polivy & Herman, 1985, 1987, 1991; Polivy, Herman, Hackett, & Kuleshnyk, 1986; Schlundt & Johnson, 1990). Laboratory research has demonstrated that normal dieters (Herman & Mack, 1975; Herman & Polivy, 1988b; Polivy & Herman, 1985, 1987, 1991; Polivy, Herman, Hackett, et al., 1986) and individuals suffering from bulimia nervosa (Kales, 1989) eat more when they have eaten something that they perceive as diet breaking or fattening than when they have eaten a food seen as acceptable or low calorie. Even just thinking that one has eaten something fattening (Knight & Boland, 1989; Polivy, 1976; Spencer & Fremouw, 1979; Woody, Costanzo, Leifer, & Conger, 1981) or planning to do so (Ruderman, Belzer, & Halperin, 1985; Tomarken & Kirschenbaum, 1984) can provoke overeating in restrained eaters.

Eating a forbidden food seems to lead to binge eating through the activation of binge eaters' all-or-none cognitions, noted earlier as a precondition. Bulimia nervosa patients have frequently been shown to think in a black-or-white, dichotomous fashion, and it has been hypothesized that such dichotomous thoughts precipitate binges (e.g., Garner & Bemis, 1985; Johnson & Connors, 1987; Johnson et al., 1987; Kales, 1990; King et al., 1987; Lingswiler et al., 1989a; Mizes, 1988; Orleans & Barnett, 1984; Schlundt & Johnson, 1990; Wilson, 1984). Once the bulimic patient has eaten something she feels is proscribed, she appears to abandon her diet as hopeless or ruined, rather than trying harder to preserve it, or compensating for the breach; in the binge eaters' dichotomous world, failure is absolute and cannot be rectified or even mitigated.

Binge eaters exhibit other cognitive distortions as well. While eating, bulimia nervosa patients think more negative thoughts about food than do normals (Willmuth et al., 1988), and they have been shown to have more distorted, irrational thoughts about food and body shape, which may trigger overeating (Zotter & Crowther, 1991).

The starve-or-binge pattern characterizing bulimia nervosa patients has been interpreted in terms of the ''abstinence violation effect,'' a construct imported from drug abuse research (Johnson et al., 1987; Schlundt & Johnson, 1990). Like drug abusers or alcoholics who strive for abstinence and then go on a drug binge if they violate this abstinence (e.g., Marlatt & Gordon, 1980, 1985; Wilson, 1984), bulimia nervosa patients' irrational thought patterns precipitate binge eating when they believe that they have ruined their diets by eating even a small quantity of forbidden food. Not all experimental attempts to link these sorts of cognitions with overeating have been successful (e.g., Jansen, Merckelbach, Oosterlaan, Tuiten, & Van den Hout, 1988), perhaps because of the inherent difficulties of inducing significant overeating in the laboratory. Nevertheless, there is a fair consensus that overindulgence is a reliable trigger for further overindulgence. Moreover, the initial overindulgence need not be substantial; for the prospective binger, a small amount of what is perceived to be a forbidden food may suffice to trigger a binge.

The ingestion of alcohol has also been cited frequently as a precipitator of binge eating (Abraham & Beumont, 1982; Johnson et al., 1987; Williamson, 1990). Forty four percent of Abraham and Beumont's (1982) bulimia nervosa patients mentioned it as a trigger, as did many of those interviewed by Williamson (1990). Laboratory studies of restrained eaters have also identified alcohol as a disinhibitor of eating, though only when it is correctly identified as alcohol (Polivy & Herman, 1976b, 1976c). It is possible that alcohol or other intoxicants operate through one of the triggering mechanisms already cited. Alcohol might impair the ability of long-term considerations to control behavior, perhaps by reducing cognitive capacity (Josephs & Steele, 1990); alternatively, it may alter the balance of motivation such that immediate attractions gain power over delayed gratifications. Alcohol may alter one's affective tone, making one feel worse and more deserving of reward, or better and therefore less in need of self-improvement through dieting. Sorting out these confusing alternatives will require sophisticated research.

Although most normal eating (and even normal overeating) occurs in social situations, and the very presence of other people seems to lead to increased intake, (De Castro, 1990), privacy or isolation, which will be discussed shortly as a maintaining factor, has also been cited as a triggering factor for binge eating. Bulimia nervosa patients are more likely to binge when home alone (e.g., Abraham & Beumont, 1982; Davis et al., 1988; Johnson et al., 1987; Johnson & Larson, 1982; Orleans & Barnett, 1984; Pyle et al., 1981; Schlundt & Johnson, 1990; Wilson, 1984), and being alone may be a factor in their negative moods (Johnson et al., 1987). Orleans and Barnett (1984) described the isolation of the bulimia nervosa patient as an "interpersonal vacuum the bulimic tries to fill with food" (p. 162). They pointed out that privacy ensures that no negative social consequences will result from a binge, at least not immediately. Being alone may exacerbate aversive self-awareness, which the binge eater will attempt to escape by retreating to lower levels of cognitive awareness (Heatherton & Baumeister, 1991), which may in turn trigger a binge, particularly if attractive food cues are present. Privacy, then, may provoke a distressing loneliness or uncomfortable self-awareness, triggers that we have already examined. Or privacy may act on its own as a trigger, without the mediation of distress, by providing an opportunity to engage in a tempting but socially unacceptable behavior pattern. Whether privacy will ultimately be classed as an independent trigger awaits further research.

There thus seems to be a variety of precipitants of binge eating behavior. Most of these triggers presupppose the presence of at least some of the preconditions outlined previously. The trigger may be thought of as an acute event that converts the latent inclination to eat into an overt binge. Just as the preconditions were seen to be intercorrelated, making it difficult to determine their separate contributions, so the triggers, although they have historically been listed separately, may under further examination prove to be complexly interrelated. As an obvious example, it may prove to be the case that overindulgence (one kind of trigger) creates distress (another kind of trigger); it is even possible that distress makes it easier to imagine that one has overindulged. For all the research that has been conducted in this area, it seems that most of the interesting questions have not even been asked, let alone answered. And we must remember further that what starts a binge (i.e., a trigger) is not necessarily what keeps it going once it has begun.

PSYCHOLOGICAL MAINTAINING FACTORS

Once a binge has been triggered, several psychological conditions are necessary for it to be maintained. We discussed distress or negative affect as a major precipitant of binge eating. The binge serves to reduce the negative affect, at least temporarily, and such affect reduction is likely to be one of the factors that maintains bingeing (e.g., Beumont, 1988; Elmore & De Castro, 1990; Fairburn & Cooper, 1987; Hawkins & Clement, 1984; Herman & Polivy, 1988a; Johnson et al., 1988; Kaye et al., 1986; Orleans & Barnett, 1984; Schlundt & Johnson, 1990; Thompson et al., 1987; Wilson, 1984). A variety of explanations have been offered for how such affect reduction occurs, but the important factor for the present discussion is the mere success of binge eating at reducing negative emotions, which is sufficient to maintain the eating behavior.

Like stress, privacy or isolation may not only precipitate binge eating; it seems also to be a requirement if a binge is to continue (Abraham & Beumont, 1982; Orleans & Barnett, 1984; Pyle et al., 1981; Wilson, 1984). Laboratory experiments have shown that dieters who feel self-conscious about the presence of another person (such as the experimenter) while they are eating are less likely to overeat than are those who are left alone to eat (Herman, Polivy, & Silver, 1979; Polivy, Herman, Hackett, et al., 1986). Most individuals with bulimia nervosa will binge only if they are alone (Abraham & Beumont, 1982; Orleans & Barnett, 1984; Pyle et al., 1981; Wilson, 1984), though a few will tolerate the presence of others (e.g., Pyle et al., 1981; Schlundt & Johnson, 1990). Privacy protects the binge eater against possible negative social consequences of binge eating (Orleans & Barnett, 1984). Such sanctions might be activated if another person appears during the binge, so the binger would most likely attempt to hide her binge-eating behavior. For the most part, if someone else intrudes while the bulimia nervosa patient is in the midst of a binge, the binge will be terminated immediately, or it will be postponed until the person leaves and the binger is alone again (Abraham & Beumont, 1982; Schlundt & Johnson, 1990). (The postponed binge raises interesting questions about triggering, most notably whether a binge currently in the pause mode requires another trigger to get it restarted, or, as suggested above, whether it simply requires the restitution of the maintaining conditions—such as privacy—that were in force when the interruption occurred.)

Rosen and Leitenberg theorize that the need for privacy is based on its being necessary to allow purging to follow the binge. (Conceivably one might binge in public and purge in private, but the likelihood of obtaining the privacy necessary for purging would seem to be greater if one is alone initially.) Rosen and Leitenberg (e.g., Leitenberg et al., 1988; Rosen & Leitenberg, 1982, 1985, 1988a, 1988b; Willmuth et al., 1988) propose that a critical maintaining factor for binge eating is the ability to vomit after the binge and have demonstrated in the laboratory that bulimia nervosa patients will not binge if they know they will be prevented from vomiting afterward (Leitenberg et al., 1988; Rosen & Leitenberg, 1982; Willmuth et al., 1988). The opportunity to purge following the binge is thus a requirement for the continuation of a binge episode. Although pleasure is rarely mentioned as a maintaining factor in binge eating, Rosen and Leitenberg do not deny that there may be pleasure during bingeing; they do insist, however, that such pleasure is possible only if the binge eater can anticipate the opportunity to vomit (Rosen & Leitenberg, 1988b).

Another factor that has been advanced as important for the maintenance of a binge is the feeling that the binge is not finished or completed (Schlundt & Johnson, 1990). Some bingers report that the binge continues until they "run out of steam" (Abraham & Beumont, 1982). The question remains, however, what exactly this means to the binge eater. What signals the completion of a binge? Obversely, how does the binge eater recognize that the binge is as yet incomplete? Johnson (Johnson et al., 1988) proposes that binges serve adaptive functions such as self-nurturance (in the absence of any other sources of self-care), expression of oppositionality, and expression of impulsivity (which may or may not be eroticized). It may be necessary for the binger to continue eating, then, until one of these functions has been fulfilled. Exactly what sensations accompany the fulfillment of these functions remains unexplored.

To summarize, the psychological factors that maintain a binge once it has begun include stress reduction, privacy, the opportunity to purge, and the feeling that the binge has not reached its conclusion.

TERMINATION

Physical factors such as the absence of any more food or the limits of the binge eater's stomach capacity may terminate a binge episode (Abraham & Beumont, 1982), but psychological factors are especially influential. As mentioned earlier, a binge will generally be terminated by the arrival of another person, but this is usually more an interruption than a true termination of the binge.

The disappearance or negation of the maintaining factors described above may result in actual termination of the binge. For example, as Abraham and Beumont (1982) described, the binge eater eventually feels finished, or "out of steam" and terminates the binge. The decision that one is finished is obviously a psychological one. Binges vary tremendously in length (Mitchell, Pyle, & Eckert, 1981; Pyle et al., 1981; Rossiter, Agras, Telch, & Bruce, 1992) and number of calories consumed (Davis et al.,

1988; Mitchell et al., 1981; Rosen & Leitenberg, 1988b; Rosen, Leitenberg, Fisher, & Khazam, 1986; Rossiter et al., 1992; Schlundt & Johnson, 1990), not only between, but even within individuals. Subjective, psychological factors clearly determine when the individual decides she has completed her binge. Even calling an eating episode a binge seems to be a subjective decision on the part of the binge eater (Jansen, Van den Hout, & Griez, 1990; Lingswiler et al., 1989a; Rosen et al., 1986; Rossiter et al., 1992; Schlundt & Johnson, 1990; Wilson, 1984). Thus, whether the binge should be deemed over or not also depends on the essentially psychological judgment of the binge eater.

Most frequently, vomiting, stomach fullness, nausea, or pain terminates the binge (Abraham & Beumont, 1982; Mitchell et al., 1981; Rosen & Leitenberg, 1985; Schlundt & Johnson, 1990). Even these physical reactions have a psychological element, however; fullness and pain, for instance, both involve subjective judgments. Vomiting in bulimia nervosa patients is generally intentional (e.g., Rosen & Leitenberg, 1985), so the decision to end the binge by vomiting also contains a voluntary (psychological) component.

Some bingers terminate their binges when their intense fear of gaining weight becomes activated by their eating (Schlundt & Johnson, 1990). This fear overwhelms the desire to binge and forces the bulimia nervosa patient to stop eating.

CONSEQUENCES

The immediate consequences of binge eating differ dramatically from its delayed longer term results. In general, it seems that while many of the immediate effects are rewarding, the more remote consequences are aversive and/or dangerous. Most reports indicate that binges do result in relief of negative affect and hunger in the short term (e.g., Abraham & Beumont, 1982; Elmore & De Castro, 1990; Hawkins & Clement, 1984; Kaye et al., 1986; Lingswiler et al., 1989b; Orleans & Barnett, 1984; Rosen & Leitenberg, 1982; Schlundt & Johnson, 1990; Steinberg et al., 1989; Wilson, 1984). Binge eating and purging relieve negative mood and anxiety, which in turn reinforces binge–purge behavior (Abraham & Beumont, 1982). Also, as Rosen noted, "Bulimia is also rewarded by some consequences that avoid negative cognitions. The bulimic woman is able to escape having to think and worry about other problems when she is engaged in the act of bingeing. Also, purging and dieting allow her to avoid unpleasant thoughts about getting fat" (Rosen & Leitenberg, 1982, pp. 174–175). The purge reduces the anxiety of having binged (Wilson, 1984).

Unfortunately, however, this relief from distress soon dissipates, to be replaced by shame, guilt, disgust, self-condemnation, and depression (e.g., Abraham & Beumont, 1982; Elmore & De Castro, 1990; Hawkins & Clement, 1984; Lingswiler et al., 1989b; Orleans & Barnett, 1984; Rosen & Leitenberg, 1982; Schlundt & Johnson, 1990; Wilson, 1984). Positive emotions have been found to be more evident immediately after a binge than 1 hour or even 30 minutes later (Lingswiler et al., 1989b). Moreover, subjects feel out of control of their eating (Hawkins & Clement, 1984; Orleans & Barnett, 1984; Rosen & Leitenberg, 1982; Schlundt & Johnson, 1990) and worry or even panic about becoming fat, causing them to return to stringent dieting, setting up the next binge (Abraham & Beumont, 1982; Lingswiler et al., 1989b; Orleans & Barnett, 1984; Schlundt & Johnson, 1990). Even later, the binge eater is likely to develop concerns about the damage she is doing to her body (Schlundt & Johnson, 1990). This discrepancy between the (positive) immediate and (negative) delayed effects of binge eating may account for apparently contradictory reports of decreased, increased, or unchanged negative affect following binge eating behaviors (e.g., Tobin, Johnson, Steinberg, Staats, & Dennis, 1991).

In the social environment, there are some initial positive effects of dieting and weight loss, such as increased attention and concern from family and friends (Schlundt & Johnson, 1990) and even admiration of the supposed dieting success (Branch & Eurman, 1980; Schlundt & Johnson, 1990). But it soon becomes apparent that bulimia interferes with the binge eater's functioning; intimate or interpersonal relationships become impaired, family problems appear or are exacerbated, and financial problems and work impairment are common (Mitchell et al., 1985; Schlundt & Johnson, 1990). It must be recognized that a preoccupation with food and a need for privacy are not conducive to positive social interactions with friends or family, and that chronic binge eating—be it ritualized or uncontrolled—may actively interfere with one's daily obligations and financial stability.

In addition to these emotional and social consequences of binges, there are also somatic ones. As above, there are immediate and delayed effects, and at the somatic level, the distinction between effects of the binge and effects of purging are notable. Positive consequences immediately after the binge include the fact that eating reduces sympathetic arousal (Orleans & Barnett, 1984; Schlundt & Johnson, 1990), and relieves hypoglycemia. The binge–purge episode may lead to an endorphin high, or at least the removal of endorphin withdrawal effects.

On the other hand, bingeing is usually followed fairly soon by abdominal pain, fatigue (Lingswiler et al., 1989b; Mitchell et al., 1985; Pyle et al., 1981), headaches, and dizziness (Lingswiler et al., 1989b), not to mention discomfort and bloating (Orleans & Barnett, 1984). Menstrual irregularities are also common in binge eaters (Garner et al., 1985). Other physical symptoms reported after repeated binge–purge episodes are primarily belated results of purging (e.g., Garner et al., 1985; Mitchell et al., 1985; Pyle et al., 1981; Schlundt & Johnson, 1990).

The cognitive consequences of binge–purge episodes show a similar pattern of immediate positive and delayed negative effects. Initially, the binge eater, particularly if she purges, can see herself as controlling her weight, avoiding her other problems, and getting away with eating all she wants (Schlundt & Johnson, 1990). This soon gives way to a negative self-evaluation, an even more distorted body image, and a sense of loss of control (Schlundt & Johnson, 1990).

In summary, the reinforcing consequences of binge eating tend to occur immediately after the episode. Relief or distraction from negative feelings about one's life or oneself are quickly supplanted by even more negative feelings and thoughts, heightened by the somatic discomforts and long term damage to the body brought about by bingeing and purging. In the next section, we will explore various explanations for such a self-defeating syndrome. For the moment, we must remember that behavior is usually maintained by its immediate consequences; delayed reinforcers (or punishers) are ordinarily less effective in controlling behavior.

MODELS OF BINGE EATING

A wide variety of models have been proposed to explain binge eating; this very variety itself requires interpretation and analysis. While the popular press focuses on the frantic eating as symbolic of such driving needs as "love hunger" (e.g., Roth, 1989), more sober scientific and clinical researchers have offered models of binge eating based on addictions, conditioning, affect regulation, escape theory, self-esteem needs, dieting, and combined biopsychosocial factors. We will review the evidence for each of these and evaluate their current status.

Addictions Model

Because of their vulnerability to dysphoria and mood fluctuations, bulimia nervosa patients have been described as at risk for addictive behavior (eating, in this case), which is used to modulate dysphoric and fluctuating mood states (Johnson & Larson, 1982; see Wilson, Chapter 6, for a full discussion of this model). The addiction model incorporates many of the above-mentioned predisposing factors, including biochemical, familial, and cultural variables. These preconditions result in food (rather than, or in addition to, some other substance) becoming a substance of abuse for these individuals; the preconditions determine not only which substance(s) will be abused but whether there will be abuse at all. In the addiction model, food is actually being used for tension reduction/regulation, as a sort of sedative, in the same way that alcoholics are presumed to use alcohol. The binge eater then purges to get rid of food so as not to become fat. Purging is thus seen as the solution to the problems created by using food as a mood regulator. It is only when she realizes that her binges are out of control that the patient begins to dread eating and to feel guilty. At this point binges are not relieving—or not only relieving—but primarily guilt inducing. Purging relieves this guilt to some extent and allows the discharge of anger. It is possible that purging eventually replaces bingeing as the principle source of tension reduction (Johnson & Larson, 1982). This model is really more an affect regulation model than an addiction one. The underlying assumption is that all addictions, or substance abuse, actually reflect attempts to regulate emotions.

Woods (Woods & Brief, 1988) has discussed the relation between eating disorders and addictive behaviors, and Wilson (1991; Chapter 6, this volume) has reviewed the application of the concept of addiction to eating disorders. Both authors analyzed the relevance of such a model for disordered eating. Drug abusers and binge eaters display notable similarities in their reports of cravings, feelings of lack of control, preoccupation with the substance, repeated unsuccessful attempts to stop, denial and secrecy, use of the substance and/or related behaviors to control emotion and stress, and general impairment of social and physical functioning; these similarities have fueled the speculation that bingeing represents a variant of addiction (Wilson, 1991; Woods & Brief, 1988).

Within this addiction model, several investigators have posited that conditioning factors such as the conditioning of cephalic-phase (anticipatory physiological) responses to the sight, smell, taste, and even the thought of food can elicit conditioned insulin responses (Jansen [1990] cited in Wilson, 1991; Woods & Brief, 1988). Even affect associated with food intake can become a conditioned stimulus for physiological responses in this fashion (Booth, 1988). Woods and Brief (1988) focused on tolerance, a major aspect of drug addiction, and argued that similar mechanisms cause tolerance to drugs and a tolerance-like syndrome that accounts for some of the symptoms of eating disorders (see Wilson, Chapter 6 for a more detailed discussion). This syndrome has been cited as both evidence and explanation of addiction in binge eaters (e.g., Booth, 1988; Wilson, 1991; Woods & Brief, 1988).

Woods and Brief (1988) point out further parallels between eating and drug taking. Once eating occurs it precipitates changes in many regulated parameters, including increases in the nutrients in the blood (glucose, in particular). The body learns to anticipate when food will be eaten (when eating occurs regularly or in response to similar cues) and counters the undesirable effects of a typical meal, in which too much nutrient enters the system at one time. (We tend to eat in oversized bouts, rather than in physiologically more appropriate bits.) Cephalic-phase insulin release provides the mechanism for countering the excessive impact of a meal, by in effect creating reactive hypoglycemia, a decrease in blood glucose rather than the normal increase associated with meals. Eating, like drug taking, thus displays the sort of habitual, predictable effects that come to elicit learned anticipatory physiological responses. These reactions are normally adaptive, but they may become associated with undesirable end results such as withdrawal or reactive hypoglycemia. "It is also possible that the addicting nature of certain habits or modes of eating may predispose individuals to certain eating disorders" (Woods & Brief, 1988, p. 313). Other similarities of eating disorders to addictions are reflected in similar descriptions in the third edition, revised of the *Diagnostic and Statistical Manual of Mental Disorders* (DSM-III-R) (American Psychiatric Association, 1987). Psychological factors precipitate the disorder in both cases, but in eating disorders, weight loss and restricted eating and starvation trigger physical reactions that maintain the cycle (Woods & Brief, 1988).

Wilson (1991; Chapter 6, this volume), however, argues that the similarities between binge eaters and drug addicts are superficial and do not necessarily mean that bulimia is an addiction or substance use disorder. Wilson concludes that bulimics do not meet the tolerance, physical dependence, loss of control, or craving criteria for an addictive disorder. Wilson concludes his review by stating that the addiction model for binge eating is a "therapeutic and conceptual dead end" (Wilson, 1991).

Conditioning Model

A simpler variant of the addiction model of binge eating focuses solely on the conditioning aspects of the behavior. This model (e.g., Booth et al., 1990; Jansen, 1990) proposes that bulimia may be merely a collection of disordered habits of eating and self-perception. Dieting and bulimia may be linked through the repeated breaches of self-imposed inhibitions on food intake that characterize both; these breaches activate "the normal appetite mechanism of nutritional conditioning of stimuli to eat" (Booth et al., 1990, p. 118). Consuming a forbidden but desired food after deprivation establishes conditioned responses of cravings for food and induces a sense of loss of control. Affective triggers become conditioned stimuli for these cravings. Repeated conditioning episodes may lead to increases in the amount of food eaten, amplifying the guilt or anxiety experienced by the binge eater. Of course, only a minority of dieters respond to their self-deprivation with snacks often enough to become addicted this way. The initiating factor beyond cyclic dieting that precipitates actual bingeing could be an interaction of dieting with the emotional turmoils of sociosexual maturation (Booth et al., 1990).

Affective Disorders/Regulation Models

One model that has received considerable attention stems from the proposition that bulimia is a variant of affective disorder (Hudson, Pope, Jonas, & Yurgelun-Todd, 1983; Tobin et al., 1991). The co-occurrence of eating disorders and depression is well established (Strober & Katz, 1988). However, many researchers have argued that this association actually indicates either that eating disorders are produced by factors that may also cause depression, or that eating disorders themselves cause depression, or that changes associated with starvation or weight loss cause depression (Laessle, Schweiger, Fichter, & Pirke, 1988; Strober & Katz, 1988). Laessle and his colleagues (Laessle et al., 1988) performed a series of experiments demonstrating the cogency of these explanations of the correlation, and concluded that depression is probably not the primary disorder underlying eating disorders. Moreover, discriminant function analyses of depressive symptoms in affective disorder patients and eating disorder patients revealed a bimodal distribution of scores, with different patterns of symptomatology characterizing the two groups of patients (Cooper & Fairburn, 1986; Laessle et al., 1988).

In their review of the evidence on the association of affective and eating disorders, Strober and Katz (1988) noted that "attempts to link eating disorders. . .to affective disorders are premature and have overlooked various noncausal interpretations of their apparent association" (p. 100). They concluded that the evidence provides little if any support for the hypothesis that eating disorders are variants of affective disorder. They point to the perceptible boundaries between these disparate conditions in symptomatology, course of illness, family history, and biology. They acknowledged that the two disorders do coexist in some individuals at some times and offered four possible explanations of this coincidence. One possibility is that depression increases the risk in some personalities for weight preoccupation and eating disorder, through the enhanced sense of effectiveness that may result from dieting, which then defends against the incipient depression. The changes in appetite and even the weight loss occasionally caused by depression may increase the value of dieting, and the eating disorder may then become self-sustaining. A second potential explanation is that nutritional deficits and surfeits may potentiate neurotransmitter imbalances, resulting in depression. This may be especially likely in those with a biological predisposition to depression. The third possibility is that the stresses associated with an eating disorder may precipitate depression. Finally, some forms of eating disorders and affective disorders may have common psychological and/or biological risk factors, which increase the likelihood of co-occurrence of the two disorders (Strober & Katz, 1988). At the moment it is not possible to distinguish among these hypotheses, but they should prove fruitful for future research.

A different type of model linking binge eating and affect postulates that binge eating serves affect-regulating functions, particularly the reduction of negative affect, which then maintains the binge eating. Many have argued that binge eaters are recruited from among those individuals who somehow learn to control their dysphoria by eating, and later, for many, by purging (e.g., Beumont, 1988; Elmore & De Castro, 1990; Fairburn & Cooper, 1987; Hawkins & Clement, 1984; Herman & Polivy, 1988a; Hsu, 1990; Johnson et al., 1988; Kaye et al., 1986; Leitenberg et al., 1988; Orleans & Barnett, 1984; Rosen & Leitenberg, 1982, 1985, 1988b; Schlundt & Johnson, 1990; Thompson et al., 1987; Wilson, 1984). A variety of theories of how distress triggers binge eating were explored earlier in this chapter, so we will not repeat them here. The general model seems to be that binge eaters learn to regulate (i.e. blunt or mask) negative emotions by using eating to reduce their unpleasant affect; the precise manner of negative affect reduction—distraction, substitution, providing comfort or tension reduction, and so on—remains in dispute. Negative affect reduction reinforces eating in response to aversive feelings, establishing a conditioned pattern. Even the long-term increase in negative affect that most studies report may be integrated into stress reduction in some models, such as those that postulate a replacement or masking of the real problem with guilt and distress about overeating (e.g., Hawkins & Clement, 1984; Herman & Polivy, 1988a).

Escape Model

A psychological model of binge eating related to the affect regulation model is offered by Heatherton and Baumeister (1991). They argue that binge eaters tend to have high standards and expectations for themselves and that they are especially sensitive to the real or perceived demands of others. It thus becomes likely that they will often experience negative self-perceptions (e.g., that they have performed inadequately, let someone down, not lived up to their own or others' expectations). This aversive awareness of the self and its inadequacies generates emotional distress, including anxiety and depression. Binge eaters attempt to escape this distress by narrowing their focus of attention to their immediate physical surroundings or stimulus environment. This narrow focus prevents their dwelling on broader, more meaningful issues (such as their personal worth and prospects) and thus facilitates escape from painful self-awareness. A by-product of the refocusing of thought away from higher levels is a release of normal inhibitions on eating, which are premised on relatively complex cognitions about the benefits of long-range goals such as weight loss. Cognitive narrowing also fosters an uncritical acceptance of irrational beliefs and thoughts, such as have been shown to characterize binge eaters (Heatherton & Baumeister, 1991).

Dieting Model

It seems to be generally agreed that dieting either contributes to (Abraham & Beumont, 1982; Davis et al., 1988; Garner et al., 1985; Hawkins & Clement, 1980; Heatherton & Polivy, 1992; Herman & Polivy, 1988a; Hsu, 1990; Johnson & Connors, 1987; Lingswiler et al., 1989a; Polivy & Herman, 1985; Polivy, Herman, Olmsted, & Jazwinski, 1984; Rosen et al., 1990; Schlundt & Johnson, 1990), or at the very least exacerbates, binge eating (e.g., Orleans & Barnett, 1984; Pyle et al., 1981; Wilson, 1991). Dieting was one of the more widely acknowledged precursors to binge eating discussed in the section of this chapter on preconditions.

Dieting serves as a central cause of or contributor to binge eating in several models. For example, Herman and Polivy (1980; 1988a) posit that those individuals who choose to diet—who generally have low self-esteem and are dissatisfied with their bodies and are using dieting to improve themselves—soon encounter consequences that arise directly from food restriction. These consequences, such as hunger, frustration, and impaired sensitivity to internal cues including those signaling satiety, all contribute to binge eating. Hunger and frustration not only make food more attractive and desirable, but raise arousal levels and emotional hyperresponsiveness, which also contribute to binge eating if the eating serves to blunt affect. Binge eating, in turn, demands more dieting (or purging) to offset the effects of the calories consumed in the binge. The failure to lose weight further lowers self-esteem, so that the cycle often becomes self-perpetuating.

Heatherton and Polivy (1992) formalized this model recently into what they refer to as a "spiral model" of dieting's effects on binge eating. They point out that individuals with high standards (or low self-evaluations) for body weight and shape tend to undertake dieting, restraining their intake in order to achieve their goal of weight loss and a thinner physique. Unfortunately, such diets are rarely successful. Dieters are prone to episodes of overeating in response to various triggers, and weight either remains stable (Heatherton, Polivy, & Herman, 1991) or even rises somewhat (Polivy & Herman, 1991). Individuals who persist in their attempts to diet thus experience more and more of these episodes of dietary failure, lowering their self-esteem, increasing their negative affect, and enhancing their susceptibility to dietary disinhibition and further failure. This negative spiral promotes the development of chronic binge eating or eating disorders in those with debilitating personality deficits that predispose them to psychopathological disorder.

A related model of binge eating hypothesizes that overweight or unassertiveness leads to a negative self-image, which in turn leads to dieting. Dieting increases the potential for losing control of one's impulses to overeat or for becoming preoccupied with food and dieting, which eventually may lead to binge eating (Hawkins & Clement, 1984).

Biopsychosocial Models

Dieting is just one of the factors incorporated into a group of more complex models of binge-eating behavior that combine biological–genetic, psychological, and social–environmental variables into a biopsychosocial causal structure. Garner et al. (1985) offered one of the earlier combinatory models, arguing that therapy for binge eating must focus on all of these factors because the evidence indicates that all are contributing in interconnected ways to the problem behavior. They discuss how for the past few decades, women have been victimized by unrealistically thin standards of appearance, a glorification of a youthful (read-slender) appearance, and a serious prejudice against fatness, placing them under intense pressure to diet and/or exercise in order to become thin (social–environmental factor). They go on to review the evidence showing that body weight generally resists change because it is defended physiologically around a set point; deviations from this defended weight trigger compensatory physiological mechanisms that attempt to return the person to their original, defended body weight (biological factor). Dieting is thus not an effective means of weight control, because it is usually opposed by these biological defenses of weight; of course, for most women the defended weight is higher than the current cultural ideal. Restrictive dieting provokes binge eating, and then vomiting, in the manner described above. Bingeing and vomiting escalate, since the vomiting allows the dieter to continue to give in to her urge to eat without having to worry about weight gain.

Johnson and Connors (1987) offer an even more intricate model, which requires over 300 pages to explicate. Basically, they propose that biogenetic predispositions such as a genetic risk for developing affective disorder combine with familial factors and sociocultural pressures toward high achievement and thinness to promote a character structure featuring affective instability and low self-esteem. When such an individual then tries to achieve thinness and all its alleged benefits, through dieting, the underlying affective instability is heightened, generating an enhanced susceptibility to disruptive events such as failure of any kind. These events trigger binge eating, panic about weight gain, and purging, which then cycles back into dieting.

Hsu (1990) maintains that ''dieting provides the entrée into an eating disorder'' (p. 77), but ''since the majority of those who embark on a diet do *not* develop an eating disorder. . . genetic, psychological, biological, personality and family factors may increase the vulnerability of a dieting individual to an eating disorder'' (p. 78). Hsu goes on to analyze the increasing adiposity of North Americans at a time when cultural preference for a slender physique has become more intense; this discrepancy produces an ever-greater need to diet in order to conform to societal ideals. The turmoil and stress of adolescence are further contributors, as is the precarious self-concept and body image, and the often-agonizing adolescent search for identity. Genetic influence, personality and psychodynamics, and familial influences are the other variables that interact with dieting to yield binge eating and eating disorders in Hsu's model.

Another integrated model is based on a systems perspective, which takes into account the interaction of biological, psychological, and environmental variables to produce symptoms or disorders such as binge eating (Schlundt & Johnson, 1990). These authors evaluate the contribution of biological, cognitive, emotional, and environmental influences on binge eating and derive a biopsychosocial functionalist model. They point out that the consequences of one behavior are often the antecedents of the next in the series. In the case of binge eating, antecedents are environmental (e.g., situational cues, social relationship systems), behavioral (e.g., previous eating or dieting, ongoing activity), cognitive (e.g., knowledge of food and dieting, expectations, body image), emotional (e.g., mood, psychopathology), and physiological (e.g., blood levels of nutrients, hunger, hormones, neurochemicals). These antecedents affect behaviors such as binge eating, fear of fat, purging, and dieting, which in turn have consequences in the same domains as the antecedent variables, and eventually have an impact on those antecedents.

Finally, a recent biopsychosocial model postulates that binge eating is a heterogeneously determined disorder with psychological, biological, familial, and sociocultural factors interacting (Tobin et al., 1991).

Factors such as family history and biology combine to place an individual at increased risk for low self-esteem, low self-efficacy, and affective instability. Adding a sociocultural preference for thinness onto this substrate encourages dieting, which leads to weight loss and hunger. Inevitably restraint breaks down and bingeing begins. Binge eating generates concern about weight gain, though, so purging starts. Bingeing and purging have negative effects on self-efficacy, self-esteem, and chronic mood, leading to yet more restraint. The result is a cyclic pathway with multiple entry sites. This model has the advantage of accommodating most of the previous unidimensional models of binge eating.

Conclusions

Of the models proposed to account for binge eating, the integrated biopsychosocial ones seem to hold out the most promise and explain the most data. The addiction model seems to have been effectively discounted by recent analysis (Wilson, 1991), as has the bulimia-as-a-variant-of-depression model (Cooper & Fairburn, 1986; Laessle et al., 1988; Strober & Katz, 1988). The conditioning model, the affective self-regulation model, and the dieting model all seem to be subsumed in the biopsychosocial models.

Although the biopsychosocial models have the virtue of inclusiveness, they all tend to blur the various causal elements into a comprehensive melange that lacks specificity. Everything is included, but at the expense of not differentiating between more and less important contributors to bingeing. These models are not especially effective at encouraging empirical research, and leave one with the impression that by including all the relevant variables, we have arrived at an explanation.

Perhaps more problematic is the fact, often lost in discussions of these models, that the biopsychosocial models—perhaps more than any of the other more specific models that have been criticized as incomplete, one sided, or inaccurate—are actually models of the binge eating syndrome (or bulimia nervosa), rather than models of binge eating per se. The biopsychosocial models explain how one becomes (and remains) a binge eater, but they do not do an adequate job of describing—let alone explaining—particular binge episodes. They deal mainly with preconditions and consequences, and have little to say about triggers, and less to say about maintaining and terminating factors. The question of who will become a binge eater is important and interesting, but it does not supplant the equally important and interesting questions regarding the behavioral analysis of the binge-eating episode.

The models all seem to attempt to organize at least some of the components of binge-eating episodes discussed here into an etiological or causal string. Unfortunately, the complex nature of the phenomenon—that is, the fact that we are dealing with a human disorder—dictates that we have access in most instances only to correlational data, making causal modeling difficult to confirm. In addition, the five stages of binge eating are all interrelated, so factors influence one another at different phases of the behavioral pattern. By examining the psychological elements at each stage of binge eating, we may eventually be able to understand more fully both the factors that contribute to the development of the syndrome in particular individuals and the conditions surrounding binge-eating behavior itself.

Even without adequate causal models for binge eating, analysis of the stages of bingeing described here can be clinically useful by improving the treatment of binge eating. Currently, therapeutic interventions tend to mirror etiological discussions, focusing generally on the personality and behavioral preconditions as well as the more distressing consequences, but paying little attention to specific triggering, maintaining and terminating factors. An understanding of all of the phases of binge eating, and the distinctions between such factors as proximate versus distal eliciting mechanisms, could provide a more complete and systematic framework for an integrated cognitive, behavioral, and experiential therapy. For example, experiential analysis of emotional preconditions (e.g., low self-esteem) and triggers (e.g., acute distress) could be combined with cognitive interventions targeting both preconditions (e.g., overvaluation of thinness) and triggers (e.g., all-or-nothing thinking, abstinence violation) and with behavioral change techniques focused on maintaining and terminating variables. A clearer analysis of the components of the bingeing cycle should clarify, in turn, the tasks of therapy.

REFERENCES

Abraham, S. F., & Beumont, P. J. V. (1982). How patients describe bulimia or binge eating. *Psychological Medicine, 12,* 625–635.

American Psychiatric Association. (1987). *Diagnostic and statistical manual of mental disorders* (3rd ed., rev.). Washington, DC: Author.

Baucom, D. H., & Aiken, P. A. (1981). Effect of depressed mood on eating among obese and nonobese dieting and nondieting persons. *Journal of Personality and Social Psychology, 41,* 577–585.

Beumont, P. J. V. (1988). Bulimia: Symptoms, syndrome, and predicament. In K. M. Pirke, W. Vandereycken, & D. Ploog (Eds.), *The psychobiology of bulimia nervosa* (pp. 2–9). Berlin: Springer-Verlag.

Booth, D. A. (1988). Culturally corralled into food abuse: The eating disorders as physiologically reinforced excessive appetites. In K. M. Pirke, W. Vandereycken, & D. Ploog (Eds.), *The psychobiology of bulimia nervosa* (pp. 18–32). Berlin: Springer-Verlag.

Booth, D. A., Lewis, V. J., & Blair, A. J. (1990). Dietary restraint and binge eating: Pseudo-quantitative anthropology for a medicalised problem habit? *Appetite, 14,* 116–119.

Branch, C. H. H., & Eurman, L. J. (1980). Social attitudes toward patients with anorexia nervosa. *American Journal of Psychiatry, 137,* 631–632.

Cash, T. F., & Brown, T. A. (1987). Body image in anorexia nervosa and bulimia nervosa: A review of the literature. *Behavior Modification, 11,* 487–521.

Cooper, P. J., & Fairburn, C. G. (1986). The depressive symptoms of bulimia nervosa. *British Journal of Psychiatry, 148,* 268–274.

Davis, R., Freeman, R. J., & Garner, D. M. (1988). A naturalistic investigation of eating behavior in bulimia nervosa. *Journal of Consulting and Clinical Psychology, 56,* 273–279.

De Castro, J. (1990). Social facilitation of duration and size but not rate of the spontaneous meal intake of humans. *Physiology and Behavior, 47,* 1129–1135.

Dykens, E. M., & Gerrard, M. (1986). Psychological profiles of purging bulimics, repeat dieters, and controls. *Journal of Consulting and Clinical Psychology, 54,* 283–288.

Edwards, F. E., & Nagelberg, D. B. (1986). Personality characteristics of restrained/binge eaters versus unrestrained/nonbinge eaters. *Addictive Behaviors, 11,* 207–211.

Eldredge, K., Wilson, G. T., & Whaley, A. (1990). Failure, self-evaluation, and feeling fat in women. *International Journal of Eating Disorders, 9,* 37–50.

Elmore, D. K. & De Castro, J. M. (1990). Self-rated moods and hunger in relation to spontaneous eating behavior in bulimics, recovered bulimics, and normals. *International Journal of Eating Disorders, 9,* 179–190.

Fairburn, C. G., & Cooper, Z. (1987). Behavioral and cognitive approaches to the treatment of anorexia nervosa and bulimia nervosa. In P. J. V. Beamont, G. D. Burrows, & R. C. Casper (Eds.). *Handbook of eating disorders* (pp. 271–298). Amsterdam: Elsevier.

Fairburn, C. G., & Garner, D. M. (1986). The diagnosis of bulimia nervosa. *International Journal of Eating Disorders, 5,* 403–419.

Frost, R. O., Goolkasian, G. A., Ely, R. J., & Blanchard, F. A. (1982). Depression, restraint, and eating behavior. *Behavior Research and Therapy, 20,* 113–121.

Garfinkel, P. E., & Garner, D. M. (1982). *Anorexia nervosa: A multidimensional perspective* New York: Brunner/Mazel.

Garfinkel, P. E., Goldbloom, D., Davis, R., Olmsted, M. P., Garner, D. M., & Halmi, K. A. (1992). Body dissatisfaction in Bulimia Nervosa: Relationship to weight and shape concerns and psychological functioning. *International Journal of Eating Disorders, 11,* 151–161.

Garner, D. M. & Bemis, K. M. (1985). Cognitive therapy for anorexia nervosa. In D. M. Garner & P. E. Garfinkel (Eds.), *Handbook of psychotherapy for anorexia nervosa and bulimia* (pp. 107–146). New York: Guilford Press.

Garner, D. M., Garfinkel, P. E., & Bonato, D. P. (1987). Body image measurement in eating disorders. *Advances in Psychosomatic Medicine, 17,* 119–133.

Garner, D. M., Rockert, W., Olmsted, M. P., Johnson, C., & Coscina, D. V. (1985). Psychoeducational principles in the treatment of bulimia and anorexia nervosa. In D. M. Garner & P. E. Garfinkel (Eds.), *Handbook of psychotherapy for anorexia nervosa and bulimia* (pp. 513–572). New York: Guilford Press.

Hawkins, R. C., & Clement, P. F. (1980). Development and construct validation of a self-report measure of binge-eating tendencies. *Addictive Behaviors, 5,* 219–226.

Hawkins, R. C., & Clement, P. F. (1984). Binge eating: Measurement problems and a conceptual model. In R. C. Hawkins, W. J. Fremouw, & P. F. Clement (Eds.), *The binge-purge syndrome* (pp. 229–251). New York: Springer.

Hawkins, R. C., Turell, S., & Jackson, L. J. (1983). Desirable and undesirable masculine and feminine traits in relation to students' dieting tendencies and body image dissatisfaction. *Sex Roles, 9,* 705–718.

Heatherton, T. F., & Baumeister, R. F. (1991). Binge-eating as escape from self-awareness. *Psychological Bulletin, 110,* 86–108.

Heatherton, T. F., Herman, C. P., & Polivy, J. (1991). Effects of physical threat and ego threat on eating behavior. *Journal of Personality and Social Psychology, 60,* 138–143.

Heatherton, T. F., & Polivy, J. (1992). Chronic dieting and eating disorders: A spiral model. In J. Crowther, S. E. Hobfall, M. A. P. Stephens, & D. L. Tennenbaum (Eds.), *The etiology of bulimia: The individual and familial context* (pp. 133–155). Washington, DC: Hemisphere.

Heatherton, T. F., Polivy, J., & Herman, C. P. (1991). Restraint, weight loss and variability of body weight. *Journal of Abnormal Psychology, 100,* 78–83.

Herman, C. P., & Mack, D. (1975). Restrained and unrestrained eating. *Journal of Personality, 43,* 647–660.

Herman, C. P., & Polivy, J. (1975). Anxiety, restraint, and eating behavior. *Journal of Abnormal Psychology, 84,* 666–672.

Herman, C. P., & Polivy, J. (1980). Restrained eating. In A. Stunkard (Ed.), *Obesity* (pp. 208–225). Philadelphia: Saunders.

Herman, C. P., & Polivy, J. (1988a). Excess and restraint in bulimia. In K. Pirke, W. Vandereycken, & D. Ploog (Eds.), *The psychobiology of bulimia* (pp. 33–41). Munich: Springer-Verlag.

Herman, C. P., & Polivy, J. (1988b). Studies of eating in normal dieters. In B. T. Walsh (Ed.), *Eating Behavior in Eating Disorders* (pp. 95–112). Washington, DC: American Psychiatric Association Press.

Herman, C. P., Polivy, J., & Heatherton, T. F. (1991). *Effects of distress on eating: Meta-analysis of the experimental literature.* Unpublished manuscript, University of Toronto.

Herman, C. P., Polivy, J., Lank, C., & Heatherton, T. F. (1987). Anxiety, hunger and eating. *Journal of Abnormal Psychology, 96,* 264–269.

Herman, C. P., Polivy, J., & Silver, R. (1979). Effects of an observer on eating behavior: The induction of "sensible" eating. *Journal of Personality, 47,* 85–99.

Hsu, L. K. G. (1990). *Eating disorders.* New York: Guilford Press.

Hudson, J. I., Pope, H. G., Jonas, J. M., & Yurgelun-Todd, D. (1983). Phenomenologic relationship of eating disorders to major affective disorder. *Psychiatry Research, 9,* 345–354.

Humphrey, L. L. (1986). Structural analysis of parent–child relationships in eating disorders. *Journal of Abnormal Psychology, 95,* 395–402.

Humphrey, L. L. (1987). Comparison of bulimic–anorexic and nondistressed families using structural analysis of social behavior. *Journal of the American Academy of Child and Adolescent Psychiatry, 26*, 248–255.

Jakobovits, C., Halstead, P., Kelley, L., Roe, D. A., & Young, C. M. (1977). Eating habits and nutrient intake of college women over a thirty-year period. *Journal of the American Dietetic Association, 71*, 405–411.

Jansen, A., Merckelbach, H., Oosterlaan, J., Tuiten, A., & Van den Hout, M. (1988). Cognitions and self-talk during food intake of restrained and unrestrained eaters. *Behaviour Research and Therapy, 26*, 393–398.

Jansen, A., Van den Hout, M., & Griez, E. (1990). Clinical and non-clinical binges. *Behaviour Research and Therapy, 28*, 439–444.

Johnson, C., & Connors, M. E. (1987). *The etiology and treatment of bulimia nervosa.* New York: Basic Books.

Johnson, C., Connors, M. E., & Tobin, D. L. (1987). Symptom management of bulimia. *Journal of Consulting & Clinical Psychology, 55*, 668–676.

Johnson, C., & Larson, R. (1982). Bulimia: An analysis of moods and behavior. *Psychosomatic Medicine, 44*, 341–351.

Johnson, C., Steinberg, S., & Lewis, C. (1988). Bulimia. In K. Clark, R. Parr, & W. Castelli (Eds.), *Evaluation and management of eating disorders.* Champaign, IL: Life Enhancement Publications.

Josephs, R. A., & Steele, C. M. (1990). The two faces of alcohol myopia: Attentional mediation of psychological stress. *Journal of Abnormal Psychology, 99*,115–126.

Kales, E. F. (1989). A laboratory study of cognitive factors in bulimia. *Annals of the New York Academy of Sciences, 575*, 535–537.

Kales, E. F. (1990). Macronutrient analysis of binge eating in bulimia. *Physiology and Behavior, 48*, 837–840.

Kaye, W. H., Gwirtzman, H. E., George, D. T., Weiss, S. R., & Jimerson, D. C. (1986). Relationship of mood alterations to bingeing behavior in bulimia. *British Journal of Psychiatry, 149*, 479–485.

King, G., Herman, C. P., & Polivy, J. (1987). Food perception in dieters and non-dieters. *Appetite, 8*, 147–158.

Klesges, R. C., Klem, M. L., & Bene, C. R. (1989). Effects of dietary restraint, obesity, and gender on holiday eating behavior and weight gain. *Journal of Abnormal Psychology, 98*, 499–503.

Knight, L., & Boland, F. (1989). Restrained eating: An experimental disentanglement of the disinhibiting variables of calories and food type. *Journal of Abnormal Psychology, 98*, 412–420.

Laessle, R. G., Schweiger, U., Fichter, M. M., & Pirke, K. M. (1988). Eating disorders and depression: Psychobiological findings in bulimia and anorexia nervosa. In K. M. Pirke, W. Vandereycken, & D. Ploog (Eds.), *The psychobiology of bulimia nervosa* (pp. 90–100). Berlin: Springer-Verlag.

Leitenberg, H., Rosen, J. C., Gross, J., Nudelman, S., & Vara, L. (1988). Exposure plus response-prevention treatment of bulimia nervosa. *Journal of Consulting and Clinical Psychology, 56*, 535–541.

Lingswiler, V. M., Crowther, J. H., & Stephens, M. A. P. (1989a). Affective and cognitive antecedents to eating episodes in bulimia and binge eating. *International Journal of Eating Disorders, 8*, 533–539.

Lingswiler, V. M., Crowther, J. H., & Stephens, M. A. P. (1989b). Emotional and somatic consequences of binge episodes. *Addictive Behaviors, 14*, 503–511.

Marlatt, G. A., Gordon, J. R. (Eds.). (1985). *Relapse prevention: Maintenance strategies in the treatment of addictive behaviors.* New York: Guilford Press.

Marlatt, G. A., & Gordon, J. R. (Eds.). (1980). *Determinants of relapse: Implications for the maintenance of behavior change.* New York: Brunner/Mazel.

Mayhew, R., & Edelmann, R. J. (1989). Self-esteem, irrational beliefs and coping strategies in relation to eating problems in a non-clinical sample. *Personality and Individual Differences, 10*, 581–584.

Miller, T. M., Coffman, J. G., & Linke, R. A. (1980). Survey on body image, weight, and diet of college students. *Journal of the American Dietetic Association, 77*, 561–566.

Mitchell, J. E., Hatsukami, D., Eckert, E., & Pyle, R. L. (1985). Characteristics of 275 patients with bulimia. *American Journal of Psychiatry, 142*, 482–485.

Mitchell, J. E., Pyle, R. L., & Eckert, E. D. (1981). Frequency and duration of binge-eating episodes in patients with bulimia. *American Journal of Psychiatry 138*, 835–836.

Mizes, J. S. (1988). Personality characteristics of bulimic and non-eating-disordered female controls: A cognitive behavioral perspective. *International Journal of Eating Disorders, 7*, 541–550.

Orleans, C. T., & Barnett, L. R. (1984). Bulimarexia: Guidelines for behavioral assessment and treatment. In R. C. Hawkins, W. J. Fremouw, & P. F. Clement (Eds.), *The binge#purge syndrome: Diagnosis, treatment and research* (pp. 144–177). New York: Springer.

Polivy, J. (1976). Perception of calories and regulation of intake in restrained and unrestrained subjects. *Addictive Behaviors, 1*, 237–244.

Polivy, J., Garner, D. M., & Garfinkel, P. E. (1986). Thinness and social behavior. In C. P. Herman, M. P. Zanna, & E. T. Higgins (Eds.), *Physical appearance, stigma, and social behavior: The Ontario symposium* (Vol. 3, pp. 89–112). Hillsdale, NJ: Erlbaum.

Polivy, J., Heatherton, T. F., & Herman, C. P. (1988). Self-esteem, restraint, and eating behavior. *Journal of Abnormal Psychology, 97*, 354–356.

Polivy, J., & Herman, C. P. (1976a). Clinical depression and weight change: A complex relation. *Journal of Abnormal Psychology, 85*, 338–340.

Polivy, J., & Herman, C. P. (1976b). The effects of alcohol on eating behavior: Disinhibition or sedation. *Addictive Behaviors, 1*, 121–125.

Polivy, J., & Herman, C. P. (1976c). Effects of alcohol on eating behavior: Influences of mood and perceived intoxication. *Journal of Abnormal Psychology, 85*, 601–606.

Polivy, J., & Herman, C. P. (1985). Dieting and binging: A causal analysis. *American Psychologist, 40*, 193–201.

Polivy, J., & Herman, C. P. (1987). The diagnosis and treatment of normal eating. *Journal of Consulting and Clinical Psychology, 55*, 635–644.

Polivy, J., & Herman, C. P. (1991). Good and bad dieters: Self-perception and reaction to a dietary challenge. *International Journal of Eating Disorders, 10*, 91–99.

Polivy, J., Herman, C. P., Hackett, R., & Kuleshnyk, I. (1986). The effects of self-attention and public attention on eating in restrained and unrestrained subjects. *Journal of Personality and Social Psychology, 50,* 1203–1224.

Polivy, J., Herman, C. P., Olmsted, M. P., & Jazwinski, C. (1984). Restraint and binge eating. In R. C. Hawkins, W. J. Fremouw, & P. F. Clement (Eds.), *The binge-purge syndrome* (pp. 104–122). New York: Springer.

Polivy, J., Herman, C. P., & Pliner, P. (1990). Perception and evaluation of body image: The meaning of body shape and size. In J. M. Olson & M. P. Zanna (Eds.), *Self-inference processes: The Ontario symposium* (pp. 87–114). Hillsdale, NJ: Erlbaum.

Pyle, R. L., Mitchell, J. E., & Eckert, E. D. (1981). Bulimia: A report of 34 cases. *Journal of Clinical Psychiatry, 42,* 60–64.

Rosen, J. C., & Gross, J. (1987). Prevalence of weight reducing and weight gaining in adolescent girls and boys. *Health Psychology, 6,* 131–147.

Rosen, J. C., Gross, J., & Vara, L. (1987). Psychological adjustment of adolescents attempting to lose or gain weight. *Journal of Consulting and Clinical Psychology, 55,* 742–747.

Rosen, J. C., & Leitenberg, H. (1982). Bulimia Nervosa: Treatment with exposure and response prevention. *Behavior Therapy, 13,* 117–124.

Rosen, J. C., & Leitenberg, H. (1985). Exposure plus response prevention treatment of bulimia nervosa. In D. M. Garner & P. E. Garfinkel (Eds.), *Handbook of psychotherapy for anorexia nervosa and bulimia* (pp. 193–212). New York: Guilford Press.

Rosen, J. C., & Leitenberg, H. (1988a). The anxiety model of Bulimia Nervosa and treatment with exposure plus response prevention. In K. M. Pirke, W. Vandereycken, & D. Ploog (Eds.), *The psychobiology of bulimia nervosa* (pp. 146–150). Heidelberg: Springer-Verlag.

Rosen, J. C., & Leitenberg, H. (1988b). Eating behavior in bulimia nervosa. In B. T. Walsh (Ed.), *Eating behavior in eating disorders* (pp. 161–173). Washington, DC: American Psychiatric Press.

Rosen, J. C., Leitenberg, H., Fisher, C., & Khazam, C. (1986). Binge-eating episodes in bulimia nervosa: The amount and type of food consumed. *International Journal of Eating Disorders, 5,* 255–267.

Rosen, J. C., Tacy, B., & Howell, D. (1990). Life stress, psychological symptoms and weight reducing behavior in adolescent girls: A prospecitve analysis. *International Journal of Eating Disorders, 9,* 17–26.

Rossiter, E. M., Agras, W. S., Telch, C. F., & Bruce, B. (1992). The eating patterns of non-purging bulimic subjects. *International Journal of Eating Disorders, 11,* 111–120.

Roth, G. (1989). *Feeding the hungry heart.* New York: NAL Dutton.

Ruderman, A. (1985a). Dysphoric mood and overeating. *Journal of Abnormal Psychology, 94,* 78–85.

Ruderman, A. J. (1985b). Restraint and irrational cognitions. *Behavior Research and Therapy, 23,* 557–561.

Ruderman, A. J. (1986). Dietary restraint: A theoretical and empirical review. *Psychological Bulletin, 99,* 247–262.

Ruderman, A. J., Belzer, L. J., & Halperin, A. (1985). Restraint, anticipated consumption, and overeating. *Journal of Abnormal Psychology, 94,* 547–555.

Ruderman, A. J., & Grace, P. S. (1987). Restraint, bulimia, and psychopathology. *Addictive Behaviors, 12,* 249–255.

Ruderman, A. J., & Grace, P. S. (1988). Bulimics and restrained eaters: A personality comparison. *Addictive Behaviors, 13,* 359–368.

Schlundt, D. G., & Johnson, W. G. (1990). *Eating disorders: Assessment and treatment.* Boston: Allyn & Bacon.

Schotte, D. E., Cools, J., & McNally, R. J. (1990). Induced anxiety triggers overeating in restrained eaters. *Journal of Abnormal Psychology, 99,* 317–320.

Silverstein, B., & Perdue, L. (1988). The relationship between role concerns, preferences for slimness, and symptoms of eating problems among college women. *Sex Roles, 18,* 101–106.

Silverstein, B., Peterson, B., & Perdue, L. (1986). Some correlates of the thin standard of bodily attractiveness for women. *International Journal of Eating Disorders, 5,* 895–905.

Slochower, J. (1983). *Excessive eating: The role of emotions and environment.* New York: Human Sciences Press.

Spencer, J. A., & Fremouw, W. J. (1979). Binge eating as a function of restraint and weight classification. *Journal of Abnormal Psychology, 88,* 262–267.

Steinberg, S., Tobin, D., & Johnson, C. (1989). The role of bulimic behaviors in affect regulation: Different functions for different patient subgroups? *International Journal of Eating Disorders, 9,* 51–55.

Striegel-Moore, R., Silberstein, L., Frensch, P., & Rodin, J. (1989). A prospective study of disordered eating among college students. *International Journal of Eating Disorders, 8,* 499–509.

Striegel-Moore, R. H., Silberstein, L. R., & Rodin, J. (1986). Toward an understanding of risk factors for bulimia. *American Psychologist, 41,* 246–263.

Strober, M., & Humphrey, L. L. (1987). Familial contributions to the etiology and course of anorexia nervosa and bulimia. *Journal of Consulting and Clinical Psychology, 55,* 654–659.

Strober, M., & Katz, J. L. (1988). Depression in the eating disorders: A review and analysis of descriptive, family and biological findings. In D. M. Garner & P. E. Garfinkel (Eds.), *Diagnostic issues in anorexia nervosa and bulimia nervosa* (pp. 80–111). New York: Brunner/Mazel.

Thompson, D. A., Berg, K. M., & Shatford, L. A. (1987). The heterogeneity of bulimic symptomatology. *International Journal of Eating Disorders, 6,* 215–234.

Tobin, D. L., Johnson, C., Steinberg, S., Staats, M., & Dennis, A. B. (1991). Multifactorial assessment of bulimia nervosa. *Journal of Abnormal Psychology, 100,* 14–21.

Tomarken, A. J., & Kirschenbaum, D. S. (1984). Effects of plans for future meals on counter-regulatory eating by restrained eaters. *Journal of Abnormal Psychology, 93,* 458–472.

Tuschl, R. J., Laessle, R. G., Kotthaus, B. C., & Pirke, K. M. (1989). Behavioral and biological correlates of restrained eating. *Annals of the New York Academy of Sciences, 575,* 580–581.

Tuschl, R. J., Platte, P., Laessle, R. G., Stichler, W., & Pirke, K. M. (1990). Energy expenditure and everyday eating behavior in healthy young women. *American Journal of Clinical Nutrition, 52,* 81–86.

Wardle, J., & Beales, S. (1988). Control and loss of control over eating: An experimental investigation. *Journal of Abnormal Psychology, 97,* 35–40.

Williamson, D. A. (1990). *Assessment of eating disorders: Obesity, anorexia and bulimia nervosa.* New York: Pergamon Press.

Willmuth, M. E., Leitenberg, H., Rosen, J. C., & Cado, S. (1988). A comparison of purging and nonpurging normal weight bulimics. *International Journal of Eating Disorders, 7,* 825–835.

Wilson, G. T. (1984). Toward the understanding and treatment of binge eating. In R. C. Hawkins, W. J. Fremouw, & P. F. Clement (Eds.), *The binge#purge syndrome* (pp. 264–289). New York: Springer.

Wilson, G. T. (1991). The addiction model of eating disorders: A critical analysis. *Advances in Behaviour Research and Therapy, 13,* 27–72.

Woods, S. C., & Brief, D. J. (1988). Physiological factors. In D. M. Donovan & G. A. Marlatt (Eds.), *Assessment of addictive behaviors* (pp. 296–322). New York: Guilford Press.

Woody, E., Costanzo, P., Leifer, H., & Conger, J. (1981). The effects of taste and caloric perceptions on the eating behavior of restrained and unrestrained subjects. *Cognitive Therapy and Research, 5,* 381–390.

Yates, A., Leehey, K., & Shisslak, C. M. (1983). Running—an analogue of anorexia nervosa? *New England Journal of Medicine, 308,* 251–255.

Zotter, D. L., & Crowther, J. H. (1991). The role of cognitions in bulimia nervosa. *Cognitive Therapy and Research, 15,* 413–426.

Binge Eating: Psychobiological Mechanisms

John E. Blundell
Andrew J. Hill

Within the domain of clinicians interested in eating disorders it is now agreed that a binge has two major properties: loss of control (difficulty in preventing an urge to initiate eating or failure to bring an episode of eating to a close) and the consumption of an objectively large amount of food (inappropriate for the circumstances)—see Fairburn and Wilson (Chapter 1, this volume). Similarly, among researchers working on appetite control it is generally regarded that mechanisms exist to control the onset and termination of episodes of eating and to limit the amount of food consumed to biologically appropriate quantities. It follows that it is worth considering the extent to which binge eating involves a failure or weakness of the biological mechanisms for the control of appetite. Initially certain characteristics of the biological processes underlying the expression of human appetite will be set out. This will permit an evaluation of three issues related to binge eating:

1. Understanding the topography and structure of a binge
2. Defining mechanisms which may be weak or dysregulated
3. Elucidating predisposing factors that create vulnerability for the occurrence of a binge

It should of course be kept in mind that mechanisms of appetite control are linked to the processes of body weight regulation. It follows that the properties of the system of weight regulation (working through appetite control mechanisms) may throw light upon the apparent ease with which binge eating can be prompted.

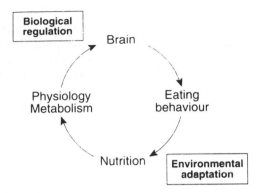

FIGURE 10.1. Outline of a system indicating the interaction between various components contributing to the expression of appetite. The system indicates that eating is adjusted in the interests of biological regulation and environmental adaptation.

REGULATORY PROPERTIES

The biology of appetite includes the operation of eating itself, motivational states that accompany feeding, peripheral physiological and metabolic processes, brain pathways and receptors, together with the nutritional influence on all of these domains. Behavior and nutrition are biological entities just as much as glands, secretions, and organs. If normal functioning can be described, then it may allow a better appreciation of disorderly or dysregulated appetite. Initially the expression of human appetite can be perceived as including a drive for energy, conscious sensations of hunger, preferences for particular tastes, selection of specific nutrients, cravings for certain foods, and a pattern of eating behavior. This pattern can be described as a profile of meals and snacks and the intervals between these eating episodes. A knowledge of the mechanisms that influence these parameters should help us to comprehend abnormalities of body weight, eating disorders and their treatments, together with the phenomenon of dieting.

Appetite can be considered as a phenomenon that links biological happenings (under the skin) with environmental events (beyond the skin). Indeed, the expression of appetite can be viewed as the end product of an intimate interaction between physiology and the environment (e.g., Blundell & Hill, 1986). The diagram in Figure 10.1 illustrates how appetite is shaped by the principles of biological regulation and environmental adaptation. On one hand all living organisms require food (a nutritional supply) for growth and maintenance of tissues. This supply is achieved through behavior (commonly called eating). The expression of this behavior is controlled according to the state of the biological system. A complex system of signals operates to ensure the appropriate direction and quality of this (eating) behavior. The extension of Claude Bernard's principle of homeostasis to include behavior is often referred to as the behavioral regulation of internal states (Richter, 1943). However, the expression of behavior is also subject to environmental demands and behavior is therefore adapted in the face of particular circumstances.

In the case of human appetite, consideration should be given to the conscious and deliberate (external) control over behavior. Human beings can decide to alter their own behavior (eating) in order to meet particular objectives, for example, a display of moral conviction (political hunger strike) or a demonstration of aesthetic achievement (dieting). In both of these cases eating is curtailed with an ensuing interruption of the nutritional supply. The regulatory properties of the system will tend to oppose this undersupply and generate a drive to eat. In the technically advanced cultures of Europe and the United States the nutritional supply may be adjusted by the environment in another way. The existence of an abundant supply of palatable, high-energy dense food promotes overconsumption. This in turn (in an interaction with genetic susceptibility) leads to an increase in fat deposition (Bouchard, 1985). However, this oversupply of calories leading to deposition of fat does not generate a biological drive to undereat. Hence, the operation of the regulatory system is not symmetrical: There is a strong defense against undernutrition and only weak response to the effects of overnutrition. These features may have important implications for binge eating. Attempts to suppress eating, as in dieting, will generate strong urges to initiate eating (biological defense) while any vicarious gain in body weight (which may promote bodily dissatisfaction) will not help to suppress appetite.

The biological drive to eat can be linked with the satiating power of food. "Satiating power" or "satiating efficiency" is the term applied to the capacity of any consumed food to suppress hunger and to inhibit the onset of a further period of eating (Kissileff, 1984; Blundell, Rogers, & Hill, 1987). Food brings about this effect by way of certain mediating processes that can be roughly classified as sensory, cognitive, postingestive, and postabsorptive (see Figure 10.2). The operation of these processes is generated by the impact of food on physiological and biochemical mechanisms. Collectively these processes have been referred to as the satiety cascade (Blundell, Hill, & Rogers, 1988). The way in which food is sensed and processed by the biological system generates signals (neural and humoral) that are utilized for the control of appetite. It follows that any self-imposed or externally applied reduction in the food supply (creating a caloric deficit) will weaken the satiating power of food.

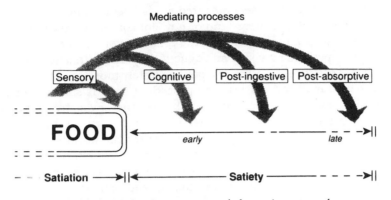

FIGURE 10.2. Components of the satiety cascade.

One consequence of this will be the failure of food to adequately suppress hunger (the biological drive). The satiety cascade appears to operate as efficiently in obese people as in lean individuals. Hence, a normal appetite response to a reduced calorie intake is evident in obese subjects.

Technically, satiety can be defined as that inhibition of hunger and eating that arises as a consequence of food consumption. It can be distinguished from satiation, which is the process that brings a period of eating to a halt. Consequently satiation and satiety act conjointly to largely determine the pattern of eating behavior and the accompanying profile of motivation. The conscious sensation of hunger is one index of motivation and reflects the strength of satiation and satiety. It is worth keeping in mind that hunger is a biologically useful sensation. It is a nagging, irritating feeling that prompts thoughts of food and reminds us that the body needs energy. The identification and management of hunger are important factors underlying normal appetite function and abnormalities of appetite and body weight. In turn, the cycle of hunger and its relationship to eating can be used as a marker of regulation or dysregulation.

NUTRITION AND SATIETY

The concept of the satiety cascade implies that foods of varying nutritional composition will engage differently with the mediating processes and will therefore exert differing effects upon satiation and satiety. There is considerable interest in whether the macronutrients—protein, fat, and carbohydrates—differ in satiating efficiency.

A procedure widely used to assess the action of food on satiety is the preload strategy. Precisely prepared foods (identical in taste and appearance but varying in energy and/or nutrient composition) can be consumed in the preload. The effects of the consumption are then measured over varying periods by visual analogue rating scales (to assess hunger and other sensations), food checklists, accurately monitored test meals, and, if necessary, food diaries. The procedure sounds simple, but the conduct of such experiments needs to be governed by a strong methodology to prevent incidental features interfering with the monitoring process. For example, it is important to prevent the occurrence of any appetite-modulating stimuli occurring during the interval between preload and test meal. Such interruption would obviously contaminate the evaluation of the satiating efficiency of the preload.

Using the preload strategy and related procedures it is possible to assess the satiating power of a wide variety of foods varying in macronutrient composition (e.g., Blundell et al., 1988). Indeed, it has been noted that "it would be of great value to have tables showing the energy–satiety ratio of all the common foods to indicate their potential for causing overnutrition" (Heaton, 1981, p. 328). Foods exerting only a weak effect on satiety would not be expected to provide effective appetite control. At the present time there is considerable theoretical and clinical interest in the effect of carbohydrates and fat upon appetite. What is the evidence? Considering carbohydrates, it is clear that following consumption the digested carbohydrates influence a number of mechanisms involved in satiety. These include glucoreceptors within the gastrointestinal tract (Mei, 1985), which send afferent information to the brain via the vagus and splanchnic nerves and glucosensitive cells in the liver, nucleus tractus solitarius, and hypothalamic regions of the brain that monitor the postabsorptive activity of glucose (e.g., Oomura, 1988). These mechanisms form the basis of the energostatic control of feeding (Booth, 1972) or what has been called the caloric control of satiety (Blundell & Rogers, 1991). Although sweet carbohydrates induce some positive feedback for eating through oral afferent stimulation, this should be countered by the potent inhibitory action via postingestive and postabsorptive mechanisms. Appropriate experiments should demonstrate whether or not this is the case.

One clear finding from these studies is that carbohydrates are efficient appetite suppressants. That is, they contribute markedly to the satiating efficiency of food and exert a potent effect on satiety (Rogers, Carlyle, Hill, & Blundell, 1988; Rogers & Blundell, 1989). This evidence indicating the potency of metabolized carbohydrate to inhibit appetite is precisely complemented by studies showing that an analogue of glucose, namely, 2-deoxy-d-glucose (which blocks the utilization of glucose by cells), actually increases hunger when given to human subjects

(Thompson & Campbell, 1977). On the basis of studies on rats it was argued some years ago that "if the cumulative inhibitory effects of carbohydrate on feeding are indeed energostatic. . .then any substance which can readily be used by the animal to provide energy should produce an appropriate food intake compensation over a period of several hours after loading" (Booth, 1972, p. 199). Studies have shown that this is exactly the case for humans. A variety of carbohydrates including glucose, fructose, sucrose, and maltodextrins have rather similar effects when given in a preload. That is, they suppress later intake by an amount roughly equivalent to their caloric value, although the time course of the suppressive action may vary a little according to the rate at which the carbohydrate loads are metabolized.

Considering the action of fat upon satiety, at the present time only a few studies have systematically investigated the extent to which dietary fat contributes to the satiating power of food. However, there is a widespread belief that high-fat diets are responsible for an elevated energy intake, which in turn leads to weight gain through fat deposition. For example, it has been shown that the "food quotient" (FQ) of a diet is inversely correlated with weight gain (Tremblay, Plourde, Despres, & Bouchard, 1989). In addition, Lissner, Levitsky, Strupp, Kackwarf, and Roe (1987) demonstrated that subjects undereat when forced to eat low-fat foods (high FQ diet) for 3 weeks and overeat (relative to a balanced diet) when obliged to consume from an assortment of high-fat foods (low FQ diet). These findings make it appear as if fat stimulates caloric intake. It is known that the fat content of food alters texture and palatability and may increase food acceptability. This factor coupled with the high caloric density of fat probably facilitates dietary excess within a meal or snack (passive overconsumption). However, it is not known to what extent fat calories impinge on the duration of the intermeal interval or subsequently reduce the quantity of food eaten. Some experiments have indicated a potent satiating action. The study of Van Stratum, Lussenburg, Van Wenzel, Vergoesen, and Cremer (1977) suggested that fat and carbohydrates are equally satiating, while Welch, Saunders, and Read (1985) demonstrated that intestinal deposition of fat suppressed intake. In animal studies fat is known to be a potent releaser of cholecystokinin (CCK). Interestingly Greenberg, Torres, Smith, and Gibbs (1989) have shown that intraduodenal placement of fat in the rat suppresses intake while intraportal infusions of the same fat (intralipid) do not. In humans a high fat preload intended to prompt CCK release allowed the trypsin inhibitor Ryan-Potato II to exert a noticeable suppression of energy intake (Hill, Peikin, Ryan, & Blundell, 1990). Consequently these various experimental outcomes appear to indicate that fat has a potent postingestive effect on intake, has equivalent satiating power to carbohydrate, or induces relatively weak caloric compensation. How can these findings be reconciled with one another and with the view that exposure to a high-fat diet favors the development of obesity? The answer seems to rest on the distinction between satiation and satiety (Figure 10.2). Satiation is the process that terminates eating within a meal, while satiety is the subsequent meal-induced inhibition over further eating. It can be deduced that, while fat does exert an effect on satiety, it only has a weak effect on satiation. Dietary fat appears to exert only a minimal inhibition over eating at the time of consumption, and therefore large quantities may be consumed with ease. After consumption the fat will begin to exert inhibition over further eating through the mediating processes of the satiety cascade.

In the case of protein, studies on animals (Geary, 1979) and lean (Hill & Blundell, 1986) and obese (Hill & Blundell, 1990) humans agree that protein has a greater satiating efficiency calorie for calorie than the other macronutrients. Collectively, these experiments on nutrients indicate that nutritional composition of food is an important biological component controlling the expression of appetite. Consequently, any self-imposed or enforced adjustment in nutritional input will have implications for eating and will be a significant factor to be considered in assessing the symptoms of eating-disordered patients. The full implications of nutritional factors can be appreciated only by considering wider aspects of appetite control.

RELEVANCE OF NUTRITION TO BINGE EATING

In the field of the biology of appetite research it has become clear that it is no longer sufficient to refer simply to food intake. The nutrient composition of the food consumed plays a significant role in the activation of mechanisms involved in good appetite control. (See Walsh, Chapter 3, this volume, for an account of the research on the composition of the binges of patients with bulimia nervosa.) For example, the above review indicates that an avoidance of carbohydrate foods will prevent carbohydrates from producing their potent and rapid postabsorptive suppression of hunger. This effect is apparent at about 2½ hours after eating and is manifest via the postingestive window. Equally an avoidance of carbohydrate foods will fail to supply the nutrient substrate required for carbohydrate oxidation and the repletion of glycogen stores. Therefore, an urge to eat and a requirement for carbohydrate will remain high. This means that postprandial satiety will remain low and hunger will stay relatively high.

While avoidance of carbohydrates or low carbohydrate intake will weaken satiety, the main action of fat is likely to be on satiation. High-fat foods can possess extremely attractive sensory properties because of the texture conferred by fat and by the appealing tastants that can be embedded in fat. High-fat foods exert a relatively weak effect on satiation (meal size). This is almost certainly because a large number of calories can be ingested very rapidly and before the inhibitory mechanisms can be brought into operation. In turn, a large amount of energy ingested as fat appears to exert a disproportionately weak effect on satiety (Blundell, Cotton, Lawton, & Burley, 1992). Since high-fat intake (unlike carbohydrate) does not appear to promote fat oxidation, the ingested fat is likely to be stored, therefore leading to weight gain.

Consequently it can be seen how an aberrant pattern of nutrient selection could give rise to an unhelpful pattern of control characterized by weak satiation and weak satiety; in turn, this would be reflected in poor control over meal size (measured in energy value) and reduced postprandial satiety (measured by a weakened suppression of hunger).This loss of control could constitute a source of vulnerability for binge eating.

THE NATURE OF THE APPETITE CONTROL SYSTEM

The biopsychological system that is concerned with the expression of appetite can be conceptualized on three levels (Figure 10.3; for a more detailed version, see Blundell [1991]). These are: the level of psychological events (hunger perception, cravings, hedonic sensations) and behavioral operations (meals, snacks, energy, and macronutrient intakes); the level of peripheral physiology and metabolic events; and the level of neurotransmitter and metabolic interactions in the brain. The essence of the approach advocated here is that appetite can best be understood by adopting a systems view in which the expression of appetite reflects the synchronous operation of events and processes in the three levels. Neural events trigger and guide behavior, but each act of behavior involves a response in the peripheral physiological system; in turn, these physiological events are translated into brain neurochemical activity. This brain activity represents the strength of motivation and the willingness to feed or refrain from feeding.

Even before food touches the mouth, the sight and smell of food generate physiological signals. These events constitute the cephalic phase of appetite (Powley, 1977). Cephalic-phase responses are generated in many parts of the gastrointestinal tract, and their function is to anticipate the ingestion of food. During and immediately after eating affer-

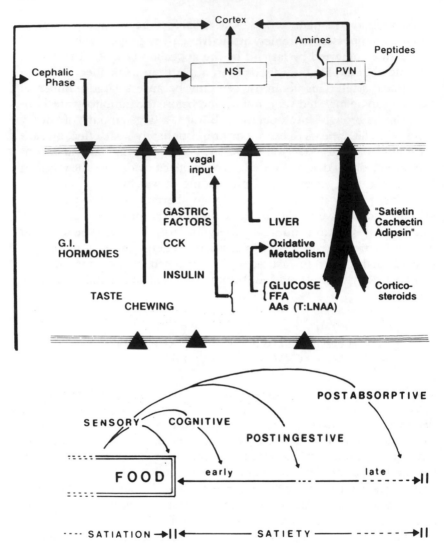

FIGURE 10.3. Conceptualization of the biopsychological system indicating the processing of nutritional information at three levels: the operations of the satiety cascade, intermediary physiological mechanisms, and brain pathways.

ent information provides the major control over appetite. It has been noted that "Afferent information from ingested food acting in the mouth provides primarily positive feedback for eating; that from the stomach and small intestine primarily negative feedback..." (Smith, Greenberg, Corp, & Gibbs, 1990, p. 63). Initially the brain is informed about the amount of food ingested and its nutrient context via afferent input. The gastrointestinal tract is equipped with specialized chemo- and mechanoreceptors that monitor physiological activity and pass information to the brain mainly via the vagus nerve (Mei, 1985). This afferent information constitutes one class of satiety signals and forms part of the postingestive control of appetite. It is usual to identify a postabsorptive, phase which arises, naturally enough, when nutrients have undergone digestion and cross the wall of the intestine to enter the circulation. These products, which accurately reflect the food that has been consumed, may be metabolized in the peripheral tissues or organs or may enter the brain directly. In either case these products constitute a further class of metabolic satiety signals. It has been argued that the degree of oxidative metabolism of glucose and free fatty acids in the liver constitutes a significant source of information useful for the control of appetite (Friedman, Tordoff, & Ramirez, 1986). Additionally, products of digestion and agents responsible for their metabolism may reach the brain and bind to specific chemoreceptors, or influence neurotransmitter synthesis, or alter some aspect of neuronal metabolism. In each case the brain is informed about some aspect of the metabolic state resulting from food consumption.

It has also been hypothesized that the blood carries specific substances that reflect the state of depletion or repletion of energy reserves and directly modulate critical brain mechanisms. These substances could include satietin (Knoll, 1979), adipsin (Cook & Spiegelman, 1987)—a more likely regulator of fat than appetite—and the sugar acids 3,4 - dihydroxybutanoic acid γ-lactone, 2-buten-4-olide, and 2,4,5 - trihydroxypentanoic acid γ-lactone (Shimizu, Oomura, & Sakata, 1984). From an evolutionary perspective it is possible to envisage that many peripheral regulators of the handling of ingested nutrients could be exploited as potential signals of food-related activities or bodily needs. One such possibility is the activation peptide of pancreatic procolipase (Erlanson-Albertsson & Larsson, 1988).

Traditional views of the neural control of appetite have been based on opposed hunger and satiety centers in the hypothalamus. These concepts are now out of date. It may be useful to recognize distinct roles for the hindbrain—particularly the nucleus of the solitary tract (NTS) and the closely associated area postrema, and the forebrain, and to consider separate processes of registration, transcription, and integration. Changes in the gastrointestinal tract resulting from food consumption are registered in the hindbrain. This information is transcribed onto neurotransmitter pathways (amines and associated peptides) and projected to primarily hypothalamic zones where integration with neuroendocrine and metabolic activity is organized. Information arriving from the periphery via neural pathways is complemented by qualitatively different types of information that can be detected in blood and cerebrospinal fluid. These include the polypeptides acidic-fibroblast growth factor (aFGF), interleukin-1 and tumor necrosis factor (cachectin) (Oomura, 1988), together with brain insulin. Another feature of the brain's detection system is the presence of so-called glucose-monitoring neurons that are also sensitive to other nutrients. These are located at strategic sites in the hindbrain and forebrain (as well as in the periphery).

A large number of neurotransmitters, neuromodulators, pathways, and receptors are implicated in the central processing of information relevant to appetite. The profile of this activity reflects the flux of physiological and biochemical transactions in the periphery and represents the pattern of behavioral events and associated motivational states.

PERIPHERAL INFLUENCES ON APPETITE

A good deal of interest in peripheral sites of action for the suppression of appetite has focused upon peptidergic inhibition of food intake. Many peripherally administered peptides lead to an anorexic response and good experimental evidence for a natural role exists for CCK, pancreatic glucagon, bombesin, and somatostatin (Smith, 1988). Recent research has now confirmed the status of CCK as a hormone mediating satiation and early-phase satiety. The consumption of protein or fat simulates the release of CCK, which activates CCK-A receptors in the pyloric region of the stomach. This signal is transmitted via vagal afferents to the NTS from where it is relayed to the medial zones of the hypothalamus including the paraventricular nucleus (PVN) and ventromedial hypothalamus (VMH). The anorexic effect of systemically administered CCK can be blocked by vagotomy (Smith, Jerome, & Norgren, 1985) and by the selective CCK-A receptor antagonist, devazepide (MK-329) (Dourish, Coughlan, Hawley, Clark, & Iverson, 1988). Significantly there now exist many reports demonstrating that the CCK-A type antagonist administered alone leads to an increase in food intake in experimental animals (Hewson, Leighton, Hill, & Hughes, 1988). Interestingly, trypsin inhibitors, which block the inactivation of CCK, produce a suppression of food intake in animals (McLaughlin, Peikin, & Baile, 1983) and humans (Hill et al., 1990). Not surprisingly considerable research activity has been directed toward the development of CCK analogues or peptoids with anorexic potency. Many products now exist, but their future as clinical appetite suppressants may depend upon finding ways to prevent adaptive responses in the pancreas that appear to develop with repeated administration. The pharmacological actions of glucagon in suppressing food intake is notable, but there is currently no evidence on how glucagon induces vagal afferent signals (Geary, 1990). Another peptide, insulin, appears to have significant peripheral and central actions. Peripheral effects on carbohydrate metabolism are well known, but it appears that an appetite or body-weight signal may be generated by CSF insulin (Woods, Lotter, McKay, & Porte, 1979).

CENTRAL ACTION

The influence of central neurochemical activity on the expression of appetite is complex and involves numerous interactions between different loci and different receptors that result in shifts in the magnitude, direction, and quality of eating behavior. A good deal of evidence has been accumulated from the direct application of chemicals to the brain either via the CSF or directly into specific sites. Most agents suppress intake, but a significant number stimulate eating, sometimes in a dramatic fashion. The most frequently demonstrated action is the stimulation of feeding following activation of alpha-2 adrenoceptors in the PVN (Leibowitz, 1978). It is also known that spontaneous feeding is associated with endogenous release of noradrenaline in the PVN and with an increase in PVN alpha-2 receptor density (Leibowitz, 1988). In turn, it appears that the PVN is a site for the long-established anorexic action of serotoninergic agents (Blundell, 1977). The PVN also contains glucosensitive neurons and therefore may be a point of interaction for neurotransmitter activity and metabolic states reflecting energy regulation. Circulating corticosteroids have been demonstrated to influence noradrenaline receptor sensitivity, and it has been argued that noradrenaline and 5-HT act antagonistically to influence the release of corticotropin releading factor (CRF). Since the PVN is also a potent anorexic drug-binding site (Angel, 1990) neurochemical activity in this area may serve to integrate behavioral, metabolic, and neuroendocrine responses. In more lateral areas of the hypothalamus (perifornical zone) feeding is suppressed by micro-injection of agents that activate dopamine D_2 or adrenergic $beta_2$ receptors (Leibowitz & Brown, 1980). Consequently, noradrenaline, 5-HT, and dopamine produce quantitative shifts in feeding from closely related sites in the hypothalamus.

Potent feeding responses can also be obtained by micro-injection of peptides to the brain. Many peptides such as insulin, CCK, calcitonin, bombesin, neurotensin, THRH, somatostatin, VIP, CRF, and glucagon suppress feeding after cerebroventricular administration (Morley, Levine, Gosnell, & Krahn, 1985). A smaller number of peptides increase food intake, and this group includes betaendorphin, dynorphin, neuropeptide-Y, peptide YY, and galanin. When injected into the PVN, NPY and PYY can induce 50% of daily food intake within 1 hour. The stimulation of feeding by galanin appears to be specific to the PVN and closely related sites (Kyrkouli, Stanley, Seirafi, & Leibowitz, 1990). Classic research of a decade ago indicated how projections between the brainstem and hypothalamic nuclei were involved in neuroendocrine regulation (Sawchencko & Swanson, 1982). This pattern of projections is also important for feeding; peptides such as NPY and galanin appear to originate (in part) in adrenergic (C1, C2) or noradrenergic (A1, A2, A6) nuclei in the brainstem. In summary, peptides such as CCK, CRF, THRH, NPY, opioids, and galanin appear to have important central roles in conjunction with noradrenaline, 5-HT, and dopamine in the organization of the expression of appetite (and energy balance more generally). These actions are generated in response to visceral and metabolic information, which reflects the immediate past history of feeding and the body's nutritional status. Other neural mechanisms involving cholinergic, benzodiazepine, and GABA-ergic receptors may also be implicated at some point.

REGULATION AND DYSREGULATION IN THE APPETITE CONTROL SYSTEM

The description of behavioral, physiological, and neurochemical events set out above indicates that eating involves a synchrony between events in each of the three levels of the system (Figure 10.3). In the normal expression of appetite, episodes of eating, accompanied by hunger, are reflected in a sequence of physiological events in the periphery together with a chain of neurotransmitter adjustments in the brain. This profile of neurotransmitter activity mediates in the expression of appetite and gives character to food-seeking behavior.

This appetite control system could become disordered or upset in various ways. First, some intrinsic part of the physiology or neurochemistry could be defective (altered enzyme production, down-regulated receptors etc.), which would impede the appropriate transmission or registration of nutritional information. Alternatively dysregulation could be induced by extrinsic forces. These could be mild or severe. An example of mild external disruption would be the confusion of taste metabolism conditioning. This would arise when the cue-consequence conditioning process (Garcia, Hankins, & Rusiniak, 1974), which allows appropriate anticipatory responses to be generated to the taste of food, is undermined by the appearance in the food supply of many consumables with identical tastes but differing metabolic properties. In addition, any food material that generated conflicting information between the ingestive, postingestive, or postabsorptive phases (e.g., Blundell et al.,

1987) would impede the optimum functioning of the system. However, the most severe dysregulation would probably arise following deliberate adjustment of the pattern of eating. This would occur in severe dieting and prolonged fasting alternating with bingeing, and would it be complicated further by vomiting.

It follows from this analysis that eating disorders such as anorexia nervosa and bulimia nervosa would necessarily involve considerable dysregulation of the appetite control system (Morley & Blundell, 1988). The initial trigger could arise from an intrinsic or extrinsic source, but consequent contamination of the behavioral pattern would engender desynchrony with the other levels. It is known that in eating-disordered patients desynchrony exists between eating behavior and subjective motivation (Owen, Halmi, Gibbs, & Smith, 1985) and between behavior and peripheral variables such as plasma amino acid ratios (Pirke, Schweiger, & Laessle, 1986) and central indices such as neurotransmitter metabolites in cerebrospinal fluid (Kaye, Ebert, Gwirtsman, & Weiss, 1984). It has been suggested that there is a serious dysregulation of serotonin in eating disorders (Brewerton et al., 1989; Blundell & Hill, 1990).

This proposal, that orderly appetite control rests upon the maintenance of synchrony in the transmission of nutritional information, also incorporates the proposition that a disordered appetite is associated with a loss of synchrony. Dysregulation or desynchrony could be brought about by chronic mild provocation (such as conflicting biological information in the food supply) or by abrupt severe behavioral disruption (such as repeated episodes of fasting, bingeing, and vomiting). It follows that the treatment of eating disorders will entail a resynchronization of events at the three levels. Such treatments could include pharmacological agents acting on central neuromodulators that would regulate the pattern of eating (Blundell, 1990).

UNCOUPLING OF BIOLOGICAL PROCESSES

It may be reasonably supposed that a well-regulated appetite control system will arise when an orderly pattern of eating generates a consequential cascade of peripheral and central physiological actions. The biological responses will therefore be entrained to the behavioral pattern. This orderly sequence allows for the possible development of good conditioning between the perceptual properties of foods and their actions on postingestive or postabsorptive receptor systems. In turn, this permits the development of useful anticipatory reactions to food, which represent one component of the so-called biological wisdom of the body.

Any disruption of the profile of eating behavior is likely to lead to a weakening of the relationship between behavior, peripheral physiology, and brain neurochemical events. It is worth keeping in mind that the pattern of neurotransmitter activity in the brain represents the way in which the structure and direction of behavior are organized. When the pattern of behavior is arbitrarily imposed from outside (by conscious decision) and is unrelated to physiological requirements, then the function of the biological processes may be undermined. It can be reasonably argued that one function of postingestive inhibitory processes of the satiety cascade is to modulate the pattern of behavior so that energy and nutrient intake is appropriate to the rate at which food can be handled by the body (rate of digestion, absorption, etc.). These postprandial events are not just a consequence of eating but have a specific biological function. In turn, the postabsorptive events signify the extent to which physiological needs are being met by the behavioral input (i.e., eating). If needs are met (detected by receptor activity, neural processing, etc.), then the drive to seek food will be modulated accordingly. Consequently, the postingestive and postabsorptive events of the satiety cascade function conjointly to maintain a biologically appropriate pattern of intake that is in synchrony with the needs of the body.

Probably the most severe disorganization of this cascade occurs when vomiting is introduced into the behavior pattern. Under these circumstances there will be an uncoupling of the relationship between behavior, some postingestive actions, and most (but not all) postabsorptive processes. Apart from the general physiological asynchrony caused by this action, vomiting may specifically lead to an intensified need state reflected in an enhanced attractiveness of certain food stimuli (increased hedonic value) and an absence of postingestive suppression of hunger and eating. It can be deduced that this state may further exaggerate the urge to eat. Thus, if binge eating does not precede vomiting, it is almost certain to arise as a consequence.

SUMMARY

The study of the biology of appetite involves the interrelationships between eating behavior and motivation to eat, nutritional composition of food, peripheral physiological events, and central neurochemical processes. The individual mechanisms that may influence the expression of appetite are many, and the conjoint operation of these mechanisms is complex. However, the principles underlying this complexity can be perceived by considering the biopsychological system, which guides the expression of appetite. This system indicates key sites in peripheral physiology or in the brain that are responsible for the maintenance of good appetite control. The system also identifies targets toward which treatments for eating or weight disorders may be directed. Disorders of appetite could arise either from an endogenous aberrant or weak mechanism or from an externally applied shift in the behavior pattern. According to this conceptualization, eating disorders reflect a dysregulation in the appetite control system. It follows that investigation of the biology of appetite can provide information to help people maintain a good control over appetite for healthy living and can also throw light upon the nature and treatment of eating disorders.

REFERENCES

Angel, I. (1990). Central receptors and recognition sites mediating the effects of monoamines and anorectic drugs on feeding behavior. *Clinical Neuropharmacology, 13,* 361–391.

Blundell, J. E. (1977). Is there a role for serotonin (5-hydroxytryptamine) in feeding? *International Journal of Obesity, 1,* 15–42.

Blundell, J. E. (1990). Pharmacology of appetite control. *Current Therapeutics, 31,* 19–21.

Blundell, J. E. (1991). Pharmacological approaches to appetite suppression. *Trends in Pharmacological Science, 12,* 147–157.

Blundell, J. E., Cotton, J. R., Lawton, C. L., & Burley, V. J. (1992). Dietary fat and appetite control: Weak effects on satiation (within meals) and satiety (following meals). In D. Mellor (Ed.), *Dietary fats: Determinants of preference, selection and consumption* (pp. 79–103). London: Elsevier.

Blundell, J. E., & Hill, A. J. (1986). BioPsychological interactions underlying the study and treatment of obesity In M. J. Christie & P. G. Mellett (Eds.), *The Psychosomatic Approach: contemporary practice of whole person care* (pp. 115–138). Chichester: Wiley.

Blundell, J. E., & Hill, A. J. (1990). Serotonin, eating disorders and the satiety cascade. In G. B. Cassano & H. S. Akisal (Eds.), *Serotonin-system-related syndromes (SRS)—Psychopathological and therapeutic links* (pp. 125–129). Royal Society of Medicine Services International Congress and Symposium Series No. 165.

Blundell, J. E., Hill, A. J., & Rogers, P. J. (1988). Hunger and the satiety cascade— their importance for food acceptance in the late 20th century. In D. M. H. Thompson (Ed.), *Food acceptability* (pp. 233–250). London: Elsevier.

Blundell, J. E., & Rogers (1991). Hunger, hedonics and the control of satiation and satiety. In M. Friedman & M. Kare (Eds.), *Appetite* (pp. 127–148). New York: Marcel Dekker.

Blundell, J. E., Rogers, P. J., & Hill, A. J. (1987). Evaluating the satiating power of foods: Implications for acceptance and consumption. In J. Solms (Ed.), *Chemical composition and sensory properties of food and their influence on nutrition* (pp. 205–219). London: Academic Press.

Booth, D. A. (1972). Post absorptively induced suppression of appetite and the energostatic control of feeding. *Physiology and behavior, 9,* 199–202.

Bouchard, C. (1985). Inheritance of fat distribution and adipose tissue metabolism. In J. Vague, P. Bjorntorp, B. Guy-Grand, M. Rebuffe-Scrive, & P. Vague (Eds.), *Metabolic complications of human obesities* (pp. 87–96). Amsterdam: Experta Medica.

Brewerton, T., Muller, E., Brandt, H., Lesem, M., Hegg, A., Murphy, D., & Jimerson, D. (1989). Dysregulation of 5-HT function in bulimia nervosa. In *The psychobiology of human eating disorders. Annals of the New York Academy of Sciences, 575,* 500–502.

Cook, K. S., Spiegelman, B. M. (1987). Adipsin, a circulating serum protease homolog secreted by adipose tissue and sciatic nerve. *Science, 237,* 402–404.

Dourish, C. T., Coughlan, J., Hawley, D., Clark, M., & Iversen, S. D. (1988). Blockade of CCK-induced hypophagia and prevention of morphine tolerance by the CCK antagonist L-364,718. In R. Y. Wang & R. Schoenfeld (Eds.), *CCK antagonists* (pp. 307–325). New York: Alan R. Liss.

Erlanson-Albertsson, C., & Larsson, A. (1988). The activation peptide of pancreatic procolipase decreases food intake in rats. *Regulatory Peptides, 22,* 325–331.

Friedman, M. I., Tordoff, M. G., & Ramirez, I. (1986). Integrated metabolic control of food intake. *Brain Research Bulletin, 17,* 855–859.

Garcia, J., Hankins, W. G., & Rusiniak, K. W. (1974). Behavioral regulation of the milieu interne in man and rat. *Science, 185,* 824–831.

Geary, N. (1979). Food intake and behavioral caloric compensation after protein repletion in the rat. *Physiology and Behavior, 23,* 1098–1098.

Geary, N. (1990). Pancreatic glucagon signals postprandial satiety. *NeuroScience and Behavioral Reviews, 14,* 323–338.

Greenberg, D., Torres, N. I., Smith, G. P., & Gibbs, J. (1989). The satiating effect of fats is attenuated by the cholecystokinin antagonist proglumide. *Annals of the New York Academy of Sciences, 575,* 517–520.

Heaton, K. W. (1981). Dietary fibre and energy intake. In P. Berchtold, M. Cairella, A. Jacobelli, & V. Silano (Eds.), *Regulators of intestinal absorption in obesity, diabetes and nutrition* (pp. 283–294). Roma: Societa Editrice Universo.

Hewson, G., Leighton, G. E., Hill, R. G., & Hughes, J. (1988). The cholecystokinin receptor antagonist L364,718 increases food intake in the rat by attenuation of the action of endogenous cholecystokinin. *British Journal of Pharmacology, 93,* 79–84.

Hill, A. J., & Blundell, J. E. (1986). Macro-nutrients and satiety: the effects of a high protein or a high carbohydrate meal on subjective motivation to eat and food preferences. *Nutrition and Behavior, 3,* 133–144.

Hill, A. J., & Blundell, J. E. (1990). Sensitivity of the appetite control system in obese subjects to nutritional and serotoninergic challenges. *International Journal of Obesity, 14,* 219–233.

Hill, A. J., Peikin, S. R., Ryan, C. A., & Blundell, J. E. (1990). Oral administration of proteinase inhibitor II from potatoes reduces energy intake in man. *Physiology and Behavior, 48,* 241–246.

Kaye, W. E., Ebert, M. H., Gwirtsman, H. E., & Weiss, S. (1984). Differences in brain serotoninergic metabolism between nonbulimic and bulimic patients with anorexia nervosa. *American Journal of Psychiatry, 141*, 1598–1601.

Kissileff, H. R. (1984). Satiating efficiency and a strategy for conducting food loading experiments. *Neuroscience and Biobehavioral Reviews, 8*, 129–135.

Knoll, J. (1979). Satietin: A highly potent anorexigenic substance in human serum. *Physiology and Behaviour, 23*, 497–502.

Kyrkouli, S. E., Stanley, B. G., Seirafi, R. D., & Leibowitz, S. F. (1990). Stimulation of feeding by Galanin: Anatomical localization and behavioral specificity of this peptide's effects in the brain. *Peptides, 11*, 995–1001.

Leibowitz, S. F. (1978). Paraventricular nucleus: a primary site mediating adrenergic stimulation of feeding and drinking. *Pharmacology, Biochemistry, and Behavior, 8*, 163–175.

Leibowitz, S. F. (1988). Hypothalamic paraventricular nucleus: interaction between alpha$_2$—noradrenergic system and circulating hormones and nutrients in relation to energy balance. *Neuroscience and Biobehavioral Reviews, 12*, 101–109.

Leibowitz, S. F., & Brown, L. L. (1980). Histochemical and pharmacological analysis of catecholaminergic projections to the perifornical hypothalamus in relation to feeding inhibition. *Brain Research, 201*, 315–345.

Lissner, L., Levitsky, D. A., Strupp, B. J., Kackwarf, H., & Roe, D. A. (1987). Dietary fat and the regulation of energy intake in human subjects. *American Journal Clinical Nutrition, 46*, 886–892.

McLaughlin, C. L., Peikin, S. R., & Baile, C. A. (1983). Trypsin inhibitor effects on food intake and weight gain in Zucker rats. *Physiology and Behaviour, 31*, 487–491.

Mei, N. (1985). Intestinal chemosensitivity. *Physiological Review, 65*, 211–237.

Morley, J. E., & Blundell, J. E. (1988). The neurobiological basis of eating disorders: Some formulations. *Biological Psychiatry, 23*, 53–78.

Morley, J. E., Levine, A. S., Gosnell, B. A., & Krahn, D. D. (1985). Peptides as central regulators of feeding. *Brain Research Bulletin, 14*, 511–519.

Oomura, Y. (1988). Chemical and neuronal control of feeding motivation. *Physiology and Behavior, 44*, 555–560.

Owen, W. P., Halmi, K. A., Gibbs, J., & Smith, G. P. (1985). Satiety responses in eating disorders. *Journal of Psychiatric Research, 19*, 279–284.

Pirke, K. M., Schweiger, U., & Laessle, R. G. (1986). Effect of diet composition on affective state in anorexia nervosa and bulimia. *Clinical Neuropharmacology, 9*, 513–515.

Powley, J. (1977). The ventromedial hypothalamic syndrome, satiety and a cephalic phase hypothesis. *Psychological Review, 84*, 89–126.

Richter, C. P. (1943). Total self-regulatory functions in animals and human beings. *Harvey Lecture Series, 38*, 63–103.

Rogers, P. J., & Blundell, J. E. (1989). Separating the actions of sweetness and calories: Effects of saccharin and carbohydrates on hunger and food intake in human subjects. *Physiology and Behavior, 45*, 1093–1099.

Rogers, P. J., Carlyle, J., Hill, A. J., & Blundell, J. E. (1988). Uncoupling sweet taste and calories: comparison of the effects of glucose and three high intensity sweeteners on hunger and food intake. *Physiology and Behavior, 43,* 547–552.

Sawchenko, P. E., & Swanson, L. W. (1982). The organization of noradrenergic pathways from the brainstem to the paraventricular and supraoptic nuclei in the rat. *Brain Research Reviews, 4,* 275–325.

Shimizu, N., Oomura, Y., & Sakata T. (1984). Modulation of feeding by endogenous sugar acids acting as hunger or satiety factors. *American Journal of Physiology, 246,* R542–R550.

Smith, G. P. (1988). Humoral mechanisms in the control of body weight. In H. Weiner & A. Baum (Eds.), *Perspectives in behavioral medicine, eating regulation and dyscontrol* (pp. 59–65). Hillsdale, NJ: Erlbaum.

Smith, G. P., Greenberg, D., Corp, E., & Gibbs, J. (1990). Afferent information in the control of eating. In G. A. Bray (Ed.), *Obesity: towards a molecular approach* (pp. 63–79). New York: Alan K. Liss.

Smith, G. P., Jerome, C., & Norgren, R. (1985). Afferent axons in abdominal vagus mediate satiety effect of cholecystokinin in rats. *American Journal of Physiology, 249,* R638–R641.

Thompson, D. A., & Campbell, R. G. (1977). Hunger in humans induced by 2-deoxy-d-glucose: Glucoprivic control of taste preference and food intake. *Science, 198,* 1065–1068.

Tremblay, A., Plourde, G., Despres, J-P, & Bouchard, C. (1989). Impact of dietary fat content and fat oxidation on energy intake in humans. *American Journal of Clinical Nutrition, 49,* 799–805.

Van Stratum, P., Lussenburg, R. N., Van Wenzel, L. A., Vergroesen, A. J., & Cremer, H. D. (1977). The effect of dietary carbohydrate: fat ratio on energy intake by adult women. *American Journal of Clinical Nutrition, 31,* 206–212.

Welch, I. 0., Saunders, K., & Read, N. W. (1985). Effect of ileal and intravenous infusions of fat emulsions on feeding and satiety in human volunteers. *Gastroenterology, 89,* 1293–1297.

Woods, S. C., Lotter, E. C., McKay, L. D., & Porte, D. (1979). Chronic intracerebroventricular infusion of insulin reduces food intake and body weight of baboons. *Nature, 282,* 503–505.

EVALUATION
AND TREATMENT

Assessment of Binge Eating

G. Terence Wilson

Much of the literature on the assessment of binge eating is based on studies of patients with bulimia nervosa. With the explosion of interest in binge eating in obese patients (see Marcus, Chapter 5, this volume) and the recent formulation of binge eating disorder (see Fairburn & Wilson, Chapter 1, this volume), research on assessment of binge eating is being extended to a much wider range of individuals with eating disorders. In contrast to increasingly intensive conceptual and experimental analyses of binge eating in these normal-weight and overweight populations, however, the assessment of binge eating in anorexia nervosa has been largely neglected (see Garner, Chapter 4, this volume). Nevertheless, it is reasonable at this point to assume that knowledge about the assessment of binge eating in bulimia nervosa and obesity is applicable to the comparable behavior in patients with anorexia nervosa.

The definition of binge eating has changed over the years. As discussed by Fairburn and Wilson (Chapter 1, this volume), a binge has two defining properties in the fourth edition of the *Diagnostic and Statistical Manual of Mental Disorders* (DSM-IV) (American Psychiatric Association, 1993):* (1) the consumption of a large amount of food given the circumstances, and (2) loss of control. This definition has specific implications for assessment. It becomes necessary to take into account the *context* within which overeating occurs in order to determine whether the amount of food consumed was large, and it is essential to assess the person's level of control over the initiation and cessation of eating. Making these judgments requires detailed information on the nature and fre-

---

*The DSM-IV criteria cited in this volume are those that were approved as final by the DSM-IV Eating Disorders Work Group and the Task Force on DSM-IV (APA, 1993). These criteria may be subject to minor editorial revisions before the publications of DSM-IV.

quency of overeating. Therefore, simply asking individuals' to report how often they binge falls far short of what is required.

There is no universally accepted "gold standard" measure of binge eating. No biological measure exists. Biochemical abnormalities in normal-weight patients who binge are relatively rare (Jacobs & Schneider, 1985) and appear to be the consequences of purging rather than excessive food intake (Mitchell, Pomeroy, & Colon, 1989). Methods for assessing binge eating can be grouped in four categories: (1) self-report questionnaires, (2) interview techniques (3) self-monitoring, and (4) observational or laboratory-based behavioral strategies. This chapter summarizes the more commonly used assessment methods within these categories, and analyzes the relative advantages and disadvantages they offer the researcher and clinician.

MEASUREMENT PROBLEMS

Regardless of the method used to assess binge eating, several measurement problems remain to be resolved. The diagnostic criteria for all eating disorders that feature binge eating refer to recurrent *episodes* of binge eating. Treatment studies of bulimia nervosa have routinely measured outcome in terms of change in the frequency of discrete binge-eating episodes. With the recent attention devoted to the diagnosis of binge eating disorder, however, it has been suggested that assessment should focus on the number of days on which binge eating occurred rather than discrete episodes of binge eating. Consistent with this view, the proposed criteria in DSM-IV for binge eating disorder specify that "binge eating occurs, on average, at least two days a week for six months."

As noted in DSM-IV, the issue of assessing episodes versus days of binge eating remains to be explored. Rossiter, Agras, Telch, and Bruce (1992) found that compared with self-monitoring data, obese binge eaters recalled almost twice as many binge episodes. In contrast, patients' recall of the number of days on which binge eating occurred was similar to that obtained from self-recording in daily diaries. The investigators concluded that the number of days of binge eating provides a more accurate measure than discrete episodes. Evidence from the assessment of alcohol abuse (Polich, 1982) similarly indicates that estimates of days will be more accurate than specific episodes. Using this rationale, Wilfley et al. (in press) used number of days of binge eating as the primary outcome measure in their comparative study of psychological treatments of binge eating in obese patients. Research using methods superior to those adopted to date is needed to examine the relative accuracy of frequency of episodes versus days in binge eaters who purge and those who do not.

The definition of binge eating proposed for both bulimia nervosa and binge eating disorder in DSM-IV specifies that the food is consumed in "a discrete period of time (e.g., within any 2-hour period)." This presents the assessor with practical difficulties. There are patients who binge over an extended period of time—a form of overeating referred to as "grazing" (Rossiter et al., 1992). For example, Marcus, Smith, Santelli, and Kaye (1992) found that in their study of patients with binge eating disorder, roughly 24% of all episodes of binge eating lasted the entire day (see Marcus, Chapter 5, this volume). These prolonged periods of overeating may be interspersed with episodes of vomiting (Garner, Shafer, & Rosen, 1992). Using the number of times the patient vomits to punctuate an episode of binge eating does not resolve the problem. An alternative is to rely on the patient's perception of whether the extended period of overeating constituted a single binge-eating episode. A preferred approach is to adopt the more specific and interviewer-determined guideline of the most recent version of the Eating Disorder Examination (EDE) (Fairburn & Cooper, Chapter 15, this volume). This guideline suggests that a gap of more than an hour between episodes, which is not due to the force of circumstances, should be regarded as a boundary between one binge and the next.

In other instances, when eating is especially chaotic, it can be extremely difficult for either the patient or the assessor to determine when one episode stops and another starts. Moreover, as Garner et al. (1992) also note, the entire eating experience is often colored by strong affect or "spacing out," which makes accurate recall of precise sequences of events even more questionable. These practical difficulties encourage the investigation of using number of days on which binge eating occurs as the unit of assessment of binge eating. The most prudent course at present would be to assess both episodes and days of binge eating in the event that any differences have clinical significance.

SELF-REPORT QUESTIONNAIRES

A variety of questionnaires have been used to assess binge eating. The first questionnaire with this aim was the Binge Scale (BS) (Hawkins & Clement, 1980). This nine-item scale was designed to measure both the behavior and attitudes associated with bulimia as described in DSM-III (APA, 1980) (see Table 11.1 for sample items). The BS has good internal consistency and test–retest reliability.

The 16-item Binge Eating Scale (BES) was devised to assess binge eating in obese subjects (Gormally, Black, Daston, & Rardin, 1982). Sample items are illustrated in Table 11.2. The BES measures both the behavioral features of binge eating and the feelings and cognitions associ-

TABLE 11.1. Sample Questions from the Binge Scale

How often do you binge?
  A. Seldom
  B. Once or twice a month
  C. Once a week
  D. Almost every day

Which best describes your feelings during a binge?
  A. I feel that I could control the eating if I chose.
  B. I feel that I have at least some control.
  C. I feel completely out of control.

Note. From Hawkins and Clement (1980). Copyright 1980 by Pergamon Press. Reprinted by permission.

ated with this behavior. The BES has good test–retest reliability, and discriminates between patients with bulimia nervosa and normal controls. It has been used extensively by Marcus and her colleagues to select and characterize patient samples in their studies of obese binge eaters (see Marcus, Chapter 5, this volume). The BES has been shown to discriminate among obese individuals assessed independently by trained clinicians to have no, moderate, or severe binge-eating problems. Marcus, Wing, and Hopkins (1988) found that 98% of patients whose score on the BES indicated severe binge eating (a score of 27 or greater) met DSM-III for bulimia, compared with none of those whose BES score was 17 or less.

The Eating Disorder Inventory (EDI) is a 64-item multiscale instrument designed to assess the psychopathological features of anorexia nervosa and bulimia (Garner, Olmstead, & Polivy, 1983). The EDI-2 is a recently revised version of the questionnaire (Garner, 1991). This instrument has good psychometric properties and discriminates between patients with clinical eating disorders and normals. Gross, Rosen, Leitenberg, and Willmuth (1986) examined its association with daily diary recordings of eating and purging behavior over a 3-week period by patients with bulimia nervosa. The Bulimia subscale (see Table 11.3) was correlated significantly with frequency of vomiting ($r = 0.38$). No correlation between the subscale and binge eating itself was reported, possibly because the investigators apparently did not assess binge-eating behavior directly from the diary recordings.

The Bulimia Test (BULIT) (Smith & Thelen, 1984) comprises 36 items designed to assess the symptoms of bulimia as described in DSM-III. It discriminates between patients with bulimia and normal controls, and has adequate reliability and validity. The test includes questions about purging and weight change in addition to items on eating habits. The Bulimic Investigatory Test (BITE) is another 36-item test (Henderson & Freeman, 1987), with adequate psychometric properties, that assesses

TABLE 11.2. Sample Questions from the Binge Eating Scale

Question 8
1. I rarely eat so much food that I feel uncomfortably stuffed afterward.
2. Usually about once a month, I eat such a quantity of food, I end up feeling very stuffed.
3. I have regular periods during the month when I eat large amounts of food either at mealtime or at snacks.
4. I eat so much food that I regularly feel quite uncomfortable after eating and sometimes a bit nauseous.

Question 10
1. I usually am able to stop eating when I want to. I know when ''enough is enough.''
2. Every so often, I experience a compulsion to eat which I can't seem to control.
3. Frequently, I experience strong urges to eat which I seem unable to control, but at other times I can control my eating urges.
4. I feel incapable of controlling urges to eat. I have a fear of not being able to stop eating voluntarily.

Question 11
1. I don't have any problem stopping eating when I feel full.
2. I usually can stop eating when I feel full but occasionally overeat leaving me feeling uncomfortably stuffed.
3. I have a problem stopping eating once I start and usually I feel uncomfortably stuffed after I eat a meal.
4. Because I have a problem not being able to stop eating when I want, I sometimes have to induce vomiting to relieve my stuffed feeling.

Note. From Gormally, Black, Daston, and Rardin (1982). Copyright 1982 by Pergamon Press. Reprinted by permission.

the psychopathology of eating disorders, including actual eating patterns. Neither the BULIT nor the BITE have been used much in research on binge eating.

The EDE-Q is 38-item, self-report measure of the specific psychopathology of eating disorders (Fairburn & Beglin, 1992). It is derived from the EDE (Fairburn & Cooper, Chapter 15, this volume). Its utility in assessing binge eating is discussed in the following section. Recently Spitzer and his colleagues (1992) have developed a questionnaire to assess the criteria for the diagnosis of binge eating disorder. It has yet to be adequately validated.

Advantages

The great appeal of self-report questionnaires is their ease of administration. They are economical and efficient ways of assessing problems with large numbers of subjects when a time-consuming clinical interview is impractical. Several of the questionnaires have adequate psychometric properties. As such they are well suited for assessing large groups

TABLE 11.3. Individual Items from the Bulimia Subscale of the Eating Disorders Inventory-2

I eat when I am upset.
I stuff myself with food.
I have gone on eating binges where I have felt that I could not stop.
I think about bingeing (overeating).
I eat moderately in front of others and stuff myself when they're gone.
I have the thought of trying to vomit in order to lose weight.
I eat or drink in secrecy.

Note. From Garner (1991). Copyright 1991 by Psychological Assessment Resources, Inc. Reprinted by permission.

of subjects as in epidemiological research. These questionnaires provide a general gauge of the overall severity of the symptoms of a bulimic eating disorder and therefore have proved useful in assessing therapeutic change. Several studies of patients with bulimia nervosa have shown that instruments such as the EDI and BES can be used as measures of overall treatment effects (Garner et al., 1993). They do not necessarily reflect changes in binge eating, however. Ortega, Waranch, Maldonado, and Hubbard (1987), for example, obtained significant changes on the BS following treatment of patients with bulimia nervosa that were not confirmed by independent ratings of the patients' daily records of food intake. Whether or not this is true only for the BS or for self-report measures in general is unknown.

Whereas questionnaires such as the EDI and BULIT have been shown to be valid measures of overall degree of disturbance in eating disorder patients (Garner, 1991; Thelen, Farmer, Wonderlich, & Smith, 1991), to my knowledge only a single study has evaluated the utility of a self-report questionnaire in assessing specific aspects of the psychopathology of eating disorders including binge eating. In this study by the Oxford group (Fairburn & Beglin, 1992), the EDE-Q and EDE were administered to a community sample of 243 women and 36 female patients with bulimia nervosa ($n = 23$) or anorexia nervosa ($n = 13$). Both assessment methods were administered within a 24-hour interval, so that they both covered the same preceding 28 days.

Data analysis focused on the correspondence between the two methods for the core features of eating disorders, namely, self-induced vomiting, laxative abuse, binge eating (uncontrolled overeating), and strict dieting. The correlations for binge eating were statistically significant, i.e., .45 and .60 for the community sample and patient sample, respectively, although there were statistically significant differences between the rates obtained by the EDE and the EDE-Q for binge eating in both the community and patient samples. It is noteworthy, however, that this correspondence was less than the very impressive correlations obtained for self-induced vomiting, i.e., .88 and .91. These results indicate that vomiting, an unambiguous and discrete action, can be assessed more accurately using self-report than binge eating, a less unambiguous behavior requiring contextual analysis. The data also suggested that the EDE-Q is more accurate in assessing binge eating in patients than in community-based subjects, possibly because the patients had a better understanding of the concept of binge eating.

Disadvantages

Standardized questionnaires have significant limitations for assessing binge eating. The terms ''binge'' and ''binge eating'' typically are not defined, a serious problem in view of the evidence that there is no generally agreed upon definition of binge eating (Fairburn & Beglin, 1992; see Fairburn & Wilson, Chapter 1, this volume). This is illustrated in the Ortega et al. (1987) finding that patients reported far more frequent binges than determined by independent raters reviewing daily eating records with diagnostic criteria in mind.

Most of the questionnaires fail to assess binge eating directly. Instead of providing a clearcut measure of the specific behavior of overeating, they yield some sort of composite index of the eating habits and attitudes and feelings associated with overeating. They do not provide the detailed descriptive information or a specific count of the frequency of binge eating that is needed to make a diagnosis, for planning therapeutic interventions or for monitoring treatment progress and outcome. Spitzer et al.'s (1992) questionnaire was specifically designed to assess the diagnosis of binge eating disorder, but it did not directly measure binge eating as it will be defined in DSM-IV. The questionnaire defined binge eating as episodes of eating a large amount of food over the past 6 months, during which subjects reported ''*usually*'' feeling that they ''couldn't stop eating or control what or how much they were eating.'' The questionnaire did not specify that each episode of overeating had to be uncontrolled, only that subjects *usually* experienced a loss of control during overeating.[1]

In addition to the lack of definition of binge eating and the failure to quantify this behavior directly, most questionnaires do not specify a consistent time frame for the occurrence of binge eating. Moreover, the descriptors of frequency of occurrence are often vague, such as ''seldom'' or ''almost every day'' (see Table 11.1).

A final caveat concerns the possibly limited value of self-report questionnaires even when they assess binge eating directly. Based on their findings, Fairburn and Beglin (1992) conclude that the EDE-Q is not a satisfactory measure of binge eating in the community. This limitation has significance that extends beyond this one study. The authors point out that most of the studies of the prevalence of binge eating and eating disorders have relied upon self-report questionnaires (see Fairburn & Beglin, 1990). These data call into question the accuracy of estimates of the prevalence of binge eating based on self-report measures.

CLINICAL INTERVIEWS

Some sort of clinical interview has been among the most widely used means of assessing binge eating in patients. These interviews vary widely in how structured they are, and whether or not they are respondent- or investigator-based. The best formulated ones are five semistructured interviews developed for assessing the specific psychopathology of eating disorders and binge eating in particular—the Clinical Eating Disorder Rating Instrument (CEDRI) (Palmer, Christie, Cordle, Davies, & Kenrick, 1987); the Structured Interview for Anorexia and Bulimia Nervosa (SIAB) (Fichter et al., 1989); Interview for Diagnosis of Eating Disorders (IDED) (Williamson, 1990); the Binge Eating Disorder (BED) Interview (Spitzer, 1992); and the Eating Disorder Examination (EDE) (Fairburn & Cooper, Chapter 15, this volume). The CEDRI, SIAB, and IDED are not commonly employed, and there is virtually no literature on their use. The BED Clinical Interview (Yanovski, 1993) has only begun to be used. Unlike the EDE, which is discussed next, in the BED Interview the patient and not the assessor judges what constitutes a binge. (The same holds true for the CEDRI and IDED.) In an initial study of obese binge eaters, Brody et al. (1992) found that the interrater reliability on the overall diagnosis of BED was .70. However, in the analysis of binge eating per se, the mean Kappa for "large amount of food" was only .58 compared with .76 for reported loss of control. The EDE is widely used in clinical and epidemiological research in North America, Europe, and Australia and has been translated into several different languages. It has also been more intensively studied than the other interviews. Accordingly, the focus in the present chapter is on the EDE.

The complete schedule of the EDE is given in Fairburn and Cooper (Chapter 15, this volume). The interview may take up to an hour or more to administer, and requires well-trained assessors who are, ideally, also knowledgeable about the nature of eating disorders. As with any clinical interview, particularly one that is investigator based, it is important for the assessor to establish an accepting and understanding relationship with the patient. Patients with eating disorders typically feel ashamed about their behavior and can be very sensitive to subtle cues of disapproval and rejection. It is not uncommon to come across eating-disorder patients who have previously received unsympathetic treatment from professionals not experienced in this area.

Advantages

The EDE has favorable psychometric properties. High interrater reliability has been demonstrated in different settings (Cooper & Fairburn, 1987; Rosen, Vara, Wendt, & Leitenberg, 1990; Wilson & Smith, 1989). The internal consistency of the five subscales is satisfactory (Cooper, Cooper, & Fairburn, 1989). Its discriminant validity as a measure of the specific psychopathology of eating disorders in general, and binge eating in particular, was established in a study of 100 patients with anorexia nervosa or bulimia nervosa versus normal controls (Cooper et al., 1989). All individual items showed significant differences between the two groups. The selection criteria for the control group in this study quite possibly resulted in the inclusion of subjects who were unconcerned about body weight or shape. However, Wilson and Smith (1989) showed that the EDE distinguished between patients with bulimia nervosa and nonbulimic subjects who were preoccupied with dieting and weight. In this study the EDI subscales did not discriminate between the two groups, indicating the superior discriminant validity of the semistructured interview over this standardized self-report questionnaire. Finally, the EDE has proved to be a sensitive measure of the effects of psychological treatment of bulimia nervosa (Fairburn et al., 1991; Garner et al., 1993; Wilson, Eldredge, Smith, & Niles, 1991).

The EDE provides depth and breadth of assessment of binge eating that no other interview or questionnaire can equal. A major advantage is that it provides a conceptual framework and definition for different forms of overeating, including binge eating. It defines four different forms of overeating depending on whether the amount of food consumed is genuinely large (objective bulimic episodes or episodes of objective overeating) or only perceived to be excessive by the individual (subjective bulimic episodes or episodes of subjective overeating), and if the person experienced a sense of loss of control at the time (bulimic episodes) or not (see Fairburn & Wilson, Chapter 1, this volume). These forms of overeating are not mutually exclusive.

Unlike other instruments, the EDE defines overeating and ensures that both interviewer and patient share the same meaning of key concepts. A "large amount" is defined by the interviewer as what other people would regard as an unusually large amount under the specific circumstances. The interviewer asks a number of probe questions to make this judgment. "Loss of control" is defined as the inability to resist an episode of overeating or to stop eating once started. Uncontrolled consumption of an objectively large amount of food is referred to as an objective bulimic episode, and as discussed by Fairburn and Wilson (Chapter 1, this volume), this defines binge eating in DSM-IV. By making distinctions among different forms of overeating, the EDE framework makes possible empirical resolution of the controversy over whether or not the amount of food consumed is a useful diagnostic or prognostic descriptor (Garner et al., 1992).

Validity studies of the EDE have used daily self-recording of eating as a comparative standard. Using a sample of unselected college students, Rosen et al. (1990) correlated self-recording of all food and liquid intake for the 7 days prior to administration of the EDE with the different subscales. The overeating subscale was significantly correlated with frequency of binge-eating episodes. According to Rosen et al. (1990), the "sum of the two EDE items for objective binge-eating episodes also predicted binge eating frequency on eating records" (p. 524). The authors state that they derived their estimate of binge eating from the students' self-recordings. Any attempt to derive a count of binge eating from self-monitoring must necessarily rely on subjects' interpretation because independent raters cannot infer loss of control, even though they can estimate amount of food consumed. However, unless the students were given a definition of binge eating (which is not made clear), it can be assumed that they reported both subjective and objective bulimic episodes as "binges." The correlation between the EDE and students' self-recordings, therefore, may actually underestimate the degree of concordance between the two forms of assessment.

In an extension of this research, Loeb, Walsh, and Pike (1992) compared EDE assessment of binge eating (objective bulimic episodes) with self-recording in bulimia nervosa patients at pre- and posttreatment. At pretreatment, the correlation between the two measures for the identical preceding seven days was an impressive .96. At posttreatment, Loeb et al. found that the two measures for the same seven and 28 days periods were .97 and .98 respectively. Such high correlations might well reflect patients' memories of self-recording binge frequencies during the preceding 7 and 28 days. As a result, the data do not directly address the question of the accuracy of recall on the EDE for the preceding time period in the absence of formal self-monitoring of binge eating.

Finally, the EDE can be extremely useful in clinical practice. The rich detail provided by the interview, and the opportunity for the assessor to probe details of eating behavior and attitudes that might otherwise remain unclear, can greatly assist the therapist in understanding the nuances of a patient's eating disorder.

Disadvantages

Clinical interviews necessarily have relied upon the global self-reports of patients. The critical question is how reliable and accurate these reports are. It would be a mistake to automatically accept the notion that self-report of binge eating is inherently distorted. The intensively studied record of the accuracy and utility of self-report of drinking by problem drinkers and alcoholics suggests otherwise (Wilson, 1987). To summarize, the reliability of self-report is high in both the general population (Williams, Aitken, & Malin, 1985) and patient populations (Skinner & Sheu, 1982). The validity of alcohol abusers' self-reports of drinking has been assessed using official records (e.g., hospitalization and driving arrests), collateral reports, and measures of blood alcohol concentration. In general, several studies have shown that self-report from sober patients correlates highly with these more objective sources of information (Wilson, 1987). Validity is especially high for self-reports of "abstinence" versus "drinking" but less so for measures of amount of alcohol consumed. When discrepancies between self-report and collateral report or blood alcohol determination were obtained, the gap was due as often to alcohol abusers overreporting as to underreporting their drinking. There is little reason to suspect that the self-reports of patients with bulimia nervosa would be any less reliable or valid than those of problem drinkers and alcoholics, populations whose motivation for treatment is probably often lower than that of many patients with eating disorders featuring binge eating.

It is difficult to investigate the accuracy of self-report of binge eating because the behavior is characteristically carried out in secrecy. The use of collateral reports by significant others in the person's natural environment is hence less of an option than it is with other more public forms of psychoactive substance abuse, such as alcohol abuse (Vuchinich, Tucker, & Harllee, 1988). In a rare case in which collateral reports were possible, Giles, Young, and Young (1985) found that they tended to validate the patient's self-report. At best, collateral reports can provide only indirect information on the course of patients' binge eating. In patients with bulimia nervosa, for example, a major goal of treatment is to establish a regular pattern of three nutritionally balanced meals a day. The pattern and content of meals are publicly observable, and in many instances collaterals will have direct and consistent access to this behavior in patients. This sort of collateral report provides indirect but nonetheless useful corroborative information about a patient's progress.

Self-report of binge eating can also be compared with objective assessment of instructed binge eating in hospitalized patients. Mitchell and

Laine (1985) found that the average amount of food in binge-eating episodes in the hospital setting was much more than what the patients claimed they normally ate. This does not necessarily indicate that their self-reports were unreliable. Equally plausible is the interpretation that eating in this artificial setting is unrepresentative of behavior in their natural environment (Rosen & Srebnic, 1990).

There is no biological marker that can be used to validate self-report, as noted above. Perhaps the best available strategy is to compare patients' self-reports of binge eating with daily recordings of all eating behavior. The Loeb et al. (1992) and Rosen et al. (1990) studies that used this strategy encourage the view that the EDE does provide a valid assessment of binge eating in patients with bulimia nervosa. Nevertheless, Rossiter et al. (1992) found a marked discrepancy between daily recordings and self-report by obese patients with binge eating. Whether the difference between these studies is a function of the type of eating disorder, the superiority of the EDE over simple self-report, or other methodological differences remains to be determined.

Rather than querying whether self-report is accurate or not, the emphasis should be on arranging conditions to optimize accuracy (Babor, Brown, & Del Boca, 1990). Establishing a good working relationship with the subject or patient is likely to enhance accuracy. It will facilitate full self-disclosure of sensitive and embarrassing information and encourage individuals to invest the necessary time and effort in recalling specific details of eating behavior. Miller and Rollnick (1992) have made a persuasive case against the not-uncommon professional view that ''all alcoholics are liars.'' They spell out the deleterious consequences of such an a priori bias for assessment and treatment. It would be a serious mistake to tar binge eaters with the same brush on the unsubstantiated grounds that as comparable addicts or substance abusers they share the denial and distortion that allegedly typifies alcoholics.

Some assessment instruments are more likely to promote accurate recall than others. Interviews are to be preferred, and the mode of questioning can facilitate accuracy. The EDE offers a good example. In its administration, accurate recall is significantly aided by following the recommended procedure of having the interviewer refer to a diary or calendar to enhance recall of the previous 28 days. Key points or events during the period can be more easily identified in this way and serve as a reminder of what happened on surrounding days. As Wilson (1987) has noted, this procedure is an adaptation of the Sobell and Sobell Time Line (TL) technique for assessing drinking in alcoholics (Sobell, Sobell, Leo, & Cancilla, 1988).

The TL technique has been shown to improve the reliability and validity of self-reported use and abuse of alcohol (Sobell et al., 1988). Furthermore, the TL has additional clinical value. Following the Time Line back on a calendar represents a form of retrospective self-monitoring or behavioral assessment. As the therapist works with the patient, the chances of uncovering clinically significant patterns of bulimic behavior are maximized. Antecedent and consequent events that might be maintaining the behavior may be identified in a way that is precluded by requests for global self-reports of past functioning.

Detailed clinical interviews such as the EDE are not appropriate for all occasions or purposes. Two relative disadvantages of the EDE are that, for research purposes, it requires raters with specific training in its administration and may take more than an hour to complete.

SELF-MONITORING

Self-monitoring consists of patients recording in eating diaries or on special monitoring forms their entire daily food and liquid intake, typically over the period of a week. Self-monitoring records should specify the following information about all eating and drinking: the time of day; the location, the type and amount consumed; and the social, emotional, and environmental context. To increase the accuracy of patients' self-monitoring, Rosen and Srebnik (1990) recommend brief training in identifying food servings in standard units of measurement. Such training is probably the exception rather than the rule, however. Self-monitoring does not include weighing food. Not only is this impractical, but it may also needlessly exacerbate patients' preoccupation with food. Calorie counting is not encouraged for the same reason.

Patients should also be asked to identify which eating episodes they viewed as excessive and whether or not they felt in control of their eating at the time. Patients should also be asked to record food intake as soon as possible after eating to maximize accuracy. It is not recommended that patients complete this recording immediately prior to eating. Clinical experience suggests that they only rarely comply with such an assignment. Moreover, if the objective is simply to obtain a measure of actual eating, postprandial assessment is preferred. Compliance with self-monitoring should be actively promoted rather than passively expected. Patients need to be given an explanation of its purpose and its importance to assessment and treatment. Potential obstacles to completing self-monitoring should be anticipated and suggestions made for overcoming them. Compliance is best when self-monitoring is embedded with an actively collaborative relationship between the assessor and the patient (Meichenbaum & Turk, 1989).

Advantages

Self-monitoring offers many advantages as an assessment technique, to the extent that it has long been the backbone of behavioral assessment strategies across a wide range of different clinical problems (Hawton, Salkovskis, Kirk, & Clark, 1989; O'Leary & Wilson, 1987). A particular advantage is that patient self-monitoring allows for immediacy of assessment of binge eating, which presumably increases accuracy. It avoids the inevitable problems of retrospective recall, possibly distorted by reactions of shame and embarrassment, inherent in clinical interviews and questionnaire administration.

The only study of the reliability of self-monitoring of binge eating showed encouraging results (Crowther, Lingswiler, & Stephens, 1984). Of a sample of 56 college students, 29 were classified as binge eaters on the basis that they responded positively to the question "Do you ever engage in periods of uncontrolled, excessive eating commonly called binge eating or bingeing?" and had a score of 10 or higher on the BS (Hawkins & Clement, 1980). Subjects were asked to complete Daily Food Schedules in which they recorded all eating episodes after they had finished eating for a 2-week period. They also indicated which episodes they considered to have been binges. Roommates or family members were given the identical Daily Food Schedules and asked to record the subjects' eating whenever they were with them. They were instructed not to discuss their observations with subjects.

The mean percentage agreement between subjects and their partners was 89.7% both for types of food and the amount consumed during binges. This finding is somewhat puzzling given that binge eating is usually a secretive activity. There were no significant differences in type or amount of food between eating episodes, matched for time of day and location, during which partners were present or absent. This finding suggests that the independent reliability checks did not significantly influence subjects' self-monitoring.

Self-monitoring has proved to be particularly useful in research on treatment outcome and in clinical assessment and intervention. A number of controlled psychological treatment studies have used self-monitoring records to determine treatment effects (e.g., Agras, Schneider, Arnow, Raeburn, & Telch, 1989; Leitenberg, Rosen, Gross, Nudelman, & Vara, 1988; Wilson, Rossiter, Kleifield, & Lindholm, 1986). Self-monitoring is especially important in the cognitive-behavioral therapy (CBT) approach to assessment and treatment. The proximal antecedents or triggers of binge eating are identified primarily by asking patients to record the circumstances in which episodes occurred. It provides the information that allows the therapist to determine when and where the episode took place; what the patient was thinking, feeling, and doing at the time; and the nature of the interpersonal context. This information is essential in CBT for selecting and implementing cognitive and behavioral change strategies.

Disadvantages

Self-monitoring can provide a detailed assessment of what food was eaten, when it was eaten, and under what circumstances. It is the patient who decides whether a particular eating episode was a binge. This procedure, therefore, differs from a clinical interview such as the EDE in which the assessor determines whether a binge occurred. It can be argued that it is difficult for eating-disordered patients to make the contextual assessment that is necessary to define their overeating. In this view, the assessor should determine what constitutes binge eating. This issue has received relatively little attention in the literature.

Some studies that have used self-monitoring to assess treatment-produced changes in binge eating have ignored the DSM-III-R requirement of an objectively large amount of food, and simply recorded patients' judgment of what constituted a binge, even if the amount eaten was only perceived to be excessive. In the terminology of the EDE, this combines objective and subjective bulimic episodes. An alternative approach, which yields data consistent with the DSM-III-R criteria, is to educate the patient about what constitutes a binge and ensure a shared understanding of what is being monitored. Fairburn and Beglin (1992) found that the EDE-Q self-report assessment of binge eating correlated more highly with the EDE interview measure for patients with eating disorders than the community sample. To the degree that this reflected the patients' superior understanding of the nature of binge eating, this result underscores the importance of ensuring such mutual understanding. In a preliminary study, Loeb et al. (1992) found an impressively high positive correlation of .96 between posttreatment EDE assessment of objective bulimic episodes (binges) and self-monitoring records for the preceding 7 days.

Several sources of potential inaccuracy with self-monitoring can be identified (Rosen & Srebnik, 1990). Instead of monitoring intake at the time of eating, patients often postpone this recording to some later time (e.g., the end of the day). Patients often report "spacing out" during binge eating. This dissociative-like state can combine with the emotional impact of binge eating (not to mention the occurrence of purging in patients with bulimia nervosa), to threaten the accuracy of recall about precisely what was eaten. Nevertheless, even if self-monitoring provides only a rough estimate of the amount of food consumed, it is reasonable to assume that it reliably reflects the frequency of binge-eating episodes.

The act of self-monitoring may itself directly influence the nature and frequency of binge eating. Daily recording is likely to prompt greater awareness of the relationship between binge eating and the situational influences that trigger this behavior. This is a disadvantage if the goal is to obtain a nonreactive estimate of binge eating. It is a plus in therapy. Self-monitoring is not merely an assessment technique in CBT. It is an integral part of attempts to help patients develop improved self-regulation over their behavior, serving as the basis of self-evaluative reactions and self-reinforcement processes (Bandura, 1986). Self-monitoring has been shown to be reactive in the assessment of obesity (Green, 1978) and cigarette smoking (Abrams & Wilson, 1979). Two studies have compared the pretreatment self-monitoring of binge eating in patients with bulimia nervosa with their self-reports of these activities during pretreatment interviews (Wilson et al., 1986; Yates & Sambrailo, 1984). In both studies the self-monitoring revealed significantly lower frequencies of both binge eating and vomiting than patients' self-reports. This finding is consistent with the notion that self-monitoring is reactive, but the possibility that self-report is simply less accurate than self-monitoring, or vice versa, cannot be ruled out.

A study of the eating behavior of obese binge eaters showed a different pattern of findings (Rossiter et al., 1992). Prior to treatment, 1 week's self-monitoring revealed that these patients had a mean of 10.6 (SD = 7.5) binges and had binged on 5 (SD = 2.2) days. In contrast, self-reported calendar recall of the 7 days preceding the week of self-monitoring indicated a mean of 5.7 (SD = 3.7) binges, and 4.4 (SD = 1.7) binge days. Rossiter and her colleagues suggest that the discrepancy between these data for obese binge eaters and those previously obtained with bulimia nervosa patients may be attributable to the former's difficulty in accurately recalling binge episodes ''when there are no discrete purging episodes to anchor them in patients' minds'' (p. 117).

The optimal length of self-monitoring is largely a function of the purpose of the assessment. Most treatment outcome studies have used periods of 1 or perhaps 2 weeks. This might be too short a time interval. Binge eating frequencies can fluctuate considerably in the short-term, suggesting that a 1-week window may not capture the overall pattern. However, more than 1 or 2 weeks is impractical in pretreatment assessment, suggesting the need for an alternative measure such as the EDE, which has a 28-day time span (Wilson et al., 1991). There are data from posttreatment assessment of binge eating in patients with bulimia nervosa, however, which suggest that a brief period of 7 days of self-monitoring may accurately reflect frequency over a longer period. Loeb et al. (1992) reported a correlation of .96 between 7 days of self-monitoring and the preceding 28 days at posttreatment assessment in patients with bulimia nervosa.

OBJECTIVE MEASURES

Laboratory Studies of Binge Eating

Direct behavioral measurement of binge eating has advantages no other form of assessment can match. Walsh (Chapter 3, this volume) summarizes the research on the experimental analysis of binge eating in patients with bulimia nervosa in laboratory or inpatient settings. The same methodology has been extended to the study of binge eating in patients with the diagnosis of binge eating disorder (Goldfein, Walsh, Devlin, LaChaussee, & Kissileff, 1992; Yanovski et al., 1992).

Advantages

The unique feature of this approach to behavioral assessment is the precision and objectivity it confers on calculation of the amount and type of food consumed under experimentally controlled conditions. This methodological rigor makes controlled behavioral measurement a powerful tool for basic research on the nature of binge eating. Several important findings have emerged from this approach. Binge eating in patients with bulimia nervosa is characterized by the overall amount of food consumed rather than differences in macronutrient content from nonbinge meals. This research has helped to disconfirm the widely held notion of "carbohydrate craving" among patients with bulimia nervosa. Another distinctive feature of patients with bulimia nervosa is that they also eat less than normal controls during nonbinge meals. This research has confirmed clinical impressions that bulimia nervosa is characterized by a pattern of dietary restriction punctuated by uncontrolled consumption of large amounts of food.

Disadvantages

Laboratory assessment of this sort represents a highly specialized research procedure and has no clinical applicability. Another limitation is that it is inevitably conducted in an artificial setting. Gone are the characteristic privacy and secrecy that are such an integral part of binge eating in the real world. In part because of these realities, many patients will not consent to participate in this type of research. Therefore, it is difficult to know how generalizable are the findings obtained from these highly selected patients studied under atypical conditions. Walsh and colleagues tried to address this issue by asking subjects to rate their eating in terms of how "typical" it was of a binge. As discussed by Walsh (Chapter 3, this volume), some patients rated their eating after the instruction to eat normally as typical of their binge eating. Others, instructed to binge, rated their eating as not at all typical of binge eating. They counted as binges only those meals consumed after the instruction to binge and rated as "moderately" or "extremely" typical of a binge. Yanovski et al. (1992) did not have to make this adjustment. They found that their BED patients rated meals following the instruction to binge as uniformly very typical of their binge eating outside of the laboratory. Despite the limitations on the generalizability of these laboratory studies of behavioral assessment of binge eating, it must be noted that the results have been comparable across different laboratories, and are also generally consistent with self-reported eating patterns.

Standardized Test Meals

Rosen and the Vermont group developed a procedure using standardized test meals to assess the eating habits of patients with bulimia nervosa (Rosen, Leitenberg, Fondacaro, Gross, & Willmuth, 1985). The test consists of asking subjects to eat as much as they "comfortably can" of a complete dinner in the laboratory on 1 day, followed by two different meals at home on the next 2 days. Patients are instructed not to vomit for at least 2½ hours after the meal. Compared to normal controls, patients ate significantly less of all three meals. Rather than assessing binge eating, these standardized test meals provide an index of dietary restraint.

CONCLUSIONS AND RECOMMENDATIONS

The relative merits of the different methods for assessing binge eating depend on the purpose of the assessment. Self-report questionnaires are useful as measures of overall severity but have major limitations when it comes to the diagnosis and clinically relevant description of binge eating.

Behavioral measurement of binge eating under laboratory conditions offers the most objective form of assessment but is limited to being a highly specialized research strategy. Of measures with broad clinical applicability, self-monitoring provides the most direct assessment of the frequency and temporal pattern of eating behavior. The limitations of self-monitoring are that the recording is often made retrospectively and that patients have to make the judgment whether a perceived overeating episode constitutes a binge as defined in DSM-III-R (APA, 1987) and DSM-IV. There is evidence that this is difficult for them to do reliably. The use of self-monitoring to assess therapeutic effects should continue in controlled treatment outcome studies, and, ideally, should be used in conjunction with a detailed clinical interview such as the EDE (Rosen & Srebnic, 1990). Self-monitoring is uniquely useful to the clinician in identifying the proximal antecedents and consequences of binge eating and in planning specific therapeutic interventions.

The EDE, a semistructured clinical interview, has several advantages over alternative methods of assessment. It is the only instrument that directly assesses the diagnostic criteria of all eating disorders. It is the only instrument that directly assesses the different forms of overeating. The conceptual framework and clear definitions it offers for assessing objectively and subjectively large eating episodes, and whether or not they are accompanied by a sense of loss of control, provide the means for ultimately establishing the diagnostic and clinical significance of these distinctions. It is unmatched in the depth and breath of assessment. In anorexia nervosa and bulimia nervosa, binge eating occurs against the backdrop of severe dietary restriction. The general consensus is that dieting is an important antecedent (if not a necessary but not sufficient cause) of binge eating (see Polivy & Herman, Chapter 9, this volume). The EDE provides the most direct and detailed assessment of dietary restriction of any assessment instrument, including searching questions about the avoidance of eating in general, avoidance of particular foods, skipping meals, attempts to impose caloric limits, reactions to violations of self-imposed dietary rules, and preoccupation with food and its caloric content. As Rosen et al. (1990) have concluded, it "appears to be the only validated measure of eating disorders that could be substituted for a battery of other measures" (p. 527).

NOTE

1. This questionnaire has been revised and now defines a binge consistently with DSM-IV (see Yanovski, in press). It is called the Questionnaire on Eating and Weight Patterns—Revised (QEWP-R).

REFERENCES

Abrams, D. B., & Wilson, G. T. (1979). Self-monitoring and reactivity in the modification of cigarette smoking. *Journal of Consulting and Clinical Psychology, 47*, 243-251.

Agras, W. S., Schneider, J. A., Arnow, B., Raeburn, S. D., & Telch, C. F. (1989). Cognitive-behavioral treatment with and without exposure plus response prevention in the treatment of bulimia nervosa: A reply to Leitenberg and Rosen. *Journal of Consulting and Clinical Psychology, 57,* 778-779.

American Psychiatric Association. (1980). *Diagnostic and statistical manual of mental disorders* (3rd ed.). Washington, DC: Author.

American Psychiatric Association. (1987). *Diagnostic and statistical manual of mental disorders* (3rd ed., rev.). Washington, DC: Author.

American Psychiatric Association. (1993). *DSM-IV draft criteria (3/1/93).* Washington, DC: Author.

Bandura, A. (1986). *Social foundations of thought and action: A social cognitive theory.* Englewood Cliffs, NJ: Prentice Hall.

Babor, T. F., Brown, J., & Del Boca, F. K. (1990). Validity of self-reports in applied research on addictive behaviors: Fact or fiction? *Behavioral Assessment, 12,* 5-31.

Cooper, Z., Cooper, P. J., & Fairburn, C. G. (1989). The validity of the Eating Disorder Examination and its subscales. *British Journal of Psychiatry, 154,* 807-812.

Cooper, Z., & Fairburn, C. (1987). The Eating Disorder Examination: A semistructured interview for the assessment of the specific psychopathology of eating disorders. *International Journal of Eating Disorders, 6,* 1-8.

Crowther, J. H., Lingswiler, V. M., & Stephens, M. A. (1984). Topography of binge eating. *Addictive Behaviors, 9,* 299-303.

Fairburn, C. G., & Beglin, S. J. (1990). Studies of the epidemiology of bulimia nervosa. *American Journal of Psychiatry, 147,* 401-408.

Fairburn, C. G., & Beglin, S. J. (1992). *The assessment of eating disorders: Interview on self-report questionnaire?* Unpublished manuscript, Oxford University.

Fairburn, C. G., Jones, R., Peveler, R. C., Carr, S., Solomon, R., O'Connor, M. E., & Hope, R. A. (1991). Three psychological treatments for bulimia nervosa: A comparative trial. *Archives of General Psychiatry, 48,* 463-469.

Fichter, M. M., Elton, M., Engel, K., Meyer, A., Poustka, F., Mall, H., & von der Heydte, S. (1989). The Structured Interview for Anorexia and Bulimia Nervosa (SIAB): Development and characteristics of a (semi-)standardized instrument. In M. M. Fichter (Ed.) *Bulimia nervosa: Basic research, diagnosis and therapy* (pp. 57-70). Chichester: Wiley.

Garner, D. M. (1991). *Eating Disorders Inventory-2.* Odessa, FL: Psychological Assessment Resources.

Garner, D. M., Olmstead, M. A., & Polivy, J. (1983). Development and validation of a multidimensional Eating Disorder Inventory for anorexia nervosa and bulimia nervosa. *International Journal of Eating Disorders, 2,* 15-34.

Garner, D. M., Rockert, W., Davis, R., Garner, M. V., Olmsted, M. P., & Eagle, M. (1993). Comparison between cognitive-behavioral and supportive-expressive therapy for bulimia nervosa. *American Journal of Psychiatry, 150,* 37-46.

Garner, D. M., Shafer, C. L., Rosen, L. W. (1992). Critical appraisal of the DSM-III-R Diagnostic criteria for eating disorders. In S. R. Hooper, G. W. Hynd, and R. E. Mattison (Eds.), *Child psychopathology, diagnostic criteria and clinical assessment* (pp. 261-302). Hillsdale, NJ: Erlbaum.

Giles, T., Young, R., & Young, D. (1985). Behavioral treatment of severe bulimia. *Behavior Therapy, 16,* 393-405.

Goldfein, J., Walsh, B. T., Devlin, M. J., LaChaussee, J., & Kissileff, H. (1992, April 24). *Eating behavior in binge eating disorder.* Paper presented at the Fifth International Conference on Eating Disorders, New York.

Gormally, J., Black, S., Daston, S., & Rardin, D. (1982). The assessment of binge eating severity among obese persons. *Addictive Behaviors, 7,* 47–55.

Green, I. (1978). Temporal and stimulus factors in self-monitoring by obese persons. *Behavior Therapy, 9,* 328–341.

Gross, J., Rosen, J. C., Leitenberg, H., & Willmuth, M. (1986). Validity of the Eating Attitudes Test and the Eating Disorders Inventory in bulimia nervosa. *Journal of Consulting and Clinical Psychology, 54,* 875–876.

Hawkins, R., & Clement, P. (1980). Development and construct validation of a self-report measure of binge eating tendencies. *Addictive Behaviors, 5,* 219–226.

Hawton, K., Salkovskis, P., Kirk, J., & Clark, D. (1989). *Cognitive behaviour therapy.* Oxford: Oxford University Press.

Henderson, M., & Freeman, C. P. L. (1987). A self-rating scale for bulimia: The BITE. *British Journal of Psychiatry, 150,* 18–24.

Jacobs, M., & Schneider, J. (1985). Medical complications of bulimia: A prospective evaluation. *Quarterly Journal of Medicine, 54,* 177–182.

Leitenberg, H., Rosen, J., Gross, J., Nudelman, S., & Vara, L. S. (1988). Exposure plus response prevention treatment of bulimia nervosa. *Journal of Consulting and Clinical Psychology, 56,* 535– 541.

Loeb, K., Walsh, T. B., & Pike, K. M. (1992, April 24). *The assessment of bulimia nervosa.* Paper presented at the Fifth International Conference on Eating Disorders, New York.

Marcus, M. D., Smith, D., Santelli, R., & Kaye, W. (1992). Characterization of eating disordered behavior in obese binge eaters. *International Journal of Eating Disorders, 12,* 249–256.

Marcus, M. D., Wing, R. R., & Hopkins, J. (1988). Obese binge eaters: Affect, cognitions and response to behavioral weight control. *Journal of Consulting and Clinical Psychology, 56,* 433–439.

Meichenbaum, D., & Turk, D. C. (1989). *Facilitating treatment adherence.* New York: Plenum Press.

Miller, W. R., & Rollnick, S. (1992). *Motivational interviewing: Preparing people to change addictive behavior.* New York: Guilford Press.

Mitchell, J. E., & Laine, D. C. (1985). Monitored binge eating behavior in patients with bulimia nervosa. *International Journal of Eating Disorders, 4,* 177–183.

Mitchell, J. E., Pomeroy, C., & Colon, E. (1989). Medical complications in bulimia nervosa. In M. M. Fichter (Ed.), *Bulimia nervosa: Basic research, diagnosis and therapy* (pp. 71–83). New York: Wiley.

O'Leary, K. D., & Wilson, G. T. (1987). *Behavior therapy: Application and outcome* (2nd ed.). Englewood Cliffs, NJ: Prentice Hall.

Ortega, D. F., Waranch, H. R., Maldonado, A. J., & Hubbard, F. A. (1987). A comparative analysis of self-report measures of bulimia. *International Journal of Eating Disorders, 6,* 301–311.

Palmer, R. Christie, M., Cordle, C., Davies, D., & Kenrick, J. (1987). The Clinical Eating Disorder Rating Instrument (CEDRI): A preliminary description. *International Journal of Eating Disorders, 6,* 9–16.

Polich, J. M. (1982). The validity of self-reports in alcoholism research. *Addictive Behaviors, 7,* 123–132.

Rosen, J. C., Leitenberg, H., Fondacaro, K. M., Gross, J., & Willmuth, M. E. (1985). Standardized test meals in assessment of eating behavior in bulimia nervosa: Consumption of feared foods when vomiting is prevented. *International Journal of Eating Disorders, 4,* 59–70.

Rosen, J. C., & Srebnik, D. (1990). Assessment of eating disorders. In P. McReynolds, J. C. Rosen, & G. Chelune (Eds.), *Advances in psychological assessment* (Vol. 7, pp. 229–259). New York: Plenum Press.

Rosen, J. C., Vara, L., Wendt, S., & Leitenberg, H. (1990). Validity studies of the Eating Disorder Examination. *International Journal of Eating Disorders, 9,* 519–528.

Rossiter, E. M., Agras, W. S., Telch, C. F., & Bruce, B. (1992). The eating patterns of non-purging bulimic subjects. *International Journal of Eating Disorders, 11,* 111–120.

Skinner, H., & Sheu, W. (1982). Reliability of alcohol use indices: The lifetime drinking history and the MAST. *Journal of Studies on Alcohol, 43,* 1157–1170.

Smith, M. C., & Thelen, M. H. (1984). Development and validation of a test for bulimia nervosa. *Journal of Consulting and Clinical Psychology, 52,* 863–872.

Sobell, L. C., Sobell, M. B., Leo, G. I., & Cancilla, A. (1988). Reliability of a timeline method: Assessment normal drinkers' reports of recent drinking and a comparative evaluation across several populations. *British Journal of Addiction, 83,* 393–402.

Spitzer, R. L. (1992). *Binge Eating Disorder Interview.* Unpublished manuscript, Columbia University.

Spitzer, R. L., Devlin, M., Walsh, B. T., Hasin, D., Wing, R., Marcus, M., Stunkard, A., Wadden, T., Yonovski, S., Agras, W. S., Mitchell, J., & Nonas, C. (1992). Binge eating disorder: A multisite field trial of the diagnostic criteria. *International Journal of Eating Disorders, 11,* 191–203.

Thelen, M. H., Farmer, J., Wonderlich, J., Smith, M. C. (1991). A revision of the Bulimia Test: BULIT-R. *Psychological Assessment, 3,* 119–124.

Vuchinich, R. E., Tucker, J. A., & Harllee, L. M. (1988). Behavioral assessment. In D. M. Donovan & G. A. Marlatt (Eds.), *Assessment of addictive behaviors* (pp. 51–83). New York: Guilford Press.

Wilfley, D. E., Agras, W. S., Telch, C. F., Rossiter, E. M., Schneider, J. A., Cole, A. G., Sifford, L. A., & Raeburn, S. D. (in press). Group cognitive-behavioral therapy and group interpersonal psychotherapy for the nonpurging bulimia: A controlled comparison. *Journal of Consulting and Clinical Psychology.*

Williams, G., Aitken, S., & Malin, H. (1985). Reliability of self-reported alcohol consumption in a general population survey. *Journal of Studies on Alcohol, 46,* 223–227.

Williamson, D. A. (1990). *Assessment of eating disorders.* New York: Pergamon Press.

Wilson, G. T. (1987). Assessing treatment outcome in bulimia nervosa: A methodological note. *International Journal of Eating Disorders, 6,* 339–348.

Wilson, G. T., Eldredge, K. L., Smith, D., & Niles, B. (1991). Cognitive-behavioral treatment with and without response prevention for bulimia. *Behaviour Research and Therapy, 29,* 575–583.

Wilson, G. T., Rossiter, E., Kleifield, E., & Lindholm, L. (1986). Cognitive-behavioral treatment of bulimia nervosa: A controlled evaluation. *Behaviour Research and Therapy, 24,* 277–288.

Wilson, G. T., & Smith, D. (1989). Assessment of bulimia nervosa and evaluation of the Eating Disorder Examination. *International Journal of Eating Disorders, 8,* 173–180.

Yanovski, S. Z., (1993). *Binge Eating Disorder Clinical Interview.* Unpublished manuscript. Division of Digestive Diseases and Nutrition, National Institute of Health, Bethesda, MD.

Yanovski, S. Z. (in press). Binge eating disorder: Current knowledge and future direction. *Obesity Research.*

Yanovski, S. Z., Leet, M., Yanovski, J. A., Flood, M., Gold, P. W., Kissileff, H. J., & Walsh, B. T. (1992). Food selection and intake in obese women with binge eating disorder. *American Journal of Clinical Nuitrition, 56,* 975–980.

Yates, A. J., & Sambrailo, F. (1984). Bulimia nervosa: A descriptive and therapeutic study. *Behaviour Research and Therapy, 22,* 502–518.

Pharmacological Treatments of Binge Eating

James E. Mitchell
Martina de Zwaan

RATIONALE FOR THE USE
OF PSYCHOPHARMACOLOGICAL DRUGS

Research in the neurosciences has begun to unravel the basic biological mechanisms, both central and peripheral, that control eating and appetite. Neurotransmitters such as norepinephrine (NE), serotonin (5-HT), and dopamine, neuropeptides such as cholecystokinin (CCK), opioids, neuropeptide Y, and peptide YY, and hormones such as cortisol and insulin have all been shown to be involved in the regulation of eating behavior in animal studies, influencing such parameters as appetite, hunger, satiety, macronutrient selection, meal frequency, meal size, meal initiation, rate of eating, meal duration, intermeal intervals, total food intake, body weight, and binge eating.

Up until recently it has been impossible to measure actual neuromodulator influences on eating behavior in humans, since there is no direct means to continuously monitor neurotransmitter activity in the human brain, and, therefore, researchers have had to speculate through analogies from animal experiments. There are, however, some indirect indicators of neuromodulator activity, although most are of uncertain value, such as measuring the cerebrospinal fluid (CSF) and plasma levels of neuromodulators and their metabolites or precursors (tryptophan, 5-HIAA, somatostatin, peptide YY), provocative challenge tests (tryptophan, m-CPP, test meals), and the examination of peripheral receptor sites (imipramine binding sites on platelets, beta-adrenergic receptors sites on lymphocytes). These approaches have suggested ways to manipulate neuromodulator functions in humans by administering drugs with specific effects on different systems, and some of this research has suggested pharmacological strategies that can be used to modify eating behavior in humans. In particular, some of this work has suggested possible ways to modify binge eating in humans.

For example, recent research has focused on the use of serotonergic drugs in the treatment of binge eating and overeating, since they have been shown to enhance satiety (Enas, Pope, & Levine, 1989; Fluoxetine Bulimia Nervosa Collaborative Study Group, 1992a; Freeman & Hampson, 1987; Wilcox, 1990). Wurtman (1987) and others have suggested that bulimics may have low levels of serotonin in the central nervous system. Because many antidepressants increase the turnover of serotonin, these drugs may reduce the frequency of binge eating, if binge eating is driven by the need to increase brain serotonin.

Many patients with eating disorders demonstrate symptoms suggestive of other psychiatric disorders, particularly affective disorders and impulse control disorders. This overlap or comorbidity has led some researchers to conceptualize eating disorders as secondary to depressive illness, or as manifestations of impulse dyscontrol. It has been established that serotonergic dysfunction can also contribute to impairment in mood (Hudson, Pope, Jonas, & Yurgelun-Todd, 1983) and impulse control. These observations have suggested possible pharmacological strategies to these problems.

Drugs that reduce hunger may also facilitate restraint and thereby affect binge eating (Craighead & Agras, 1991). Two controlled studies of such drugs, one with methylamphetamine and the other with fenfluramine, have been conducted under laboratory conditions (Ong, Checkley, & Russell, 1983; Robinson Checkley, & Russell, 1985). These drugs have different effects on brain neurotransmitters, methylamphetamine acting mainly on dopamine and noradrenaline, and fenfluramine mainly on serotonin.

Like the serotonergic system, the endogenous opioid peptide system appears to be important in the control of feeding behavior, in particular stress-induced feeding (Fullerton, Getto, Swift, & Carlson, 1985). Selective opiate antagonists including naloxone, naltrexone, and nalmefene have proven to have robust short-term effects in reducing food consumption. These observations have led to the hypothesis that opioid antagonists might decrease eating and/or stress-induced overeating. Studies that address this hypothesis will be examined below.

GENERAL REMARKS

Most studies on the psychopharmacological treatment of binge eating have been conducted with patients with bulimia nervosa, even though binge eating has been associated with a variety of clinical syndromes including anorexia nervosa, obesity, seasonal affective disorder, premenstrual syndrome, and certain organic disorders.

The studies reviewed in this chapter have generally used criteria for bulimia nervosa from the third edition and third edition, revised, of the *Diagnostic and Statistical Manual of Mental Disorders* (DSM-III; DSM-III-R) (American Psychiatric Association, 1980, 1987). In some studies additional criteria such as vomiting, a minimum frequency of three binge eating/vomiting episodes per week, and a duration of illness of more than 1 year have been required to assure homogeneity and a certain degree of severity among the subjects (Mitchell et al., 1990; Walsh et al., 1988). Some studies have used Russell's criteria (Ong et al., 1983; Russell, Checkley, Feldman, & Eisler, 1988; Sabine, Yonace, Farrington, Barratt, & Wakeling, 1983), or their own criteria for binge eating or compulsive eating (Wermuth, Davis, Hollister, & Stunkard, 1977), which have generally required both overeating and and a sense of lack of control over eating.

Assessment of abnormal eating behaviors in these studies has usually relied on self-report methods, often daily diaries. It must be pointed out that the validity of self-reported eating behavior is still unclear (see Wilson, Chapter 11, this volume).

RESEARCH FINDINGS

Overview

Many different drugs have been used in the treatment of binge eating among bulimic, anorexic, and obese subjects. These include tricyclic antidepressants (amitriptyline, imipramine, desipramine), nontricyclic antidepressants (mianserin, fluoxetine, fluvoxamine, phenelzine, trazodone, bupropion, tryptophan, lithium), appetite suppressants (fenfluramine, methylamphetamine), as well as anticonvulsants (carbamazepine, phenytoin), cyproheptadine, and opioid antagonists (naloxone, naltrexone).

Antidepressants

The results of most of the controlled trials reported to date indicate that antidepressants show at least some superiority over placebo in reducing the frequency of binge eating episodes, as well as the intensity of some other symptoms commonly seen in eating disorder patients, such as preoccupation with food and depressive symptoms (Table 12.1). The dosage levels needed to achieve an effect appear to be similar to those required in the treatment of major depression with a tendency for higher

TABLE 12.1. Controlled Trials of Antidepressants in Patients with Binge Eating

Author(s) (year)	Drug	Dosage (mg/day)	Duration (weeks)	Diagnosis	Assessment of binge eating	Change in binge-eating frequency (no. of patients)
Tricyclics						
Bulimia (nervosa)						
Pope, Hudson, Jones, & Yurgelun-Todd (1983)	Imipramine	200	6	DSM-III	Daily episodes interview	red. >75% (4), red. >50%(4), red. <50%(1)
	Placebo					red. >50%(1), red. <50%(8), incr.(1)
Mitchell & Groat (1984)	Amitriptyline	150	8	DSM-III	Daily episodes EB-III	m.red. 72%(16)
	Placebo					m.red. 52%(16)
Hughes et al. (1986)	Desipramine	200	2–6	DSM-III	Daily episodes diary	red. ≥80%(9), red. <80%(1)
	Placebo					red. ≥80%(0), red. <80%(12)
Agras et al. (1987)	Imipramine	$m = 167$	16	DSM-III	Daily episodes diary	m.red. 72%(10).rem 30%
	Placebo					m.red. 43%(10)
Kaplan et al. (1987)	Imipramine	Plasma levels	6 (CO)	DSM-III	—	imi. sig. > plac.(11)
	Placebo					
Blouin et al. (1988)	Desipramine	150	6 (CO)	DSM-III	Daily episodes diary; Bulimia subscale of EDI	sig. red.(10)
	Placebo					n.i.
Barlow et al. (1988)	Desipramine	150	6 (CO)	DSM-III	Weekly episodes weekly questionnaire	red >80%(3), red. >50%(8), red. <50%(13) n.i.(24)
	Placebo					
Walsh et al. (1991)	Desipramine	200–300	6	DSM-III-R	Daily episodes diary	m.red. 47%(40), rem. 12.5%(5)
	Placebo					m.incr. 7%(38), rem. 7.5%(3)
Alger et al. (1991)	Imipramine	100–150	6	DSM-III-R	Daily episodes diary	m.red. 26%(7)
	Placebo					m.red. 30%(7)
Obese binge eaters						
McCann & Agras (1990)	Desipramine	$m = 188$ 100–300	12	DSM-III-R no purging	No. of days with binge-eating diary	m.red. 63%(10), rem. 60%
	Placebo					m.incr. 16%(13), rem.15%
Alger et al. (1991)	Imipramine	100–150	6	BES ≥ 25	Daily episodes diary	m.red. 73%(12)
	Placebo					m.red. 50%(11)

(cont.)

253

TABLE 12.1. (cont.)

Author(s) (year)	Drug	Dosage (mg/day)	Duration (weeks)	Diagnosis	Assessment of binge eating	Change in binge-eating frequency (no. of patients)
MAOIs						
Bulimia (nervosa)						
Walsh et al. (1988)	Phenelzine	60–90	8	DSM-III	Daily episodes diary	m.red. 64.2%(23), rem. 35%
	Placebo					m.red. 5.5%(27), rem. 4%
Kennedy et al. (1988)	Isocarboxazid	60	6 (CO)	DSM-III	Daily episodes diary and interview	red. >50%(10), red. <50%(2), rem. 33%
	Placebo					red. >50%(5), red. <50%(7)
Serotonin reuptake inhibitors						
Bulimia nervosa						
FBNC Study Group (1992a)	Fluoxetine	60	8	DSM-III-R	Daily episodes patient's own definition	med. red. 67%
	Fluoxetine	20				med. red. 45%
	Placebo					med. red. 33%
FBNC Study Group (1992b)	Fluoxetine	60	16	DSM-III-R	Daily episodes diary	med. red. 50%(290)
	Placebo					med. red. 18%(100)
Obese binge eaters						
Marcus et al. (1990)	Fluoxetine	60	52	BES≥27	Bulimia subscale of EDI	sig. red.(4)
	Placebo					sig. red.(5?)
Other antidepressants						
Bulimia (nervosa)						
Sabine et al. (1983)	Mianserin	60	8	Russell	No. of days with binge-eating diary	n.i.(14)
	Placebo					n.i.(22)
Horne et al. (1988)	Bupropion	450	8	DSM-III	Daily episodes diary	m.red. 67%(37)
	Placebo					m.red. 2%(12)
Pope et al. (1989)	Trazodone	200–400	6	DSM-III-R	Daily episodes diary	m.red. 31%(20), rem. 10%(2)
	Placebo					m.incr. 21%(22), rem. 0%

Note. BES, Binge Eating Scale; CO, crossover; EB-III, Eating Behavior III; EDI, Eating Disorder Inventory; incr., increase; m., mean; n.i., not improved; med., median; red., reduction; rem., remission; sig., significant.

dosages to be more effective. The time course of action of the medication also appears to be similar to that found in the treatment of depression, with improvement occurring after 1 and 3 weeks of treatment.

One study did not find an effect for antidepressants (Sabine et al., 1983). In this study the number of days per week the subjects reported bingeing and vomiting did not change throughout the 8-week period for either group; however, the dosage of 60 mg may have been subtherapeutic. Two other studies, one using amitriptyline and the other imipramine, obtained equivocal results (Alger, Schwalberg, Bigaoutte, Michalek, & Howard, 1991; Mitchell & Groat, 1984). However, these studies also used dosages that may have been below the therapeutic range (100–150 mg).

Tricyclic Antidepressants

Imipramine and desipramine are the best studied tricyclic drugs in the treatment of normal-weight and overweight subjects with binge-eating problems (four and five controlled studies, respectively). Most of these studies have shown a significant superiority for imipramine and desipramine over placebo in the reduction of binge-eating frequency (Table 12.1). Alger et al.'s (1991) results, however, did not confirm these findings, in that imipramine treatment was no different from placebo in the reduction of binge-eating frequency, both in normal-weight and obese binge eaters. However, they did report a significant reduction in binge eating frequency from baseline in all patients, irrespective of weight status and medication, and in imipramine-treated obese binge eaters they found a significant reduction in binge duration compared to placebo subjects. McCann and Agras (1990), on the other hand, found a striking superiority for desipramine over placebo in subjects with nonpurging bulimia nervosa. The patients who received desipramine reduced their frequency of binge eating by 63%, whereas patients receiving placebo increased their frequency of binge eating by 16%. At the end of the 12-week program, 60% of the active drug group but only 15% of the placebo group were abstinent from binge eating. In the desipramine group there was a significant increase in dietary restraint and a reduction in the tendency for stressors to trigger binge eating. After discontinuation of the drug, binge eating frequency rapidly increased again. These findings suggest that antidepressants might work by enhancing adherence to dietary rules.

The tricyclic antidepressant amitriptyline has been used in the treatment of bulimic anorexics, and appears to be superior to placebo in promoting weight gain (Halmi, Eckert, Ladu, & Cohen, 1986). Consistent with the effect in patients with bulimia nervosa, there was no increase in kilocalories consumed, suggesting no change in dietary restraint.

Monoamine Oxidase Inhibitors

A large number of uncontrolled studies have shown improvement in bulimic symptoms with monoamine oxidase inhibitors (MAOIs) (Brotman, Herzog, & Woods, 1984; Jonas, Hudson, & Pope, 1983; Kennedy, Piran, & Garfinkel, 1985; Pope, Hudson, & Jonas, 1983; Roy-Byrne, Gwirtsman, Edelstein, Yager, & Gerner, 1983; Shader & Greenblatt, 1982; Stewart, Walsh, Wright, Roose, & Glassman, 1984; Walsh et al., 1982). In addition, the MAO inhibitors phenelzine and isocarboxazide have been shown to be significantly superior to placebo in controlled trials using patients with bulimia nervosa (Kennedy et al., 1988; Walsh et al., 1988). In Walsh et al.'s (1988) study the effect of phenelzine was particularly striking, with a mean reduction of binge eating of 64.2% and a remission rate of 35.0% compared to only 5.5% reduction and 4.0% remission rate in the placebo group. A similar remission rate of 33% was obtained in Kennedy et al.'s study with isocarboxazid. In both the Kennedy et al. (1988) and Walsh et al. (1988) studies, however, side effects posed a major clinical problem, particularly orthostatic hypotension, insomnia, and sedation. Many patients discontinued the active drug shortly after the end of the double-blind trial, mainly because the side effects were difficult to tolerate.

In clinical practice MAO inhibitors are not often used to treat patients who binge eat because of the dietary restrictions required. Foods containing a high concentration of tyramine or dopamine may cause rapid and extreme rises in blood pressure that may be life threatening. Especially in outpatients who do not have sufficient control over their food intake, there is a risk of hypertensive crises. However, it must be noted that few bulimics binge eat on high tyramine foods such as aged cheese, beer, and chicken liver.

Serotonin Re-uptake Inhibitors

There has been recent interest in the use of serotonin reuptake inhibitors in the treatment of binge eating and bulimia nervosa. Fluoxetine hydrochloride has been shown to be effective in the treatment of bulimia nervosa at high dosages (60 mg/day). In a large multicenter placebo-controlled trial involving 387 patients, 60 mg of fluoxetine proved significantly superior to 20 mg fluoxetine and to placebo (FBNC Study Group, 1992a). The median reduction in binge-eating frequency was 67% and 45%, respectively, for the fluoxetine-treated patients, and 33% for the group receiving placebo. Subjects tolerated 60 mg well, even though therapy was initiated at this dosage. Thirty percent of patients discontinued participation during the 8-week study. However, discontinuation due to adverse events was rare (5%), and did not differ between the placebo-treated patients and those receiving fluoxetine. A 60-mg dose of fluoxetine has been shown to be effective and safe even over an extended period of 16 weeks in a subsequent study of 398 patients with bulimia nervosa (unpublished double-blind multicenter study). The median reduction of binge eating was 50% in fluoxetine-treated patients and 18% in placebo-treated patients. The drop-out rate was high, with 40% of patients on active drug and 52% on placebo discontinuing early. However, discontinuation associated with adverse events was low.

In the treatment of obese binge eaters Marcus et al. (1990) found no differences in the reduction of scores on the Bulimia subscale of the Eating Disorder Inventory in patients treated with fluoxetine or placebo. Fluoxetine-treated patients lost significantly more weight than those treated with placebo, but the drug did not appear to have a particular benefit for binge eaters. Furthermore, the authors observed that the effect on weight occurred primarily during the first 20 weeks of fluoxetine treatment with almost no effect thereafter. This observation seems to parallel the attenuation of the antibinge effect of antidepressants over time (Pope, Hudson, Jonas, & Yurgelun-Todd, 1985; Pyle et al., 1990; Walsh, Hadigan, Devlin, Gladis, & Roose, 1991).

Other Antidepressants

Bupropion, an antidepressant chemically unrelated to tricyclics and MAO inhibitors, cannot be recommended in the treatment of patients with binge-eating episodes, despite its significant superiority to placebo in patients with bulimia nervosa. In a multicenter-controlled trial (Horne et al., 1988), 5.8% of subjects experienced grand mal seizures during treatment with 450 mg bupropion, leading to early termination of the study. Trazodone produces few adverse effects in bulimic patients, but appears to be modest in its beneficial effects. Even though trazodone was significantly superior to placebo in reducing binge-eating frequency, Pope, Keck, McElroy, and Hudson (1989) found that only 2 out of 20 patients assigned to trazodone achieved a remission of bulimic symptoms.

Comparisons of Antidepressant Drugs and Psychological Treatments

Three recent studies have compared the relative effectiveness of cognitive-behavioral therapy (CBT) and antidepressant drugs (imipramine, desipramine, and fluoxetine) in normal-weight subjects with bulimia nervosa. The results of the two outpatient studies suggest superiority of CBT, with or without the antidepressant, over drug therapy alone, but with the suggestion that the drug does add to psychotherapy in some patients on certain variables (Agras et al., 1992; Mitchell et al., 1990). In Fichter et al.'s (1991) study of inpatients, the addition of fluoxetine did not augment improvement, possibly owing to a "ceiling effect." Hudson and Pope (1990) have suggested that the design of these comparison studies may underestimate the efficacy of drug treatment, since subjects are offered only a single drug, rather than different antidepressants or other agents if they fail to respond, as would be the case in clinical practice.

Lithium Carbonate

Hsu, Clement, Santhouse, and Ju (1991) reported the results of a study comparing lithium carbonate and placebo in 68 patients with bulimia nervosa some of whom had relapsed or failed to improve with behavior therapy (Table 12.5). As in Mitchell and Groat's (1984) study with amitriptyline, a minimal behavioral therapy was used in addition to pharmacotherapy. In both treatment groups the mean decrease in binge eating and purging was similar, reaching about 60%, whether or not the patient was depressed.

Given these findings there is little reason to use lithium in the treatment of patients with bulimia nervosa. Moreover, lithium should be used cautiously, given the fluid and electrolyte abnormalities to which these patients are prone (Mitchell, Pyle, Eckert, Hatsukami, & Lentz, 1983).

Anticonvulsants

Green, Rau, and colleagues (Green & Rau, 1974; Rau & Green, 1975; Rau & Green, 1978; Rau, Struve, & Green, 1979) reported epileptiform abnormalities in electroencephalographs (EEG) in 64% of a series of 59 patients with compulsive eating. More patients with abnormal EEGs at baseline improved on phenytoin than did patients with normal EEGs (70% vs. 35%, respectively). There has been only one controlled trial of phenytoin in binge eating, by Wermuth et al. (1977) using a double-blind cross-over design. Overall, the effectiveness of phenytoin was considerably less in this study than in Green and Rau's open studies. Furthermore, only a few patients exhibited abnormal EEGs, and these abnormalities did not correlate with treatment response. Kaplan, Garfinkel, Darby, and Garner (1983) published a pilot double-blind, cross-over study in six patients using carbamazepine. Only one patient with a concurrent diagnosis of affective disorder showed a response.

In summary, there is no convincing evidence to date for a relation between seizure disorder (or EEG abnormalities) and binge eating, or convincing evidence for the utility of anticonvulsants in these patients (Table 12.2).

Opiate Antagonists

One experimental study involved the short-term intravenous administration of the short-acting narcotic antagonist naloxone (Table 12.3). This study demonstrated a decrease in the amount of calories consumed during an eating binge in a series of patients hospitalized on a metabolic research ward. The comparison drugs were placebo and CCK-8, the putative satiety peptide. The decrease in kilocalories was significant for naloxone, but not CCK-8 (Mitchell, Laine, Morley, & Levine, 1986).

There have been several clinical studies using the long-acting orally active narcotic antagonist naltrexone hydrochloride. The results of three consecutive open label treatment studies by Jonas and Gold (1986, 1987, 1988) suggest that high-dose naltrexone therapy in the range to 200–300 mg a day will significantly reduce binge-eating behavior in normal-weight bulimic women. However, three controlled trials using lower dosages (50–150 mg a day) did not find a significant superiority over placebo (Alger et al., 1991; Igoin-Apfelbaum & Apfelbaum, 1987; Mitchell, Christenson, et al., 1989). Unfortunately, naltrexone carries a risk of hepatotoxicity at the higher dosages and therefore cannot be recommended for clinical usage in this population.

Appetite Suppressants

Two controlled investigations, one with methylamphetamine and the other with fenfluramine, have been conducted under laboratory conditions (Ong et al., 1983; Robinson et al., 1985) (Table 12.4). No patient experienced a binge-eating episode during the test meal following administration of active drug, whereas approximately 50% of patients did following placebo. Fenfluramine and d-fenfluramine have been found to be effective in reducing the frequency of binge-eating and vomiting episodes in two controlled trials using patients with bulimia nervosa (Blouin et al., 1988; Russell et al., 1988). One of these studies showed a reduction of associated symptoms such as depression (Blouin et al., 1988), whereas the other did not (Russell et al., 1988).

Fenfluramine has been extensively used in the treatment of obesity. To our knowledge there have been no reports examining its relative effectiveness in binge-eating and non-binge-eating obese patients.

TABLE 12.2. Controlled Trials of Anticonvulsants in Patients with Binge Eating

Author(s) (year)	Drug	Dosage (mg/day)	Duration (weeks)	Diagnosis	Assessment of binge eating	Change in binge-eating frequency (no. of patients)
Bulimia (nervosa)						
Wermuth et al. (1977)	Phenytoin	Plasma level 10–20ug/ml	6 (CO)	Compulsive eating (own)	daily episodes diary and interview	red. >75%(6), red. >50%(2), red. >20%(6), red. <20%(5)
	Placebo					red <20%(19)
Kaplan et al. (1983)	Carbamazepine	Plasma level 6–10ug/ml	6 (CO)	DSM-III	daily episodes diary	rem. (1), n.i.(5)
	Placebo					rem. (0), n.i.(6)

Note. CO. crossover: n.i.. not improved: red.. reduction: rem.. remission

TABLE 12.3. Controlled Trials of Opiate Antagonists in Patients with Binge Eating

Author(s) (year)	Drug	Dosage (mg/day)	Duration (weeks)	Diagnosis	Assessment of binge eating	Change in binge-eating frequency (no. of patients)
Bulimia (nervosa)						
Mitchell et al. (1986)	Naloxone Cholecysto-kinin-8	18 120	Single dose (CO)	DSM-III	Induction of binge-eating episode	red. of kcal consumed nal. >plac., CCK-8
Igoin-Apfelbaum & Apfelbaum (1987)	Naltrexone Placebo	120	4 (CO)	DSM-IV	–	nal. = plac.
Mitchell, Christenson, et al. (1989)	Naltrexone Placebo	50	3 (CO)	DSM-III-R	Daily episodes EB-III	nal. not sig. >plac.
Alger et al. (1991)	Naltrexone Placebo	150–200	6	DSM-III-R	Daily episodes diary	m.red. 30%(8) m.red. 30%(7)
Obese binge eaters						
Alger et al. (1991)	Naltrexone Placebo	150–200	6	BES ≥25	Daily episodes diary	m.red. 48%(10) m.red. 50%(11)

Note. BES. Binge Eating Scale: CCK-8: cholecystokinin-8: CO. crossover: EB-III. Eating Behavior III: m.. mean: nal.. naloxone/naltrexone: red.. reduction: sig.. significant

TABLE 12.4. Controlled Trials of Appetite Suppressants in Patients with Binge Eating

Author(s) (year)	Drug	Dosage (mg/day)	Duration (weeks)	Diagnosis	Assessment of binge eating	Change in binge-eating frequency (no. of patients)
Bulimia (nervosa)						
Ong et al. (1983)	Amphetamine Placebo	0.2/kg i.v.	Single dose (CO)	Russell	Test meal after 120 min.	no episodes(8), episode(0) no episode(4), episode(4)
Robinson et al., (1985)	Fenfluramine Placebo	60	Single dose (CO)	Russell and DSM-III	Test meal for 5 hours	no episodes(14), episode(1) no episode(5), episode(10)
Blouin et al. (1988)	Fenfluramine Desipramine	60	6 (CO)	DSM-III	Daily episode diary	sig. red.(12)
Russell et al. (1988)	d-fenfluramine Placebo	30	12	Russell	No. of days with binge eating	m.red. 31.6% m.red. 23.9%

Note. CO, crossover; m., mean; red., reduction; sig., significant

TABLE 12.5. Controlled Trials of Other Drugs in Patients with Binge Eating

Author(s) (year)	Drug	Dosage (mg/day)	Duration (weeks)	Diagnosis	Assessment of binge eating	Change in binge-eating frequency (no. of patients)
Bulimia (nervosa)						
Krahn & Mitchell (1985)	L-tryptophan Placebo	3000	4	DSM-III	Daily episodes diary	tryp. = plac.
Hsu et al. (1991)	Lithium Placebo	600–1200 plasma level $m = 0.62$	8	DSM-III	Daily episodes diary and interview	sig. red. lith.(38) = plac.(30) red. approx. 60%
Halmi et al. (1986)	Cyproheptadine Amitriptyline Placebo	8–32 40–160	≤12	DSM-III AN	Body weight	weight gain NB>B weight gain B>NB cyp. sig. >plac.

Note. AN, anorexia nervosa; B, bulimics; cyp., cyproheptadine; lith., lithium; m., mean; NB, nonbulimics; plac., placebo; red., reduction; sig., significant; tryp., tryptophan

Cyproheptadine

Cyproheptadine (Table 12.5), a serotonin and histamine antagonist, has been investigated in patients with anorexia nervosa in three double-blind, placebo-controlled studies (Goldberg, Halmi, Eckert, Casper, & Davis, 1979; Halmi et al., 1986; Vigersky & Loriaux, 1977). Only in the Halmi et al. (1986) study was cyproheptadine found to be significantly superior to placebo, but this effect was of marginal clinical significance. The study is mentioned in this chapter because cyproheptadine increased treatment efficacy only in the nonbulimic subgroup and seemed to impair treatment outcome in the bulimic subgroup.

Tryptophan

Tryptophan (Table 12.5) is a serotonin precursor and therefore acts via a serotonergic mechanism. Two uncontrolled trials reported that the drug did have a positive effect (Cole & Lapierre, 1986; Kaye, Gwirtsman, Brewerton, George, & Wurtman, 1988), but this was not confirmed in a small double-blind, placebo-controlled cross-over study (Krahn & Mitchell, 1985) using patients with bulimia nervosa.

BINGE EATING AND DEPRESSION

Antidepressant drugs were first used to treat patients with bulimia nervosa because of the association of the disorder with depressive symptoms (Pope, Hudson, Jonas, & Yurgelun-Todd, 1983). Controlled and uncontrolled studies suggest that the majority of drugs effective in the treatment of bulimia nervosa have in common thymoleptic properties. It is therefore surprising that these drugs are equally effective whether or not the patient is depressed at presentation (FBNC Study Group, 1992a; Horne et al., 1988; Hsu et al., 1991; Hughes, Wells, Cunningham, & Ilstrup, 1986; Mitchell & Groat, 1984; Walsh et al., 1988). This finding suggests that they are having an ''antibulimic'' effect separate from their antidepressive effect, a conclusion supported by the observation that in some studies antidepressants exert antibinge properties somewhat more quickly than their known antidepressant effects (e.g., Barlow, Blouin, Blouin, & Perez, 1988). It must also be noted that even in nondepressed bulimic patients, significant changes in emotional state occur during treatment with these drugs and that these changes may enhance control over eating. For instance, Walsh et al. (1988) suggested that phenelzine might work by reducing the anxiety and tension that frequently precedes the onset of an eating binge.

SHORTCOMINGS OF DRUG TREATMENT

Remission Rates

Although many patients respond to antidepressant drugs in terms of percentage reductions in binge eating and purging, in most studies only
a minority of patients are free from the behavior at the end of treatment.
The mean percentage reduction in binge eating across active treatment
cells is approximately 70%, but only 22% of patients are in complete
remission at the end of treatment (Mitchell, Pyle, et al., 1989). However,
patients who display a less than complete response to an initial antidepressant may respond to a second antidepressant (Mitchell, Pyle, et
al., 1989; Pope et al., 1985; Pyle et al., 1990) or to treatment with a different class of drug.

Predictors of Response

No variables have been identified that consistently predict response to
drug treatment. Furthermore, the choice of agents remains empirical
(Hudson & Pope, 1990).

Placebo Response

There have been differences in placebo response rates across studies, suggesting differences in patient populations and the psychotherapeutic
component of treatment. For example, Mitchell and Groat (1984) obtained a reduction of binge-eating frequency of 52% in subjects receiving placebo compared with a 72% reduction in patients receiving
amitriptyline, suggesting a considerable effect of the accompanying
minimal behavioral treatment. A similar result was reported by Alger
et al. (1991) in obese binge eaters with a 50% reduction of binge-eating
episodes in patients receiving placebo compared to 73% in patients on
imipramine. Hsu et al. (1991) obtained a reduction of binge-eating frequency of 60% in bulimia nervosa patients receiving minimal behavioral
intervention whether they received lithium carbonate or placebo. On the
other hand several treatment studies have demonstrated lack of improvement or even worsening of bulimic symptoms in patients receiving placebo (McCann & Agras, 1990; Pope et al., 1989; Walsh et al., 1991).

Adverse Effects

Another factor limiting the usefulness of medication is side effects. Side
effects that pose clinical problems are orthostatic hypotension and se-

dation, as well as the risk of a hypertensive crisis and insomnia with MAOIs, anticholinergic effects with tricyclics, and nausea and vomiting with selective serotonin reuptake inhibitors. No study using tricyclic antidepressants has reported weight gain or carbohydrate craving, side effects frequently seen in depressed patients. Naltrexone at high dosages carries a risk of hepatotoxicity, lithium carbonate may cause fluid and electrolyte abnormalities, and some appetite suppressants have been shown to have potential for abuse.

Plasma Levels

There can be problems in the management of patients who purge, since vomiting and laxative abuse can compromise the amount of drug remaining for absorption. However, only one study has found a relationship between serum drug levels and response (Hughes et al., 1986).

Acceptance of Drugs and Attrition

In controlled studies, drop-out rates have ranged from 0% to 50% for patients receiving active medication. Similar rates (0% to 34%) have been obtained with CBT (Agras et al., 1992). One study reported that as many as 34% of the drop outs were due to intolerance of side effects (Barlow et al., 1988). In other studies, only a minority of drop outs could be attributed to the adverse effects of the drug used (e.g., fluoxetine in FBNC Study Group [1992a]). The acceptance of drug therapy by bulimic patients has not been systematically studied. Subjects volunteering for drug or psychotherapy studies are a biased group. In our clinical experience, patients generally expect and prefer referral for counseling.

MAINTENANCE OF CHANGE

Few studies have systematically examined the maintenance of change following drug treatment, or the effects of drug discontinuation. Pope, Hudson, Jonas, and Yurgelun-Todd (1983) reported that at 1 to 8-month follow-up, 90% of their original sample of patients treated with imipramine had responded to imipramine or some other antidepressant including desipramine, nortriptyline, tranylcypromine, and trazodone. They subsequently reported a 2-year follow-up wherein they found that although some patients could be effectively withdrawn from medication and maintain their improvement, a sizable subgroup relapsed when taken off drugs (Pope et al., 1985). Furthermore, many required several medication changes or dosage adjustments to maintain their improvement.

Walsh et al. (1991) demonstrated limited improvement and considerable relapse with continued treatment with desipramine. As many as 29% of the patients who entered an open maintenance phase after successful initial treatment relapsed within 4 months. This relapse rate is similar to that reported by Pyle et al. (1990) for patients maintained on imipramine following successful initial treatment. They found that even after 6 months of sustained improvement it is not possible to discontinue medication successfully in many patients. These observations suggest that antidepressant drugs are of limited value when used in isolation.

Treatment Recommendations

Given the relatively low cost of medication therapy compared to psychotherapy, one could argue for a strategy of using antidepressants as the first step in the treatment of patients with binge-eating episodes. However, it has to be noted that most patients will require further treatment, perhaps with cognitive-behavioral therapy. Given this observation and the high relapse rate on antidepressants, we currently believe that psychotherapy is the treatment of choice for most patients. We suggest that antidepressants be prescribed when there is clear evidence of a coexisting affective disorder, in particular if there is evidence that the affective disorder preceded the onset of the eating disorder. In addition, antidepressants may be helpful for patients who remain depressed despite improvement in their eating symptoms in response to other forms of treatment, as well as for those patients who show only partial response or a lack of response to a psychotherapeutic intervention, whether or not they are depressed (Mitchell, 1990).

When prescribing medication, we generally prefer serotonin reuptake inhibitors such as fluoxetine or fluvoxamine, given their favorable side effect profile. Using fluoxetine as an example, a dosage of 60 mg is generally needed and well tolerated, and we often initiate patients at this dose. If the response is encouraging we generally recommend this dosage be continued for 6 months to 1 year before a trial of discontinuation. While blood levels of fluoxetine have not been shown to be useful, we do routinely monitor levels of tricyclics to avoid toxicity. There is no convincing evidence of a correlation between tricyclic serum levels and response.

REFERENCES

Agras, W. S., Dorian, B., Kirkley, B. G., Arnow, B., & Bachman, J. (1987). Imipramine in the treatment of bulimia: A double-blind controlled study. *International Journal of Eating Disorders, 6,* 29–38.

Agras, W. S., Rossiter, E. M., Arnow, B., Schneider, J. A., Telch, C. F., Reaburn, S. D., Bruce, B., Perl, M., & Koran, L. M. (1992). Pharmacological and cognitive-behavioral treatment for bulimia nervosa: A controlled comparison. *American Journal of Psychiatry*, 149, 82–87.

Alger, S. A., Schwalberg, M. D., Bigaoutte, J. M., Michalek, A. V., & Howard, L. J. (1991). Effects of a tricyclic antidepressant and opiate antagonist on binge-eating behavior in normoweight bulimic and obese, binge-eating subjects. *American Journal of Clinical Nutrition*, 53, 865–871.

American Psychiatric Association. (1980). *Diagnostic and statistical manual of mental disorders* (3rd ed.). Washington, DC: Author.

American Psychiatric Association. (1987). *Diagnostic and statistical manual of mental disorders* (3rd ed. rev.). Washington, DC: Author.

Barlow, J., Blouin, J. H., Blouin, A. G., & Perez, E. L. (1988). Treatment of bulimia with desipramine: A double-blind cross over study. *Canadian Journal of Psychiatry*, 33, 129–133.

Blouin, A. G., Blouin, J. H., Perez, E. L., Bushnik, T., Zuro, C., & Mulder, E. (1988). Treatment of bulimia with fenfluramine and desipramine. *Journal of Clinical Psychopharmacology*, 8, 261–269.

Brotman, A. W., Herzog, D. B., & Woods, S. W. (1984). Antidepressant treatment of bulimia: The relationship between bingeing and depressive symptomatology. *Journal of Clinical Psychiatry*, 45, 7–9.

Cole, W., & Lapierre, Y. D. (1986). The use of tryptophane in normal-weight bulimia. *Canadian Journal of Psychiatry*, 31, 755–756.

Craighead, L. W., & Agras, W. S. (1991). Mechanisms of action in cognitive-behavioral and pharmacological interventions for obesity and bulimia nervosa. *Journal of Consulting and Clinical Psychology*, 39, 115–125.

Enas, G. G., Pope, H. G., & Levine, L. R. (1989). Fluoxetine in bulimia nervosa: Double blind study. In *New Research Program and Abstracts, 142nd Annual Meeting of the American Psychiatric Association*. Washington, DC: American Psychiatric Association.

Fichter, M. M., Leibl, K., Rief, W., Brunner, E., Schmidt- Auberger, S., & Engel, R. R. (1991). Fluoxetine versus placebo: A double-blind study with bulimic inpatients undergoing intensive psychotherapy. *Pharmacopsychiatry*, 24, 1–7.

Fluoxetine Bulimia Nervosa Collaborative Study Group. (1992a). Fluoxetine in the treatment of bulimia nervosa: A multicenter, placebo-controlled, double-blind trial. *Archives of General Psychiatry*, 49, 139–147.

Fluoxetine Bulimia Nervosa Collaborative Study Group. (1992b). Unpublished raw data. Indianapolis, IN.

Freeman, C. P. L., & Hampson, M. (1987). Fluoxetine as a treatment for bulimia nervosa. *International Journal of Obesity*, 11(suppl. 3), 171–177.

Fullerton, D. T., Getto, C. J., Swift, W. J., & Carlson, I. H. (1985). Sugar, opioids and binge eating. *Brain Research Bulletin*, 14, 673–680.

Goldberg, S. C., Halmi, K. A., Eckert, E. D., Casper, R., & Davis, J. M. (1979). Cyproheptadine in anorexia nervosa. *British Journal of Psychiatry*, 134, 67–70.

Green, R. S., & Rau, J. H. (1974). Treatment of compulsive eating disturbances with anticonvulsant medication. *American Journal of Psychiatry*, 131, 428–432.

Halmi, K. A., Eckert, E., Ladu, T., & Cohen, J. (1986). Treatment efficacy of cyproheptadine and amitriptyline. *Archives of General Psychiatry*, 43, 177–181.

Horne, R. L., Ferguson, J. M., Pope, H. G. Jr., Hudson, J. I., Lineberry, C. G., Ascher, J., & Cato, A. (1988). Treatment of bulimia with bupropion: A multicenter controlled trial. *Journal of Clinical Psychiatry, 49,* 262–266.

Hsu, L. K. G., Clement, L., Santhouse, R., & Ju, E. S. Y. (1991). Treatment of bulimia nervosa with lithium carbonate: A controlled study. *Journal of Nervous and Mental Disease, 179,* 351–355.

Hudson, I. J., & Pope, H. G., Jr. (1990). Psychopharmacological treatment of bulimia. In M. Fichter (Ed.), *Bulimia nervosa: Basic research, diagnosis & therapy* (pp. 331–342). Chichester: Wiley.

Hudson, I. J., Pope, H. G., Jr., Jonas, J. M., & Yurgelun-Todd, D. (1983). Phenomenologic relationship of eating disorders to major affective disorder. *Psychiatry Research, 9,* 345–354.

Hughes, P. L., Wells, L. A., Cunningham, C. J., & Ilstrup D. M. (1986). Treating bulimia with desipramine: A placebo-controlled double-blind study. *Archives of General Psychiatry, 43,* 182–186.

Igoin-Apfelbaum, L., & Apfelbaum, M. (1987). Naltrexone and bulimic symptoms. *Lancet,* 1087–1088.

Jonas, J. M., & Gold, M. S. (1986). Naltrexone reverses bulimic symptoms. *Lancet, 1,* 807.

Jonas, J. M., & Gold, M. S. (1987). Treatment of antidepressant-resistant bulimia with naltrexone. *International Journal of Psychiatry in Medicine, 16,* 305–309.

Jonas, J. M., & Gold, M. S. (1988). The use of opiate antagonists in treating bulimia: A study of low-dose versus high-dose naltrexone. *Psychiatry Research, 24,* 195–199.

Jonas, J. M., Hudson, J. I., & Pope, H. G., Jr. (1983). Response to "Psychiatrist as a mind sweeper": Eating disorders and antidepressants. *Journal of Clinical Psychopharmacology, 3,* 59–60.

Kaplan, A. S., Garfinkel, P. E., Darby, P. L., & Garner, D. M. (1983). Carbamazepine in the treatment of bulimia. *American Journal of Psychiatry, 140,* 1225–1226.

Kaplan, A. S., Garfinkel, P. E., & Garner, D. M. (1987, May 13). *Bulimia treated with carbamazapine and imipramine.* Paper presented at the American Psychiatric Association Annual Meeting, Chicago.

Kaye, W. H., Gwirtsman, H. E., Brewerton, T. D., George, D. T., & Wurtman, R. J. (1988). Bingeing behaviour and plasma amino acids: A possible involvement of brain serotonin in bulimia nervosa. *Psychiatry Research, 23,* 31–43.

Kennedy, S. H., Piran, N., & Garfinkel, P. E. (1985). Monoamine oxidase inhibitor therapy for anorexia nervosa and bulimia: A preliminary trial of isocarboxazid. *Journal of Clinical Psychopharmacology, 5,* 279–285.

Kennedy, S. H., Piran, N., Warsh, J. J., Prendergast, P., Mainprize, E., Whynot, C., & Garfinkel, P. E. (1988). A trial of isocarboxazid in the treatment of bulimia nervosa. *Journal of Clinical Psychopharmacology, 8,* 391–396.

Krahn, D., & Mitchell, J. E. (1985). Use of L-tryptophan in treating bulimia. *American Journal of Psychiatry, 142,* 1130.

Marcus, M. D., Wing, R. R., Ewing, L., Kern, E., McDermott, M., & Gooding, W. (1990). A double-blind, placebo-controlled trial of fluoxetine plus behavior modification in the treatment of obese binge-eaters and non-binge-eaters. *American Journal of Psychiatry, 147,* 876–881.

McCann, U. D., & Agras, W. S. (1990). Successful treatment of nonpurging bulimia nervosa with desipramine: a double-blind, placebo-controlled study. *American Journal of Psychiatry, 147*, 1509–1513.

Mitchell, J. E. (1990). *Bulimia nervosa*. Minneapolis: University of Minnesota Press.

Mitchell, J. E., Christenson, G., Jennings, J., Huber, M., Thomas, B., Pomeroy, C., & Morley, J. (1989). A placebo-controlled, double-blind crossover study of naltrexone hydrochloride in outpatients with normal weight bulimia. *Journal of Clinical Psychopharmacology, 9*, 94–97.

Mitchell, J. E., & Groat, R. (1984). A placebo-controlled, double-blind trial of amitriptyline in bulimia. *Journal of Clinical Psychopharmacology, 4*, 186–192.

Mitchell, J. E., Laine, D. E., Morley, J. E., & Levine, A. S. (1986). Naloxone but not CCK-8 may attenuate binge-eating behavior in patients with the bulimia syndrome. *Biological Psychiatry, 21*, 1399–1406.

Mitchell, J. E., Pyle, R. L., Eckert, E. D., Hatsukami, D., & Lentz, R. (1983). Electrolyte and other physiological abnormalities in patients with bulimia. *Psychological Medicine, 13*, 273–278.

Mitchell, J. E., Pyle, R. L., Eckert, E. D., Hatsukami, D., Pomeroy, C., & Zimmerman, R. (1989). Response to alternative antidepressants in imipramine nonresponders with bulimia nervosa. *Journal of Clinical Psychopharmacology, 9*, 291–293.

Mitchell, J. E., Pyle, R. L., Eckert, E. D., Hatsukami, D., Pomeroy, C., Zimmerman, R. (1990). A comparison study of antidepressants and structured intensive group psychotherapy in the treatment of bulimia nervosa. *Archives of General Psychiatry, 47*, 149–157.

Ong, Y. L., Checkley, S. A., & Russell, G. F. M. (1983). Suppression of bulimic symptoms with methylamphetamine. *British Journal of Psychiatry, 143*, 288–293.

Pope, H. G., Jr., Hudson, J. I., & Jonas, J. M. (1983). Antidepressant treatment of bulimia: Preliminary experience and practical recommendations. *Journal of Clinical Psychopharmacology, 3*, 274–281.

Pope, H. G., Jr., Hudson, J. I., Jonas, J. M., & Yurgelun-Todd, D. (1983). Bulimia treated with imipramine: A placebo-controlled, double-blind study. *American Journal of Psychiatry, 140*, 554–558.

Pope, H. G., Jr., Hudson, J. I., Jonas, J. M., & Yurgelun-Todd, D. (1985). Antidepressant treatment of bulimia: A two-year follow-up study. *Journal of Clinical Psychopharmacology, 5*, 320–327.

Pope, H. G., Jr., Keck, P. E., Jr., McElroy, S. M., & Hudson, J. I. (1989). A placebo-controlled study of trazodone in bulimia nervosa. *Journal of Clinical Psychopharmacology, 9*, 254–259.

Pyle, R. L., Mitchell, J. E., Eckert, E. D., Hatsukami, D., Pomeroy, C., & Zimmerman, R. (1990). Maintenance treatment and 6 month outcome for bulimic patients who respond to initial treatment. *American Journal of Psychiatry, 147*, 871–875.

Rau, J. H., & Green, R. S. (1975). Compulsive eating: A neuropsychological approach to certain eating disorders. *Comprehensive Psychiatry, 16*, 223–231.

Rau, J. H., & Green, R. S. (1978). Soft neurological correlates of compulsive eating. *Journal of Nervous and Mental Disease, 166*, 435–437.

Rau, J. H., Struve, F. A., & Green, R. S. (1979). Electroencephalographic correlates of compulsive eating. *Clinical Electroencephalography, 10*, 180–189.

Robinson, P. H., Checkley, S. A., & Russell, G. F. M. (1985). Suppression of eating by fenfluramine in patients with bulimia nervosa. *British Journal of Psychiatry, 146*, 169–176.

Roy-Byrne, P., Gwirtsman, H., Edelstein, C. K., Yager, J., & Gerner R. H. (1983). Eating disorders and antidepressants. *Journal of Clinical Psychopharmacology, 3*, 60–61.

Russell, G. F. M., Checkley, S. A., Feldman, J., & Eisler, I. (1988). A controlled trial of d-fenfluramine in bulimia nervosa. *Clinical Neuropharmacology, 11*(suppl. 1), S146–S159.

Sabine, E. J., Yonace, A., Farrington, A. J., Barratt, K. H., & Wakeling, A. (1983). Bulimia nervosa: A placebo controlled double-blind therapeutic trial of mianserin. *British Journal of Clinical Pharmacology, 15*(suppl. 2), 195S–202S.

Shader, R. J., & Greenblatt, D. J. (1982). The psychiatrist as a mind sweeper. *Journal of Clinical Psychopharmacology, 2*, 233–234.

Stewart, J. W., Walsh, B. T., Wright, L., Roose, S. P., & Glassman, A. H. (1984). An open trial of MAO inhibitors in bulimia. *Journal of Clinical Psychiatry, 45*, 217–219.

Vigersky, R. A., & Loriaux, D. L. (1977). The effect of cyproheptadine in anorexia nervosa: A double-blind trial. In R. Vigersky (Ed.), *Anorexia nervosa* (pp. 349–356). New York: Raven Press.

Walsh, B. T., Gladis, M., Roose, S. P., Stewart, J. W., Stetner, F., & Glassman, A. H. (1988). Phenelzine vs. placebo in 50 patients with bulimia. *Archives of General Psychiatry, 45*, 471–475.

Walsh, B. T., Hadigan, C. M., Devlin, M. J., Gladis, M., & Roose, S. P. (1991). Long-term outcome of antidepressant treatment for bulimia nervosa. *American Journal of Psychiatry, 148*, 1206–1212.

Walsh, B. T., Stewart, J. W., Wright, L., Harrison, W., Roose, S. & Glassman, A. H. (1982). Treatment of bulimia with monoamine oxidase inhibitors. *American Journal of Psychiatry, 139*, 1629–1630.

Wermuth, B. M., Davis, K. L., Hollister, L. E., & Stunkard, A. J. (1977). Phenytoin treatment of the binge-eating syndrome. *American Journal of Psychiatry, 134*, 1249–1253.

Wilcox, J. A. (1990). Fluoxetine and bulimia. *Journal of Psychoactive Drugs, 22*, 81–82.

Wurtman, R. J. (1987). Nutrients affecting brain composition and behavior. *Integrative Psychiatry, 5*, 226–257.

Short-Term Psychological Treatments for Binge Eating

W. Stewart Agras

Research into the treatment of binge eating and bulimia nervosa has progressed from a pleasing simplicity just 10 years ago, when there were few treatment studies, to a bewildering complexity today, with many studies of seemingly different procedures. Indeed, many of the original studies focused solely on the more dramatic behavior of purging, rather than on what is generally considered today to be the centrally important behavior, namely, binge eating. The rediscovery of binge eating in the obese (Stunkard, 1959; Spitzer et al., 1992), the recognition that such behavior is linked to adiposity (Bruce & Agras, 1992; Kolotkin, Revis, Kirkley, & Janick, 1987; Telch, Agras, & Rossiter, 1988) and indeed may be a risk factor for obesity, and the fact that treatments effective in bulimia nervosa are also effective in those who binge eat (McCann & Agras, 1990; Telch, Agras, Rossiter, Wilfley, & Kenardy, 1990; Smith, Marcus, & Kaye, 1992) all suggest that binge eating and bulimia nervosa may be aspects of the same core disorder. Hence, no distinction will be made between these two problems in this review of the short-term psychological treatment of binge eating.

Ten years ago, it was commonly thought that cognitive-behavioral therapy (CBT) was a specific approach to the treatment of binge eating in bulimia nervosa, based as it was on a particular view of the genesis of binge eating. Today the situation is not as clear and at least two more complex questions must be posed. The first of these questions is whether some treatments are better than others, or whether all treatments are equally effective. This issue is often discussed as one of specific versus nonspecific effects, the latter being due to procedures common to all therapies such as a therapeutic relationship, a therapeutic rationale, therapeutic instructions, goal setting, reinforcement of progress, and so on. It is now recognized that although commonalities may account for equivalent effectiveness in some cases, in others an alternative explanation is likely. Thus, two different therapies may be equally effective yet attain that effectiveness through the use of different procedures and by means of different therapeutic processes. Hence, a second question to be posed today is whether treatments exert specific or nonspecific effects and whether they work by the same or different processes. These questions inevitably lead to a consideration of the factors maintaining binge eating and the way in which a particular therapy may influence these factors.

Before beginning this review of the literature it is important to note that the assessment of binge eating leaves much to be desired, a problem that may affect the apparent outcomes of studies in unknown ways, and that may ultimately distort our understanding of the efficacy of treatment. Two main approaches to the assessment of binge eating exist, interview-based recall most commonly using the Eating Disorder Examination (EDE) (Cooper & Fairburn, 1987) and self-monitoring of binge episodes. In the case of interview-based assessment, the period of recall is often 4 weeks. Given the vagaries of human memory it is quite possible that recall over such an extended period is not accurate. On the other hand, self-monitoring assessment is usually over a 1-week period. Given the individual variability in bulimic episodes this would seem to be too short a period of assessment. Moreover, the EDE classifies binges into objective and subjective types depending on the size of the binge, a typology not used in self-monitoring assessment. Indeed, self-monitoring studies often use the apparently more reliable assessment of binge days rather than the absolute number of binges (Rossiter, Agras, Telch, & Bruce, 1992). Such variation in assessment methods between studies obviously makes comparison across studies difficult and potentially misleading. Urgently needed are comparisons between the various methods of assessing binge eating, so that the most accurate method can be used in future treatment studies. Given this caveat, the various psychological treatments and their relative success in reducing binge eating and its associated psychopathology will be addressed.

WHAT TREATMENTS HAVE BEEN USED AND HOW DO THEY DIFFER?

Among the early studies of the treatment of bulimia nervosa, CBT, first proposed by Fairburn (1981), stands out as being the best described as to its procedures, and the most frequently studied in controlled trials.

One of the main components of treatment is self-monitoring of food intake, binge-eating episodes, and triggers of those episodes. This information is used (1) to shape three or more meals per day, (2) to gradually introduce feared foods into the diet (exposure treatment), and (3) to identify and rectify distorted cognitions about food intake, weight, and body shape. In later sessions, relapse prevention procedures are introduced. This treatment has been applied both individually and in groups. To this basic package a variety of other procedures have been added by various research groups, including relaxation training and response prevention of purging.

The second approach to the treatment of binge eating involves treatments that stress one or more of the components of CBT, often used within dismantling studies. These treatments include behavior therapy, which omits the cognitive procedures, and psychoeducational therapy, which is usually provided in groups and involves education, discussion (of symptoms, behaviors, and common problems), and often behavioral prescriptions including eating three meals a day. Psychoeducational therapy may also include attention to distorted cognitions regarding weight and shape; hence, some of these treatment packages more resemble behavior therapy, while others more resemble a stripped-down version of cognitive-behavioral therapy. Other forms of psychoeducational therapy are purely educational in nature, offering information but no individualized therapeutic advice.

The third major approach to treatment includes various forms of manualized psychotherapy. Few controlled studies of these approaches exist at present, although as will be seen later in this chapter, the results of such studies are of great theoretical importance. The first of these approaches is Interpersonal Psychotherapy (IPT), which was first introduced as a nonintrospective, short-term psychological treatment for depression (Klerman, Weissman, Rounsaville, & Chevron, 1984). In its adaptation to the treatment of binge eating, IPT is described as having three stages (Fairburn, in press). In the first stage, the interpersonal difficulties involved in the development and maintenance of the eating disorder are identified. In the second stage, a contract to work on these problems is made and they become the focus of treatment. Finally, in the third stage, issues of termination are addressed. In its research usage, there is no focus whatsoever on the eating problem. A second psychotherapy that has been used in the treatment of binge eating is supportive–expressive therapy of which a manualized version exists (Luborsky, 1984). This is a nondirective, interpretive psychotherapy in which no specific advice is given (Garner et al., 1993). Eating disorders are viewed as disguising underlying interpersonal problems. In distinction to IPT, which focuses on the here and now, the past is explored to illuminate interpersonal difficulties and a core conflictual relationship theme is established. As is the case in IPT, expression of feelings is encouraged. Hence, supportive–expressive therapy shares some features with IPT, but also differs from it. The third manualized therapy has been used as a control group in two studies (Kirkley, Schneider, Agras, & Bachman, 1985; Agras, Schneider, Arnow, Raeburn, & Telch, 1989). This treatment consisted of a nondirective therapy in which no direct advice was given, combined with self-monitoring of binge eating and antecedent events.

The final distinct approach to the treatment of binge eating is the use of family therapy (Russell, Szmukler, Dare, & Eisler, 1987). In this approach to treatment, all the available family members are involved. The first phase of treatment consists in gaining the cooperation of the family. To accomplish this, the dangers of the patient's condition are stressed. In the second phase of treatment, the family organization is assessed, particularly focusing on the manner in which the family is organized around the patient's symptomatic behaviors. Finally, various interventions are used to help the family change, focusing on their behavior toward the patient.

HOW EFFECTIVE ARE THESE TREATMENTS IN THE SHORT TERM?

Because CBT has been the most studied form of treatment for binge eating, this approach necessarily forms the standard for comparisons across studies. It should be noted, however, that treatment procedures, treatment length, and the population treated may differ considerably between studies that are purportedly of the same procedure. Drop-out rates range from 0% to 34% in the studies examined, with a median drop-out rate of 16% (Agras et al., 1992; Agras et al., 1989; Fairburn, Kirk, O'Connor, & Cooper, 1986; Fairburn et al., 1991; Freeman, Barry, Dunkeld-Turnbull, & Henderson, 1988; Garner et al., 1993; Kirkley et al., 1985; Mitchell et al., 1990; Olmsted et al., 1991; Smith et al., 1992; Telch et al., 1990; Wilfley et al., in press; Wilson, Rossiter, Kleifield, & Lindholm, 1986; Wilson, Eldredge, Smith, & Niles, 1991; Wolf, & Crowther, 1992). Of those remaining in treatment, abstinence rates range from 20% to 76%, with a median rate of 47%. Thus, if we take a hypothetical cohort of 100 binge eaters and treat them with CBT, we would expect 16 to drop out of treatment and 40 to be abstinent at the end of treatment. A 40% abstinence rate suggests that we are far from having found the ideal treatment for binge eating.

The results of behavior therapy, nutritional counseling, or their combination, are similar to those for cognitive-behavioral therapy, with drop outs ranging from 0% to 24%, and abstinence rates ranging from 51% to 100% (Dalvit-McPhillips, 1984; Fairburn et al., 1991; Freeman et al., 1988; Mitchell et al., 1990; Wolf & Crowther, 1992). The study in which 100% abstinence was found, it should be noted, was conducted entirely by telephone; hence, there is some question as to the accuracy of initial diagnosis, treatment compliance, and outcome (Dalvit-McPhillips, 1984). However, whether comparing across studies that have used CBT, it appears that behavior therapy, nutritional counseling, or some combination of these procedures achieves comparable effects.

The next group of therapies, manualized psychotherapies, has a drop-out rate ranging from 7% to 23%, with a median of 17%, and an abstinence rate ranging from 12% to 44%, with a median of 24% (Mitchell et al., 1990; Wolf & Crowther, 1992; Agras et al., 1989; Fairburn et al., 1991; Garner et al., 1993; Kirkley et al., 1985; Laessle et al., 1991; Wilfley et al., in press). The somewhat poorer abstinence rates achieved in these studies, would appear to indicate that as a group the structured psychotherapies are less effective than CBT. However, it should be noted that several different types of treatment are grouped together in this comparison. Finally, in the one controlled family therapy study, there was a high drop-out rate of 44% and a very low abstinence rate of 9%, a recovery rate not dissimilar to that found in participants allocated to a waiting list (Russell et al., 1987).

Overall, it appears that there may be several effective psychological therapies for the treatment of binge eating. Their comparative effectiveness, as determined from controlled studies, will be examined in a later section of this chapter.

DO THE EFFECTS OF TREATMENT PERSIST?

Very few investigators report the long-term results of treatment in a comprehensive manner. Such reports should include the number of patients who continue improved at follow-up in relation to those who improved with treatment. In addition, it is necessary to include the number of patients who are improved at follow-up in relation to those who did not improve with treatment. The first proportion indicates how well patients maintain their gains; the second proportion indicates either a delayed effect of treatment or spontaneous recovery. Reports should also document the treatments that have occurred in the maintenance period and the effects of those treatments. In addition, it is necessary to choose a reasonable criterion for successful initial outcome. It is proposed here that abstinence from binge eating is a useful criterion, although more comprehensive outcome indicators taking into account improvements in related psychopathology should be added.

Olmsted et al. (1991) present a detailed account of maintenance following individual CBT. At posttreatment assessment 36% of the patients were abstinent. Sixty-seven percent of these recovered patients were still abstinent at 3-month follow-up. In addition, 19% of those who were not abstinent posttreatment now were, giving a total of 32% abstinent at follow-up, a slight drop from the 36% abstinent at posttreatment. In the absence of this detailed account one might conclude that the relapse rate was 11% (neglecting those who recover during the follow-up period) rather than 33%. Unlike the closed follow-up study of Fairburn, Jones, Peveler, Hope, and O'Connor (in press) it is not clear whether any of those who recovered during the maintenance period had received additional treatment. While the remaining studies do not categorize outcome in this detailed manner, for the most part patients treated with CBT maintain their gains reasonably well. One of the highest relapse rates was reported by Telch et al. (1990), who found a 54% relapse rate for patients with nonpurging bulimia nervosa treated with CBT in the 10 weeks following the end of therapy. One reason noted by the authors for this high relapse rate may have been the relatively short length of treatment, namely, 10 weeks, which precluded the teaching of adequate maintenance skills. Overall, taking our cohort of 100 patients into the follow-up period we would expect 32 to be abstinent.

A similar picture emerges for the group of behavior therapy/nutritional treatments, and for those treated with structured psychotherapies. Once treatment has resulted in the cessation of binge eating, the majority of patients continue to be abstinent at follow-up. This suggests that once improvement has occurred through any form of psychological intervention, reasonable maintenance of improvement is the rule.

ARE ALL TREATMENTS EQUALLY EFFECTIVE?

The comparison of two treatments in a randomized design has usually involved a comparison of a variant of CBT with either a modification of CBT, e.g., a behavior-therapy condition that omits the cognitive procedures, or with a manualized psychotherapy. Three studies have compared behavior therapy with CBT (Freeman et al., 1988; Fairburn et al., 1991; Wolf & Crowther, 1992) In the first two of these studies, behavior therapy and CBT were found to be equally effective in reducing the frequency of binge eating. Fairburn et al. (1991) noted, however, that there was an advantage for CBT in reducing concerns about weight and shape. This is particularly interesting, since the cognitive components of treatment are specifically directed toward ameliorating such concerns. In the third study (Wolf & Crowther, 1992) behavior therapy was superior to CBT in reducing binge eating. This is a somewhat unusual finding in that a therapy containing all the behavior-therapy components was less effective than behavior therapy itself. It is possible therefore that this finding is due to unknown extraneous factors or variation within the populations randomized to the two treatment groups. These authors also reported that CBT was more effective than behavior therapy in reducing preoccupation with dieting and general psychopathology. Overall, then, there is no evidence that CBT is more efficacious in the short term at reducing binge eating than behavior therapy. In other words, addition of the cognitive components of therapy does not add to effectiveness in reducing binge eating, although there is evidence that the cognitive component is superior in modifying concerns with shape and weight and preoccupation with dieting. Whether or not such effects contribute to better maintenance of improvement is unclear at present.

A second, and distinctly different type of behavior therapy with which CBT has been compared is exposure and response prevention (ERP). This treatment was introduced by Rosen and Leitenberg (1982) and is based on an anxiety model of bulimia nervosa, in which binge eating is postulated to increase anxiety, which in turn is relieved by purging. Hence, purging is viewed in this model as maintaining binge eating by means of anxiety relief. Although treatment procedures have varied between studies, patients either bring, or are served, binge food during a treatment session, and time is allowed for anxiety (and the urge to induce vomiting) to dissipate once food is eaten. Four studies have now compared CBT with ERP (Agras et al., 1989; Leitenberg, Rosen, Gross, Nudelman, & Vara, 1988; Wilson et al., 1986; Wilson et al., 1991). In the first of these (Wilson et al., 1986) ERP was found to be more effective than CBT. However, as the authors note, the form of CBT used in this study omitted some of the critical behavioral procedures usually included in the treatment package. The second study, found equivalent results for CBT and ERP on a variety of measures including binge frequency (Leitenberg et al., 1988). The third study (Agras et al., 1989) found that only CBT was more effective than a waiting list group in reducing binge eating, with ERP showing no differences. Since CBT was combined with ERP in this study, it appeared that ERP had detracted from the effects of CBT. The authors surmised that, since therapy time had been held equal between the two groups, ERP prevented patients in the combined group from receiving the full cognitive-behavioral treatment. This hypothesis was recently tested by Wilson et al. (1991), who found no difference between CBT and ERP in a study that allowed extra time for the ERP procedures. There is, then, little evidence that ERP adds to the effectiveness of CBT. This is not surprising, since the latter treatment also exposes patients to their feared foods, albeit in a less structured way. Moreover, these studies do little to confirm the anxiety reduction model of bulimia nervosa postulated by Rosen and Leitenberg (1982).

The second set of studies compares CBT with different psychotherapies. In the first of these studies, cognitive-behavioral group therapy was compared with a nondirective group therapy, with both groups self-monitoring eating behavior (Kirkley et al., 1985). The purpose of this study was to omit the specific behavior change procedures associated with CBT while maintaining other less specific elements of therapy including self-monitoring. CBT was found superior to the nondirective approach in reducing binge eating. In a partial replication of this study using individual therapy it was found that CBT was more effective than a wait-list control group, while the nondirective therapy (plus self-monitoring) was not (Agras et al., 1989). Both studies suggest that the behavior change procedures used in CBT (over and above the use of self-monitoring) are important in reducing the frequency of binge eating.

Fairburn et al. (1986) compared a focal psychotherapy with CBT, although there was some procedural overlap between the two treatment conditions. No difference was found between the two treatments in the reduction of binge eating, although CBT produced greater reductions in psychopathology and depression. The problem with procedural overlap was rectified in a later study from the same group of investigators who took great care to separate out the specific features of the two therapies (Fairburn et al., 1991; Fairburn et al., in press). In this study, IPT suitably modified for application to eating disorders, and that did not address eating problems directly, was compared with CBT. No difference was found between these two therapies in reducing binge-eating frequency, and on other measures while CBT was superior at the end of treatment, there was no difference between CBT and IPT over the closed 1-year follow-up. A similar comparison, again with no procedural overlap between treatments, was made in patients with nonpurging bulimia nervosa (Wilfley et al., in press). Once more the two therapies were equivalent in their effectiveness in reducing binge eating. One further study compared supportive–expressive therapy with CBT (Garner et al., 1993). No difference was found between the two therapies in reducing the frequency of binge eating. Once again CBT was more effective in reducing a variety of psychopathology including anxiety, dysthymia and self-esteem.

A final study compared nutritional counseling (a treatment concentrating on decreasing restrained eating) with stress management (Laessle et al., 1991). Nutritional counseling attained an abstinence rate of 50% compared with 27% for stress management, differences that were statistically significant or approached significance at several points from posttreatment to 1-year follow-up. Stress management was superior in reducing anxiety and feelings of ineffectiveness.

Overall, it appears that CBT is no better than a variety of manualized psychotherapies in reducing binge eating, including focal psychotherapy, supportive–expressive therapy, and IPT, although CBT generally leads to broader gains in associated psychopathology. It should be noted, however, that this conclusion would be somewhat different were the focus of this chapter on bulimia nervosa, since the results for purging are often more supportive of CBT than other forms of psychotherapy. This may be due to the differences in accuracy of measurement of purging versus binge eating, since episodes of purging are easier to define than are episodes of binge eating. Stress management fares less well in this regard, being significantly less effective than nutritional management in reducing binge eating.

Given these findings one might argue that there is little evidence of specificity for any psychotherapeutic treatment of binge eating and that the treatment results are due to nonspecific factors shared by the various psychotherapies. There are two arguments against this proposition. First, two studies have shown that CBT is superior to antidepressant medication, and one of these demonstrated that the psychological therapy was superior to a combination of therapist support plus a placebo (Agras et al., 1992; Mitchell et al., 1990). Hence, it is not likely that the results of CBT are due either to a placebo effect, or to shared elements among therapies. Second, it appears that certain components of CBT are needed to obtain its treatment effects. Thus, in two studies it has been shown that that the specific cognitive-behavioral procedures add to the effects of the combination of self-monitoring plus nondirective therapy (Agras et al., 1989; Kirkley et al., 1985). Finally, procedures central to the effectiveness of CBT have been deliberately excluded from the comparison psychosocial therapies that have demonstrated equal effectiveness to CBT (Fairburn et al., 1991; Fairburn et al., in press; Garner et al., 1993; Wilfley et al., in press). This strongly suggests that while CBT and some psychosocial therapies are of equal effectiveness in reducing binge eating, they attain these effects through the use of different procedures and by means of different mechanisms.

DIFFERENTIAL THERAPEUTIC MECHANISMS IN THE TREATMENT OF BINGE EATING

The thesis underlying the cognitive-behavioral approach to the treatment of binge eating is that cultural expectations regarding the body shape of women shifted in the 1960s, 1970s, and 1980s toward thinness.

At the same time, dieting, rather than other methods such as changing clothing styles, became the way to achieve thinness. In some women, dieting becomes associated with rigid food rules and presumably excessive caloric deprivation, leading to cycles of dieting followed by binge eating when food rules are broken. While it is not known how the binge-eating pattern is set into motion (i.e., what the exact risk factors are, whether psychosocial or biological), it is clear from descriptive studies that binge eaters alternate between caloric restriction and binge eating (Rosen, Leitenberg, Fisher, & Khazam, 1986; Rossiter & Agras, 1990; Rossiter et al., 1992). CBT is directed specifically toward this abnormal eating pattern, by shaping three meals per day, slowly introducing feared foods into the diet, and correcting the distorted thinking regarding food, body shape, and weight (Fairburn, 1981). While, as we have seen, the evidence for the effectiveness of the cognitive components of therapy in reducing binge eating is not strong, it does appear that CBT reduces the dietary restraint associated with binge eating, with significantly more calories being eaten posttreatment (and not purged) following therapy (Rossiter, Agras, & Losch, 1988). In addition, in many of the studies of CBT, measures of dietary restraint have been found to be significantly reduced posttreatment. These findings are certainly consistent with theoretical expectations regarding the mechanism of CBT.

It is, therefore, surprising that manualized psychotherapies, procedurally and conceptually distinct from CBT, appear equally effective in reducing binge eating, even when no attention is paid to eating behavior. The thesis behind the use of IPT (the most studied psychotherapy in relation to binge eating) is that eating disorders appear during late adolescence, when interpersonal issues loom large. It is hypothesized that binge eating is triggered by, and becomes a means of coping with, the negative affect associated with faulty interpersonal responding. IPT is directed toward ameliorating the faulty interpersonal responding and the associated negative affect (Klerman et al., 1984). There is evidence that personality disorder, particularly borderline personality, is particularly prevalent in bulimia nervosa (e.g., Cooper et al., 1988) and that major depression is also prevalent in obese patients who binge eat (Marcus et al., 1990). Additionally, interpersonal difficulties have been shown to be common in patients with bulimia nervosa (Norman & Herzog, 1986) and have been implicated in its etiology (Striegel-Moore, Silberstein, & Rodin, 1986). All this suggests that interpersonal difficulties play an important role in the maintenance of binge eating and that therapies directed toward ameliorating these difficulties should reduce the tendency to binge eat.

These therapeutic studies suggest that there are two factors that may lead to the disinhibition of eating behavior: dietary restriction, presumably resulting in excessive hunger and preoccupation with food, and negative affect stemming from interpersonal difficulties. It seems likely that these factors may also disinhibit eating behavior in normals, but to a greater extent in binge eaters, perhaps because of predisposing factors. In this theory of binge eating, either or both factors may be present in any one individual, and we would expect different responses to treatment based on which of these factors is present and to what degree, and what form of treatment is used.

A PSYCHOLOGICAL TREATMENT MODEL FOR BINGE EATING

While it is clear that CBT is the most researched psychological method of treatment for binge eating, with growing support for the effectiveness of IPT, the question remains just how treatment should be most effectively administered, in an individual or group format. This question has not been directly addressed in controlled treatment trials. Indeed, it should be noted that there have been very few studies in which group and individual forms of therapy have been compared, and in all of these studies there has been a confound between group or individual application and the type of therapy used (e.g., Olmsted et al., 1991). While this subject needs further research, a recent meta-analysis of group therapy reported drop-out rates comparable to individual therapy, although abstinence rates and effect size appeared somewhat lower (Fettes & Peters, 1992). In addition, there was a suggestion that when other therapy modes were added to group therapy (e.g., individual therapy or another form of psychological treatment), the results of group treatment were improved. Hence, it is not clear that group and individual forms of treatment are equally effective. On the other hand, since weight-loss therapy is usually group oriented, patients with binge eating disorder who have both weight and binge-eating problems may be more appropriately treated in a group setting than with individual therapy.

The next question that arises is whether an even more cost-effective approach (namely, a brief group psychoeducational therapy) may not have a place in the treatment of binge eating. This question has been addressed in a recent study from Toronto (Olmsted et al., 1991) in which a 5-session group psychoeducational treatment was compared with 19 sessions of individual CBT. While CBT was more effective than psychoeducational therapy, there were no differences in comparative effectiveness for patients with less severe binge-eating problems, in the region of five episodes per week or less. This suggests that one possible model of treatment would be to select less severe patients and treat them with brief psychoeducational group therapy, followed by CBT if there is not full recovery. Similarly, should CBT not be effective, a subsequent trial of IPT could be considered. It should be noted that there may be a down side to this approach, since unsuccessful attempts at treatment may undermine self-efficacy, which may in turn diminish the effectiveness of subsequent therapy.

While there is presently no evidence relating to personal factors that might indicate a differential outcome for CBT or IPT, on theoretical grounds a further triage might be considered. Hence, patients with major interpersonal problems (associated in some instances with borderline personality disorder) might be triaged to IPT, while patients in which dietary problems with their associated cognitions predominate, might be triaged to CBT.

Finally, there is the special problem of the overweight binge eater, a person who usually does not purge, but rather alternates between days of excessive caloric intake, and days in which dietary restriction predominates (Rossiter et al., 1992). It would seem reasonable to suppose that such patients would find it easier to lose weight if their binge eating was treated first. While it is clear that the binge eating of such patients can be treated effectively (Smith et al., 1992; Telch et al., 1990; Wilfley et al., in press), it is not known whether this results in weight loss, or whether adding weight loss therapy at the same time or afterward would convey benefits.

Taking all these factors into consideration, the treatment model for binge eating shown in Figure 13.1 emerges.

CLINICAL IMPLICATIONS

There are several clinical implications of the treatment system outlined in Figure 13.1. First, there is a need for the clinician to carefully assess not only the eating behavior of patients presenting with binge eating, but also to assess more broadly current interpersonal problems and personality disorder. Useful structured interviews in this regard are the Eating Disorder Examination covered in detail in Chapter 15 of this volume, and the Personality Disorders Examination (Loranger, Sussman, & Oldham, 1985). Second, for the overweight binge eater, the question of weight loss will need to be addressed. This may not be a priority for some patients, but in our experience it is a priority for the great majority. Third, only CBT and two forms of manualized psychotherapy have been found effective in the treatment of binge eating; hence, the clinician needs to become familiar with these manualized treatments. A cognitive-behavioral approach to the treatment of binge eating is

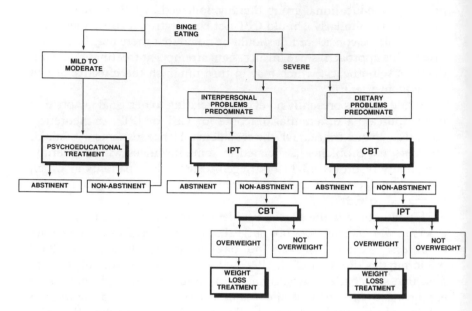

FIGURE 13.1. A flow chart illustrating a hypothetical comprehensive model of the psychological treatment of binge eating.

described in detail by Fairburn, Marcus, and Wilson (Chapter 16, this volume). An adaptation of IPT has also been described in some details (Fairburn, in press). Finally, the only study of family therapy does not suggest that this approach to the treatment of binge eating is particularly useful.

IMPLICATIONS FOR PSYCHOTHERAPY RESEARCH

In some senses research into the psychological treatment of the binge eater is at a crossroads. Sufficient initial research has now been completed to indicate that CBT effectively reduces binge eating and that the results of treatment are fairly stable. However, only some 32 patients out of every 100 entering treatment will remain abstinent 1 year later. This poses the first set of research questions, namely, how can treatment be made more effective initially, and how can the results of treatment be better maintained? The finding that other forms of manualized psychotherapy are equally effective in reducing binge eating opens the possibility that either combining elements from different therapeutic approaches (e.g., from CBT and IPT) or forming a sequential treatment process as outlined in Figure 13.1, may more effectively reduce binge eating. Both of these propositions require testing in well-controlled studies with a sufficient sample size. It should be noted in this regard that the sample size of many studies in the literature has been too small to allow firm conclusions to be drawn, and that some of the new generation of studies will of necessity involve more than one center in order to achieve a sufficient sample size. Since almost nothing is known about factors that influence maintenance of gains once treatment has been completed, another step is to identify such factors and perhaps by appending descriptive studies on future large-scale outcome studies. Once such factors have been identified, treatment procedures to improve maintenance could be developed and tested.

The second set of questions emerges from the findings of equivalent effectiveness of CBT and IPT. While this finding requires replication, of even more interest is the identification of the processes by which each of these quite different therapies works, and of patient factors that might predict differential outcome with one or the other therapy. Again, to achieve sufficient sample size, a multicenter study may be required. The third set of questions concerns the relationship between reduction in binge eating and weight loss in the overweight binge eater. This is an important health problem, since binge eating is more prevalent in the severely obese and may be a risk factor for obesity. Clearly one initial question has been answered, namely, that CBT and IPT both reduce binge-eating frequency in the overweight binge eater. The next question is whether the combination of a psychological therapy and a weight-loss therapy would be better than either therapy alone in the treatment of these individuals, particularly with respect to weight loss.

Finally, the question regarding the relative efficacy of group and individual treatment for all the effective treatment approaches to binge eating requires study. This question, unanswered after more than 10 years of research, addresses important issues of cost-effectiveness.

Overall, much progress has been made over the past decade in defining effective psychological treatment approaches to binge eating. However, design and assessment problems cloud the interpretation of the literature. Given the overall finding that less than a third of patients entering treatment will be abstinent from binge eating at follow-up, there is evidently a long way to go before we can consider that a satisfactory psychological treatment is available to help patients attain total and lasting relief from binge eating and its associated psychopathology.

ACKNOWLEDGMENT

The preparation of this chapter was partially supported by a grant from the National Institute of Mental Health (MH 38637).

REFERENCES

Agras, W. S., Rossiter, E. M., Arnow, B., Telch, C. F., Raeburn, S. D., Schneider, J., Bruce, B., Perl, M., & Koran, L. (1992). Pharmacologic and cognitive-behavioral treatment for bulimia nervosa: A controlled comparison. *American Journal of Psychiatry, 149,* 82–87.

Agras, W. S., Schneider, J. A., Arnow, B., Raeburn, S. D., Telch, C. F. (1989). Cognitive-behavioral and response-prevention treatments for bulimia nervosa. *Journal of Consulting and Clinical Psychology, 57,* 215–221

Bruce, B., & Agras, W. S. (1992). Binge eating in females: A population-based investigation. *International Journal of Eating Disorders, 12,* 365–374.

Cooper, J. L., Morrison, T. L., Bigman, O. L., Abramowitz, S. I., Blunden, D., Nassi, A., & Krener, P. C. (1988). Bulimia and borderline personality disorder. *International Journal of Eating Disorders, 7,* 43–49.

Cooper, Z., & Fairburn, C. G. (1987). The Eating Disorder Examination: A semi-structured interview for the assessment of the specific psychopathology of eating disorders. *International Journal of Eating Disorders,6,* 1–8

Dalvit-McPhillips, S. (1984). A dietary approach to bulimia nervosa. *Physiology and Behavior, 33,* 769–775.

Fairburn, C. G. (1981). A cognitive-behavioral approach to the management of bulimia. *Psychological Medicine, 11,* 707–711.

Fairburn, C. G. (in press). Interpersonal psychotherapy for bulimia nervosa. In G. R. Klerman & M. M. Weissman, *New applications of interpersonal psychotherapy,* Washington DC: American Psychiatric Press.

Fairburn C. G., Jones, R., Peveler, R. C., Carr, S. J., Solomon, R. A., O'Connor, M. E., Burton, J., Hope, R. A. (1991). Three psychological treatments for bulimia nervosa: a comparative trial. *Archives of General Psychiatry, 48,* 463–469

Fairburn, C. G, Jones, R., Peveler, R. C. Hope, R. A., O'Connor, M. (in press). Psychotherapy and bulimia nervosa: The longer-term effects of interpersonal psychotherapy, behavior therapy and cognitive behavioral therapy. *Archives of General Psychiatry.*

Fairburn, C. G., Kirk, J., O'Connor, M., & Cooper, P. (1986). A comparison of two psychological treatments for bulimia nervosa. *Behaviour Research and Therapy, 24,* 629–643.

Fettes, P. A, & Peters, J. M. (1992). A meta-analysis of group treatments for bulimia nervosa. *International Journal of Eating Disorders, 11,* 97–110.

Freeman, C. P. L., Barry, F., Dunkeld-Turnbull, J., & Henderson, A. (1988). Controlled trial of psychotherapy for bulimia nervosa. *British Medical Journal, 296,* 521–525.

Garner, D. M., Rockert, W., Davis, R., Garner, M. V., Olmsted, M. P, & Eagle, M. (1993). Comparison between cognitive-behavioral and supportive-expressive therapy for bulimia nervosa. *American Journal of Psychiatry, 150,* 37–46.

Kirkley, B. G., Schneider, J. A., Agras, W. S., & Bachman, J. A. (1985). Comparison of two group treatments for bulimia. *Journal of Consulting and Clinical Psychology, 53,* 43–48

Klerman, G. L., Weissman, M. M., Rounsaville, B. J., & Chevron, E. S. (1984). *Interpersonal psychotherapy of depression.* New York: Basic Books.

Kolotkin, R. L., Revis, E. S., Kirkley, B. G., & Janick, L. (1987). Binge eating in obesity: Associated MMPI characteristics. *Journal of Consulting and Clinical Psychology, 55,* 872–876.

Laessle, P. J., Beumont, P. J. V., Butow, P., Lennerts, W., O'Connor, M., Pirke, K. M., Touyz, S. W., & Waadt, S. (1991). A comparison of nutritional management with stress management in the treatment of bulimia nervosa. *British Journal of Psychiatry, 159,* 250–261.

Leitenberg, H., Rosen, J., Gross, J., Nudelman, S., & Vara, L. (1988). Exposure plus response-prevention treatment of bulimia nervosa. *Journal of Consulting and Clinical Psychology, 56,* 535–541.

Loranger A. W., Susman, V. L., & Oldham, J. M., (1985). *Personality Disorder Examination (PDE): A structured interview for DSM-III personality disorders.* White Plains, NY: Hospital–Cornell Medical Center.

Luborsky, L. (1984). *Principles of psychoanalytic psychotherapy: A manual for supportive-expressive treatment.* New York: Basic Books.

Marcus, M. D., Wing, R. R., Ewing, L., Kern, E., Gooding, W., & McDermott, M. (1990). Psychiatric disorders among obese binge eaters. *International Journal of Eating Disorders, 9,* 69–77.

McCann, U. D., & Agras, W. S. (1990). Successful treatment of compulsive binge eating with desipramine: A double-blind placebo-controlled study. *American Journal of Psychiatry, 147,* 1509–1517,.

Mitchell, J. E., Pyle, R. L., Eckert, E. D., Hatsukami, D., Pomeroy, C., & Zimmerman, R. (1990). A comparison study of antidepressants and structured intensive group psychotherapy in the treatment of bulimia nervosa. *Archives of General Psychiatry, 47,* 149–157

Norman, D. K., & Herzog, D. B. (1986). A 3–year outcome study of normal-weight bulimia: Assessment of psychosocial functioning and eating attitudes. *Psychiatric Research, 19,* 199–205.

Olmsted, M. P., Davis, R., Rockert, W., Irvine, M. J., Eagle, M., & Garner, D. M. (1991). Efficacy of a brief group psychoeducational intervention for bulimia nervosa. *Behaviour Research and Therapy, 29,* 71–83.

Rosen, J. C., & Leitenberg, H. (1982). Bulimia nervosa: Treatment with exposure and response prevention. *Behavior Therapy, 13,* 117–124.

Rosen, J. C, Leitenberg, H., Fisher, C., & Khazam, C. (1986). Binge-eating episodes in bulimia nervosa: The amount and type of food consumed. *International Journal of Eating Disorders, 5,* 255–267

Rossiter, E. M., & Agras, W. S. (1990). An empirical test of the DSM-III-R definition of binge. *International Journal of Eating Disorders, 9,* 513–518.

Rossiter, E. M., Agras, W. S., & Losch, M. (1988). Dietary restraint of bulimic subjects following cognitive-behavioral or pharmacological treatment. *Behaviour Research and Therapy, 26,* 495–498.

Rossiter, E. M., Agras, W. S., Telch, C. F., & Bruce, B. (1992). The eating patterns of non-purging bulimic subjects. *International Journal of Eating Disorders, 11,* 111–120.

Russell, G. F. M., Szmukler, G. I., Dare, C., & Eisler, I. (1987). An evaluation of family therapy in anorexia nervosa and bulimia nervosa. *Archives of General Psychiatry, 44,* 1047–1056.

Smith, D. E., Marcus, M. D., & Kaye, W. (1992). Cognitive-behavioral treatment of obese binge eaters. *International Journal of Eating Disorders, 12,* 257–262.

Spitzer, R. L., Devlin, M., Walsh, B. T., Hasin, D., Wing, R., Marcus, M., Stunkard, A., Wadden, T., Yanovski, S., Agras, W. S., Mitchell, J., & Nonas, C. (1992). Binge eating disorder: A multisite field trial of the diagnostic criteria. *International Journal of Eating Disorders, 11,* 191–203.

Striegel Moore, R. H., Silberstein, L. R., & Rodin, J. (1986). Toward an understanding of risk factors for bulimia. *American Psychologist, 41,* 246–263.

Stunkard, A. J. (1959). Eating patterns and obesity. *Psychiatric Quarterly, 33,* 284–292.

Telch, C. F., Agras, W. S., & Rossiter, E. M. (1988). Binge eating increases with increasing adiposity. *International Journal of Eating Disorders, 7,* 115–119.

Telch, C. F., Agras, W. S., Rossiter, E. M., Wilfley, D., & Kenardy, J. (1990). Group cognitive-behavioral treatment for the non-purging bulimic: An initial evaluation. *Journal of Consulting and Clinical Psychology, 58,* 629–635.

Wilfley, D. E., Agras, W. S., Telch, C. F., Rossiter, E. M., Schneider, J. A., Cole, A. B., Sifford, L., & Raeburn, S. D. (in press). Group cognitive-behavioral therapy and group interpersonal therapy for the non-purging bulimic: A controlled comparison. *Journal of Consulting and Clinical Psychology*

Wilson, G. T., Eldredge, K. L., Smith, D., & Niles, B. (1991). Cognitive-behavioral treatment with and without response prevention for bulimia. *Behaviour Research and Therapy, 29,* 575–583, 1991.

Wilson, G. T., Rossiter, E., Kleifield, E. I., & Lindholm, L. (1986). Cognitive-behavioral treatment of bulimia nervosa: A controlled evaluation. *Behaviour Research and Therapy, 24,* 277–288.

Wolf, E. M., & Crowther, J. H. (1992). An evaluation of behavioral and cognitive-behavioral interventions for the treatment of bulimia nervosa in women. *International Journal of Eating Disorders, 11,* 3–15.

Psychodynamic Psychotherapy and Binge Eating

David L. Tobin

This chapter departs from many previous psychodynamic papers on the eating disorders in that it integrates research and theoretical perspectives. In contrast to many research-oriented papers, the chapter maintains the view that much is to be gained by entertaining hypotheses about the function of symptomatic behavior that are drawn from psychodynamic points of view.

An assumption of the chapter is that psychodynamic influences on the thoughts, feelings, and behaviors of eating disorder patients, including binge eaters, are only one part of a larger number of influences. The psychodynamic domain of influences is regarded as resting within a "biopsychosocial" context (Johnson & Connors, 1987; Johnson & Maddi, 1986). Though the chapter will not present the other components of the biopsychosocial model in detail, they serve to anchor psychodynamic hypotheses about binge eaters.

One aspect of the biopsychosocial context that will be attended to is weight. Consistent with current and future diagnostic guidelines (American Psychiatric Association, 1987; 1993),* three categories of binge eaters will be considered in descriptions of psychopathology and treatment. These are based on body weight. They include low-weight binge eaters (i.e., patients with the binge-eating/purging type of anorexia nervosa), normal-weight binge eaters (mostly patients with bulimia nervosa), and obese binge eaters. One additional category that will not be

*The DSM-IV criteria used in this volume are those that were approved as final by the DSM-IV Eating Disorders Work Group and the Task Force on DSM-IV (APA, 1993). These criteria may be subject to minor editorial revisions before the publication of DSM-IV.

addressed in the chapter involves a small but very pathological population of obese binge eaters who are 300% or more of normal body weight. Body weight is considered for two reasons: (1) Research has tended to focus on particular weight categories, and (2) there are different treatment considerations among the different weight groups. However, it should be noted that these categories are artificial and that binge eaters are continuously distributed across the groups.

Despite this descriptive categorization, the chapter dispenses with the assumption that morphology or behavioral symptoms necessarily indicate a specific underlying psychopathology. The idea that a particular constellation of symptoms indicates a specific conflict or character is a common viewpoint in psychoanalytic writings (for review, see Schwartz, 1988). However, research suggests this is very unlikely. In the most thoroughly studied group of binge eaters, bulimia nervosa patients, there is considerable evidence to suggest heterogeneous personality structures (Herzog, Keller, Lavori, Kenny, & Sacks, 1992; Johnson, Tobin, & Enright, 1989, Johnson, Tobin, & Dennis, 1990; Steinberg, Tobin, & Johnson, 1990; Wonderlich & Swift, 1990). There is less research on the other groups of binge eaters, but psychopathological features are similarly hypothesized to be distributed both across and within the various subgroups. Though body weight is not hypothesized to reflect specific personality structures, it is speculated that the two extremes (i.e., patients with anorexia nervosa and binges eaters who are at least 300% of normal body weight) may have a concentration of certain psychopathologic types.

PROXIMAL VERSUS DISTAL ANTECEDENTS

A conceptual model of the psychopathology of binge eating may include both proximal and distal influences on the patient's binge-eating behavior (e.g., Jessor, 1981; Singer-Kaplin, 1983). Proximal influences include the immediately precipitating or consequent maintaining influences on binge eating. These influences have been the primary interest of cognitive-behavioral and biological conceptualizations and include body image difficulties (Fairburn, 1985; Cash & Brown, 1987), hunger (e.g., Johnson & Maddi, 1986), sociocultural pressures (Striegel-Moore, Silberstein, & Rodin, 1986), dieting behavior (e.g., Ruderman, 1985), and affective symptoms (Pope & Hudson, 1985). Cognitive-behavioral approaches to treatment directly address these proximal influences. Treatment goals include reducing hunger, managing dysphoric mood states, managing body-image difficulties, and coping with environmental sources of stress (Fairburn, 1985; Rosen & Leitenberg, 1982).

Psychodynamic theorists have been more interested in the distal influences on binge eating. Distal influences include the dynamic processes that form the patient's psychostructural organization (e.g., Chatham, 1985; Dennis & Sansone, 1991; Kernberg, 1988; Stone, 1980) and the corresponding historical context of the patient's personality organization. Attempts to intervene at the level of personality organization involve the assessment of personality structure, style, conflicts, deficits, defenses, and symptoms, and the analysis of these various aspects of personality. This is accomplished primarily through the development and analysis of the patient's transference to the therapist. Preliminary steps in this process may involve the analysis of both the patient's resistance to developing a transference (Gill, 1982) and the therapist's countertransference and counterresistance to the patient (Hoffman, 1983). In contrast to the externally focused approach in cognitive-behavioral therapy (CBT), the primary mechanism for therapeutic change in psychodynamic psychotherapy involves a focus on what happens during the therapy session itself.

A traditional analytic characterization of distal factors is described by Schwartz (1988): "It is the paradigm of mental functioning that recognizes the role that the unawareness of unconscious ideation has in the formation of symptoms" (p. 1). The historical method for identifying these unconscious influences involves the same method for influencing them in turn, namely, psychoanalysis and psychodynamic psychotherapy. Such an approach risks tautology and iatrogenic conclusions and is one of the challenges of psychoanalytic psychotherapy. However, researchers are beginning to make headway with more rigorous methods for assessing both personality attributes and change processes in psychotherapy that reflects a psychodynamic conceptualization (e.g., Benjamin, 1974; Neiman & Howard, 1991; Horowitz, Rosenberg, Ureno, Kalehzan, & O'Halloran, 1989; Tally, Strupp, & Morey, 1990; Weiss, Sampson, & Mount Zion Psychotherapy Research Group, 1986).

From a traditional psychodynamic perspective, it is of limited use to try to directly modify the proximal triggers of binge-eating symptoms without trying to provide patients with an understanding of the more distal influences, the historical and unconscious influences on their behavior. Rapid symptom change is expected to be either short-lived or substituted for with another difficulty (e.g., Wilson, 1988). However, recent contributions to psychoanalytic approaches have altered these assumptions. Shifting the view that transference is a wholly pathognomic process to the view that it is an interpersonal process (Gill, 1982; Hoffman, 1983; Strupp, 1989; Sullivan, 1953; Wachtel, 1977, 1987) has provided psychodynamic psychotherapists with justification for introducing symptom-oriented work early in the treatment process (Johnson, Connors, & Tobin, 1987; Tobin & Johnson, 1990; Wachtel, 1977, 1987). This justification has been most thoroughly articulated by Wachtel (1977,

1987), who proposes that personality processes are often maintained by both intrapsychic and interpersonal factors. The implication of this viewpoint is that not only will psychodynamic psychotherapy be less effective without utilization of behavioral interventions, it may even result in iatrogenic insults to the transference such that analytic work is impeded. Moreover, it is quite clear that many patients can be helped with brief, symptom-oriented approaches to treatment. Despite the success of such brief treatments (e.g., Fairburn et al., 1991), there are subgroups of binge-eating patients who are not aided by symptom-oriented approaches who may benefit from a psychotherapy that attends to both the proximal and the more distal, unconscious mediators of behavioral symptoms (e.g., Johnson et al., 1990; Tobin & Johnson, 1991).

Among clinicians working with the eating disorders, it is Johnson and his colleagues (Johnson & Connors, 1987; Johnson et al., 1987; Tobin & Johnson, 1990) who have been the most outspoken advocates of integrating psychodynamic and behavioral interventions. A related contribution involves the work of experiential therapists who incorporate a variety of in vitro and in vivo experiential activities into a psychodynamic conceptualization (e.g., Hornyak & Baker, 1989). Paralleling these developments have been the contributions of behavioral clinicians who have introduced the analysis of patient–therapist interactions as both a source of information and an opportunity for therapeutic work (Beck, Freeman, and associates, 1990; Garner & Bemis, 1985; Kohlenberg & Tsai, 1987).

The remainder of this chapter will outline psychodynamic approaches to understanding personality and the impact that such forces have on binge-eating symptoms. This model will then be applied to the three groups of binge eaters. To a considerable degree, descriptions of the treatment process will have to be brief, but a longer discussion of some of the considerations for integrative psychotherapy can be found in a previous paper (Tobin & Johnson, 1990).

PSYCHOSTRUCTURAL THEORY

The first phase of psychodynamic psychotherapy involves the assessment of the personality processes that mediate symptoms. This process of diagnosis involves the identification of the patient's psychostructural organization. Psychostructural theory is based on the stages of development that have been described by a number of psychoanalytic writers, many of whom have competed or disagreed with one another. Given the limited empirical evidence for any particular model, the notion that alternative models are in competition will be replaced in this chapter by the idea that each model may have strengths and weaknesses, or describe a particular phase of development better than the others. It should be noted that a thorough review of these models is well beyond the scope of this chapter, but an outline of useful constructs will be presented.

Psychostructural organization can be divided into at least four levels: psychotic, borderline, narcissistic, and neurotic (e.g., Dennis & Sansone, 1991). These categories are clinical descriptions of personality constructs that assume a developmental etiology. As noted, disagreement exists among psychoanalytic theorists as to the significance of specific components of personality development. Competing conceptualizations of personality development include drive theory, object relations theory, ego psychology, and self-psychology. Though each developmental model may add something to our understanding of each developmental stage, the developmental stages will be discussed in the following way: Descriptions of psychosis and borderline personality will emphasize object relations theory; descriptions of narcissistic personality will emphasize self-psychology; and descriptions of neurosis will emphasize drive theory. Thus, the descriptions here represent an amalgam of the major developmental theories. Similar to the weight categorization presented earlier, the psychostructural categories are assumed to represent prototypes or nodes of a continuously distributed set of psychopathological features.

To a certain extent, each of these developmental theories, or metapsychologies, has also been associated with a variation of psychoanalytic practice. However, in this chapter clinical practice will be detached from metapsychology. This allows one to draw on the various metapsychologies for hypotheses about psychopathology while maintaining a unified theory of clinical practice. Distinguishing clinical practice from metapsycholgy also helps to justify the integration of psychodynamic psychotherapy with other approaches to treatment.

Psychosis and Borderline Personality

Psychosis and borderline personality disorders are considered together because the personality organizations and psychoanalytic treatment of these subgroups are the primary focus of object relations theorists (e.g., Kernberg, 1988). The descriptions draw heavily on the work of Klein (e.g., 1975), Mahler (e.g., Mahler, Pine, & Bergman, 1975), and Winnicott (e.g., 1965). Within this categorization a rough outline of subtypes would include paranoid disorders and paranoid–schizoid personalities, manic and depressive personalities, and borderline personality. This list is not intended to be exhaustive but to highlight important subtypes that represent increasing levels of developmental achievement. Further, the model presented here does not disavow the potential contribution of biological factors, but will ignore them for heuristic purposes.

Object relations theory describes personality development as a parallel to cognitive development. However, in addition to basic cognitive–perceptual processes, personality development must also assimilate and accommodate the infant's affective involvement with other people. As in the process by which the infant acquires the ability to comprehend and remember physical objects, so must the infant develop an understanding and memory of "libidinal objects," or people.

Despite her inconsistent use of drive and object relations constructs, Klein (1975) provides the first detailed description of early psychostructural development from an object relations perspective. Klein's interest in childhood psychopathology began as an extension of Freud's drive theory. She speculated that oedipal concerns were present in children at a much earlier age than previously hypothesized. However, without trying to be controversial, Klein radically shifted the focus of early childhood development from drive gratification and regulation to childhood fantasies and memories of parental involvement.

For Klein, normal development is predicated on the mother providing adequate feeding. She wrote,

> The hypothesis that the infant's first experiences of feeding and of his mother's presence initiated an object relation to her is one of the basic concepts put forward in this book. The relation is at first a relation to a part object, for both the oral-libidinal and oral-aggressive impulses from the beginning of life are directed toward the mother's breast. (Klein, 1975, p. 62)

Because infants cannot learn to trust that which they cannot perceive, they must both intellectually and emotionally accommodate the perception that people are more than just a breast, or part object. This maturational process involves the transition from primitive affective-cognitive organizations of self and others to increasingly more complex organizational strategies. Though Klein's mixture of drive theory and object relations constructs makes her theoretical work cumbersome, her descriptions of primitive psychopathology are useful for understanding the clinical characteristics and treatment process for some binge eaters.

Klein (1975) divided her attention between the first and second 6 months of life. She stated that in the first 6 months "the fixation-points for all psychotic disorders can be found" (p. 1). Klein outlined the process by which primitive object relations are developed in the following lines:

> I have often expressed my view that object-relations exist from the beginning of life, the first object being the mother's breast which to the child becomes split into a good (gratifying) and bad (frustrating) breast...object-relations are moulded by an interaction between introjection and projection, between internal and external objects. These processes participate in the

building up of the ego and superego and prepare the ground for the onset of the Oedipus complex in the second half of the first year of life. (p. 2)

Of particular importance is Klein's notion that the infant is at first unable to tolerate the complexity of good and bad in the same object or person. She proposes that the infant's sense of survival depends on their ability to isolate the good from the bad. Furthermore, the overwhelming sense of helplessness encourages the infant's normal hallucination of possession and omnipotent control over the good breast. In simplified terms, protecting the good may mean keeping it to oneself, and projecting the bad into other people. This is the developmental template for paranoid–schizoid personality.

Learning to recognize that good and bad may coexist in the same person coincides with the task of learning to recognize and accept lack of control over others, both of which are milestones in psychological development. These psychological events normally occur sometime in the second 6 months of life and mark the transition from the paranoid-schizoid to the depressive position. The child is hypothesized to become depressed as a result of the realization that the part object that is desired (i.e., the good breast), is the same part object that is hated and feared (i.e., the bad breast). Fantasies to destroy the bad breast are reluctantly abandoned as the child realizes that this would also destroy the good breast. In other words, the child must learn to manage intense anger that accompanies frustration, and to prevent this anger from destroying positive feelings toward the parents. The child's growing realization of both the importance of dependency on other people and the anxieties that accompany the sense of loss that occurs when the parent is not immediately available result in frantic efforts at denial. This forms the developmental template for both manic defenses and many kinds of depressive experiences.

Klein's description is highly specific, and the theory has little research to support her observations. However, the idea that very early childhood experiences are manifest in certain types of adult psychopathology can be useful in understanding the experiences of patients with profound personality disturbance. This is particularly true with regard to patients' experience of other people, including their experience of the therapist. Klein's developmental model offers therapists a language for understanding the experience of patients with psychosis and personality disorders, which if not taken literally, can provide an experiential referent for discussing important experiences that first occurred when language was largely undeveloped (i.e., the first year of life). Moreover, the introduction of relational constructs into the psychodynamic formulations has revolutionized analytic thinking.

Other theorists have also contributed to object relations theory and descriptions of primitive psychopathology. One modification involves the recognition that the relationship fantasies Klein discusses may not be present in the newborn (e.g., Winnicott, 1965). These fantasies are dependent upon cognitive-perceptual capacities that Winnicott believed to be limited in the infant. He believed that infants do not at first perceive the distinction between the mother as someone or even something outside the infant, and therefore cannot have the fantasies that Klein discussed. As such, newborn infants do not at first have selves or mothers; there are only tensions and tension reduction.

Nevertheless, Winnicott agreed with Klein that the formation of self and of early object relationships rests on the infant's experiences around early maternal caretaking. For Winnicott, normal development was predicated on the child being so completely taken care of that the need to recognize another person does not exist. Such experience provides the nucleus for a cohesive sense of self–a self that is not jeopardized by tension frustration. Of course, no caretaker is perfect, and infants inevitably experience some tension. If this tension is not too severe, they will not be traumatized by the gradual recognition of their separateness from other people. However, in order to maintain a sense of emotional well-being, helpless infants must first have the illusory experience of having omnipotent control over the primary caretaker, and only gradually become disillusioned over their lack of omnipotence. This occurs as the result of the normal frustration that any child experiences, even with the most watchful of mothers. If these experiences of frustration do not generally go beyond the infants' ability to soothe and manage physical and emotional tension, psychological growth and maturation can occur. However, if the caregiver is either too intrusive, too neglectful, or too inconsistent, then the infant may retreat from psychological advancement.

Mahler and her colleagues (e.g., Mahler et al., 1975) also described a sequence of maturation that is helpful in understanding primitive psychopathology. Similar to Klein and Winnicott, Mahler retained certain aspects of drive theory while continuing to develop an interpersonal model of infant development and psychopathology. In addition to refining theoretical elements of development during the first year, Mahler also outlined child development from the second year until the beginnings of the oedipal period. Like Winnicott, Mahler described the infant as being unaware of external reality during the first few weeks of life, a period she calls the ''normal autistic phase.'' The ''normal symbiotic phase'' occurs from the second until the fourth or fifth month and is marked by infants' increasing awareness of the outside world. However, during this period infants still cannot distinguish between inside and outside events, and so perceive the outside world to be a part of them.

Like Klein and Winnicott, early psychological experience is divided into good and bad, and out of these experiences form the precursors of self and other. From 4 or 5 months until 10 months comes the "differentiation subphase," at which time the child begins to distinguish self from other. A prominent marker during this period is the appearance of "stranger anxiety," when the child develops the ability to locate on a more or less consistent basis the provider of good experiences within the mother and to fear other people as a source of bad experience.

Later phases include the "early" and "late practicing subphases" in which infants continue to develop cognitive and emotional capacities that allow them to function with increasingly greater autonomy. These periods are marked by their increased motor capabilities and a continued utilization of parental resources that provide powerfully reinforcing experiences of self-initiated action. However, with increasing cognitive abilities, the children eventually rediscover their limited abilities to navigate life's challenges without parental help. The "rapprochement subphase," occurring somewhere during the second year and continuing until the third year, ushers in a new sense of concern about separateness. Children must renegotiate the boundaries around when, what, and how parents are willing to respond to their wishes. It is during the rapprochement subphase that children begin to develop a more realistic appraisal of self-abilities and to modulate earlier grandiose expectations regarding their abilities. An intense struggle arises during this period around their wish to function independently on the one hand, and the desire to be taken care of on the other. During the rapprochement subphase, children fear for their safety if the mother is not there to provide caretaking, but also fear a return to symbiosis if she hovers too close. Alternating or even simultaneous anxieties over separation and fusion are the developmental template for borderline personality disorder. If children learn to manage these anxieties, and to tolerate positive and negative feelings toward the parents, they may proceed to the phase of "libidinal object constancy." During this stage they must be able to combine both positive and negative feelings toward the self and other, and thus be able to achieve a stable sense of both. This psychological milestone is the object relations counterpart to Piaget's notion of "object permanence."

The differentiating fulcrum for varieties of psychosis and borderline personality rests on the extent to which mother and infant are able to manage the separation–individuation process. While drive models tend to emphasize the child's contribution to this process vis-a-vis the pattern and strength of instinctual drives, object relations theorists shift the emphasis from instinct to parental responsiveness. Though neither Klein, Winnicott, nor Mahler completely abandoned drive theory, the importance each one placed on the ability of parents to adapt to a child's maturational needs dramatically shifted the thrust of psychoanalytic approaches to treatment from a focus on oedipal conflict to the relational vicissitudes of separation–individuation. (For a detailed review of object relations theory the reader may consult Greenberg & Mitchell [1983].)

Clinically, the evaluation of patients with primitive personality disorders is complicated by the inverse relationship between the level of depressive symptoms and the developmental stage at which personality functions were compromised. Thus, the most severely disturbed patients, such as those with paranoid disorders, are likely to demonstrate less depression than patients with borderline, dependent, or other depressive personality disorders. Paranoid patients rely on defenses such as projection and splitting that ward off depressive experiences. Patients who demonstrate manic defenses are also highly capable of limiting their experience of depression, though they are likely to have experienced depression and to fear its onset. From an object relations perspective, when binge eating is part of a paranoid personality structure, there are likely to be conscious or unconscious fantasies that may include the following: engulfing the other, controlling the other, fear of being controlled by the other, or defensively destroying the other. When binge eating serves a more manic function, it may reflect a preoccupation with excessive behavioral activity organized around the binge. An important function of binge eating for patients with manic defenses is to deny the importance of other people, and thereby avoid feeling depressed. Patients are more generally unaware of their attempts to avoid depression to the extent that they are more primitive (i.e., paranoid–schizoid) in their personality organization. To the extent that patients are able to accept their need for other people (even when they are behaviorally withdrawn), depression becomes an important part of the clinic picture.

Thus, patients with primitive psychostructural organizations can present with either florid psychotic symptoms (e.g., paranoid delusions), latent paranoid or schizoid attitudes, manic or hypomanic mood states, or significant affective symptoms. In addition to these intrapersonal difficulties, patients with primitive psychostructural organizations have limited interpersonal skills. These interpersonal deficits may or may not be immediately obvious, and patients with profound personality disturbance often have the capacity to function reasonably well in social situations where there are limited demands for close interpersonal contact. Though these patients may be able to manage the interpersonal involvement of certain occupational settings, they have limited ability to maintain a healthy family life.

Such patients may have any of a variety of interpersonal difficulties, including fear of being close (e.g., schizoid or paranoid personality), fear of being alone (e.g., dependent personality), or an oscillating fear of both closeness and separation (e.g., borderline personality). The application of object relations theory to the understanding of these patients is especially helpful when evaluating their interpersonal difficulties. In that the experiences that shape many of these personality structures occur before the development of verbal language, the therapist is often confronted with a language of behavioral enactment that reflects the reenactment of infant–parent relationship patterns. These behaviors can manifest themselves in many ways both inside and outside the session, including avoidant behavior (e.g., missing sessions), frequent requests for attention between sessions (e.g., frequent telephone calls), passive–aggressive behavior (e.g., not paying bills), suicidal or self-mutilating behavior, somatic preoccupation, abusive language, and even physical threats. These primitive, concrete, behavioral communications have a variety of interpersonal functions including demanding attention, maintaining distance, and infusing the therapist with unwanted emotional tension by way of projective identification. Such activity can be understood as a reenactment of the infant's primitive wishes to manipulate, control, incorporate, or destroy the primary caretaker. It is important for the therapist to appreciate how such behaviors are understood by patients, both consciously and unconsciously. One of the tasks of psychoanalytic psychotherapy is to translate these behavioral communications into verbal language.

For descriptions of the psychoanalytic treatment of primitive patients the reader is urged to consider Kernberg (e.g., 1988). Of particular value is Kernberg's (1988) notion that it is object *relationships* and not objects with which individuals identify. Moreover, there is usually one part of the object relationship that is more comfortably identified with by a patient and another part that is habitually projected onto other people. Understanding this process can help therapists appreciate not only those concerns a patient identifies consciously, but also those concerns that patients project onto other people. Therapists can understand these split-off affects by examining their countertransference. Therapists must limit the reenactment of these projections and attempt to bring them into the patient's awareness by interpretation, thereby interrupting the maladaptive interpersonal cycle that brought the patient into treatment. Interpretation of transference and countertransference in psychotic and borderline patients facilitates their integration of positive and negative feelings toward self and others (i.e., the good and the bad breast) in their struggle for object constancy. As they learn to tolerate periodic loss of the good object (in this case the therapist), and to manage the depressive affects that accompany separation, the focus of treatment can move from the patient's difficulties with object constancy to narcissistic deficits (e.g., Adler, 1985).

Narcissistic Personality Deficits

One example of the very divergent perspectives among psychodynamic theorists is Kernberg and Kohut's views on borderline and narcissistic personality disorders (Adler, 1986). Kernberg (1975) views narcissistic personality disorder from his object relations perspective and regards it as a variation of borderline personality disorder with a pathological grandiose self. Kohut (1971) views patients with borderline personality disorder as psychotic and untreatable by analytic techniques, whereas patients with narcissistic personality disorder are in a spectrum of analyzable patients that also includes neurotic patients. For Kohut, the difference between narcissistic and neurotic patients involves what he called disturbances of the self. While it would be difficult to do justice to the nuances of Kohut's theory in this paper, it is necessary to go beyond saying that patients with narcissistic personality structures have difficulties with self-esteem.

For Kohut (1977), the self takes on many of the psychic functions of the ego of previous theorists—"a center of initiative and recipient of impressions" (p. 99). The self is hypothesized to develop in relation to self-objects of which there are two primary types. One self-object relationship comprises the infant's display of evolving abilities and the subsequent admiration by the caretaker. The other type comprises the infant's admiration of a caretaker and subsequent identification. The life-and-death struggle that characterizes the omnipotence and grandiosity of borderline personality disorder gives way to the struggle for personal competence and self-esteem. Without adequate mirroring and admiration of the early grandiose self, the child's acceptance of realistic ideals and standards is never achieved. Without realistic modification of early grandiose ideals and standards, self-esteem is forever out of reach.

According to Kohut (1977), treatment of the narcissistic personality disorders requires certain modifications of traditional analytic technique. It is critical that the therapist allow the patient to reexperience early narcissistic aspects of the self, an experience that is only possible with much patience and tolerance on the part of the therapist. Kohut describes two primary transferences that develop—mirror and idealizing. In the mirror transference the therapist must endeavor to admire the patient's grandiosity, and in the idealizing transference the therapist must tolerate the patient's need to admire the therapist. Change does not come from interpretation but rather through the interpersonal participation of the therapist with the patient. The toleration of the therapist's narcissistic tensions that arise in the countertransference are an essential aspect of the treatment process in that they allow patients to explore their own primitive narcissistic concerns. Active participation by therapists is also required when the therapist's attention lapses and empathic failure results. At this time therapists must acknowledge this failure, and provide patients with a working model for accepting their limitations. When sufficient attention has been paid to narcissistic concerns, the patient can move on to more oedipal concerns. It should be noted that narcissistic and oedipal difficulties are not necessarily exclusive and that sometimes the two have to be addressed in tandem.

Narcissistic personality structures have a been a particular interest to clinicians working in the eating disorders (e.g., Goodsitt, 1985; Johnson & Connors, 1987; Tobin & Johnson, 1990). Drawing on the work of Kohut and Winnicott, Johnson and Connors (1987) described a group of patients who present with a veneer of integration and adjustment that reflects an expertise at adapting to the needs of others. Their experience of others is not malevolent as in patients with borderline personality structures, but reveals an attitude that other people would not be interested in them if they truly knew them. Such patients will present only a ''false self'' to other people, including the psychotherapist. For false-self/narcissistic patients, a binge-eating disorder may serve a number of functions, including (1) presenting a socially acceptable physical self (e.g., thin), (2) maintaining the attention of others on superficial (i.e., physical) aspects of self, and (3) finding a somatic compensation for narcissistic tensions. These patients do not fear annihilation as do borderline or psychotic patients; they fear humiliation. And though oedipal concerns may be part of the overall symptom picture, the interest in physical attractiveness that is typical of patients with eating disorders does not primarily correspond to sexual or competitive feelings, but rather to self-esteem needs. Thus, physical attractiveness is not sought as a means of engaging the opposite sex but to provide a narcissistic definition of the patient's self.

Neurotic Structure

Patients with neurotic personality structures have mastered the ego-organizational difficulties of psychotic patients, the difficulties with object constancy that characterize borderline patients, and have overcome the self-difficulties of false-self/narcissistic patients. Patients with neurotic levels of personality functioning present with oedipal conflicts that have been within the traditional purview of classical psychoanalysis. Anxiety over sexual/romantic involvement and achievement dominate the clinical picture. The pursuit of thinness thus becomes not so much a definition of self as in narcissistic personality deficits as it does to provide a competitive edge in attracting the opposite sex. Alternatively, binge eating in neurotic patients who are obese may help to manage conflicts over sexuality by maintaining what is conventionally regarded as a sexually unappealing body shape.

Patients who have a neurotic personality structure respond to a wide variety of treatment approaches. They do well in brief cognitive-behavioral therapy and they are probably the one-third of psychotherapy patients who do very well in any kind of treatment. While cognitive-behavioral therapies may be the most expedient of therapies for neurotic patients with binge-eating disorders, this does not necessarily indicate that neurotic-level patients should be excluded from psychodynamic psychotherapy, given sufficient interest and resources. Furthermore, there may be subgroups of neurotic patients who may be unable to make use of self-management skills until neurotic conflicts are explored and worked through.

BINGE-EATING DISORDERS

Despite the suggestion that those with binge-eating symptoms do not have a characteristic personality structure or specific unconscious conflicts, there may be a concentration of personality subtypes in certain binge-eating subgroups. This is hypothesized to be especially true of those at the two extremes of body weight: namely, anorexic patients who binge eat and those binge-eating patients who are 300% or more of normal body weight. Binge eaters at less extreme weights are hypothesized to have a broad range of personality subtypes.

Anorexic Nervosa (Binge-Eating/Purging Type)

There are a small number of empirical studies suggesting that patients with the binge-eating/purging form of anorexia nervosa have the greatest prevalence of primitive personality structures of eating-disordered patients. Studies that have compared anorexic patients who do and do not have binge-eating/purging symptoms have consistently found that the latter are more disturbed on a variety of psychiatric indices. These findings target a very difficult to treat group of patients, since anorexia nervosa is considered more difficult to treat than the other eating disorders. In summarizing the literature, DaCosta and Halmi (1992) conclude that "impulsive behaviors including stealing, drug abuse, suicide attempts, self-mutilations, . . . mood lability are more prevalent anorectic-bulimics than anorectic-restrictors" (p. 311). DaCosta and Halmi also find that anorexic bulimics have a "higher prevalence of or premorbid obesity, familial obesity, debilitating personality traits, and familial psychopathology" (p. 311). In their review of the literature, Johnson and Connors conclude that binge-eating/purging anorexics have a greater incidence of affective disorder and impulsive behaviors, show greater life impairment; and have a poorer prognosis (see Garner, Chapter 4, this volume).

Clinicians who treat these patients report that a large percentage have severe personality difficulties, often in the borderline to paranoid-schizoid range, and that inpatient hospitalization is often required. From a proximal, symptom-oriented approach one might assume the difficulty in treating these patients are a result of the cognitive changes that accompany semistarvation. From an object relations perspective, the difficulty in treating these patients results from personality traits. It is probably most useful to consider both factors as contributing to the maintenance of the patient's symptoms. In addition to the holding milieu of the inpatient ward, intensive psychotherapy (i.e., five times per week) and pharmacological interventions can be useful in helping them manage the terrifically dysphoric mood states that occur during recovery. While there is little research to support the efficacy of family therapy, there is a growing body of data to suggest that binge-eating/purging anorexic patients often have very pathological family systems (DaCosta & Halmi, 1992). Clinical experience suggests that individual therapy may be ineffective for many patients in the absence of family therapy. Once both normal-weight and a stable eating pattern is achieved, outpatient follow-up care in twice-a-week, psychodynamically oriented psychotherapy can help promote further development of the patient's sense of object constancy. Patients tend to have a better prognosis if they can remain in either a full or partial hospital program long enough to achieve a normal weight.

Bulimia Nervosa

Bulimia nervosa represents the most thoroughly studied subgroup of binge eaters. As previously noted, there is no evidence to support the idea that a particular personality structure is characteristic of bulimic patients. Given that dieting, binge eating, and even self-induced vomiting are normative in western culture (e.g., Johnson, Tobin, & Lipkin, 1989; Pyle, Mitchell, Eckert, & Halverson, 1983), it is no surprise that the clinical presentation of bulimic symptoms occurs with every possible personality structure. Further, level of depression and/or anxiety is not correlated with the severity or constellation of binge-eating symptoms in clinical samples (Garfinkel, Moldofsky, & Garner, 1980; Johnson et al., 1989, Johnson et al., 1990; Steinberg et al., 1990; Levin & Hyler, 1986; Pope, Frankenberg, & Hudson, 1987; Swift & Stern, 1982; Wonderlich & Swift, 1990).

The treatment of patients with bulimia nervosa must therefore address a wide variety of patient needs (see Tobin, Johnson, & Franke, 1990). Though a traditional psychoanalytic perspective suggests that symptom-oriented work will be unsuccessful or perhaps undermine the analysis of transference, there is no empirical evidence to support this assumption. Furthermore, important theoretical advances within psychoanalysis have emphasized the interpersonal aspects of the therapeutic relationship (e.g., Wachtel, 1977, 1987) such that attending to a patient's symptoms may be promote the development and analysis of transference.

Thus, developments from within both psychodynamic and behavioral approaches to treatment suggest that a cognitive-behavioral approach is warranted in the early stages of treatment for patients with bulimia nervosa. Clinical trials with cognitive-behavioral therapy (CBT) indicate that many patients will be helped in 20 sessions or less (Fairburn, Agras, & Wilson, 1992). From an interpersonal psychodynamic perspective, the withholding of self-management skills (e.g., Kanfer & Hagerman, 1981; Kanfer & Scheft, 1987; Tobin, Reynolds, Holroyd, & Creer, 1986) is often experienced by patients as very neglectful. The skills are simple and in many cases may not involve more than a few sessions (e.g., Fairburn, 1985; Tobin & Johnson, 1990). If patients are not successful in remitting their symptoms with a trial of CBT, then other approaches should be considered, including both psychodynamic and family systems approaches. Family systems approaches are indicated to the extent that a patient is living within a family structure that maintains bulimic symptoms and is usually a necessary adjunct for adolescent and young adult patients who live at home. Psychodynamic approaches should be considered when focusing on the proximal antecedents of a patient's bulimic symptoms proves unsuccessful. Pharmacological treatments may be a useful adjunct to psychosocial interventions as a way of helping some personality-disordered patients manage very dysphoric mood states while they are struggling to achieve behavioral control.

Obese Binge Eaters

Between a third and a half of obese individuals who seek treatment report regular episodes of binge eating, and this group appears to have greater levels of psychopathology and a poorer response to treatment than those obese individuals who do not binge eat (see Marcus, Chapter 5, this volume). The treatment of these patients not only demands the elimination of binge-eating behaviors but also some use of the very weight-control strategies one may wish to eliminate in bulimic or anorexic patients (i.e., dieting; for a detailed description of the cognitive-behavioral treatment of these patients, see Fairburn, Marcus, & Wilson, Chapter

16, this volume). For patients with primitive personality structures who use their binge eating as a way of managing separation/fusion anxiety, education about the use of efficient weight control strategies can result in these patients becoming bulimic or even anorexic. Such patients need more than just symptom-oriented interventions. Instead, they may require one to several years of psychodynamically oriented psychotherapy to address their profound interpersonal and intrapersonal deficits. Pharmacotherapy with antidepressants and occasionally low-dose neuroleptics can also be useful when mood states are so dysphoric as to prevent psychotherapeutic work. Brief CBT is often sufficient for patients with narcissistic or neurotic-level personality structure. However, higher functioning patients may benefit from psychodynamic psychotherapy or a treatment that integrates psychodynamic and behavioral therapies.

TREATMENT APPROACHES

Psychodynamic Psychotherapy

As noted earlier, the approach of this chapter differs from many other psychoanalytic papers in that it attempts to integrate psychosocial research into a broadly defined psychoanalytic approach to understanding patient psychopathology. In this way divergent metapsychological assumptions of different psychoanalytic approaches are balanced by empirical findings. The assumptions regarding theoretical implications for treatment are similarly based and reflect a highly descriptive and more readily observable process than employed by many psychoanalytic writers. Unfortunately, there is little outcome research with binge eaters to substantiate the following model, though such an approach has generated a number of treatment manuals as well as outcome research in more general populations (e.g., Luborsky, 1984; Strupp & Binder, 1984).

A description of clinical process in psychodynamic psychotherapy reflects the following assumptions as put forth by Strupp (1989) and thoroughly articulated in the Strupp and Binder (1984) treatment manual. First, the focus of treatment is on the interactions between the patient and therapist, with primary importance being given to the patient's affective experience. Second, a primary activity by the therapist is empathic listening. Third, efforts to interpret the emerging transferential material should be free of jargon and be closely linked to readily observable events. And fourth, the therapist must overcome the interpersonal pressures emanated by patients to reenact past history (e.g., countertransference) and draw these experiences into the therapeutic work. This latter point is particularly important with more primitive personality organizations because the precipitating developmental experiences may have occurred before the development of language and therefore transferential material may be largely understood in the context of the therapist's experience of the countertransference (e.g., Greenspan, 1989; Kernberg, 1988).

Strupp's description of the therapeutic process is consistent with at least one behavior therapist's vision of a radical behavioral therapy that addresses therapy process. Kohlenberg proposes that the therapist attend to and intervene with examples of the problem behavior that led them to seek treatment, as they emerge in the therapy process (Kohlenberg & Tsai, 1987). While other behavior therapists have attended to this aspect of binge-eating difficulties when it has concretely reflected binge-eating behavior (e.g., Rosen & Leitenberg, 1982), they have generally been less attentive to the interpersonal processes that may mediate binge eating when they emerge in the therapy sessions themselves.

Integrative Psychotherapy

In returning to the proximal and distal factors that may influence binge eating, one can observe a complementary reversal of what is proximal and what is distal to the treatment process when comparing psychodynamic and behavioral (or cognitive-behavioral) approaches to treatment. The efforts of behavioral therapists typically include the teaching of self-control skills (see Fairburn, Marcus, & Wilson, Chapter 16, this volume). The skills training process is directed toward helping patients achieve greater control over the precipitating and maintaining factors that promote binge eating that occur in the patient's day-to-day experiences, and is consequently directed away from the therapy process. A primary goal of behavioral therapies is to help patients transfer the skills they learn in therapy sessions into their day-to-day environment.

Psychodynamic psychotherapy takes a markedly different approach by helping patients transfer into the therapy process the precipitating and maintaining factors that are likely to promote binge eating. The empathic listening described by Strupp is designed to help the patient experience an important interpersonal encounter during the therapy hour. This provides a setting for patients to try to solve both intrapersonal and interpersonal difficulties, and to allow the therapist to make observations about maladaptive patterns. The interpersonal setting provides a powerful emotional experience so that insight does not remain intellectualized. In this way, the activities of the psychodynamic psychotherapist bear a strikingly proximal relationship to the patient's symptoms, though they are more distal to the environmental conditions outside of therapy that trigger binge eating.

There is a growing body of evidence to suggest that brief CBT is the initial treatment of choice for patients with bulimia nervosa (for review, see Fairburn et al., 1992) and obese binge eaters. Training in self-management is also useful for the binge-eating/purging type of anorexia nervosa but will often prove unsuccessful as an initial intervention. Furthermore, treatment studies of bulimia nervosa typically report that a significant minority of patients do not remit their symptoms (e.g., Fairburn et al., 1992). Though these studies have typically not evaluated personality disorders as a mediator of treatment outcome, it has been my clinical experience and that of many colleagues that patients with personality disorders do less well in CBT than patients without personality disorders. If, for example, frequent binges are utilized in the service of managing primitive separation fears, then self-monitoring and self-reinforcement will ultimately be abandoned as the patient learns that these behaviors lead to self-sufficiency, something the patient desperately wants to avoid. The underlying concerns about separation will first have to be addressed if the patient is going to see the benefit from giving up binge-eating symptoms. The same may be true for binge-eating or dieting efforts that are utilized to manage narcissistic tensions.

The findings of one open study suggest that when psychodynamic psychotherapy is added to CBT, a significant percentage of personality-disordered patients are able to improve (Johnson et al., 1990). The study further found that patients who improved needed an average of 100 sessions during the first year, while patients who received an average of 50 sessions remained symptomatic, the difference being between once- and twice-a-week psychotherapy over the course of 1 year. These findings suggest that not only is a focus on the patient–therapist relationship an important ingredient of behavior change for bulimia nervosa patients with personality disorders, but that the "dosage" of psychotherapy (Howard, Kopta, Krouse, & Orlinsky, 1986), both in terms of the frequency of sessions and duration of treatment, is also important.

Apart from a study by Olmsted and colleagues (Olmsted et al., 1991) comparing the effects of brief psychoeducational treatment with those of standard CBT, there is no other empirical work that has examined whether frequency of sessions and duration of treatment can affect treatment outcome for binge-eating patients, and very little that has specifically addressed the issue in other populations. In the past 25 years, psychotherapy research has concentrated on brief, time-limited psychotherapies, primarily as a way of achieving control over the experimental conditions related to studying psychotherapy, but probably also as a way of controlling costs and maximizing research output. In that controlling costs remains a vital consideration, it may seem that research on longer term models of psychotherapy is anachronistic. However, binge eaters who go untreated face many health difficulties, especially those patients at very low and very high weights. To the extent that binge-eating patients have significant personality disturbance, they will be resistant to brief, ambulatory approaches to treatment. Longer term psychotherapy is a cost-effective alternative when compared to long or repeated hospitalizations. In order to help patients overcome binge eating, therapists may need to attend to factors that are proximal to both the therapy process as well as to symptoms in the day-to-day environment. The indications for choosing either one or both are not well understood, and empirical studies have looked primarily at behavioral and cognitive-behavioral models of treatment. However, there are a number of reasons for selecting a cognitive-behavioral approach as the first intervention strategy. First, from an empirical perspective CBT has been shown to help many patients (Fairburn et al., 1992). Second, it is not possible to predict who will benefit from CBT, even among patients with primitive personality structures. Third, from an interpersonal, psychodynamic theoretical perspective, it is negligent to withhold training in self-control skills that may benefit patients. Finally, it may be easier to shift from an active, behavioral approach to treatment to a psychodynamic one than from the latter to the former.

Indications for beginning treatment with psychodynamic psychotherapy include previous treatment failure with CBT. Also, if a patient says that an active, behavioral intervention would not be appreciated or demonstrates significant difficulty in complying with treatment goals, then it may be more productive to seek an understanding of this difficulty rather than to pursue cognitive-behavioral goals. In the integrative model of psychotherapy that I am proposing, a patient's readiness for active suggestion is assessed before, during, and after the implementation of behavioral suggestions (Molteni, 1991; Prochaska & Norcross, 1983). For example, a patient's negative reaction to doing homework should be understood before pursuing further goals. Such a reaction may offer significant clues to the transference and should be analyzed and interpreted before proceeding. (See Tobin & Johnson [1990] for a detailed description of an integrative approach to the treatment of bulimia nervosa.)

CASE EXAMPLE

The patient was a 25-year-old professional woman who had major depression, bulimia nervosa, and a personality disorder characterized by dependency and paranoia. A diabetic, she had a severe form of bulimia nervosa in which she purged by letting her blood sugar rise. The patient had difficulties with concentration and memory, anhedonia, and insomnia, and she was frequently suicidal. She would remain in bed for days in an anaclitic, paranoid state, getting up only to binge eat. The patient could not tolerate separation from her mother or her therapist and spent most of the first year of treatment on an inpatient, psychiatric unit. Treatment lasted approximately 3 years, during which she was seen twice a week in the clinic and five times a week when in the hospital. The patient had been in a weight-loss program prior to entering treatment and was transferred to another therapist when I took a new position in another geographic area.

Treatment involved a variety of modalities, including psychodynamic, behavioral, family systems, and pharmacological interventions. Behavioral self-management training was initially effective in helping the patient regain control of her diabetes, but she quickly relapsed because she utilized diabetic crises to maintain contact with her doctors. Thus, successful management of her diabetes provoked separation anxiety and suicidality. The patient required a long period of hospitalization (10 out of the next 12 months) subsequent to these efforts.

The second phase of treatment began when she was in the hospital and emphasized the evaluation of the object-relational aspects of her self-destructive behavior. Self-destructive acts such as binge eating, neglect of her insulin regimen, and cutting were utilized in attempts to control both internalized and real objects. The patient's wishes to control her therapist and her mother were explored, but she had difficulty tolerating the intense anxiety and depression that accompanied thoughts of separation. Both antidepressant and neuroleptic medications were added to help the patient manage her dysphoria. Family treatment was initiated in the hospital, but the patient's mother had limited motivation or resources for change. Individual therapy had to proceed under constant harassment from the patient's mother, who perceived the patient's efforts to achieve autonomy as a threat to her own survival. Thus, while the patient's mother was incapable of participating directly in the treatment, the individual therapy frequently had to proceed as if her mother was present in the room. Any efforts to facilitate the patient's separation/individuation had to respect the mother's fragility. This is an example of the functional overlap between individual and family systems therapies.

After discharge from the hospital, the patient continued to struggle with her wish to have omnipotent control over the therapist. This wish was reflected in a persistent desire to return to the hospital and a resistance to expending any effort that might be self-nurturing. The emergence and working through of a primitive, paranoid transference was crucial to the patient's improvement. The patient's wishes to omnipotently control her mother emerged through the acting out of the following drama. Rather than coming to both her twice weekly sessions, the patient would remain in bed. The therapist's reaction to this repeated event was to lose patience and become angry, which was assumed to be the way that the patient was feeling toward the therapist. These feelings were explored with the patient as a way of trying to understand her experience of the acting out. After several months of exploration, she was able to articulate her wish to force the therapist to come to her house whenever she felt the need. Once this wish was explicit, the patient was gradually able to allow herself to feel anger toward the therapist and experience a sense of separation that was not catastrophic. This process helped her explore separation from her mother, which in turn facilitated a slow process toward self-regulation of her eating, her diabetes, and her interpersonal life.

The use of behavioral strategies was complicated for a number of reasons. First, the patient needed to change so many behaviors that it was difficult to know where to start. She struggled chronically with uncontrolled binge eating and purging by letting her blood sugar rise. In addition, she was habitually late for work and appointments. The therapist decided that her getting up in the morning and coming to sessions were of primary importance and refused to introduce other goals until this had been accomplished. This enraged the patient who experienced the therapist's limited activity as abandonment. However, once the patient made progress toward letting go her omnipotent fantasies of controlling the therapist, she was able to self-regulate both her diabetes and her eating difficulties with little help. Many of the patient's depressive symptoms remitted during this working-through process near the end of the second and beginning of her third year of treatment. While the patient had thorough training in self-management skills earlier in treatment, she was not ready to implement these skills until she had started working through her difficulties with separation. Of course, it must be noted that while withholding certain behavioral interventions was at times in this patient's best interests, for other patients this strategy may be a mistake. (For additional considerations in treating diabetic bulimics, see Peveler & Fairburn, 1992.)

CONCLUSIONS

For many patients who binge eat, their symptoms are related to a variety of complex interpersonal and intrapersonal concerns. Though neglecting to address symptomatic behaviors can be understood by patients as a lack of interest or expertise on the part of the therapist, rigid focus on behavioral goals often proves fruitless with those who have primitive personality structures. While it may be possible to address primitive psychostructural concerns through proximally mediated cognitions such as irrational concerns about body shape, it may be more productive to retreat from behavioral or cognitive goals and focus instead on the interpersonal issues that emerge both in the patient's day-to-day experience and in the therapy relationship itself. Given the limited empirical support for the superior efficacy of any particular approach to psychotherapy, whether in the treatment of binge eaters or any other patient population, it is important to keep in mind that patients may need a range of therapeutic activities that goes beyond traditionally defined models of treatment.

ACKNOWLEDGMENTS

I wish to thank Sandra Schein, Christopher Fairburn, and Terence Wilson for their helpful editorial comments.

REFERENCES

Adler, G. A. (1985). *Borderline psychopathology and its treatment.* Northvale, NJ: Jason Aronson.

Adler, G. A. (1986). Psychotherapy of the narcissistic personality disorder patient: Two contrasting approaches. *American Journal of Psychiatry, 143,* 430–436.

American Psychiatric Association. (1987). *Diagnostic and statistical manual of mental disorders* (3rd ed.). Washington, DC: Author.

American Psychiatric Association. (1993). *DSM-IV draft criteria (3/1/93).* Washington, DC: Author.

Beck, A. T., & Freeman, A., and associates. (1990). *Cognitive therapy of personality disorders.* New York: Guilford Press.

Benjamin, L. S. (1974). Structural analysis of social behavior. *Psychological Review, 81,* 392–425.

Cash, T. F., & Brown, T. A. (1987). Body image in anorexia nervosa and bulimia nervosa: A review of the literature. *Behavior Modification, 11,* 487–521.

Casper, R. C., Eckert, E. D., Halmi, K. A., Goldberg, S. C., & Davis, J. M. (1980). Bulimia: Its incidence and significance in patients with anorexia nervosa. *Archives of General Psychiatry, 37,* 1030–1035.

Chatham, P. M. (1985). *Treatment of the borderline personality.* New York: Jason Aronson.

DaCosta, M., & Halmi, K. A. (1992). Classification of anorexia nervosa: Question of subtypes. *International Journal of Eating Disorders, 11,* 305–314.

Dennis, A. B., & Sansone, R. A. (1991). The clinical stages of treatment for the eating disorder patient with borderline personality disorder. In C. Johnson (Ed.), *Psychodynamic treatment of anorexia nervosa and bulimia nervosa* (pp. 128–164). New York: Guilford Press.

Fairburn, C. G. (1985). Cognitive-behavioral treatment for bulimia. In D. M. Garner & P. E. Garfinkel (Eds.), Handbook of psychotherapy for anorexia nervosa and bulimia (pp. 160–192). New York: Guilford Press.

Fairburn, C. G., Agras, W. S., & Wilson, G. T. (1992). The research on the treatment of bulimia nervosa: Practical and theoretical implications. In G. H. Anderson & S. H. Kennedy (Eds.), The biology of feast and famine (pp. 317–340). New York: Academic Press.

Fairburn, C. G., Jones, R., Peveler, R. C., Carr, S., Solomon, R. A., O'Connor, M. E., & Burton, J. (1991). Three psychological treatments for bulimia nervosa. Archives of General Psychiatry, 48, 463–469.

Garfinkel, D. M., Moldofsky, & Garner, D. M. (1980). The heterogeneity of anorexia nervosa. Archives of General Psychiatry, 37, 1036–1040.

Garner, D. M., & Bemis, K. M. (1985). Cognitive therapy for anorexia nervosa. In D. M. Garner & P. E. Garfinkel (Eds.), Handbook of psychotherapy for anorexia nervosa and bulimia (pp. 107–146). New York: Guilford Press.

Gill, M. M. (1982). Analysis of transference: I. Theory and technique. New York: International Universities Press.

Goodsitt, A. (1985). Self psychology and the treatment of anorexia nervosa. In D. M. Garner & P. E. Garfinkel (Eds.), Handbook of psychotherapy for anorexia nervosa and bulimia (pp. 55–82). New York: Guilford Press.

Greenberg, J. R., & Mitchell, S. A. (1983). Object relations in psychoanalytic theory. Cambridge, MA: Harvard University Press.

Greenspan, S. I. (1989). Ego psychology: Implications for personality theory, psychopathology and the therapeutic process. Madison, CT: International Universities Press.

Gwirtsman H. E., Roy-Byrne P., Yager J., & Gerner, R. H. (1983). Neuroendocrine abnormalities in bulimia. American Journal of Psychiatry, 140, 559–563.

Herzog, D. B., Keller, M. B., Lavori, P. W., Kenny, G. M., & Sacks, N. R. (1992). The prevalence of personality disorders in 210 women with eating disorders. Journal of Clinical Psychiatry, 53, 147–152.

Hoffman, I. Z. (1983). The patient as interpreter of the analyst's experience. Contemporary Psychoanalysis, 19, 389–422.

Hornyak, L. M., & Baker, E. K. (Eds.). (1989). Experiential therapies for the eating disorders. New York: Guilford Press.

Horowitz, L. M., Rosenberg, S. E., Ureno, G., Kalehzan, B. M., & O'Halloran, P. (1989). Psychodynamic formulation, consensual response method, and interpersonal problems. Journal of Consulting and Clinical Psychology, 57, 599–606.

Howard, K. I., Kopta, S. M., Krause, M. S., & Orlinsky, D. E. (1986). The dose-effect relationship in psychotherapy. American Psychologist, 41, 159–164.

Jessor, R. (1981). The perceived environment in psychological theory and research. In D. Magnasson (Ed.), Toward a psychology of situations: An interactional perspective. Hillsdale, NJ: Erlbaum.

Johnson, C., & Connors, M. (1987). The etiology and treatment of bulimia nervosa: A biopsychosocial perspective. New York: Basic Books.

Johnson, C., Connors, M., & Tobin, D. L. (1987). Symptom management of bulimia. Journal of Consulting and Clinical Psychology, 55, 668–676.

Johnson, C., & Maddi, K. (1986). The etiology of bulimia: A bio-psycho-social perspective. *Annals of Adolescent Psychiatry, 13,* 253–273.

Johnson C., Tobin, D. L., & Enright, A., (1989). Prevalence and clinical characteristics of borderline patients in an eating disordered population. *Journal of Clinical Psychiatry, 50,* 9–15.

Johnson, C. L., Tobin, D. L., & Dennis, A. B. (1990). Differences in treatment outcome between borderline and nonborderline bulimics at one year follow-up. *International Journal of Eating Disorders 9,* 617–628.

Johnson, C. L., Tobin, D. L., & Lipkin, J. (1989). Epidemiologic changes in bulimic behavior over a five year period. *International Journal of Eating Disorders, 8,* 647–655.

Kanfer, F. H., Schefft, B. K. (1987). Self-management therapy in clinical practice. In N. S. Jacobson (Ed.), *Psychotherapists in clinical practice: Cognitive and behavioral perspectives* (pp. 10–77). New York: Guilford Press.

Kanfer, F. H., Hagerman, S. (1981). The role of self-regulation. In P. L. Rehm (Ed.), *Behavior therapy for depression: Present status and future directions* (pp. 79–105). New York: Academic Press.

Kernberg, O. F. (1975). *Borderline conditions and pathological narcissism.* New York: Jason Aronson.

Kernberg, O. F. (1988). Object relations theory in clinical practice. *Psychoanalytic Quarterly, 57,* 481–505.

Klein, M. (1975). *Envy and gratitude and other works. Vol. IV: 1942#1963.* New York: Dellacorte.

Kohlenberg, R. J., & Tsai, M. (1987). Functional analytic psychotherapy. In N. S. Jacobson (Ed.), *Psychotherapists in clinical practice: Cognitive and behavioral perspectives* (pp. 388–443). New York: Guilford Press.

Kohut, H. (1971). *The analysis of the self.* New York: International Universities Press.

Kohut, H. (1977). *The restoration of the self.* New York: International Universities Press.

Levin A. P., & Hyler S. E. (1986). DSM III personality diagnosis in bulimia. *Comparative Psychiatry, 27,* 47–53.

Luborsky, L. (1984). *Principles of psychoanalytic psychotherapy: A manual for supportive/expressive treatment.* New York: Basic Books.

Mahler, M. S., Pine, F., & Bergman. (1975). *The psychological birth of the human infant: Symbiosis and individuation.* New York: Basic Books.

Molteni, A. (1992). *Experiential approaches to the treatment of eating disorders.* Workshop presented at the Tenth Annual National Conference on Eating Disorders, Columbus, OH.

Neiman, F. L., & Howard, K. I. (1991). Introduction to the special section on seeking new clinical research methods. *Journal of Consulting and Clinical Psychology, 59,* 8–11.

Olmsted, M. P., Davis, R., Garner, D. M., Eagle, M., Rockert, W., & Irvine, M. J. (1991). Efficacy of a brief group psychoeducational intervention for bulimia nervosa. *Behaviour Research and Therapy, 29,* 71–83.

Peveler, R. C., & Fairburn, C. G. (1992). The treatment of bulimia nervosa in patients with diabetes mellitus. *International Journal of Eating Disorders, 11,* 45–54

Pope, H. G., Frankenberg, F. R., & Hudson. (1987). Is bulimia associated with borderline personality disorder? A controlled study. *Journal of Clinical Psychiatry, 48*, 181–184.

Pope, H. G., Jr., & Hudson, J. I. (1985). *New hope for binge eaters.* New York: Harper & Row.

Prochaska, J. O., & Norcross, J. C. (1983). Contemporary psychotherapies: A national survey of characteristics, practices, orientations, and attitudes. *Psychotherapy: Theory, Research, and Practice, 20*, 161–173.

Pyle, R. L., Mitchell, J. E., Eckert, E. D., & Halverson. P. A. (1983). The incidence of bulimia in freshman college students. *International Journal of Eating Disorders, 2*, 75–85.

Rosen, J., & Leitenberg, H. (1982). Bulimia nervosa: Treatment with exposure plus response prevention. *Behavior Therapy, 13*, 117–124.

Ruderman, A. (1985). Restraint, obesity, and bulimia. *Behavior Research and Therapy, 23*, 151–156.

Schwartz, H. J. (1988). *Bulimia: Psychoanalytic treatment and theory.* Madison, CT: International Universities Press.

Singer-Kaplan, H. (1983). *Evaluation of sexual dysfunction: Psychological and medical aspects.* New York: Brunner/Mazel.

Steinberg, S. L., Tobin, D. L., & Johnson, C. (1990). The role of bulimic behaviors in affect regulation: Different functions for different patient subgroups. *International Journal of Eating Disorders, 9*, 51–55.

Stone, M. H. (1980). *The borderline syndromes: Constitution, adaptation, and personality.* New York: McGraw-Hill.

Striegel-Moore, R. H., Silberstein, L. R., & Rodin, J. (1986). Toward understanding the risk factors for bulimia nervosa. *American Psychologist, 41*, 246–263.

Strupp, H. H. (1989). Psychotherapy: Can the practitioner learn from the researcher? *American Psychologist, 44*, 717–724.

Strupp, H. H., & Binder, J. L. (1984). *Psychotherapy in a new key: A guide to time limited psychotherapy.* New York: Basic Books.

Sullivan, H. S. (1953). *The journal of psychiatry.* New York: Norton.

Swift, W. J., & Stern, S. (1982). The psychodynamic diversity of anorexia nervosa. *International Journal of Eating Disorders, 2*, 17–35.

Tally, P. F., Strupp, H. H., & Morey, L. C. (1990). Matchmaking in psychotherapy: Patient–therapist dimensions and their impact on outcome. *Journal of Consulting and Clinical Psychology, 58*, 182–188.

Tobin, D. L., & Johnson, C. L. (1991). The integration of psychodynamic and behavior therapy in the treatment of eating disorders: Clinical issues versus theoretical mystique. In C. L. Johnson (Ed.), *Psychodynamic treatment of anorexia nervosa and bulimia* (pp. 374–397). New York: Guilford Press.

Tobin, D. L., Johnson, C. L., & Franke, K. (1990). Development of an eating disorder program. In J. J. Sweet, R. H. Rozensky, & S. M. Tovian (Eds.), *Handbook of clinical psychology in medical settings* (pp. 315–330). New York: Plenum Press.

Tobin, D. L., Reynolds, R., Holroyd, K. A., & Creer, T. L. (1986). Self-management and social learning theory. In K. A. Holroyd & T. L. Creer (Eds.), *Self-management of chronic disease* (pp. 29–55). Orlando, FL: Academic Press.

Wachtel, P. L. (1977). *Psychoanalysis and behavior therapy: Toward an integration.* New York: Basic Books.

Wachtel, P. L. (1987). *Action and insight.* New York: Guilford Press.

Weiss, J., Sampson, H., & the Mount Zion Psychotherapy Research Group. (1986). *The psychoanalytic process: Theory, clinical observation, and empirical research.* New York: Guilford Press.

Wilson, C. P. (1988). Bulimic equivalents. In H. J. Schwartz (Ed.), *Bulimia: Psychoanalytic treatment and theory.* Madison, CT: International Universities Press.

Winnicott, D. W. (1965). *The maturational processes and the facilitating environment.* New York: International Universities Press.

Wonderlich, S. A., & Swift, W. J. (1990). Borderline versus other personality disorders in the eating disorders. *International Journal of Eating Disorders, 9,* 617–628.

TWO APPROACHES TO ASSESSMENT AND MANAGEMENT

The Eating Disorder Examination (12th Edition)

Christopher G. Fairburn
Zafra Cooper

The psychopathology of anorexia nervosa and bulimia nervosa is complex and varied in form, with both specific and general components. The specific psychopathology is peculiar to these disorders and comprises characteristic disturbances in eating behavior and attitudes to food, eating, shape, and weight. The general psychopathology consists of features found in other psychiatric disorders, for example, depressive and anxiety symptoms. A prerequisite of research into the nature and treatment of eating disorders is a detailed and standardized description of this specific and general psychopathology. The assessment of the latter may be accomplished with the use of one of a number of well-established standardized instruments available for this purpose. The Eating Disorder Examination (EDE) was devised to provide a standardized instrument for the assessment of the specific psychopathology of eating disorders. A detailed description of the development of the measure has been provided elsewhere (Cooper & Fairburn, 1987).

The EDE assesses a broad range of the specific psychopathology of anorexia nervosa and bulimia nervosa and their variants. It is an investigator-based interview (see section on Instructions for Interviewers), which is suitable for use in both community and clinical settings. The instrument has been progressively refined over the past 8 years to maximize its reliability and validity and is now in its 12th edition. The EDE has been used in descriptive studies (e.g., Beumont, Kopec-Schrader, Talbot, & Touyz, in press; Marcus, Smith, Santelli, & Kaye, 1992; Taylor, Peveler, Hibbert, & Fairburn, in press; Wilson & Smith, 1989) and research on treatment (e.g., Fairburn, Jones, Peveler, Hope,

& O'Connor, in press; Garner et al., 1993; Wilson, Eldredge, Smith, & Niles, 1991). Adaptations have been devised for those who are pregnant and those with diabetes mellitus (Fairburn, Peveler, Davies, Mann, & Mayou, 1991; Fairburn, Stein, & Jones, 1992; Peveler, Fairburn, Boller, & Dunger, 1992; Striegel-Moore, Nicholas, & Tamborlane, 1992).

In its original form, the EDE was designed to assess present state and as such focused exclusively on the previous 4 weeks. In this form the instrument generated basic descriptive information on the degree of behavioral disturbance (e.g., frequency of various forms of overeating, self-induced vomiting, etc.) as well as a profile of individuals in terms of their scores on five subscales designed to assess key aspects of eating disorder psychopathology (Bulimia, Restraint, Eating Concern, Shape Concern, and Weight Concern). More recently a diagnostic version of the EDE has been developed that also generates operationally defined eating disorder diagnoses. As a result, certain features of diagnostic importance are assessed over a 3-month period.

This chapter presents the latest edition (12th) of the EDE (EDE 12.0D) (see pp. 333–356). The main change from earlier editions is that the interview has been shortened to include only those items required for the assessment of key behavior, the creation of subscales, and the derivation of eating disorder diagnoses. In addition, the Bulimia subscale has been dropped (see EDE Subscales below). An outline of the differences between the previous version of the EDE (11.5D) and the current one is given in the appendix I at the end of this chapter.

KEY BEHAVIOR

The EDE assesses two key behavioral aspects of eating disorders and provides frequency ratings for their occurrence. These are overeating and the use of extreme methods of weight control. Three forms of overeating (objective and subjective bulimic episodes, and episodes of objective overeating) are measured both in terms of their absolute frequency and the number of days on which they occurred. Four extreme methods of weight control (self-induced vomiting, laxative misuse, diuretic misuse, and intense exercizing) are assessed.

EDE SUBSCALES

A set of five subscales was originally derived from the EDE by grouping items together to represent the major areas of specific psychopathology (Cooper, Cooper, & Fairburn, 1989). This rational assignment of items to subscales was checked empirically by examining the internal consistency of the subscales and as a result certain minor adjustments were made. Four of these original subscales remain unchanged in EDE 12.0D. The Bulimia subscale has been omitted because it does not add further descriptive information beyond that which can be derived from the frequencies of the various forms of overeating. Listed in Table 15.1 are the current subscales and the items comprising them. (Instructions about how to derive subscale scores are provided in the section on Data Processing and Analysis.)

EATING DISORDER DIAGNOSES

Version 12.0D of the EDE may be used to generate operationally defined eating disorder diagnoses. The rules currently in use in Oxford for generating DSM-III-R and DSM-IV diagnoses are given below.*

DSM-III-R Eating Disorder Diagnoses

Anorexia Nervosa

A. "Refusal to maintain body weight over a minimal normal weight for age and height, e.g., weight loss leading to maintenance of body weight 15% below that expected; or failure to make expected weight gain dur-

---

TABLE 15.1. The Four Subscales of EDE 12.0D

Restraint	*Shape Concern*
Restraint over eating	Flat stomach
Avoidance of eating	Importance of shape
Food avoidance	Preoccupation with shape or weight
Dietary rules	Dissatisfaction with shape
Empty stomach	Fear of weight gain
	Discomfort seeing body
Eating Concern	Avoidance of exposure
Preoccupation with food, eating,	Feelings of fatness
or calories	
Fear of losing control over eating	*Weight Concern*
Social eating	Importance of weight
Eating in secret	Reaction to prescribed weighing
Guilt about eating	Preoccupation with shape or weight
	Dissatisfaction with weight
	Desire to lose weight

---

*The DSM-IV criteria used in this volume are those that were approved as final by the DSM-IV Eating Disorders Work Group and the Task Force on DSM-IV (APA, 1993). These criteria may be subject to minor editorial revisions before the publication of DSM-IV.

ing period of growth, leading to body weight 15% below that expected.'' (American Psychiatric Association [APA], 1987, p. 67)

Definition. The subject's height and weight should have been measured and reference made to tables of population norms to determine whether body weight is 15% or more below that expected. ''Maintained low weight'' should have been rated 1.

B. ''Intense fear of gaining weight or becoming fat, even though underweight.'' (p. 67)

Definition. ''Fear of weight gain'' should have been rated 4, 5, or 6 for each of the past 3 months.

C. ''Disturbance in the way in which one's body weight, size, or shape is experienced, e.g., the person claims to 'feel fat' even when emaciated, believes that one area of the body is 'too fat' even when obviously underweight.'' (p. 67)

Definition. ''Feelings of fatness'' should have been rated 4, 5, or 6 for each of the past 3 months.

D. ''In females, absence of at least three consecutive menstrual cycles when otherwise expected to occur (primary or secondary amenorrhea). (A woman is considered to have amenorrhea if her periods occur only following hormone, e.g., estrogen, administration.)'' (p. 67)

Definition. ''Menstruation'' should have been rated 0 or 7.

Bulimia Nervosa

A. ''Recurrent episodes of binge-eating (rapid consumption of a large amount of food in a discrete period of time).'' (p. 67)

Definition. Presence of recurrent ''Objective bulimic episodes'' (see item D for definition of ''recurrent'').

B. ''A feeling of lack of control over eating behavior during the eating binges.'' (p. 68)

Definition. Presence of recurrent ''Objective bulimic episodes'' (see item D for definition of ''recurrent'').

C. ''The person regularly engages in either self-induced vomiting, use of laxatives or diuretics, strict dieting or fasting, or vigorous exercise in order to prevent weight gain.'' (p. 69)

Definition. Presence of any one of items 1, 2, 3, 4, or 5. In addition, ''Abstinence from extreme weight-control behavior'' should have been rated 0, 1, or 2.

1. *Self-induced vomiting.* ''Self-induced vomiting'' should have occurred on average at least weekly over the past 3 months.
2. *Laxative misuse.* ''Laxative misuse'' should have occurred on average at least weekly over the past 3 months.

3. *Diuretic misuse.* "Diuretic misuse" should have occurred on average at least weekly over the past 3 months.
4. Strict dieting or fasting. "Dietary restriction outside bulimic episodes" should have been rated 1 or 2 for each of the past 3 months.
5. *Vigorous exercise.* "Intense exercising to control shape or weight" should have occurred on average at least 5 days a week over the past 3 months.

D. "A minimum average of two binge eating episodes a week for at least three months." (p. 69)

Definition. At least 12 "Objective bulimic episodes" should have occurred over the past 3 months and the longest continuous period free from such episodes (not due to force of circumstances) should have been no greater than 2 weeks.[1]

E. "Persistent overconcern with body shape and weight." (p. 69)

Definition. "Importance of shape" or "Importance of weight" should have been rated 4, 5, or 6 for each of the past 3 months.

DSM-IV Eating Disorder Diagnoses

Anorexia Nervosa

A. "Refusal to maintain body weight at or above a minimally normal weight for age and height (e.g., weight loss leading to maintenance of body weight less than 85% of that expected; or failure to make expected weight gain during period of growth, leading to body weight less than 85% of that expected)."

Definition. The subject's height and weight should have been measured and reference made to tables of population norms to determine whether body weight is 15% or more below that expected. "Maintained low weight" should have been rated 1.

B. "Intense fear of gaining weight or becoming fat, even though underweight."

Definition. "Fear of weight gain" should have been rated 4, 5, or 6 for each of the past 3 months.

C. "Disturbance in the way in which one's body weight or shape is experienced, undue influence of body shape or weight on self-

[1]Although the third edition of the *Diagnostic and Statistical Manual of Mental Disorders* (DSM-III-R) (American Psychiatric Association, 1987) requires two binge-eating episodes a week to make a diagnosis of bulimia nervosa, the Oxford definition is that there should have been at least 12 "objective bulimic episodes" over the past 3 months with no longer than a 2-week gap between them.

evaluation, or denial of the seriousness of current low body weight.

Definition. "Importance of shape," "Importance of weight," or "Feelings of fatness" should have been rated 4, 5, or 6 for each of the past 3 months.

D. "In post-menarchal females, amenorrhea, i.e., the absence of at least three consecutive menstrual cycles. (A woman is considered to have amenorrhea if her periods occur only following hormone, e.g., estrogen, administration.)"

Definition. "Menstruation" should have been rated 0 or 7.

No operational definition is given for the two subtypes of anorexia nervosa. Not enough information is available to provide a basis for a specific definition.

Bulimia Nervosa

A. "Recurrent episodes of binge eating. An episode of binge eating is characterized by both of the following:

1. Eating, in a discrete period of time (e.g., within any 2-hour period), an amount of food that is definitely larger than most people would eat during a similar period of time in similar circumstances
2. A sense of lack of control over eating during the episode (e.g., a feeling that one cannot stop eating or control what or how much one is eating)."

Definition. Presence of recurrent "objective bulimic episodes" (see item C for defintion of "recurrent").

B. "Recurrent inappropriate compensatory behavior in order to prevent weight gain, such as: self-induced vomiting; misuse of laxatives, diurectics or other medications; fasting; or excessive exercise."

Definition. Presence of any one of items 1, 2, 3, 4, or 5.

1. *Self-induced vomiting.* "Self-induced vomiting" should have occurred on average at least weekly over the past 3 months.
2. *Laxative misuse.* "Laxative misuse" should have occurred on average at least weekly over the past 3 months.
3. *Diuretic misuse.* "Diuretic misuse" should have occurred on average at least weekly over the past 3 months.
4. *Fasting.* "Dietary restriction outside bulimic episodes" should have been rated 1 or 2 for each of the past 3 months.
5. *Excessive exercise.* "Intense exercising to control shape or weight" should have occurred on average at least 5 days a week over the past 3 months.

C. "The binge eating and inappropriate compensatory behaviors both occur, on average, at least twice a week for 3 months."

Definition. At least 12 "objective bulimic episodes" should have occurred over the past 3 months and the longest continuous period free from such episodes (not due to force of circumstances) should have been no greater than 2 weeks.[2] In addition, "Abstinence from extreme weight-control behavior" should have been rated 0, 1, and 2.

D. "Self-evaluation is unduly influenced by body shape and weight."

Definition. "Importance of shape" or "Importance of weight" should have been rated 4, 5, or 6 for each of the past 3 months.

E. "The disturbance does not occur exclusively during episodes of anorexia nervosa."

Definition. The person should not meet diagnostic criteria for anorexia nervosa.

No operational definition is given for the two subtypes of bulimia nervosa. Not enough information is available to provide a basis for a specific definition.

Eating Disorders, NOS

No operational definition is given. Not enough information is available to provide a basis for a specific definition.[3]

DATA PROCESSING AND ANALYSIS

The EDE provides three levels of descriptive data concerning current eating disorder psychopathology.

---

[2]Although DSM-IV requires two binge-eating episodes per week to make a diagnosis of bulimia nervosa, the Oxford definition is that there should have been at least 12 "objective bulimic episodes" over the past 3 months with no longer that a 2-week gap between them. A similar frequency requirement is made for the "compensatory behavior."

[3]It is possible to provide a working definition for so-called "binge eating disorder" which is in line with the general definition provided under Eating Disorders, NOS (example 6):

"Recurrent episodes of binge eating in the absence of inappropriate compensatory behaviors characteristic of bulimia nervosa."

Definition.
1. At least twelve "objective bulimic episodes" should have occurred over the past 3 months and the longest continuous period free from such episodes (not due to force of circumstances) should have been no greater than 2 weeks.
2. Criterion B for bulimia nervosa should not be met.
3. The person should not meet diagnostic criteria for anorexia nervosa.

This definition differs from that provided in the Appendix of DSM-IV. It is designed to complement the diagnostic criteria for anorexia nervosa and bulimia nervosa.

Scores on Individual Items

The EDE provides either frequency or severity ratings for key behavioral and attitudinal aspects of eating disorders. In the case of certain frequency scores (e.g., those for bulimic episodes and self-induced vomiting), it may be difficult to obtain an accurate estimate of the rate of the behavior especially if it is occurring very frequently. In such cases it is recommended that frequencies are reported for the number of days on which the behavior occurred.

Subscale Scores

These provide a profile of individuals in terms of four major areas of eating disorder psychopathology. To obtain a particular subscale score, the ratings for the appropriate items should be added together and the sum divided by the total number of items forming the subscale. If ratings are only available on some items of a subscale, a score may nevertheless be obtained by dividing the resulting total by the number of rated items so long as more than half the items have been rated.

Global Score

This provides a measure of the overall severity of the eating disorder psychopathology (e.g., Fairburn, Peveler, Jones, Hope, & Doll, in press). To obtain a total score on the EDE the subscale scores should be summed and the resulting total divided by the number of subscales (i.e., four). If data are only available on some subscales, a global score may still be derived provided that at least three subscale scores are available. It is recommended that the global score should always be reported in conjunction with detailed EDE data for both individual subscales and key behavior.

Note

EDE data may not meet accepted criteria for normality. In this case either nonparametric statistical tests should be used or the data should be transformed.

RELIABILITY OF THE EDE

Interrater Reliability

There have been four studies of the interrater reliability of the EDE, all of which support its use. Cooper and Fairburn (1987) reported the reliability of individual EDE items using 3 trained raters and 12 subjects of whom 9 met diagnostic criteria for anorexia nervosa or bulimia nervosa and 3 had no eating disorder. Agreement between raters was calculated using the Pearson product moment coefficient. Correlation coefficients only dropped below .9 for three items, two of which were subsequently dropped from the instrument.

Beglin (1990) reported interrater reliability for both individual items and for subscale scores. Five interviewers made the original ratings for 29 subjects of whom 4 had an eating disorder of clinical severity. Agreement was calculated between these ratings and those of an independent rater. The majority of items were classified as having excellent agreement (Kappa value above .75), three items had good agreement (Kappa value above .70) and in only one case did the value of Kappa fall below .70. This item has been dropped from the EDE. Agreement for items where Kappa could not be calculated, and for the EDE subscales, was examined using the Pearson product moment coefficient and paired t tests. All correlation coefficients were above .95 and none of the t tests was significant.

Wilson and Smith (1989) conducted a study of interrater reliability on a small sample of subjects with either bulimia nervosa or restrained eating and reported Pearson product moment correlations for subscale scores ranging between .97 and .99. Rosen, Vara, Wendt, and Leitenberg (1990) reported interrater reliability coefficients, obtained from ratings of 20 interviews, ranging between .83 for the Bulimia subscale and .99 for the Shape Concern subscale.

Test–Retest Reliability

There have been no studies of the test–retest reliability of the EDE.

Internal Consistency of Subscales

A study of the internal consistency of the original five subscales was conducted to check empirically the assignment of items to subscales (Cooper et al., 1989). Alpha coefficients were calculated for each subscale using a sample of 100 patients with eating disorders and 42 controls. The coefficients were Restraint (.75), Bulimia (.90), Eating Concern (.78), Weight Concern (.68), and Shape Concern (.82), indicating a satisfactory degree of internal consistency and providing empirical justification for the rational grouping of items. A recent study of 116 patients with eating disorders reported alpha coefficients similar to those originally reported for the Restraint and Weight Concern subscales (.78 and .70, respectively) but rather lower coefficients for Bulimia (.76), Eating Concern (.68), and Shape Concern (.70) (Beumont et al., in press).

VALIDITY OF EDE

Discriminant Validity

Four studies of the discriminant validity of the EDE have been conducted. Cooper et al. (1989) demonstrated with a group of 100 patients with eating disorders and 42 normal controls that all items of the EDE, as well as the five subscales, discriminated well between these two groups.

The EDE has been shown to make finer distinctions. Wilson and Smith (1989) found significant differences between 15 patients with bulimia nervosa and 15 highly restrained controls on four of the five subscales of the EDE. As would be expected, the Restraint subscale did not discriminate between the two groups. In contrast, a self-report measure of eating disorder psychopathology performed poorly. In a further study, the EDE Weight Concern and Shape Concern subscales were shown to discriminate between 20 women with bulimia nervosa and 29 restrained controls (Rosen et al., 1990).

We have recently compared the EDE subscale scores of 125 women with bulimia nervosa with those of three groups of women without a current eating disorder: 337 normal controls, 57 dieters, and 15 women with a body mass index of 30 and above. All five subscales discriminated well between those with bulimia nervosa and each of the three groups without a current eating disorder (data adapted from Fairburn & Cooper, 1992).

Concurrent Validity

The concurrent validity of the EDE has been examined by Rosen and colleagues (1990). Certain EDE items (dietary rules, self-induced vomiting) and subscales (Restraint, Bulimia, Eating Concern) were correlated with a number of self-report measures of eating behavior derived from eating diaries. Since the eating diaries only recorded behavior occurring during the previous week, while the EDE assesses behavior and attitudes over the previous 4 weeks, there was only 1 week of overlap between the two forms of measurement. The test of concurrent validity was thus only partial. EDE subscale scores were modestly associated with the self-report measures of dietary restraint and overeating (including average calorie intake, avoidance of regular meals, and frequency and size of binge-eating episodes). EDE ratings of vomiting were highly associated with frequency of vomiting episodes.

Sensitivity to Change

In a study of outcome at 1 year after three forms of treatment for bulimia nervosa, those who had a good outcome defined in terms of no longer having objective or subjective bulimic episodes and no longer vomiting

TABLE 15.2. EDE Norms for Anorexia Nervosa

	Cooper et al., 1989 (n = 47)		Beumont et al., in press (n = 50)	
	Mean	SD	Mean	SD
Restraint	3.17	1.47	3.8	1.7
Bulimia[a]	1.58	1.55	1.9	0.9
Eating Concern	2.17	1.62	2.8	1.4
Weight Concern	2.40	1.48	2.9	1.5
Shape Concern	2.85	1.22	3.5	1.6

[a]It should be noted that different studies have used different versions of the Bulimia subscale.

or misusing laxatives, also had substantially decreased EDE subscales scores (Fairburn, Peveler, et al., in press). These EDE subscale scores were within one standard deviation of the scores obtained from a general population sample of women of the same age.

EDE NORMS

Tables 15.2 to 15.4 give norms for the EDE subscales.

INSTRUCTIONS FOR INTERVIEWERS

The EDE is an *investigator-based interview*. This contrasts with respondent-based interviews in which the subject's answers to specified questions are rated without additional questioning. Respondent-based interviews are in essence verbally administered self-report questionnaires. They work well where the concepts being assessed are simple and there is general agreement as to their meaning, but they are unsatisfactory when the concepts are complex or key terms do not have a generally accepted specific meaning. With investigator-based interviews, interviewers need training to ensure that they fully understand the concepts being assessed. The structure in such interviews lies in the detailed specifications provided for the interviewer of the concepts to be rated and the rating scheme, rather than in the precise wording of individual questions (Hill, Harrington, Fudge, Rutter, & Pickles, 1989). In summary, investigator-based interviews such as the EDE require that interviewers be trained both in the technique of interviewing and in the concepts and rules governing the ratings.

When using the EDE, it is essential that the subject understands the purpose of the interview. The interviewer should explain why the interview is being conducted and, before starting formal questioning, should aim to establish good rapport. The interviewer and subject together

TABLE 15.3. EDE Norms for Bulimia Nervosa

	Cooper et al., 1989 (n = 53)		Wilson & Smith, 1989 (n = 15)		Beumont et al., in press (n = 28)		Fairburn & Cooper, 1992 (n = 125)	
	Mean	SD	Mean	SD	Mean	SD	Mean	SD
Restraint	3.14	1.22	3.27	0.26	3.7	1.7	3.45	1.18
Bulimia[a]	3.42	0.79	2.61	0.22	3.4	0.9	2.17	0.86
Eating Concern	2.43	1.30	2.40	0.34	3.5	1.4	2.63	1.42
Weight Concern	3.14	1.44	3.96	0.34	3.8	1.7	3.73	0.39
Shape Concern	3.55	1.35	3.82	0.31	4.1	1.1	3.90	1.28

[a]It should be noted that different studies have used different versions of the Bulimia subscale.

TABLE 15.4. EDE Norms for Other Groups

	Normal controls[a] (n = 42)		Restrained controls[b] n = 15		Normal controls[c] (n = 337)		Dieters[d] (n =57)		Overweight subjects[e] (n = 15)	
	Mean	SD	Mean	SD	Mean	SD	Mean	SD	Mean	SD
Restraint	0.91	0.91	3.15	0.33	0.79	0.97	1.66	1.07	1.69	1.35
Bulimia[f]	0.41	0.87	0.14	0.10	—	—	—	—	—	—
Eating Concern	0.22	0.33	1.25	0.23	0.20	0.51	0.50	0.84	0.64	0.86
Weight Concern	0.52	0.62	2.12	0.19	1.00	0.87	1.79	0.92	1.92	1.24
Shape Concern	0.64	0.75	2.55	0.20	1.14	0.98	1.99	1.13	1.97	1.33

[a]Cooper et al. (1989)
[b]Wilson & Smith (1989)
[c]Fairburn & Cooper (1992)
[d]Fairburn & Cooper (1992)
[e]Fairburn & Cooper (1992); overweight defined as a body mass index of 30 or above.
[f]It should be noted that different studies have used different versions of the Bulimia subscale and the study by Fairburn and Cooper (1992) used EDE 12.OD.

should be trying to obtain an accurate picture of the subject's current eating behavior and attitudes. It is important to explain that a standard set of questions is being asked and that some may not apply.

The interviewer should explain that the interview is mainly concerned with the preceding 4 weeks (28 days). To help the subject accurately recall this period, time should be devoted at the beginning of the interview to the identification of events that have taken place during these 28 days. For example, the interviewer should establish whether the subject has been at home or away and what has happened on each of the four weekends. It is often helpful to refer to a diary or calendar to locate the 4 weeks in question. If the instrument is being used for diagnostic purposes (the relevant sections of the schedule are bounded by double lines), certain questions will cover a 3-month time period. Again, the interviewer should ensure that the subject is fully aware of the period under consideration. When asking about the past 3 months, it is best to focus on each month in turn starting with the most recent month and working backward.

Each of the items in the EDE has one or more (asterisked) obligatory questions that must be asked. Special emphasis should be placed upon the words and phrases that are underlined. The obligatory questions should be supplemented with additional questions of the interviewer's choice. The phrase ''over the past 4 weeks,'' which precedes each obligatory question, may be varied as seems appropriate (e.g., ''over the past month'' or ''over the past 28 days'') and inserted at any point within the question, but otherwise the obligatory questions should be asked as specified in the schedule. The items in the EDE may be covered in any order, although for most purposes the sequence presented in the schedule will be found to be satisfactory. It is perfectly appropriate to return to earlier items if further information emerges during the interview that is of relevance to prior ratings. The interview should never be undertaken in the absence of the full schedule as even the most experienced interviewers need to refer to the questions, definitions, and rating schemes.

The interviewer should pay careful attention to everything that the subject says. The interview should never be hurried. It should proceed at a steady, relaxed pace with the interviewer not moving on to the next item until he or she is satisfied that all the necessary information has been obtained. The interviewer should not be rushed along by rapid, and possibly impatient, replies. Apparently glib answers that do not seem to have been given thought should be sensitively explored. Conversely, subjects who are loquacious and overdetailed in their replies need to be kept to the point. Care must always be taken to ensure that the subject understands what information the interviewer is trying to elicit. It

TABLE 15.5. The EDE Rating Scheme

Severity ratings	Frequency ratings
0 - Absence of the feature	0 - Absence of the feature
1 - Feature almost, but not quite, absent	1 - Feature present on 1–5 days
2 -	2 - Feature present on 6–12 days
3 - Severity midway between 0 and 6	3 - Feature present on 13–15 days
4 -	4 - Feature present on 16–22 days
5 - Feature present to a degree not quite severe enough to justify a rating of 6	5 - Feature present almost every day (23–27 days)
6 - Feature present to an extreme degree	6 - Feature present every day

Note: Rate 8 if, despite adequate questioning, it is impossible to decide upon a rating. Rate 9 for missing values (or "not applicable"). If it is difficult to choose between two ratings, the lower rating (i.e., less symptomatic) should be used.

is good practice to check back with the subject before making each rating.

Guidelines for making ratings are provided for each item. Ratings should be made as the interview proceeds (although certain calculations may be delayed until afterward). The instructions for making each rating are given in square brackets and they are followed by the rating scheme itself. The majority of items are rated on a seven-point scale ranging from 0 to 6 on which either frequency or severity are rated. In most instances 0 represents the absence of the feature in question and 6 represents its presence to an extreme degree. Frequency ratings should be based on a 28-day month: If a feature is not present, rate 0; if a feature is present on up to and including 5 days, rate 1; if it is present half the time, rate 3; if it is present almost every day (with up to and including 5 exceptions), rate 5; if it is present every day, rate 6. As regards severity ratings, a rating of 1 should be made only if the feature is barely present, and a rating of 5 should be made if the feature is present to a degree not quite severe enough to justify a rating of 6. A rating of 3 should be used for degrees of severity midway between 0 and 6. *If it is difficult to decide between two ratings, the lower rating (i.e., the less symptomatic) should be chosen.* If, despite adequate questioning, it is still impossible to decide upon a rating, use the rating 8 (i.e., the symptom cannot be excluded). Missing values (or "not applicable") should be rated as 9. This rating scheme is summarized in Table 15.5. A coding sheet is included in Appendix II at the end of this chapter.

ACKNOWLEDGMENT

The authors are grateful to the Wellcome Trust for their support.

REFERENCES

American Psychiatric Association. (1987). *Diagnostic and statistical manual of mental disorders* (3rd ed., rev.). Washington, DC: Author.

American Psychiatric Association. (1993). *DSM-IV draft criteria (3/1/93)*. Washington, DC: Author.

Beglin, S. J. (1990). *Eating disorders in young adult women*. Unpublished doctoral dissertation, Oxford University, Oxford.

Beumont. P. J. V., Kopec-Schrader, E. M., Talbot, P., & Touyz, S. W. (in press). Measuring the specific psychopathology of eating disorder patients. *Australian and New Zealand Journal of Psychiatry*.

Cooper, Z., Cooper P. J., & Fairburn, C. G. (1989). The validity of the Eating Disorder Examination and its subscales. *British Journal of Psychiatry, 154*, 807–812.

Cooper, Z., & Fairburn, C. G. (1987). The Eating Disorder Examination: A semistructured interview for the assessment of the specific psychopathology of eating disorders. *International Journal of Eating Disorders. 6*, 1–8.

Fairburn, C. G., & Cooper, Z. (1992). *Further validity studies of the Eating Disorder Examination*. Manuscript in preparation.

Fairburn, C. G., Jones, R., Peveler, R. C., Hope, R. A., & O'Connor, M. (in press). Psychotherapy and bulimia nervosa: The longer-term effects of interpersonal psychotherapy, behaviour therapy and cognitive behaviour therapy. *Archives of General Psychiatry*.

Fairburn, C. G., Peveler, R. C., Davies, B., Mann, J. I., & Mayou, R. A. (1991). Eating disorders in young adults with insulin dependent diabetes mellitus: A controlled study. *British Medical Journal, 303*, 17–20.

Fairburn, C. G., Peveler, R. C., Jones, R., Hope, R. A., & Doll, H. A. (in press). Predictors of twelve-month outcome in bulimia nervosa and the influence of attitudes to shape and weight. *Journal of Consulting and Clinical Psychology*.

Fairburn, C. G., Stein, A. P., & Jones, R. (1992). Eating habits and eating disorders during pregnancy. *Psychosomatic Medicine, 54*, 665–672.

Garner, D. M., Rockert, W., Davis, R., Garner, M. V., Olmsted, M. P., & Eagle, M. (1993). A comparison between cognitive-behavioural and supportive-expressive therapy for bulimia nervosa. *American Journal of Psychiatry, 150*, 37–46.

Hill, J., Harrington, R., Fudge, H., Rutter, M., & Pickles, A. (1989). Adult Personality Functioning Assessment (APFA): An investigator based standardised interview. *British Journal of Psychiatry, 155*, 24–35.

Marcus, M. D., Smith, D., Santelli, R., & Kaye, W. (1992). Characterization of eating disordered behaviour in obese binge eaters. *International Journal of Eating Disorders, 12*, 249–256.

Peveler, R. C., Fairburn, C. G., Boller, I., & Dunger, D. (1992). Eating disorders in adolescents with insulin-dependent diabetes mellitus: a controlled study. *Diabetes Care, 15*, 1356–1360.

Rosen, J. C., Vara, L., Wendt, S., & Leitenberg, H. (1990). Validity studies of the Eating Disorder Examination. *International Journal of Eating Disorders, 9*, 519–528.

Striegel-Moore, R. H., Nicholas, T. J., & Tamborlane, W. V. (1992). Prevalence of eating disorder symptoms in preadolescent and adolescent girls with IDDM. *Diabetes Care, 15,* 1361–1368.

Taylor, A. V., Peveler, R. C., Hibbert, G. A., & Fairburn, C. G. (in press). Eating disorders among women receiving treatment for an alcohol problem. *International Journal of Eating Disorders.*

Wilson, G. T., Eldredge, K. L., Smith, D., & Niles, B. (1991). Cognitive-behavioural treatment with and without response prevention for bulimia. *Behaviour Research and Therapy, 29,* 575–583.

Wilson, G. T., & Smith, D. (1989). Assessment of bulimia nervosa: An evaluation of the Eating Disorder Examination. *International Journal of Eating Disorders, 8,* 173–179.

The Eating Disorder Examination (12.0D)

Interview Schedule

INTRODUCTION

[Having oriented the subject to the specific time period being assessed, it is best to open the interview by asking a number of introductory questions designed to obtain a general picture of the subject's eating habits. Suitable questions are suggested below.]

To begin with I should like to get a general picture of your eating habits over the last 4 weeks.

Have your eating habits varied much from day to day?

Have weekdays differed from weekends?

Have there been any days when you haven't eaten anything?

What about the previous 2 months?

Copyright 1993 by Christopher G. Fairburn and Zafra Cooper.

PATTERN OF EATING

* I would like to ask about your pattern of eating. Over the past 4 weeks which of these meals or snacks have you eaten on a regular basis?

- breakfast (meal eaten shortly after waking)   [ ]
- mid-morning snack   [ ]
- lunch (mid-day meal)   [ ]
- mid-afternoon snack   [ ]
- evening meal   [ ]
- evening snack   [ ]
- nocturnal snack (i.e., a snack eaten after the subject has been to   [ ]
  sleep)

[Rate each meal and snack separately, usually accepting the subject's classification (within the guidelines above). Ask about weekdays and weekends separately. Meals or snacks should be rated even if they lead on to a "binge." "Brunch" should generally be classed as lunch. With this item, rate up (i.e., give a higher rating) if it is difficult to choose between two ratings. Rate 8 if meals or snacks are difficult to classify (e.g., due to shift work).]

0 - Meal or snack not eaten

1 -

2 - Meal or snack eaten on less than half the days

3 -

4 - Meal or snack eaten on more than half the days

5 -

6 - Meal or snack eaten every day

RESTRAINT OVER EATING   (Restraint subscale)

 * Over the past 4 weeks have you been <u>consciously trying</u> to restrict what you eat, whether or not you have succeeded?

Has this been to influence your shape or weight?

[Rate the number of days on which the subject has *consciously attempted* to restrict his or her food intake, whether or not he or she has succeeded. The restraint should have been intended to influence shape, weight, or body composition, although this may not have been the sole or main reason. It should have consisted of planned attempts at restriction, rather than spur-of-the-moment attempts such as the decision to resist a second helping.]

0 - No attempt at restraint
1 -
2 - Attempted to exercise restraint on less than half the days
3 -
4 - Attempted to exercise restraint on more than half the days
5 -
6 - Attempted to exercise restraint every day   [ ]

AVOIDANCE OF EATING   (Restraint subscale)

 * Over the past 4 weeks have you gone for periods of 8 or more <u>waking</u> hours without eating anything?

Has this been to influence your shape or weight?

[Rate the number of days on which there has been at least 8 hours abstinence from eating food (soup and milkshakes count as food, whereas drinks in general do not) during waking hours. It may be helpful to illustrate the length of time (e.g., 9 A.M. to 5 P.M.). The abstinence must have been at least partly *self-imposed* rather than being due to force of circumstances. It should have been intended to influence shape, weight, or body composition, although this may not have been the sole or main reason.]

0 - No such days
1 -
2 - Avoidance on less than half the days
3 -
4 - Avoidance on more than half the days
5 -
6 - Avoidance every day   [ ]

EMPTY STOMACH   (Restraint subscale)

✻ Over the past 4 weeks have you wanted your stomach to be <u>empty</u>?

Has this been to influence your shape or weight?

[Rate the number of days on which the subject has had a *definite desire* to have a completely empty stomach for reasons to do with dieting, shape, or weight. *This should not be confused with a desire for the stomach to feel empty or be flat.*]

0 - No definite desire to have an empty stomach

1 -

2 - Definite desire to have an empty stomach on less than half the days

3 -

4 - Definite desire to have an empty stomach on more than half the days

5 -

6 - Definite desire to have an empty stomach every day   [ ]

FOOD AVOIDANCE   (Restraint subscale)

✻ Over the past 4 weeks have you <u>tried</u> to avoid eating any foods that you like, whether or not you have succeeded?

Has this been to influence your shape or weight?

[Rate the number of days on which the subject has actively *attempted* to avoid eating specific foods (which he or she likes) whether or not he or she succeeded. The goal should have been to *avoid the foods altogether* and not merely to restrict their consumption. Drinks do not count as food. The avoidance should have been intended to influence shape, weight, or body composition, although this may not have been the sole or main reason.]

0 - No attempts to avoid food

1 -

2 - Attempted to avoid food on less than half the days

3 -

4 - Attempted to avoid food on more than half the days

5 -

6 - Attempted to avoid food every day   [ ]

DIETARY RULES   (Restraint subscale)

* Over the past 4 weeks have you tried to follow certain <u>definite</u> rules regarding your eating, for example, a calorie limit, preset quantities of food, or rules about what you should eat or when you should eat?

* Have there been occasions when you have been aware that you have broken a dietary rule that you have set for yourself?

How have you felt about breaking them? How would you have felt if you had broken one of your dietary rules?

What are these rules? Why have you tried to follow them? Have they been designed to influence your shape or weight?

Have they been definite rules or general principles? Examples of definite rules would be "I must not eat eggs" or "I must not eat cake," whereas you could have the general principle "I should try to eat healthy food."

[Dietary rules should be rated as present if the subject has been attempting to follow "definite" (i.e., specific) dietary rules regarding his or her food intake. The rules should have been self-imposed, although originally they may have been prescribed. They should have concerned what the subject should have eaten or when eating should have taken place. They might consist of a calorie limit (e.g., below 1,200 kcals), not eating before a certain time of day, not eating certain types of food, or not eating at all. They should have been specific rules and not general guidelines, and there may have been distress should they have been broken. If the subject is aware that he or she has occasionally broken a personal dietary rule, this suggests that one or more specific rules has been present. In such cases the interviewer should ask in detail about the transgression in an attempt to identify the underlying rule. The rules should have been intended to influence shape, weight, or body composition, although this may not have been the sole or main reason. It should be noted that *"dietary rules" are regarded as having been present if there have been clear attempts to obey specific dietary rules.*

Rate 0 if no dietary rule can be identified. If there has been more than one rule straddling different time periods within the 4 weeks, these periods should be summated to make the rating.]

0 - Has not attempted to obey such rules
1 -
2 - Attempted to obey such rules on less than half the days
3 -
4 - Attempted to obey such rules on more than half the days
5 -
6 - Attempted to obey such rules every day   [ ]

PREOCCUPATION WITH FOOD,   (Eating Concern subscale)
EATING, OR CALORIES

* Over the past 4 weeks have you spent much time between meals thinking about food, eating, or calories?

* Has thinking about food, eating, or calories <u>interfered</u> with your ability to concentrate? How about concentrating on things that you are interested in, for example, reading, watching television, or following a conversation?

[Concentration is regarded as impaired if there have been *intrusive thoughts about food, eating, or calories that have interfered with activities.* Rate the number of days on which this has happened, whether or not bulimic episodes occurred.]

0 - No concentration impairment
1 -
2 - Concentration impairment on less than half the days
3 -
4 - Concentration impairment on more than half the days
5 -
6 - Concentration impairment every day   [ ]

FEAR OF LOSING CONTROL   (Eating Concern subscale)
OVER EATING

* Over the past 4 weeks have you been <u>afraid</u> of losing control over eating?

[Rate the number of days on which *definite fear* has been present, irrespective of whether the subject feels he or she has been in control. *"Loss of control" involves a sense that one will not be able to resist or stop eating.* If the subject feels unable to answer this question because he or she has already lost control, rate 9.]

0 - No fear of losing control
1 -
2 - Fear of losing control present on less than half the days
3 -
4 - Fear of losing control present on more than half the days
5 -
6 - Fear of losing control every day   [ ]

BULIMIC EPISODES AND OTHER EPISODES OF OVEREATING

(Diagnostic item)

GUIDELINES FOR INTERVIEWERS

[Four forms of episodic "overeating" are distinguished. The distinction is based upon the presence or absence of two characteristics:

(i) **Loss of control** (required for both types of "bulimic episode")

(ii) **The consumption of what would generally be regarded as a "large" amount of food** (required for "objective bulimic episodes" and "objective overeating")

The classificatory scheme is summarized in Figure 15.1 and key terms are defined below.

The interviewer should ask about each form of overeating. It is important to note that *the forms of overeating are not mutually exclusive:* It is possible for subjects to have had several different forms over the preceding month. With some subjects it is helpful to explain the classificatory scheme. Then, using the probe questions given below, the number of each type of episode may be determined and checked back with the subject.

Definition of Key Terms

"**Loss of control.**" The interviewer should ask the subject whether he or she experienced a sense of loss of control over eating *at the time* that the episode

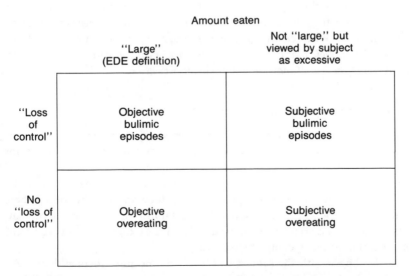

FIGURE 15.1.. The EDE scheme for classifying episodes of overeating.

occurred. If this is clearly described, loss of control should be rated as present. Loss of control may be rated positively even if the episode had been planned. If the subject uses terms such as "driven to eat" or "compelled to eat," loss of control should be rated as present.

For chronic cases only: If the subject reports no sense of loss of control yet describes having not been able to stop eating once eating had started or having not been able to prevent the episode from occurring, loss of control should be rated as present. If subjects report that they are no longer trying to control their eating because overeating is inevitable, loss of control should be rated as present.

If the interviewer is in doubt, loss of control should be rated as absent.

"Large amount of food." The decision whether or not the amount eaten was large should be made by the interviewer and does not require the agreement of the subject. Large may be used to refer to the amount of any particular type of food or the overall quantity of food consumed. *The interviewer should take into account what would be the usual amount eaten under the circumstances.* This requires some knowledge of the eating habits of the subject's general (but not necessarily immediate) social group. What else was eaten during the day is not of relevance to this rating. The speed of eating and whether or not the subject subsequently spits out or vomits the food are not of relevance.

If the interviewer is in doubt, the amount should not be classified as large.

The number of episodes of overeating. When calculating the number of episodes of overeating, the subject's definition of separate episodes should be accepted unless (within a period of eating) there was an hour or more when the subject was not eating. In this case the initial episode should be regarded as having been completed. When estimating the length of any gap, do not count the time spent vomiting. *Note that purging (self-induced vomiting or laxative misuse) is not used to define the end of individual episodes of overeating.*

Guidelines for Rating the Overeating Section

First, ask the asterisked questions to identify episodes of perceived or true overeating that have occurred over the previous 28 days. Note down all the forms of overeating on the blank section of the coding sheet.

Second, obtain detailed information about each form of overeating to decide whether it involved eating large amounts of food and whether or not there was loss of control (as defined above). Then establish for each form of overeating the number of days on which it occurred and the total number of occasions. It is advisable to make comprehensive notes.

Finally, check with the subject to ensure that no misunderstandings have arisen.]

QUESTIONS FOR RATING ITEMS

[*The asterisked questions must be asked in every case.*]

Main Probe Questions

    * I would like to ask you about any episodes of overeating that you may have had over the past 4 weeks.

    * Different people mean different things by overeating. I would like you to describe any times when you have <u>felt</u> that you have eaten too much in one go.

    * Have there been any times when you have felt that you have eaten too much, but others might not agree?

[*If there have been no such times, skip to "social eating."*]

[*n.b. For subjective bulimic episodes to be eligible, they must have been viewed as having involved eating an excessive amount of food.*]

Subsidiary Probe Questions

To assess the amount of food eaten:

    Typically what have you eaten at these times?

    What were others eating at the time?

To assess loss of control:

    Did you have a sense of loss of control at the time?

For chronic cases only:

    Could you have stopped eating once you had started?

    Could you have prevented the episode from occurring?

[For objective bulimic episodes, subjective bulimic episodes, and episodes of objective overeating make the following two ratings:

    (i) Number of days (rate 00 if none)   [ ][ ]

    (ii) Number of episodes (rate 000 if none)   [ ][ ][ ]

In general, it is best to calculate the number of days first and then the number of episodes. Rate 777 if the number of episodes is so great that their frequency cannot be calculated. Episodes of subjective overeating are not rated.]

[*Ask about the preceding 2 months.*]

For objective bulimic episodes, rate the number of episodes over the preceding 2 months and the number of days on which they occurred. (Rate 0 if none and 9 if not asked.)

Days - Month 2	[ ][ ]
Month 3	[ ][ ]
Episodes - Month 2	[ ][ ][ ]
Month 3	[ ][ ][ ]

Also rate the longest continuous period in weeks free (not due to force of circumstances) from objective bulimic episodes over the past 3 months. (Rate 99 if not asked.)   [ ][ ]

DIETARY RESTRICTION OUTSIDE BULIMIC EPISODES   (Diagnostic item)

[*Only rate this item if there have been objective bulimic episodes over the past 3 months.*]

Outside the times when you have lost control over eating (refer to objective and subjective bulimic episodes), **how much have you been restricting the amount that you eat?**

Typically, what have you eaten?

Has this been to influence your shape or weight?

[Ask about actual food intake outside the objective and subjective bulimic episodes. Rate the *average* degree of dietary restriction. This should have been intended to influence shape, weight, or body composition, although this may not have been the sole or main reason. Rate each of the past 3 months separately whether or not it included a bulimic episode. Rate 9 if not asked.]

0 - No extreme restriction outside objective bulimic episodes
1 - Extreme restriction outside objective bulimic episodes (i.e., low energy intake (< 1,200 kcal) due to infrequent eating and/or consumption of low-calorie foods)
2 - No eating outside objective bulimic episodes (i.e., fasting)

Month 1	[ ]
Month 2	[ ]
Month 3	[ ]

SOCIAL EATING   (Eating Concern subscale)

* Over the past 4 weeks have you been concerned about other people seeing you eat?

Have you avoided such occasions?

[Rate the degree of concern about eating normal or less than normal amounts of food in front of others (e.g., family) and whether this has led to avoidance. This should represent the *average* for the entire month. If the possibility of eating with others has not arisen, rate 9. *Do not consider objective bulimic episodes or episodes of objective overeating.*]

0 - No concern about being seen eating by others and no avoidance of such
    occasions

1 -

2 - Has felt slight concern at being seen eating but no avoidance

3 -

4 - Has felt definite concern and has avoided some such occasions

5 -

6 - Has felt definite concern and has avoided all such occasions   [ ]

EATING IN SECRET   (Eating Concern subscale)

* Over the past 4 weeks have you eaten in secret?

[Rate the number of days on which there has been at least one episode of secret eating. Secret eating refers to eating that is furtive and which the subject wishes to conceal. Avoidance of eating in front of others should be rated under "Social eating." If the possibility of eating with others has not arisen, rate 9. *Do not consider objective bulimic episodes.*]

0 - Has not eaten in secret

1 -

2 - Has eaten in secret on less than half the days

3 -

4 - Has eaten in secret on more than half the days

5 -

6 - Has eaten in secret every day   [ ]

GUILT ABOUT EATING   (Eating Concern subscale)

* Over the past 4 weeks have you felt guilty after eating?

Have you felt that you have done something wrong? Why?

On what <u>proportion</u> of the times that you have eaten have you felt guilty?

[Rate the *proportion of times* on which feelings of guilt have followed eating. These feelings of guilt should relate to the effects of eating on shape, weight, or body composition. *Do not consider objective bulimic episodes,* but do consider other episodes of overeating. *Distinguish guilt from regret:* Guilt refers to a feeling that one has done wrong. *N.B. This rating is based on occasions.*]

0 - No guilt after eating

1 -

2 - Has felt guilty after eating on less than half the *occasions*

3 -

4 - Has felt guilty after eating on more than half the *occasions*

5 -

6 - Has felt guilty after eating on every *occasion*   [ ]

SELF-INDUCED VOMITING   (Diagnostic item)

* Over the past 4 weeks have you made yourself sick as a means of controlling your shape or weight?

[Rate the number of days on which there has been one or more episodes of self-induced vomiting as a means of controlling shape, weight, or body composition. Rate 00 if no vomiting.]

[ ][ ]

[Rate the number of discrete episodes of self-induced vomiting. Accept the subject's definition of an episode. Rate 777 if the number is so great that it cannot be calculated. Rate 000 if no vomiting.]

[ ][ ][ ]

[*Ask about the preceding 2 months if practicing self-induced vomiting to influence shape, weight, or body composition.*]

[Rate the number of discrete episodes of self-induced vomiting over each of the 2 preceding months. Rate 999 if not asked.]

Month 2   [ ][ ][ ]
Month 3   [ ][ ][ ]

LAXATIVE MISUSE   (Diagnostic item)

* Over the past 4 weeks have you taken laxatives as a means of controlling your shape or weight?

[Rate the number of days on which laxatives have been taken as a means of controlling shape, weight, or body composition. This should have been the *main* reason, although it may not have been the sole reason. Rate 00 if there was no laxative use or there is doubt whether the laxative taking was primarily to influence shape, weight, or body composition.]

[ ][ ]

[Rate the number of individual episodes of laxative misuse (as defined above). Rate 777 if the number is so great that it cannot be calculated. Rate 000 if no such laxative misuse.]

[ ][ ][ ]

[Rate the average number of laxatives taken on each occasion. Rate 999 if not applicable. Rate 777 if not quantifiable, e.g., use of bran.]

[ ][ ][ ]

[Note the type of laxative taken.]

[*Ask about the preceding 2 months if taking laxatives to influence shape, weight, or body composition.*]

[Rate the number of discrete episodes of laxative misuse over each of the two preceding months. Rate 000 if no such laxative misuse. Rate 999 if not asked.]

Month 2   [ ][ ][ ]
Month 3   [ ][ ][ ]

DIURETIC MISUSE **(Diagnostic item)**

* Over the past 4 weeks have you taken diuretics as a means of controlling your shape or weight?

[Rate the number of days on which diuretics have been taken as a means of controlling shape, weight, or body composition. This should have been the *main* reason, although it may not have been the sole reason. Rate 00 if there was no diuretic use or there is no doubt whether the diuretic taking was primarily to influence shape, weight, or body composition.]

[ ][ ]

[Rate the number of individual episodes of diuretic misuse (as defined above). Rate 777 if the number is so great that it cannot be calculated. Rate 000 if no such diuretic misuse.]

[ ][ ][ ]

[Rate the average number of diuretics taken on each occasion. Rate 999 if not applicable. Rate 777 if not quantifiable.]

[ ][ ][ ]

[Note the type of diuretic taken.]

[*Ask about the preceding 2 months if taking diuretics to influence shape, weight or body composition.*]

[Rate the number of discrete episodes of diuretic misuse over each of the 2 preceding months. Rate 000 if no such diuretic misuse. Rate 999 if not asked.]

Month 2   [ ][ ][ ]
Month 3   [ ][ ][ ]

INTENSE EXERCISING TO CONTROL SHAPE OR WEIGHT

(Diagnostic item)

* Over the past 4 weeks have you exercised as a means of controlling your weight, altering your shape or amount of fat, or burning off calories?

Typically, what form of exercise have you taken?

[Rate the number of days on which the subject has engaged in *intense* exercise that was *predominantly* intended to use calories or change shape, weight, or body composition. The decision whether the exercising was ''intense'' should be made by the interviewer. If in doubt, the exercising should not be classed as intense. Rate 00 if no such exercising.]

[ ][ ]

[Rate the *average* amount of time (in minutes) per day spent exercising in this way. Only consider days on which the subject exercised. Rate 999 if no such exercising.]

[ ][ ][ ]

[*Ask about the preceding 2 months if there has been exercising of this type.*]

[Rate the number of days on which the subject has exercised in this manner over each of the 2 preceding months. If not asked, rate 99.]

Month 2   [ ][ ]
Month 3   [ ][ ]

ABSTINENCE FROM EXTREME   (Diagnostic item)
WEIGHT-CONTROL BEHAVIOR

[*Only ask this question if at least one of the key forms of weight-control behavior has been rated positively at the specified severity level over the past 3 months (see the section on "eating disorder diagnoses").*]

[The five forms of behavior are as follows:
- fasting
- self-induced vomiting
- laxative misuse
- diurectic misuse
- excessive exercise]

Over the past 3 months has there been a period of 2 or more weeks when you have not . . .

[Ask as for individual items.]

[Ascertain the number of consecutive weeks over the past 3 months "free" (i.e., not above threshold levels) from *all* five forms of extreme weight-control behavior. Do not rate abstinence due to force of circumstance. Rate 99 if not applicable.]

[ ][ ]

DISSATISFACTION WITH   (Weight Concern subscale)
WEIGHT

* Over the past 4 weeks have you been dissatisfied with your weight?
Have you been so dissatisfied that it has made you unhappy?

[Only rate dissatisfaction due to weight being regarded as too high. Assess the subject's attitude to his or her weight and rate accordingly. This should represent the *average* for the entire month. Only rate 4, 5, or 6, if there has been distress. Do not prompt with the terms "slight," "moderate," or "marked." Rate 9 if the subject is unaware of his or her weight.]

0 - No dissatisfaction

1 -

2 - Slight dissatisfaction (no associated distress)

3 -

4 - Moderate dissatisfaction (some associated distress)

5 -

6 - Marked dissatisfaction (extreme concern and distress, weight totally
     unacceptable)   [ ]

DESIRE TO LOSE WEIGHT   (Weight Concern subscale)

* Over the past 4 weeks have you wanted to lose weight?

Have you had a <u>strong desire</u> to lose weight?

[Rate the number of days on which there has been a *strong desire* to lose weight.]

0 - No strong desire to lose weight
1 -
2 - Strong desire present on less than half the days
3 -
4 - Strong desire present on more than half the days
5 -
6 - Strong desire present every day   [ ]

DESIRED WEIGHT

* What weight would you like to be?

[Rate weight in kilograms. Rate 888 if the subject is not interested in his or her weight. Rate 777 if no specific weight would be low enough. Rate 666 if the subject is primarily interested in his or her shape but has some concern about weight (but not a specific weight).]

[ ][ ][ ]

REACTION TO PRESCRIBED   (Weight Concern subscale)
WEIGHING

* How would you feel if you were asked to weigh yourself once each week for the next 4 weeks?

[Rate the strength of reaction. Positive reactions should be rated 9. Check whether other aspects of the subject's life would be influenced. Ask the subject to describe in detail how he or she would react and rate accordingly. Do not prompt with the terms "slight," "moderate," or "marked." If the subject would not comply with prescribed weighing because it would be extremely disturbing, rate 6.]

0 - No reaction
1 -
2 - Slight reaction
3 -
4 - Moderate reaction (definite reaction, but manageable)
5 -
6 - Marked reaction (pronounced reaction which would affect other aspects of
     the subject's life)   [ ]

DISSATISFACTION WITH SHAPE   (Shape Concern subscale)

* Over the past 4 weeks have you been dissatisfied with your shape? Have you been so dissatisfied that it has made you unhappy?

[Only rate dissatisfaction with shape and not that concerning body tone. Assess the subject's attitude to his or her shape and rate accordingly. This should represent the *average* for the entire month. Only rate 4, 5, or 6, if there has been associated distress. Do not prompt with the terms "slight," "moderate," or "marked."]

0 - No dissatisfaction with shape

1 -

2 - Slight dissatisfaction with shape (no associated distress)

3 -

4 - Moderate dissatisfaction with shape (some associated distress)

5 -

6 - Marked dissatisfaction with shape (extreme concern and distress, shape totally unacceptable)   [ ]

PREOCCUPATION WITH   (Shape Concern and
SHAPE OR WEIGHT   Weight Concern subscales)

* Over the past 4 weeks have you spent much time thinking about your shape or weight?

* Has thinking about your shape or weight <u>interfered</u> with your ability to concentrate? How about concentrating on things you are interested in, for example, reading, watching television, or following a conversation?

[Concentration is regarded as impaired if there have been *intrusive thoughts about shape or weight that have interfered with activities.* Rate the number of days on which this happened.]

0 - No concentration impairment

1 -

2 - Concentration impairment on less than half the days

3 -

4 - Concentration impairment on more than half the days

5 -

6 - Concentration impairment every day   [ ]

IMPORTANCE OF SHAPE

(Diagnostic item)
(Shape Concern subscale)

* Over the past 4 weeks has your shape been important in influencing how you feel about (judge, think, evaluate) yourself as a person?

... * If you imagine the things that influence how you feel about (judge, think, evaluate) yourself—such as (your performance at work, being a parent, your marriage, how you get on with other people)—and put these things in order of importance, where does your shape fit in?

If, over the past 4 weeks, your shape had changed in any way, would this have affected how you feel about yourself?

Is it important to you that your shape does not change?

[Rate the degree of importance the subject has placed on body shape and its position in his or her scheme for *self-evaluation*. To make this rating, comparisons may be made with other aspects of the subject's life that are of importance in his or her scheme for self-evaluation (e.g., quality of relationships, being a parent, performance at work, or leisure activities). The rating should represent the *average* for the entire month. Do not prompt with the terms "some," "moderate," or "supreme." If the subject has regarded both shape and weight as being of equivalent supreme importance, rate 6 on this item and on "Importance of weight."]

0 - No importance
1 -
2 - Some importance (definitely an aspect of self-evaluation)
3 -
4 - Moderate importance (definitely one of the main aspects of self-evaluation)
5 -
6 - Supreme importance (nothing is more important in the subject's scheme
    for self-evaluation)   [ ]

[*Ask about the preceding 2 months.*]

[Rate preceding 2 months. Rate 9 if not asked.]

Month 2	[ ]
Month 3	[ ]

IMPORTANCE OF WEIGHT

(Diagnostic item)
(Weight Concern subscale)

* Over the past 4 weeks has your weight been important in influencing how you feel about (judge, think, evaluate) yourself as a person?

. . . * If you imagine the things that influence how you feel about (judge, think, evaluate) yourself—such as (your performance at work, being a parent, your marriage, how you get on with other people)—and put these things in order of importance, where does your weight fit in?

If, over the past 4 weeks, your weight had changed in any way, would this have affected how you feel about yourself?

Is it important to you that your weight does not change?

[Rate the degree of importance the subject has placed on weight (i.e., actual or presumed weight) and its position in his or her scheme for *self-evaluation*. To make this rating, comparisons may be made with other aspects of the subject's life that are of importance in his or her scheme for self-evaluation (e.g., quality of relationships, being a parent, performance at work, or leisure activities). The rating should represent the *average* for the entire month. Do not prompt with the terms "some," "moderate," or "supreme." If the subject has regarded both weight and shape as being of equivalent supreme importance, rate 6 on this item and on "Importance of shape."]

0 - No importance
1 -
2 - Some importance (definitely an aspect of self-evaluation)
3 -
4 - Moderate importance (definitely one of the main aspects of self-evaluation)
5 -
6 - Supreme importance (nothing is more important in the subject's scheme for self-evaluation)   [ ]

[*Ask about the preceding 2 months.*]

[Rate preceding 2 months. Rate 9 if not asked.]

Month 2   [ ]
Month 3   [ ]

FEAR OF WEIGHT GAIN
(Diagnostic item)
(Shape Concern subscale)

[*Shorten the question if the subject is obviously overweight.*]

* Over the past 4 weeks have you been <u>afraid</u> that you might gain weight (or become fat)?

[Rate the number of days on which a *definite fear* has been present. Exclude reactions to actual weight gain.]

0 - No definite fear of fatness or weight gain

1 -

2 - Definite fear of fatness or weight gain present on less than half the days

3 -

4 - Definite fear of fatness or weight gain present on more than half the days

5 -

6 - Definite fear of fatness or weight gain present every day   [ ]

[*Ask about the past 2 months*]

[Rate preceding 2 months. Rate 9 if not asked.]

Month 2	[ ]
Month 3	[ ]

DISCOMFORT SEEING BODY   (Shape Concern subscale)

* Over the past 4 weeks have you felt uncomfortable seeing your body, for example, in the mirror, in shop window reflections, while undressing, or while taking a bath or shower?

Have you avoided seeing your body? Why?

[The discomfort should be due to the subject's sensitivity about the overall appearance of his or her shape or figure. It should not stem from sensitivity about specific aspects of appearance (e.g., acne) or from modesty.]

0 - No discomfort about seeing body

1 -

2 - Some discomfort about seeing body

3 -

4 - Definite discomfort about seeing body

5 -

6 - Definite discomfort about seeing body, and has attempted to avoid all such occasions (i.e., the subject has attempted not to see his or her body at all even when washing)   [ ]

AVOIDANCE OF EXPOSURE   (Shape Concern subscale)

* Over the past 4 weeks have you felt uncomfortable about <u>others</u> see-ing your body, for example, in communal changing rooms, when swimming, or when wearing clothes that show your shape? What about your partner or friends seeing your body?

Have you avoided such situations? Why?

[The discomfort should be due to the subject's sensitivity about the overall appearance of his or her shape or figure. It should not stem from sensitivity about specific aspects of appearance (e.g., acne) or from modesty. If the possibility of "exposure" has not arisen, rate 9.]

0 - No discomfort about others seeing body

1 -

2 - Some discomfort about others seeing body

3 -

4 - Definite discomfort about others seeing body

5 -

6 - Definite discomfort about others seeing body, and has attempted to avoid all such occasions   [ ]

FEELINGS OF FATNESS   (Diagnostic item)
(Shape Concern subscale)

[*Omit this item if the subject is* <u>*obviously*</u> *overweight and rate 7.*]

* Over the past 4 weeks have you felt fat?

[Rate the number of days on which the subject has "felt fat" accepting his or her use of this expression. Distinguish feeling fat from feeling bloated premen-strually, unless this is experienced as feeling fat.]

0 - Has not felt fat

1 -

2 - Has felt fat on less than half the days

3 -

4 - Has felt fat on more than half the days

5 -

6 - Has felt fat every day   [ ]

[*Ask about the preceding 2 months.*]

[Rate preceding 2 months. Rate 9 if not asked.]

Month 2   [ ]
Month 3   [ ]

FLAT STOMACH　　　　　　　　　　　(Shape Concern subscale)

[*Omit this item if the subject is* <u>obviously</u> *overweight and rate 7.*]

Over the past 4 weeks have you had a definite desire to have a flat stomach?

[Rate the number of days on which the subject has had a *definite desire to have a flat or concave stomach*. Do not rate simply the desire to have a flatter stomach.]

0 - No definite desire to have a flat stomach

1 -

2 - Definite desire to have a flat stomach on less than half the days

3 -

4 - Definite desire to have a flat stomach on more than half the days

5 -

6 - Definite desire to have a flat stomach every day　　　　　　　　[　]

WEIGHT AND HEIGHT

[The subject's weight and height should be measured.]

Weight in kg　[　][　][　]
Height in cm　[　][　][　]

MAINTAINED LOW WEIGHT　　　　　　　　(Diagnostic item)

[*Rate for subjects who may be underweight.*]

Over the past 3 months have you been trying to lose weight?

If no: **Have you been trying to make sure that you do not gain weight?**

[If weight is low, rate presence of attempts either to lose weight or to avoid weight gain. Rate 9 if not asked.]

0 - No attempts either to lose weight or to avoid weight gain over the past 3 months

1 - Attempts either to lose weight or to avoid weight gain over the past 3 months for reasons concerning shape or weight

2 - Attempts either to lose weight or to avoid weight gain over the past 3 months for other reasons　　　　　　　　　　　　　　　　　[　]

MENSTRUATION   (Diagnostic item)

Have you missed any menstrual periods over the past few months?

How many periods have you had?

Are you taking an oral contraceptive (the "pill")?

[With post-menarchal females, rate number of menstrual periods over the past three expected menstrual cycles. Rate 7 if the subject is pre-menarchal, if she has been taking an oral contraceptive, or if she has been pregnant or breast feeding.]   [ ]

END OF SCHEDULE

Differences between EDE
Versions 11.5D and 12.0D

The main changes to 11.5D are summarized below.
1. The following items have been omitted:
    "Subjective loss of control over eating"
    "Subjective overeating"
    Ratings of "duration," "fullness," and "distress" in the overeating section
    "Exercising to control shape or weight"
    "Solitary exercising exclusively to control shape or weight"
    "Other extreme methods for controlling shape or weight"
    "Subjective weight"
    "Weighing"
    "Vigilance about shape"
    "Regional fatness"
    "Body composition"
2. The following item has been added:
    "Intense exercizing to control shape or weight"
3. The following items have been renamed:
    "Dietary restraint outside bulimic episodes"—now "Dietary restriction outside bulimic episodes"
    "Abstinence from weight-control behavior"—now "Abstinence from extreme weight-control behavior"
    "Pursuit of weight loss"—now "Desire to lose weight"
    "Fear of fatness"—now "Fear of weight gain"

In addition, version 12.0D incorporates minor changes both to the questions themselves, to the definitions of certain items, and to the operational DSM-III-R criteria. The revisions to the overeating section are of particular importance. The changes stem from accumulated experience using the instrument in a variety of clinical and community-based settings.

Coding Sheet (EDE-12.0D)

Pattern of eating
  - breakfast   [ ]
  - mid-morning snack   [ ]
  - lunch   [ ]
  - mid-afternoon snack   [ ]
  - evening meal   [ ]
  - evening snack   [ ]
  - nocturnal snack   [ ]
Restraint over eating   [ ]
Avoidance of eating   [ ]
Empty stomach   [ ]
Food avoidance   [ ]
Dietary rules   [ ]
Preoccupation with food, eating, or calories   [ ]
Fear of losing control over eating   [ ]
Overeating section

Notes

Objective bulimic episodes
- number of days [ ][ ]
- number of episodes [ ][ ][ ]
- [number of days over preceding 2 months] month 2 [ ][ ]
  month 3 [ ][ ]
- [number of episodes over preceding 2 months] month 2 [ ][ ][ ]
  month 3 [ ][ ][ ]
- [longest continuous period free from objective bulimic episodes
    over past 3 months] [ ][ ]

Subjective bulimic episodes
- number of days [ ][ ]
- number of episodes [ ][ ][ ]

Episodes of objective overeating
- number of days [ ][ ]
- number of episodes [ ][ ][ ]

[Dietary restriction between bulimic episodes] month 1 [ ]
  month 2 [ ]
  month 3 [ ]

Social eating [ ]
Eating in secret [ ]
Guilt about eating [ ]

Self-induced vomiting
- days [ ][ ]
- episodes [ ][ ][ ]
- [episodes over the preceding 2 months] month 2 [ ][ ][ ]
  month 3 [ ][ ][ ]

Laxative misuse
- days [ ][ ]
- episodes [ ][ ][ ]
- average number taken per occasion [ ][ ][ ]
- type of laxative . . . .
- [episodes over the preceding 2 months] month 2 [ ][ ][ ]
  month 3 [ ][ ][ ]

Diuretic misuse
- days [ ][ ]
- episodes [ ][ ][ ]
- average number taken per occasion [ ][ ][ ]
- type of diuretic . . . .
- [episodes over the preceding 2 months] month 2 [ ][ ][ ]
  month 3 [ ][ ][ ]

Note. The items in square brackets are those *required* for diagnostic purposes.

Intense exercising to control shape or weight
  – days   [ ][ ]
  – time   [ ][ ][ ]
  – [days over the preceding 2 months]   month 2   [ ][ ]
                                                month 3   [ ][ ]
Abstinence from extreme weight-control behavior   [ ][ ]
Dissatisfaction with weight   [ ]
Desire to lose weight   [ ]
Desired weight   [ ][ ][ ]
Reaction to prescribed weighing   [ ]
Dissatisfaction with shape   [ ]
Preoccupation with shape or weight   [ ]
Importance of shape   [ ]
  – [preceding 2 months]   month 2   [ ]
                                                month 3   [ ]
Importance of weight   [ ]
  – [preceding 2 months]   month 2   [ ]
                                                month 3   [ ]
Fear of weight gain   [ ]
  – [preceding 2 months]   month 2   [ ]
                                                month 3   [ ]
Discomfort at seeing body   [ ]
Avoidance of exposure   [ ]
Feelings of fatness   [ ]
  – [preceding 2 months]   month 2   [ ]
                                                month 3   [ ]
Flat stomach   [ ]
Objective weight (kg)   [ ][ ][ ]
Objective height (cm)   [ ][ ][ ]
[Maintained low weight]   [ ]
[Menstruation]   [ ]

CHAPTER 16

Cognitive-Behavioral Therapy for Binge Eating and Bulimia Nervosa: A Comprehensive Treatment Manual

Christopher G. Fairburn
Marsha D. Marcus
G. Terence Wilson

This is a detailed manual describing the cognitive-behavioral approach to the treatment of binge eating and bulimia nervosa. It is designed to supplant earlier versions of the manual (Fairburn, 1985; Fairburn & Cooper, 1989). The manual focuses of the treatment of bulimia nervosa, but it also includes details of how the treatment should be adapted to suit obese patients who binge eat as well as binge eating in anorexia nervosa.

The manual opens with a review of the current status of this form of cognitive-behavioral therapy (CBT). This is followed by a description of the treatment itself.

THE CURRENT STATUS OF THE COGNITIVE-BEHAVIORAL APPROACH

Bulimia Nervosa

The cognitive-behavioral approach to the treatment of binge eating was developed as a treatment for bulimia nervosa. It was the first promising treatment for bulimia nervosa (Fairburn, 1981), and it is the most extensively studied of the psychological treatments for the disorder. On the basis of the findings of these studies (reviewed in Fairburn, Agras, & Wilson [1992]), cognitive-behavioral therapy is generally regarded as the treatment of choice for bulimia nervosa. It has been a consistent finding that most patients improve substantially and that these improvements are well maintained, at least for the first year after treatment. Information on the long-term maintenance of change is needed. CBT has been shown to be at least as effective, if not more effective, as all the treatments with which it has been compared. These have included supportive psychotherapy, two forms of focal psychotherapy, exposure with response prevention, behavior therapy, and treatment with antidepressant drugs. Combining CBT and antidepressant drugs appears to convey no clear benefit.

It is important to stress that CBT is no panacea. Some patients fail to benefit and others make only limited gains. Some general prognostic factors have been identified, the most potent appearing to be the patient's pretreatment level of self-esteem (Fairburn, Kirk, O'Connor, Anastasiades, & Cooper, 1987; Fairburn, Peveler, Jones, Hope, & Doll, in press), with those patients having lowest self-esteem faring least well. However, even though patients with low self-esteem respond least well, there is no reason not to treat them with CBT, since there is no evidence that they would respond better to any other approach. The same applies to patients with frank personality disorders: Clinical experience suggests that they do less well than those without personality disorders, and there is evidence that they are more likely to drop out (Fairburn, Peveler, et al., in press), but there is no evidence that they do better with any other treatment approach.

CBT may be an unnecessarily intensive form of treatment for some patients with bulimia nervosa. A minority of patients respond extremely quickly and appear not to need the full treatment. It is therefore of note that simple psychoeducational programs, even those involving a lecture format (Olmsted et al., 1991), are sufficient in certain cases. However, it must be noted that maintenance of change after brief treatment of this type has not been adequately studied.

Given current knowledge, it is reasonable to use CBT as the first-line approach when treating patients with bulimia nervosa. The only patients to exclude are the few patients who need partial or full hospitalization. There are four indications for hospitalization: if the patient is too depressed to be managed as an outpatient or there is a risk of suicide; if the patient's physical health is a cause for concern, severe electrolyte disturbance being the most common problem; if the patient is in the first trimester of pregnancy and her eating habits are severely disturbed, because of the risk of a spontaneous abortion; or if the eating disorder proves refractory to outpatient care. In our experience these criteria do not often apply: in less than 5% of cases in the first author's experience. In such cases there should be an initial period of inpatient or day patient treatment followed by outpatient care probably along cognitive-behavioral lines.

How CBT operates is not clear. (See Wilson & Fairburn [in press] for an account of possible mechanisms.) It is not likely to be through non-specific mechanisms common to many psychological treatments, although these are probably responsible in part for the symptomatic improvement seen in the first few weeks (Jones, Peveler, Hope, & Fairburn, in press).

Other Patient Groups

Anorexia Nervosa (Binge-Eating/Purging Type)

Much less is known in general about the treatment of other patients who binge eat. (See Fairburn & Wilson, Chapter 1, this volume, for an account of the classification of patients who binge eat.) The treatment of patients with the binge-eating/purging type of anorexia nervosa has not been studied in its own right. They are thought to respond less well than patients who neither binge nor purge (see Garner, Chapter 4, this volume). They can be managed using the form of CBT used to treat bulimia nervosa, although (as described later in this chapter) it needs to be adapted in certain ways.

Eating Disorders Not Otherwise Specified, Binge Eating Disorder, and Obesity

Within "eating disorders not otherwise specified" there are many individuals with recurrent episodes of binge eating including those with binge eating disorder (Fairburn, Welch, & Hay, in press; see Fairburn & Wilson, Chapter 1, this volume). The eating problems of these individuals have not been well characterized. It is likely that they would respond well to an adaptation of CBT for bulimia nervosa. The subgroup that is also obese (see Marcus, Chapter 5, this volume) has very particular needs, since treatment has to address not only this group's eating problem but also its obesity (see later in this chapter). There is preliminary evidence that these patients respond well to CBT (Telch, Agras, Rossiter, Wilfley, & Kenardy, 1990; Smith, Marcus, & Kaye, 1992; Wilfley et al., in press) at least as far as their eating disorder is concerned. The effects of treatment on their weight are not yet clear, since follow-up has not been sufficiently long.

PRACTICAL DETAILS
OF THE COGNITIVE-BEHAVIORAL APPROACH
—
BULIMIA NERVOSA

The Use of This Manual

There follows a detailed description of the standard form of CBT used to treat patients with bulimia nervosa. The description takes the form of a treatment manual based on one used in a recent treatment trial (Fairburn et al., 1991; Fairburn, Jones, Peveler, Hope, & O'Connor, in press) As such, it will be unusually specific in its description of what CBT involves. Throughout the manual it is assumed that the patient is female, since male cases of bulimia nervosa are not often encountered.

In everyday clinical practice it is possible to implement treatments more flexibly than is possible within the context of most treatment trials. This is not necessarily an advantage to the patient. Since it is clear from the findings of recent treatment trials that CBT applied in a standard way benefits most patients, therapists not encumbered by the constraints of a research protocol should think carefully before introducing modifications to the treatment. Changes may not result in an improved outcome. For example, when used in treatment trials CBT usually has a preset duration and number of sessions and, as in many short-term psychotherapies, this arrangement is made clear to the patient at the outset and at regular intervals throughout treatment. Few therapists normally work this way, yet in our opinion it has definite advantages. For example, it concentrates the minds of the patient and therapist, tending to make them work harder in therapy. It also has certain specific advantages when treating patients with bulimia nervosa. These stem from the finding that many patients continue to improve over the months following treatment, even though they are having no further therapy. We believe that the continuing improvement may be attributed to treatment having disrupted certain key mechanisms that maintain the disorder ("breaking the back of the disorder") and that as a result the disorder is no longer self-perpetuating; instead, it begins to disintegrate. This process starts during treatment, but it takes time for its full effect to be seen. If treatment is continued until maximum benefit is obtained (i.e., usual clinical practice), the tendency would be for the patient (and therapist) to ascribe the continuing improvement to the ongoing therapy, whereas it might well have occurred anyway. It is our belief that it is preferable for patients to see that the continuing improvement stems from the progress that *they* have made overcoming the disorder. We therefore advocate for most patients a fixed number of sessions (usually 20) followed by a limited number of bimonthly posttreatment review appointments designed to monitor progress. Once the final outcome is clear 6 to 8 months later, further treatment can be arranged if needed.

Despite urging caution before making significant changes to the treatment described in this manual, we appreciate the need to adapt the treatment to suit the individual patient's characteristics. The adaptations most commonly required are specified at the end of each section of the manual.

Some Preliminary Points about the Treatment

Treatment usually lasts about 20 weeks. As in all cognitive-behavioral treatments, it is semistructured, problem-oriented, and mainly concerned with the patients' present and future rather than their past. The focus is on the factors and processes that are maintaining the eating problem rather than on those that operated earlier in its evolution. Treatment is an active process, with responsibility for change residing with the patient; the therapist provides information, guidance, support, and encouragement.

Three stages in the treatment may be distinguished. In the first, the main emphasis is on presenting the cognitive view on the maintenance of bulimia nervosa, since this underpins the entire treatment. In addition, behavioral techniques are used to replace binge eating with a stable pattern of regular eating. In the second, further attempts are made to establish healthy eating habits with there being particular emphasis on the elimination of dieting. It is at this stage that cognitive procedures are most extensively used, the focus being on the thoughts, beliefs, and values that are maintaining the problem. The final stage is concerned with the maintenance of change following treatment. In general, the treatment is additive, with procedures being added to previous ones rather than being introduced and then withdrawn. While the precise timing of the introduction of techniques is not critical, their order is important, since they are designed to build upon one another.

As in all cognitive-behavioral treatments, it is essential that the patient and therapist establish an effective working relationship in which they are collaborators with a common goal, that of overcoming the eating problem. Mutual trust and respect are important. A sound relationship is important since many of the behavioral assignments are not only difficult to accomplish but also run directly counter to these patients' beliefs and values. There is no evidence that the sex of the therapist is relevant to outcome. Any influence of this type is likely to be small in comparison with the effect of the therapist's level of competence at executing the key treatment procedures.

Therapists require some knowledge and understanding of the physiological disturbances seen in bulimia nervosa. These patients are at risk of a variety of physical complications. In addition, therapists need to educate patients about body weight regulation, dieting, and body image disturbance, since many harbor significant misconceptions about food and eating and their shape and weight. Clearly, to educate patients, therapists must themselves be well informed about these matters.

Stage 1 (Sessions 1 to 8)

There are two major aims. The first is to explain the rationale underlying the cognitive-behavioral treatment approach, and the second is to replace binge eating with a stable pattern of regular eating. More detailed aims are listed in Table 16.1.

In the original form of the treatment, the appointments in Stage 1 were held twice a week. More experience suggests that such frequent appointments are generally only needed for those patients whose eating habits are severely disturbed, in particular, those patients who overeat many times each day. These patients need to be seen more often than once a week; otherwise, the gains made after one session tend not to endure until the next, and patients tend instead to slip back to how they were some days earlier. On the other hand, the majority of patients may be managed successfully with weekly sessions. If the therapist is in doubt about the optimal frequency of sessions for a particular patient, it is suggested that they be held twice weekly at first and reduced to weekly in the light of progress. Patients who are having days free from episodes of overeating can usually be managed from the outset with weekly sessions.

Session 1

Prior to starting treatment the patient should have been comprehensively assessed. This includes taking a full history, completing a mental state

---

TABLE 16.1. The Aims of Stage 1

To establish a sound therapeutic relationship

To educate the patient about the cognitive view on the maintenance of bulimia nervosa and to explain the need for both behavior and cognitive change

To establish regular weekly weighing

To educate the patient about body weight regulation, the adverse effects of dieting, and the physical consequences of binge eating, self-induced vomiting, and laxative abuse

To reduce the frequency of overeating by introducing a pattern of regular eating and the use of alternative behavior

To reduce secrecy and enlist the cooperation of friends and relatives.

---

examination, assessing the patient's physical health, and checking that she is fit to be managed on an outpatient basis. In addition, she should have treatment options outlined and their relative merits discussed. If it is decided that CBT is the approach of choice, then the optimal time to start treatment should be reviewed, since CBT requires a high level of commitment with few, if any, interruptions to the pattern of appointments. If the patient has competing commitments that are going to interfere with treatment, it is sometimes better to postpone starting CBT until these have passed.

ORIENTING THE PATIENT

The patient should be provided with the following information:

1. *Treatment structure.* Treatment comprises 19 sessions over about 20 weeks. Stages 1 and 2 consist of eight sessions each, and Stage 3 consists of three sessions. The sessions are up to 50 minutes in length. They always begin on time and never extend beyond the allocated 50 minutes.

2. *Treatment content.* At first, the rationale underlying CBT will be explained and the patient will be helped to regain control over eating largely by establishing a pattern of regular eating. Specific advice will be given on how this may be achieved. Once overeating is intermittent, attention will be directed to those factors that have been maintaining the eating problem. The patient will be helped to cope more effectively with the circumstances that tend to result in binge eating; and attempts will be made to identify, question, and modify relevant behaviors, thoughts, and attitudes. The final stage in treatment will be concerned with ensuring that the changes are maintained, or even built upon.

3. *Likely outcome.* Patients should be told that when using this treatment approach, most improve markedly and the improvements are usually well maintained. However, two further points need to be made. First, it is common for difficulties with eating to still be present at the end of treatment, but it is equally common for there to be continuing improvement over the following 4 to 8 months. Second, patients should not expect to be "cured" in the conventional sense: At times of stress, they may deteriorate, but between such times their eating should not be a problem. Patients should be told that they are likely to remain more sensitive than the average person about food and eating, and shape and weight.

4. *Treatment style and need for commitment.* It should be emphasized that this type of treatment requires full commitment: It needs to be given priority. Half-hearted attempts at treatment tend to fail. Regular homework assignments will be set after each treatment session, and the pa-

tient should do her utmost to complete them. The more effort that is put into treatment, the greater are likely to be the rewards. The therapist will provide information, advice, and encouragement, but it is up to the patient to make the most of this opportunity to change.

ESTABLISHING A COLLABORATIVE THERAPEUTIC RELATIONSHIP

Considerable effort should be put into establishing an effective working relationship. However, while genuine interest and concern are important, the therapist should be capable of being firm and authoritative, particularly with regard to the setting and reviewing of homework assignments.

TAKING A HISTORY

If the therapist was not involved in the assessment of the patient, information will need to obtained about the eating problem and its development. The following topics should be covered:

- the current state of the eating problem
- the patient's psychosocial adjustment, physical health, and current social circumstances
- the patient's prior experience of treatment
- the patient's attitude toward the eating problem and how it should be managed
- the evolution of the eating problem since its onset
- the patient's weight and menstrual history
- the patient's personal and family history

In addition, whenever possible, supplementary information should be obtained from an informant. At first, many patients are unwilling for others to be involved; indeed, it is common for no one to know that they have an eating problem or are seeking help. Under these circumstances, there is no need at this stage to interview an informant.

OUTLINING THE RATIONALE UNDERLYING
THE COGNITIVE-BEHAVIORAL APPROACH TO TREATMENT

The first step is to explain the cognitive view of the maintenance of bulimia nervosa. This is illustrated in Figure 16.1. The therapist should draw out this figure in stages incorporating the patient's own experiences and terms. The best starting point is the patient's complaint, binge eating itself, and the various forms of purging (self-induced vomiting, and

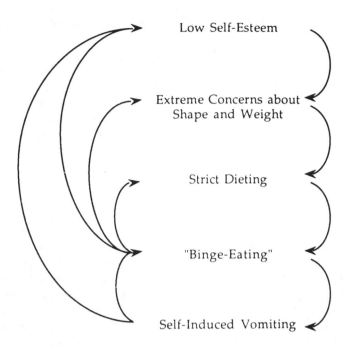

Low Self-Esteem

Extreme Concerns about
Shape and Weight

Strict Dieting

"Binge-Eating"

Self-Induced Vomiting

FIGURE 16.1. The cognitive view of the maintenance of bulimia nervosa.

the misuse of laxatives and diuretics). Most patients will accept that there is a vicious circle operating with their practice of compensatory purging serving either to promote overeating or, at the very least, to erode constraints against overeating (because of their belief in the effectiveness of purging as a means of weight control).

Next the relationship between binge eating and dieting needs to be discussed. There is no difficulty proposing that binge eating encourages dieting, but much more problematic is the notion that dieting itself encourages binge eating. (This connection is discussed by Polivy and Herman, Chapter 9, this volume.) The link between dieting and binge eating needs to be stressed since eliminating dieting is a major goal of treatment. One way of beginning to persuade patients that their form of dieting is a problem is to review the precipitants of their episodes of binge eating. Many patients report that a common trigger is breaking a personal dietary rule, for example, the eating of a "banned" food. The therapist can point out that had the food not been banned, the episode might well not have occurred. The notion should be introduced that the rule-ridden type of dieting practiced by patients with bulimia nervosa actively promotes overeating. The therapist should return to this point at repeated intervals during treatment especially when it is exemplified by the patient's behavior.

Generally the next part of the figure to consider is the relationship between dieting and concerns about shape and weight. This vicious circle is usually self-evident. Lastly, for patients in whom low self-esteem is clearly a problem, the therapist should note that low self-esteem and extreme concerns about shape and weight tend to be intimately related. It should be pointed out that episodes of loss of control over eating tend to worsen self-esteem, thereby exaggerating feelings of ineffectiveness and intensifying concerns about shape and weight.

Once the figure has been fully discussed, the therapist should review its implications. The major point to stress is that there is more to the patient's eating problem than just binge eating. While most patients will present complaining of binge eating (and possibly purging), they need to appreciate the need for change in other areas if they are to make a lasting recovery. Tackling binge eating in isolation is likely to produce only temporary benefits since the factors that promote binge eating will still be in place. There needs to be a reduction in their dietary restraint, otherwise they will be prone to binge eat, and to achieve this reduction, concerns about body shape and weight (and possibly self-esteem) will also need to be addressed. Thus treatment needs to focus on both behavior (e.g., eating and purging) and thoughts and feelings (e.g., concerns about shape and weight).

The therapist should explain that treatment tends to work from the bottom of Figure 16.1 upward. The initial focus is on the patient's presenting complaint of binge eating (which probably accounts in part for the acceptability of this approach), but by Stage 2 the emphasis will have extended to tackling dieting and concerns about shape and weight. The therapist should emphasize that the entire treatment derives logically from the cognitive account of the disorder and that if the patient does not understand the rationale for any procedure she should question the therapist who will in all likelihood refer back to the figure. To reinforce further this account of bulimia nervosa and its implications for treatment, the therapist should indeed return to the figure at regular intervals and, whenever possible, illustrate it with examples drawn from the patient's behavior.

INTRODUCING MONITORING

Toward the end of the first session, the patient should be given her first homework assignment. This is to start monitoring her eating. The rationale for monitoring should be clearly explained: first, it helps the therapist and patient examine her eating habits and the circumstances under which problems arise; and second, and more importantly, between sessions it helps the patient modify her eating habits and problematic thoughts and feelings.

It is not uncommon for patients to be reluctant to monitor, especially if they are ashamed of the way that they eat. The therapist should anticipate this response by assuring the patient that there is no need to be ashamed of her behavior, and by telling her that recording what actually happens is an essential first step in addressing the eating problem and overcoming it. Some patients respond by saying that they have monitored in the past and did not find it helpful. The reply should be that it is most unlikely that they will have monitored in the way that is being proposed and with this use of the information thereby gained. If the therapist detects any reluctance to monitor, it should be stressed that self-monitoring is the cornerstone of treatment and is essential for progress to be made.

To help the patient monitor, she should be given written instructions describing what is involved (see Table 16.2) together with an example monitoring sheet (see Figure 16.2).

Session 2

REVIEWING THE MONITORING SHEETS

Session 2 and all subsequent sessions open with a review of the monitoring sheets completed since the last session. At this stage each sheet should be discussed in great detail, and this especially applies to Session 2. The quality of a patient's monitoring is directly related to the degree of attention that the therapist pays it. For this reason the therapist should be painstaking when reviewing the first set of monitoring sheets. It should be checked when food items were written down (i.e., how long after they were consumed), the accuracy of the description, and whether there are any omissions. The monitoring must not have been retrospective; instead, the patient should be writing down what she eats immediately after she has eaten it. Any difficulties in monitoring should be explored and solutions sought. Accurate monitoring should be praised. In general, it is best if patients guide the therapist through each day's monitoring sheets, thereby ensuring they are active participants in the review process. The aim is to get a full understanding of the patient's current eating habits. Episodes of ''excessive eating'' (signified by asterisks in the fourth column) should be discussed in particular detail to understand why they were viewed as excessive and what might have precipitated them.

Some patients return having not monitored. The therapist must try to understand why this has happened. Often it is appropriate to react

---

TABLE 16.2. Instructions for Monitoring

The purpose of self-monitoring is twofold: First, it provides a detailed picture of how you eat, thereby bringing to your attention and that of your therapist the exact nature of your eating problem; and second, by making you more aware of what you are doing at the very time that you are doing it, self-monitoring helps you change behavior that previously seemed automatic and outside your control. Accurate self-monitoring is central to treatment.

At first, writing down everything you eat may well be irritating and inconvenient, but soon it will become second nature and of obvious value. We have yet to encounter anyone whose lifestyle makes monitoring truly impossible.

A sample monitoring sheet is shown overleaf. A new sheet should be started each day. Column 1 is for noting the time when you eat or drink anything, and Column 2 is for recording the nature of the food and liquid consumed. Calories should not be recorded: Instead, you should provide a simple (nontechnical) description of what you ate or drank. Each item should be written down as soon as possible after its consumption. Recalling what you ate or drank some hours earlier is not satisfactory, since it will not help you change your behavior. Episodes of eating that you viewed as meals should be identified with brackets. Snacks and other episodes of eating should not be bracketed.

Column 3 should specify where the food or liquid was consumed. If this was in your home, the room should be specified.

Asterisks should be placed in Column 4 adjacent to any episodes of eating that you felt at the time were excessive. It is essential to record all the food that you eat during binges.

Column 5 is for recording when you vomit, or take laxatives or diuretics (water tablets).

Column 6 should be used as a diary to record events that influenced your eating; for example, if an argument precipitated a binge, you should note that down. You may wish to record other important events, even if they had no effect on your eating. Indeed, it is a good idea noting down all strong feelings, for example, feelings of depression, anxiety, boredom or loneliness, or feeling fat. Column 6 should also be used to record your weight each time that you weigh yourself.

Obviously, if you are to record in the way that you are being asked, you will have to carry your monitoring sheets with you. Every treatment session will include a review of your latest monitoring sheets. You must therefore remember to bring them.

---

with some surprise, since not monitoring will effectively sabotage treatment. Under these circumstances the rationale for monitoring must be restated, and any misunderstandings and difficulties resolved.

INTRODUCING WEEKLY WEIGHING

With this form of treatment patients are not weighed by the therapist (except at assessment and perhaps also at the end of treatment). This is in part because sessions can become dominated by the subject of weight

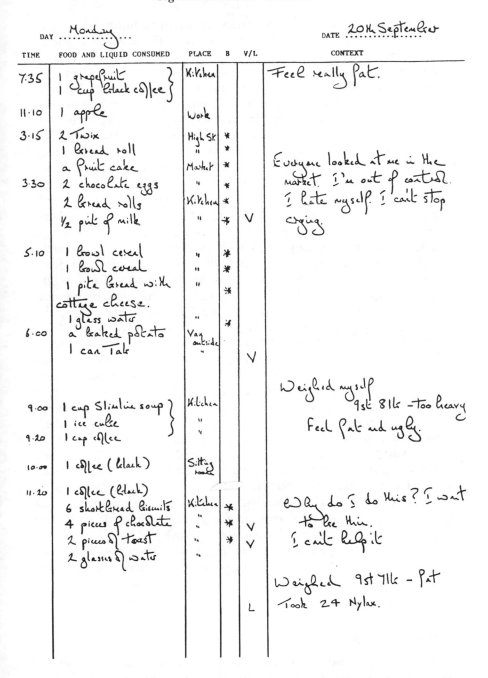

DAY Monday

DATE 20th September

TIME	FOOD AND LIQUID CONSUMED	PLACE	B	V/L	CONTEXT
7.35	1 grapefruit 1 cup black coffee	Kitchen			Feel really fat.
11.10	1 apple	Work			
3.15	2 Twix 1 bread roll a fruit cake	High St. " Market	* * *		Everyone looked at me in the market. I'm out of control. I hate myself. I can't stop crying.
3.30	2 chocolate eggs 2 bread rolls ½ pint of milk	" Kitchen "	* * *	V	
5.10	1 bowl cereal 1 bowl cereal 1 pita bread with cottage cheese. 1 glass water	" " " "	* * * *		
6.00	a baked potato 1 can Tab	Van outside "		V	
9.00	1 cup Slimline soup 1 ice cube	Kitchen "			Weighed myself 9st 8lb –too heavy Feel fat and ugly.
9.20	1 cup coffee	"			
10.00	1 coffee (black)	Sitting room			
11.20	1 coffee (black) 6 shortbread biscuits 4 pieces of chocolate 2 pieces of toast 2 glasses of water	Kitchen " " " "	* * *	V V	Why do I do this? I want to be thin. I can't help it
				L	Weighed 9st 7lb – fat Took 24 Nylax.

FIGURE 16.2. A typical monitoring sheet.

at the expense of other more important issues. In addition, advantages come from having the patient weigh herself between sessions. (A different strategy is used when treating patients with the bulimic type of anorexia nervosa.) Instead, patients are asked to weigh themselves once a week on a morning of their choice. (In practice, a weekday morning usually works out best.) There is often some resistance to this suggestion. By definition, patients with bulimia nervosa are overconcerned with their shape and weight, and this concern is expressed in their weighing habits. There is a tendency for them either to check their weight daily or more often, or to avoid weighing altogether while nevertheless remaining highly concerned about their weight. Both groups of patients find it difficult adjusting to weekly weighing. Patients who have been avoiding weighing should be forewarned that they may well experience a short-lived increase in their concern about their weight and an urge to weigh themselves more often than once a week. Patients who have been weighing themselves frequently find it difficult weighing themselves once a week, since they fear that they will gain inordinate amounts of weight between weighings. Some patients will need to purchase weighing scales; others will need to take them out of hiding. Many will need to keep the scales out of sight to help them resist weighing themselves too often.

Weighing at weekly intervals is an important part of treatment. Since these patients' eating habits will be changing markedly, and since certain of the behavioral instructions are designed to activate the patients' concerns about shape and weight, it is reasonable that they monitor their weight so as to have accurate knowledge about what is happening. However, patients also need to address their overconcern with their weight; they have to tolerate some degree of uncertainty about what they weigh rather than focusing on inconsequential day-to-day fluctuations in weight. Indeed, because of their tendency to draw major conclusions on the basis of trivial short-term fluctuations in weight, patients should be advised against making inferences about their weight on the basis of less than four consecutive weekly readings (i.e., they should draw conclusions only on the basis of longer-term trends).

Weekly weighing is a good example of how a simple behavioral instruction can highlight an underlying psychopathological feature and bring about change. During the more cognitively oriented phase of treatment (Stage 2), patients' reactions to weighing are examined.

OTHER ELEMENTS

In Session 2, it is usually sufficient to concentrate exclusively upon the two procedures described above. If time allows, and monitoring is satisfactory, some education may also be provided (see Sessions 3 to 8).

Sessions 3 to 8

During Sessions 3 to 8, the therapist should introduce the principal behavioral strategies for regaining control over eating. At the end of each session, the patient should be set a limited number of clearly specified tasks. (Some patients benefit from having these tasks written down.) At the subsequent session, the therapist and patient together should review her attempts to fulfill these tasks, and further ones should be set. Since patients with bulimia nervosa tend to be excessively self-critical, all progress, however modest, should be highlighted and praised.

REVIEWING THE MONITORING SHEETS AND HOMEWORK ASSIGNMENTS

All sessions should open with a detailed review of the monitoring sheets. The aim is to assess problems and progress. All homework tasks must be reviewed with difficulties being explored and new tasks set. In general, it is best not to move on to new tasks until the previous ones have been at least partly accomplished.

CLARIFYING THE COGNITIVE VIEW OF BULIMIA NERVOSA

The therapist should repeatedly return to the cognitive view of the disorder. When information emerges that reinforces some aspect of this view, it should be discussed with the patient and lessons drawn. For example, if an episode of overeating was precipitated by the breaking of a dietary rule, this may be used to make the important point that the patient's attempts to follow rigid dietary rules result in her being prone to binge eat. The aim is to help the patient gain an understanding of the mechanisms that perpetuate the eating problem and to appreciate the need for both behavior and cognitive change.

EDUCATING THE PATIENT ABOUT WEIGHT AND EATING

Early in this phase of treatment the patient should be provided with information on the following topics.

1. *Body weight.* The patient should be told about the body mass index and its use in place of weight tables (Garrow, 1988). (The body mass index is weight in kg/[height in m]^2). She should be told her body mass index and given the accepted figures for being underweight (below 18), a healthy weight (20 to 27), and overweight (27 or more). She should be advised against having an exact desired weight, since this does not allow for natural day-to-day fluctuations in weight. Instead, she should be advised to accept a weight range of approximately 6 lb (or 3 kg) in

magnitude. This weight range should not extend below a body mass index of 18, since at such a weight she will be prone to experience the physiological and psychological sequelae of starvation, which would worsen the eating problem. These sequelae include delayed gastric emptying, preoccupation with food and eating, and depressed mood. The patient should also be advised against choosing a weight range that necessitates anything more than slight dietary restraint, since for people who binge eat restraint often leads to overeating. In practice, it is best that she postpone deciding upon a specific weight range until she has regained control over eating and learned to eat more healthily, since only then will she be able to evaluate the amount that she can eat in order to keep her weight relatively stable. The patient should be told that in most cases treatment has little or no effect on body weight, either during treatment itself or afterward (Fairburn, Jones, et al., in press).

In the course of these discussions the therapist should mention the arbitrary nature of most desired weights. They tend to be located just under a significant threshold figure (just like prices in shops). Thus, in the United States women often wish to weigh below 100, 110, 120, or 130 lb, whereas in Great Britain women usually choose to weigh just below 7, 8, or 9 stone (equivalent to 98, 112, or 126 lb, respectively).

2. *The physical consequences of binge eating, self-induced vomiting, and laxative abuse.* All patients should be informed about the common physical complications of bulimia nervosa. These include electrolyte abnormalities in those who vomit or take laxatives; salivary gland enlargement, which can give the patient's face a chubby appearance; erosion of the dental enamel of the inner surface of the front teeth; intermittent edema, particularly in those who take large quantities of purgatives or diuretics; ovarian abnormalities; and menstrual disturbance. Only the electrolyte abnormalities are medically serious and, even so, they rarely need treatment in their own right. Usually it is sufficient to focus on the treatment of the eating problem itself, since normalization of eating behavior will result in their reversal. The same is true of the other physical complications other than the dental damage, which is permanent. In the case of menstruation, there may be a significant delay before the onset of regular monthly periods.

3. *The ineffectiveness of vomiting and laxative abuse as means of weight control.* With respect to vomiting, the main point to emphasize is that binges usually involve the consumption of a large amount of energy (it can be salutary for patients to calculate the calorie content of a typical binge) and that self-induced vomiting does not retrieve everything that has been eaten. This accounts for why those patients who vomit every time that they eat are not necessarily underweight. The explanation is that these patients are living off the residue of their binges. It should

also be pointed out (with reference to Figure 16.1) that among patients with bulimia nervosa, self-induced vomiting is habit-forming, since it encourages overeating through two mechanisms. First, since patients think that by vomiting they will avoid absorbing what they have eaten, they tend to relax their dietary controls and become more prone to overeat; and second, they discover that it is easier to vomit if their stomach is full. As a result, a vicious cycle is established with patients becoming increasingly dependent on vomiting to compensate for their increased food intake. A specific point is worth making to those patients that eat "marker" foods (e.g., tomatoes) at the beginning of their binges and subsequently vomit until these foods (i.e., the tomato skins) appear in their vomitus. This is that their geological view on how food is laid down in the stomach is ill founded: Instead, the stomach contents are churned about and what goes in first does not necessarily come out last.

With regard to laxatives, patients should be informed that they have little or no effect on energy absorption and that, like diuretics, their influence on weight is short term and the result of temporary shifts in fluid balance.

4. *The adverse effects of dieting.* There are three forms of dieting: avoiding eating for long periods of time, avoiding eating certain types of food, and restricting the total amount of food eaten. Most patients with bulimia nervosa practice all three forms of dieting, usually to an extreme degree. Typically they have rigid rules about what and when they should eat, and these are impossible to obey, particularly at times of stress. Patients tend to view deviations from these rules as evidence of their poor self-control rather than realizing that the rules themselves are at fault, and they usually react by temporarily abandoning self-control. Patients regard themselves as having broken their diet and they give up, resolving to restart dieting either later that day or the next morning. Once control has been relinquished, other factors actively encourage overeating. These include the pleasure that comes from eating the banned foods, distraction from current problems, and the temporary alleviation of feelings of depression and anxiety. The point that the therapist needs to stress is that dieting encourages overeating, the aim being to help patients arrive at the conclusion that dieting is not advisable for them.

GIVING ADVICE REGARDING EATING, VOMITING, AND PURGATIVE USE

This advice is central to treatment and should be introduced gradually over Sessions 3 to 8.

1. *The prescription of a pattern of regular eating.* This is probably the single most effective procedure in the treatment program, and it therefore needs considerable emphasis.

The patient should be asked to restrict her eating to three planned meals each day, plus two or three planned snacks. These meals and snacks should not be followed by vomiting or any other compensatory behavior. There should rarely be more than a 3-hour interval between the planned meals and snacks, and the patient should always know when she is next going to have a meal or snack. This eating pattern should take precedence over other activities; irrespective of her circumstances or appetite, the patient should not skip the meals or snacks. Conversely, between these times she should do her utmost to refrain from eating. Thus, her day should be structured by this pattern of regular eating.

Introducing this eating pattern has the effect of displacing the alternating overeating and dietary restriction that characterizes these patients' eating habits. Obviously the pattern must be tailored to suit the patient's daily commitments, and usually it needs to be modified to accommodate weekends. If a particular day is unpredictable, the patient should plan ahead as far as possible and identify a time to take stock when she can then plan the remainder of the day. Patients whose eating habits are severely disturbed should introduce this eating pattern in gradual stages. First, they should concentrate on the part of the day when their eating is least disturbed, which is usually the morning; then they should gradually extend the eating pattern until it encompasses the entire day.

Some patients are reluctant to eat meals or snacks, since they think that this will result in weight gain. They can be reassured that this rarely occurs, since the introduction of a pattern of regular eating will decrease their frequency of binge eating and thereby significantly reduce their overall energy intake. Despite such reassurances, however, it is common for patients to select meals and snacks that are low in energy. There need be no objection to this practice, since at this stage in treatment the emphasis is on establishing regular eating (i.e., the emphasis is on *when* the patient eats rather than on *what* she eats). If the patient does seek advice on what to eat, she should be encouraged to adopt a varied diet with the minimum number of proscribed foods. Patients should always be discouraged from counting calories, and especially from any tendency to keep a running total. During treatment they will discover that they can eat much more than they thought without gaining weight; in the past, they had failed to take account of the calories that they had absorbed from their binges. Occasionally patients seek advice about the quantity they should eat, and in particular whether they should eat until they feel full. They should be told that their sensations of appetite, hunger, and fullness are all likely to be disturbed, and that for the meantime they should not be used to determine when they should start or stop eating. Instead, the patient should adhere to the prescribed pattern of eating and should consume no more than average-sized portions of food. (The size of an average portion can be determined from the eating habits of friends or relatives, from recipes, or from the instructions on food packages.) A common problem is that patients are liable to feel full after eating relatively little, and that this feeling of fullness results in an urge to vomit. Feelings of fullness appear to be especially likely to develop after eating foods perceived as fattening. This reaction is likely to be largely cognitive in nature and the result of paying undue attention to abdominal sensations that would normally pass unnoticed. Patients who are troubled by feelings of fullness often benefit from wearing loose clothes at mealtimes and from engaging in distracting activities immediately afterward. They may be reassured that feelings of fullness usually subside within an hour.

The introduction of this pattern of regular eating may be set up as a behavioral experiment designed to demonstrate to patients that they can eat meals and snacks without gaining weight.

2. *The use of alternative behavior.* To help patients adhere to the pattern of regular eating, they should be asked to identify pleasurable activities that are incompatible with binge eating. Such activities may be used to cope with times between meals and snacks when they have an urge to overeat, thereby reducing the likelihood of binge eating. It is especially important to encourage patients to keep "one step ahead of the problem": They should predict when difficulties are likely to arise and at these times engage in activities incompatible with binge eating. Such activities may include telephoning or visiting friends, taking some form of exercise, or having a bath or shower.

3. *Stimulus control and allied measures.* The well-known stimulus control techniques used in the treatment of obesity may be employed, when applicable, to help patients adhere to the prescribed eating pattern. Such measures include not engaging in other activities while eating, restricting eating to one room in the house, limiting the amount of food available while eating, practicing leaving food on the plate, and discarding leftover food. In addition, the patient should limit the quantity of "dangerous" food in the house (i.e., food liable to be consumed when binge eating), she should make such food relatively inaccessible, and she should have substitute supplies of "safe" food. She should carefully plan her shopping and use a shopping list. She should avoid shopping when she is hungry or feels liable to overeat, and she should buy foods that need preparation rather than those that can be eaten immediately. When she senses that her control is poor, she should carry as little money as possible.

4. *Advice regarding vomiting.* In the great majority of cases, vomiting does not need to be tackled, since it ceases once the patient has stopped overeating. Nevertheless, it is important to ask patients to choose meals

and snacks that they are prepared not to vomit. If the patient feels tempted to vomit after eating, she should engage in a distracting activity for the following hour or so until the urge to vomit has passed.

5. *Advice regarding laxatives and diuretics.* Having explained the ineffectiveness of these drugs at preventing food absorption, the therapist should ask patients to cease taking them and throw away their supplies. It is surprising how many can do so with no further help. Those patients who find this instruction impossible to follow should be given a fixed withdrawal schedule during which the drugs are gradually phased out. A small number of regular users experience a temporary period of weight gain following their discontinuation that can be attributed to rebound fluid retention. It is therefore worth forewarning patients of this possibility to help them cope with the associated weight gain.

INTERVIEWING THE PATIENT'S FRIENDS OR RELATIVES

Toward the end of Stage 1 (around Sessions 7 or 8), the therapist should consider arranging one or two joint interviews with the patient and the people with whom she lives. These interviews serve three functions. First, they encourage the patient to bring the problem into the open, thereby removing the secrecy that typically accompanies and maintains the problem. By "coming out," it is more difficult for the patient to revert to secretive binge eating and purging. Second, by getting the patient to explain the rationale and principles of treatment, the therapist can check that they have been fully understood. Third, by educating the friends or relatives and answering their questions, they can be helped to provide an environment that will facilitate the patient's own efforts at overcoming the problem. For a variety of reasons, some patients will be reluctant to involve others, but by this point in treatment it may be possible to persuade them to divulge the problem and thereby enlist further help.

Progress during Stage 1

In the great majority of cases, Stage 1 results in a marked reduction in the frequency of binge eating and purging and an associated decrease in the level of general psychiatric symptoms. In those cases in which significant depressive symptoms persist, the possibility that they have a coexisting depressive disorder must be considered. Such patients sometimes benefit from the prescription of an antidepressant drug. Alternatively, the focus of CBT can be shifted to concentrate on depressive features. (See Fennell [1989] for a good description of CBT for depression.)

Patients whose eating has not improved during Stage 1 rarely benefit from going on to Stage 2. Instead, other treatment options should be considered. For example, it may be appropriate to arrange a period of full or partial hospitalization during which there will be more intensive treatment and some degree of external control over eating.

It is appropriate to extend Stage 1 in those cases in which significant gains are being made but the patient is still binge eating at least once per day. However, it is important to stress that protracted intensive contact is rarely helpful: If the patient's eating has not significantly improved after 8 weeks of treatment, this approach should be abandoned.

Stage 2 (Sessions 9 to 16)

In this stage in treatment there is continuing emphasis on regular eating, the use of alternative behavior, and weekly weighing, but in addition the focus broadens to address all forms of dieting, concerns about shape and weight, and more general cognitive distortions. The techniques consist of a combination of behavioral and cognitive procedures. The behavioral procedures are mostly forms of exposure. The cognitive procedures follow the principles devised by Beck and colleagues (e.g., Beck, Rush Shaw, & Emery, 1979) for the treatment of depression. In addition, training in problem solving may be of value in helping patients cope with day-to-day difficulties that would otherwise tend to precipitate episodes of binge eating.

In general, it is best to start with the procedures for tackling dieting. Then, after one or two sessions, training in cognitive restructuring may begin. Training in problem solving is best done once clear precipitants for individual binges can be identified. The behavioral techniques for addressing concerns about shape and weight may be introduced at any stage.

As in Stage 1, each treatment session opens with a review of the monitoring sheets completed since the last session in order to allow a detailed examination of the patient's progress at achieving the homework tasks. This review is followed by the introduction of new or modified treatment techniques as dictated by the patient's progress and the stage in treatment. At the end of the session, the therapist and patient agree upon a set of homework tasks. Appointments are weekly.

Tackling Dieting

A major goal of treatment is to reduce, if not eliminate altogether, the strong tendency of these patients to diet. The adverse effects of their characteristically rigid form of dieting will have been emphasized in Stage

1. The cardinal feature is the attempt to obey strict, precisely defined dietary rules and to react to the inevitable transgressions by throwing in the towel and temporarily abandoning all attempts at controlling food intake. It is this extreme response to perceived overeating, however minor, that is one of the major factors that accounts for the characteristic eating pattern of these patients, namely, intense dietary restriction punctuated by bouts of overeating (see Polivy & Herman, Chapter 9, this volume).

The therapist should discuss with the patient the relationship between dieting and binge eating, illustrating where possible with specific examples from the patient's behavior. In doing so it is important to identify the thoughts that actually pass through the patient's mind at the point at which she abandons her attempts to control her eating. Typically, these will take the form "I've blown my diet" or "I'm out of control," examples of dichotomous reasoning (black and white thinking) in which only extremes are perceived. This is the style of dysfunctional reasoning that is most characteristic of patients with eating disorders. It is important to encourage patients to spot when they think this way so that they can begin to counter this style of thinking (see Cognitive Restructuring below).

The aim is to help the patient arrive at the conclusion that dieting makes her prone to binge eat and that to reduce this vulnerability she must cease to diet. (The treatment of overweight patients is discussed later in the chapter.) The patient will be afraid that ceasing to diet will result in weight gain. This is rarely the case, since much of her energy intake will have come from binges and she will be much less vulnerable to binge once she ceases to diet. The patient should be reminded that in most cases there is minimal weight change as a result of treatment.

In Stage 1 one form of dieting will have been addressed, the tendency to avoid eating for long periods of time. Early in Stage 2 is the time to address the two other forms, avoiding specific types of food and attempting to maintain a low energy intake. To tackle food avoidance, the first step is to identify the foods being avoided. A good way of doing this is to ask the patient to visit a local supermarket and note down all foods that she would be reluctant to eat because of their possible effect on her shape or weight. She should then be asked to rank the avoided foods in order of the degree of reluctance that she would have eating them. At the next treatment session this list (usually composed of 40 or so items) should be broken down into four groups of foods of increasing difficulty, and then over the following weeks the patient should progressively introduce these foods into her diet, starting with the easiest and moving on to the most difficult. The foods should be eaten as part of her planned meals or snacks and only at times when she feels that she has a reasonable degree of control over eating. At first the amount of the food eaten is not important, although the eventual goal is that the patient should be capable of eating normal quantities with impunity. The systematic introduction of avoided foods should continue until the patient is no longer anxious about eating them. Thereafter, the patient may choose to eat a narrower diet.

The elimination of the third form of dieting, restriction over the total amount eaten, is achieved in a similar fashion. By direct questioning and detailed scrutiny of the monitoring sheets, it should be possible to determine whether the patient is eating too little. If this is the case, she should be asked to eat more until she is consuming at least 1,500 kcal each day, and preferably nearer 1,800 kcal.

A small number of patients find it impossible to obey these behavioral instructions. They may prove unable to introduce banned foods, or they may go on to binge and perhaps purge afterward. With such patients a form of therapist-assisted exposure may be helpful. This involves arranging for the patient to eat the avoided foods in the treatment session and then helping her combat the urge to overeat or vomit. Such sessions need careful planning, with the patient being made fully aware of what is being proposed and the rationale for it. The food to be eaten should be consumed early in the session, the remainder of which is devoted to helping her cope with the resulting feelings and to the identification and questioning of associated thoughts (see cognitive restructuring below). Usually a series of such sessions is required, with different types of food being dealt with in turn. Between sessions, the patient should practice eating these foods without subsequently binge eating or purging, and without adjusting her pattern of regular eating.

Patients should be encouraged to relax certain other controls over eating. For example, some patients who are highly calorie conscious dislike eating foods whose calorie content is uncertain. They may even insist on preparing all their own food so that they know its exact composition. Such patients should be encouraged to eat foods whose calorie content is difficult to determine. All patients should practice eating in a wide variety of circumstances (e.g., restaurants, dinner parties, picnics, etc.), and they should eat as varied a diet as possible.

Enhancing Problem-Solving Skills

Once patients are binge eating on an intermittent rather than regular basis, the therapist and patient together should attempt to identify the precipitants of individual episodes. While the immediate antecedents can usually be identified as specific thoughts (typically of the type described above) and changes in mood, these are often provoked by external problems of an interpersonal character. Developing the patient's problem-solving skills helps her cope more effectively with such problems, thereby further reducing her vulnerability to binge eat. An important byproduct of training in problem solving is that difficulties that have often gone unnoticed or unaddressed now are faced and tackled, thereby reducing external sources of stress and improving self-esteem.

The first step in training in problem solving is to identify a recent episode of poor control over eating that was precipitated by an external stressor. Then, using this example, the therapist should teach the patient the principles of problem solving. The therapist should explain that while many problems seem overwhelming at first, if they are approached systematically they usually turn out to be manageable. Training in problem solving helps the patient tackle day-to-day difficulties. If she learns to use the technique effectively, it will further reduce her vulnerability to binge eat by improving her ability to cope with situations that would previously have triggered episodes of overeating.

Efficient problem solving follows these commonsense steps:

Step 1—The problem should be identified and specified as soon as possible after it has occurred. It may emerge that there are two or more coexisting problems, in which case each should be addressed separately. Rephrasing the problem is often helpful.

Step 2—All ways of dealing with the problem should be considered. The patient should generate as many potential solutions as possible. Some solutions may immediately seem nonsensical or impracticable. Nevertheless, they should be included in the list of possible alternatives. The more solutions that are generated, the more likely a good one will emerge.

Step 3—The likely effectiveness and feasibility of each solution should be considered.

Step 4—One alternative should be chosen. This is often an intuitive process. Sometimes a combination of solutions is best.

Step 5—The steps required to carry out the chosen solution should be defined.

Step 6—The solution should be acted upon.

Step 7—The entire problem-solving process should be evaluated the following day in the light of subsequent events. This is a crucial step, since the goal is not simply to resolve the specific problem in question: Rather, it is to become skilled at problem solving. The patient should therefore review each of the steps of problem solving and consider how the entire process could have been improved.

Using the example problem, the therapist should go over these seven steps and demonstrate how the patient should apply problem solving to future difficulties. If time allows, another recent problem should be identified and approached in the same way but with the patient taking the lead. Then, as homework, the patient should be asked to practice problem solving whenever the opportunity arises. If any difficulty occurs or is foreseen, she should write "problem" in column 6 of her monitoring sheet, and then on the back write out each of the problem-solving steps. She should be told that her problem-solving skills will improve with practice, and that the technique may be applied to any day-to-day difficulty.

In subsequent sessions the therapist should review in detail the patient's attempts at problem solving and suggest improvements as appropriate. It is important to keep in mind that the goal is not the solution of individual problems, although this is obviously desirable, but rather the acquisition and refinement of problem-solving skills.

Addressing Concerns about Shape and Weight

These patients' extreme concerns about shape and weight are often described as their core psychopathology, since they appear to play a fundamental role in the maintenance of the disorder. A central prediction of the cognitive view on eating disorders is that relapse is likely unless these concerns are successfully addressed (Fairburn, 1988). Recent data from the follow-up phase of a treatment trial support this prediction (Fairburn, Peveler, et al., in press).

To address the extreme concerns, behavioral and cognitive procedures are used. Indeed, it is in this context that cognitive restructuring seems to be of most value. Therefore, a brief account of the principles of cognitive restructuring will be given. (Readers unfamiliar with cognitive restructuring are recommended the book edited by Hawton, Salkovskis, Kirk, & Clark [1989].)

The first step in training patients in cognitive restructuring is to identify a representative problematic thought. Usually many such thoughts will have emerged in the course of treatment, in which case a typical example may be chosen. If no suitable thought is available, then it is usually possible to elicit one, for example, by asking patients to think exactly what would go through their mind if they got on weighing scales and discovered that their weight had increased by 2 lb. Once a suitable thought has been identified, then it should be examined using the following four steps:

1. *The thought itself should be noted down.* It is most important that it is the actual thought that passed through the patient's mind and not a distillation of it.

2. *Arguments and evidence to support the thought should be marshalled.* For example, if the patient has gained weight, this fact could be said

to support the thought "I am getting fat" (or more accurately "I have gained weight"), although it does not justify the thought that "I am fat."

3. *Arguments and evidence that cast doubt on the thought should be identified.* Here it is important to examine what the thought means to the patient. For example, the thought "I feel fat" may have various different meanings including "I am overweight" or "I look overweight," or it may refer to unpleasant affective states that make the patient feel unattractive. The notion of feeling fat should be distinguished from being fat, and being fat should be distinguished from being overweight from a health perspective and also from gaining weight. Problematic thoughts are typically pejorative and undermining and not truly applicable to the situation that provoked them, yet because they tend not to be scrutinized they are believed and acted upon. Using the example above, if the patient had gained a few pounds, this cannot be equated with imminent obesity. Using a Socratic style of questioning the therapist should encourage the patient to consider such issues as "At what stage does one become fat?" "Can fatness be equated with a specific shape or weight (e.g., clothes size)?", and if so, "Am I actually approaching this shape or weight?"

Once the true meaning of the thought in question has been identified (and in many cases this is straightforward), the patient should consider what other people would think given the circumstances. Would others conclude she was fat if she had gained a few pounds in weight? The patient should ask herself whether she is applying one set of standards to herself while applying another, less rigorous set to others. She should check that she is not confusing subjective impression (e.g., feeling fat) with objective reality (e.g., being statistically overweight). She should also look out for errors of attribution: For example, could the weight gain be due to premenstrual fluid retention rather than overeating? In addition, it is essential that she check for logical errors in her thinking, by far the most common being dichotomous reasoning.

4. *The patient should reach a reasoned conclusion that should then be used to govern her behavior.* On the basis of this analysis of the appropriateness of the thought in question, the patient should decide what is reasonable to think under the circumstances. Patients should remind themselves of their reasoned conclusion each time that the problematic thought occurs. At this stage it is not to be expected that the patient will necessarily believe the reasoned conclusion: Instead, it is sufficient that she knows that this is the appropriate thing to think and that she uses it to govern her behavior.

Having illustrated the four steps of cognitive restructuring using a typical thought, and ensured that the patient understands them, the therapist should ask her to practice the procedure between sessions. It is essential that she records these efforts. There are various ways that this can be done, the most conventional being to use so-called dysfunctional thought records (see Clark, 1989). These forms have the advantage of providing an appropriate framework, although this framework can be restricting. What is essential is that the patient understands the steps involved and systematically practices them. It is the therapist's role to review at each session the patient's attempts at cognitive restructuring in order to work with the patient at refining the skill.

A common problem is that patients are not good at spotting problematic thoughts at the time that they happen. They occur naturally under many circumstances, for example, when the patient thinks she has overeaten (signified by an asterisk on the monitoring sheets), when she sees her reflection in a mirror or window, and when she receives comments about her appearance. However, it is worth giving the patient homework assignments that will be likely to provoke problematic thoughts. Many such assignments will have already been set, including weekly weighing and eating avoided foods. Other potent tasks include inspecting herself in a full-length mirror, comparing her figure with that of other women, wearing clothes that reveal her shape (e.g., a leotard or swimming costume), engaging in activities that invite comparison of her figure with that other women (e.g., exercise classes), and trying on clothes in shops. The patient should be asked to record on her monitoring sheets the actual thoughts that pass through her mind at such times and to subject them to examination using the steps outlined above. With patients who deny having problematic thoughts, it may be worthwhile attempting to provoke such thoughts in a treatment session. For example, the patient may be asked to imagine being told that she looks more healthy than she used to or that her appetite has improved. She may also be asked to imagine putting on clothes that feel tight or discovering that her weight has increased.

Occasionally, behavioral experiments may be used to test the thought in question. For example, many patients are convinced that they are fat or that parts of their bodies are fat. Often they have never previously voiced this thought. In such cases it may be appropriate to suggest that the patient ask a trusted female friend for her uncensored view on her shape. It is also common for patients to insist that on some days they are fat and that on others they are thin or less fat. This proposition can be tested by suggesting that, for a period of a week or two, the patient decide each morning whether or not she is fat and then see whether this impression matches up with her actual weight. Almost invariably, the two are found not to be closely related.

Underpinning the problematic thoughts are certain characteristic attitudes and assumptions. Typical examples include the view that all the patient's problems will be solved once she reaches her goal weight; that all her difficulties are a result of her eating (or weight) problem; that people who are thin are happy and successful, and content with their appearance; and that people who are overweight are unhappy and unsuccessful. Clearly such beliefs are extreme forms of widely held views. It is their strength, personal significance, and inflexibility that make them problematic.

The techniques used to question problematic attitudes closely resemble those used with other disorders. They cannot be identified using the approach used to identify problematic thoughts. This is because they do not tend to pass fully formed through one's mind. They are implicit, unarticulated underlying rules. They are so much a part of these patients' conceptual scheme that they are unable to step back and analyze them. For this reason they have to be inferred from their behavior (e.g., the avoidance of weighing) and the nature of their problematic thoughts (e.g., those equating fatness with being a failure) rather than identified directly.

When examining problematic attitudes, the same principles are used as when addressing problematic thoughts, although most of the work has to take place in treatment sessions. An additional feature is that the therapist should help the patient consider whether she gains anything by holding these attitudes. For example, if the patient judges her self-worth in terms of her shape or weight, she is provided with an objective and simple measure of her strengths and weaknesses; and if she equates control over eating with self-control in general, then if she diets successfully she demonstrates to herself that she is in control generally. In contrast, patients who label themselves as fat are often providing themselves with a convenient and simple excuse for a host of interpersonal problems.

Usually it becomes clear that most of the benefits of the problematic attitudes and assumptions are short term, whereas the long-term consequences are usually disadvantageous. The therapist should try to help the patient articulate these disadvantages. For example, most patients will admit that they are unlikely ever to be satisfied with their shape or weight. Thus, if they are to retain a value system in which shape and weight are given prominence, they are likely to remain perpetually dissatisfied with themselves. Furthermore, by being preoccupied with shape and weight, patients may well fail to recognize and address specific underlying problems, for example, unassertiveness, low self-esteem, and difficulties with relationships.

In some cases the origin of the attitudes and assumptions may be usefully explored. This helps give the patient some degree of understanding of her past as well as some guidelines as to how to ensure that the problem does not recur in the future. The patient should be asked to reflect on the development of the eating problem. She should consider the influence of her family and peers, and the role of social pressures to be slim. She should distinguish factors that are likely to have contributed to the onset of the problem from factors that have served to maintain it.

When examining problematic thoughts and attitudes it is always important that conclusions be drawn. In general, the therapist should encourage the patient to adopt less extreme and more flexible beliefs and values. For example, with regard to the issue of self-control, the patient may decide that some degree of self-control is desirable, but it is counterproductive to demand of oneself total self-control in all spheres at all times. Having reached a conclusion, the patient should repeatedly remind herself of it and use it to govern her behavior. Occasionally this may mean behaving in a manner that seems alien. For example, if the patient discovers that she has gained some weight, she may decide that it would be a useful test of people's response to her to wear clothes that highlight her figure rather than clothes that disguise it.

Cognitive restructuring usually reveals a limited number of relatively stereotyped problematic thoughts. As a result, after several weeks of regular practice the patient's repertoire of such thoughts should have been uncovered and explored. The same is true of the problematic attitudes. Nevertheless, it is important to persist with the procedure, since different nuances of specific thoughts often emerge and new ways of challenging them may come to light.

Some patients are resistant to cognitive restructuring. Usually this resistance stems from a fear of the unknown, a feeling that therapy is becoming unacceptably intrusive, and a realization that certain fundamental and private aspects of themselves are going to be brought out into the open. This reluctance to embark on cognitive restructuring is understandable. Nevertheless, patients should be reminded of the importance of exploring their thoughts and attitudes and they should be encouraged to do their best to do so. They may be informed of the recent finding that CBT appears to be markedly more effective than a purely behavioral version of the treatment (Fairburn, Jones, et al., in press).

A minority of patients seem incapable of engaging in cognitively oriented tasks. While they appear to understand the rationale and are willing to do the necessary homework, they seem unable to identify and examine their thoughts. As a result cognitive restructuring is impossible. With such patients this part of the treatment is best abandoned: Instead, the therapist should concentrate on those behavioral interventions that seem most likely to produce cognitive change.

In tandem with the cognitive procedures for addressing concerns with shape and weight, the therapist should apply relevant behavioral techniques. As with dieting, these involve the use of exposure. For example, some patients actively avoid others seeing their shape and so never wear tight clothes, avoid activities such as swimming, and minimize any physical contact. This avoidance of exposure to others can extend even to themselves with the result that in extreme cases the patient dresses and undresses in the dark, avoids mirrors, wears shapeless clothes, and may bathe or shower wearing a chemise. As with weighing, the obverse is also seen with some patients expressing their extreme concerns by paying minute attention to possible changes in their shape. Such patients use various methods for assessing their shape, including putting on clothes of known tightness, measuring parts of their body (e.g., their thighs), and scrutinizing themselves in mirrors. Treatment of all these patients involves helping them seek out opportunities to reveal themselves, for example, by wearing more revealing clothes and by going to swimming pools and exercise classes. In addition, those who avoid seeing their body should be progressively exposed to it with mirror and self-massage exercises. Conversely, those who frequently monitor their shape should be helped to limit this behavior. In every case the patient should be encouraged to inspect other women's bodies to put her own in perspective. Swimming pools and exercise classes are useful in this regard. The patient should be asked to identify an attractive woman and then scrutinize her body, paying particular attention to the appearance of her stomach, hips, and thighs. Typically the patient will discover that many attractive women have large hips, flesh that is dimpled, and areas that wobble.

All these behavioral techniques should be dovetailed with cognitive work. The exposure exercises will almost invariably provoke important problematic thoughts that will need to be examined there and then and reviewed at the following treatment session.

A minority of these patients exhibit true body image misperception in which they unequivocally overestimate the size of part or all their body. Clinical experience with patients with anorexia nervosa suggests that this disturbance fails to respond to direct modification, and the same appears to be true of this patient group. However, it also seems that in patients who respond to treatment, the body-image misperception resolves of its own accord. If the problem is particularly prominent, the therapist should help the patient recognise that she misperceives her shape so that she can function appropriately despite it. The patient should be provided with all the evidence indicating that she misperceives her shape, and she should be helped to reattribute the misperception to the eating disorder. As suggested by Garner and Bemis (1982, 1985), she should be encouraged to regard herself as ''color blind'' with respect to her shape. Whenever she sees herself as fat, she should remind herself that she misperceives her shape and that she should judge her size using other yardsticks, for example, according to the opinions of trusted others and the information provided by weekly weighing.

Addressing Other Cognitive Distortions

With some patients, but not all, it is important to address general cognitive distortions not directly related to the specific psychopathology of the eating disorder. The most common are dichotomous reasoning (discussed earlier), extreme perfectionism, and low self-esteem. These distortions may be addressed using the cognitive procedures already outlined. Again the reader is recommended the book by Hawton et al. (1989). In addition, Garner and Bemis (1982, 1985) provide useful guidelines from the perspective of the treatment of anorexia nervosa.

Progress during Stage 2

In the majority of cases, Stage 2 results in a consolidation of the gains made during Stage 1. Binge eating and purging become infrequent or cease altogether, while problematic thoughts and attitudes become less prominent. Occasionally progress is sufficiently rapid to justify abbreviating the course of treatment. However, the therapist should beware of judging progress simply in behavioral terms. Patients may improve behaviorally while retaining the problematic attitudes that maintain the disorder. Such patients are at risk of relapse (Fairburn, Peveler, Jones, Hope, & Doll, in press). On the other hand, if behavioral and cognitive problems remain, despite the completion of Stage 2, this is not necessarily an indication for extending treatment. As discussed earlier, further improvement often occurs even after treatment has ended.

Stage 3 (Sessions 17 to 19)

Stage 3, the final stage in treatment, consists of three interviews at 2-week intervals. The aim is to ensure that progress is maintained in the future. With patients who are still symptomatic (the majority) and who are concerned at the prospect of finishing treatment, further reassurance should be given that it is usual for there to be continuing improvement in the months following treatment.

The patient should be encouraged to practice the techniques learned in Stages 1 and 2 while the therapist takes more of a back-seat role. The patient should be asked to consider how she will manage once treatment has finished. Obviously, she will not want to continue self-monitoring indefinitely. When she decides it is the right time to stop (which is often at the end of treatment), she should be advised to check her motives: The desire to stop may stem from a reluctance to acknowledge that there has been a deterioration in the eating problem. The patient should be told that normal sensations of hunger and fullness will gradually return, if they have not done so already; once they are established, they may be used to help her decide when to eat, as long as a pattern of regular eating is maintained.

Preparing for Difficulties in the Future—Relapse Prevention

It is important to ensure that patients have realistic expectations for the future. Many expect never to binge or purge again. This expectation should be challenged, since it makes them vulnerable to relapse. Patients with bulimia nervosa have a tendency to react to any deterioration in their control over eating (any lapse) by viewing it as a relapse. The importance of the distinction between a lapse and relapse needs to be emphasized. Underlying the former term is the notion that there are degrees of deterioration, whereas the latter term has the (dichotomous) connotation that one has either recovered or has returned to square one. The two terms also have different implications for action: A lapse or slip can be corrected, whereas a relapse requires outside help.

The patient should be reminded that at times most people eat more than they think they should, and that if she does so this is neither abnormal nor a sign that her control over eating is deteriorating, even if she purges afterward. Patients are liable to be acutely sensitive to any sign that they are overeating and are prone to label any tendency of this sort as binge eating. This is not appropriate. Indeed, at times they should allow themselves to overeat and not view this negatively.

Patients should also be asked to consider what elements of the treatment they found most helpful. They should prepare a written plan for dealing with times when they sense their eating is becoming a problem. In the penultimate session this plan should be reviewed and on this basis the patient and the therapist should prepare a maintenance sheet in which the plan is formally set out. (See Table 16.3 for a typical maintenance sheet.)

The patient should be told to expect occasional setbacks. The eating problem will be an Achilles' heel, with overeating and purging being her response to stress. She should be reminded that during treatment she developed skills for dealing with the eating problem and that she should be able to use these skills again. In addition, she should be encouraged to review why setbacks occur and how she might prevent them from occurring again.

TABLE 16.3. An Illustrative Maintenance Plan

Eating problems may recur at times of stress. You should regard your eating problem as an Achilles' heel: It is the way you are prone to react at times of difficulty. You discovered during treatment that certain techniques helped you regain control over eating. The techniques that you found most helpful are listed below. These should be reinstituted under two sets of circumstances:

1. If your eating problem is getting worse
2. If you sense you are at risk of relapse

At such times there will often be some underlying problem. You must therefore examine what is happening in your life and look for any events or difficulties that might be of relevance. If any problems seem relevant, you should consider all possible solutions in order to construct a plan of action. In addition, you should use one or more of the following strategies to address your eating:

1. Set some time aside so that you can reflect on the current situation. You need to devise a plan of action. Reckon on formally reevaluating your progress every day or so. Some strategies may have worked; some may not.
2. Restart monitoring everything you eat, when you eat it.
3. Confine your eating to three planned meals each day, plus two planned snacks.
4. Plan your days ahead. Avoid both long periods of unstructured time and overbooking. If you are feeling at risk of losing control, plan your meals in detail so that you know exactly what and when you will be eating. In general, you should try to keep one step ahead of the problem.
5. Identify the times at which you are most likely to overeat (from recent experience and the evidence provided by your monitoring sheets) and plan alternative activities that are not compatible with eating, such as meeting friends, exercising, or taking a bath or shower.
6. If you are thinking too much about your weight, make sure that you are weighing yourself no more than once a week. If necessary, stop weighing altogether. If you want to reduce weight, do so by cutting down the quantities that you eat at each meal rather than by skipping meals or avoiding certain foods. Remember, you should accept a weight range, and gradual changes in weight are best.
7. If you are thinking too much about your shape, this may be because you are anxious or depressed. You tend to feel fat when things are not going well. You should try problem solving in order to see whether you can identify any current problems and do something positive to solve, or at least minimize, them.
8. If possible, confide in someone. Talk through your problem. A trouble shared is a trouble halved. Remember, you would not mind any friend of yours sharing his or her problems with you.
9. Set yourself limited realistic goals. Work from hour to hour. One failure does not justify a successsion of failures. Note down any progress, however modest, on your monitoring sheets.

As a matter of routine the risks of dieting must be stressed. It should be explained that she may well be tempted to diet at some time in the future (e.g., after childbirth), but must have serious reservations about doing so. Reasonable indications for dieting should be discussed: These are if one is clearly overweight compared to one's own norm, or if there are medical reasons to diet. The type of diet least liable to provoke binge eating may be discussed (see section on binge eating in obesity), so long as this discussion does not encourage the patient to diet unnecessarily.

OTHER PATIENT GROUPS

The cognitive-behavioral approach to the treatment of bulimia nervosa can be regarded to some extent as modular in form, since it contains groups of procedures directed at particular facets of the specific psychopathology of the disorder. Thus, there are techniques for addressing binge eating, the various forms of dieting, the extreme concerns about shape and weight, and the risk of relapse. These techniques may be used, as applicable, and from within a cognitive-behavioral perspective, with patients who show just some of these features. As a result the treatment has a wide application, since there are many patients who have a clinically significant eating disorder yet do not meet diagnostic criteria for anorexia nervosa or bulimia nervosa. Included among this group are those with binge eating disorder (see Fairburn & Wilson, Chapter 1, this volume), many of whom are overweight.

The treatment of two particular groups will be outlined, since they pose certain specific problems. First, the treatment of obese binge eaters will be considered where the patients' desire to lose weight complicates treatment. Then the treatment of anorexia nervosa will be discussed where the additional problems are the need for weight gain and the problem motivating patients to change.

Binge Eating in Obesity

Obese patients who binge eat have many features in common with patients with bulimia nervosa (see Marcus, Chapter 5, this volume), and the cognitive-behavioral view of the maintenance of bulimia nervosa appears to apply equally well to them. It follows therefore that it should be possible to adapt CBT for bulimia nervosa to suit this patient group. Three preliminary studies using forms of CBT have yielded promising results (Telch et al., 1990; Smith et al., 1992; Wilfley et al., in press).

Certain differences between patients with bulimia nervosa and obese patients who binge eat necessitate modifying the standard CBT approach. The main differences of relevance to treatment are as follows:

1. The difference in goals. The primary complaint of most patients with bulimia nervosa is of binge eating. Obese patients who binge eat typically have weight loss as their primary goal.

2. Differences in the eating behavior of the two groups. Obese binge eaters engage in less extreme weight control behavior than patients with bulimia nervosa. They diet less intensely and purging is uncommon.
3. Differences in their attitudes to shape and weight. While most obese binge eaters are highly concerned about their shape and weight, few show the overvalued ideas characteristic of patients with anorexia nervosa and bulimia nervosa.

The following section will outline the ways that CBT for bulimia nervosa has to be adapted to suit this patient group.

Modifications to Stage 1

BODY WEIGHT AND THE GOALS OF TREATMENT

The most important difference between patients with bulimia nervosa and obese binge eaters is the obesity of the latter group. Obese binge eaters have two goals, to lose weight and to stop binge eating, and weight loss is generally the more important of the two. The question of weight loss, and how it relates to binge eating, must be addressed from the outset. Therapists must emphasize that the primary aim of treatment is to eliminate binge eating and establish more healthy eating habits. In presenting this stance, therapists must be firm but empathic. They must communicate to patients that they appreciate the adverse personal, social, and physical consequences of obesity. They must demonstrate that they understand the patient's desire to lose weight, and they should point out that they will be making suggestions about nutrition, exercise, and eating, all of which should help patients control their weight. Nevertheless, therapists must be clear and consistent in emphasizing that control over eating needs to be regained before any attempts are made to lose weight. Indeed, patients should be discouraged from having a goal weight at this point. Their focus should be on their eating habits.

To help patients put aside weight loss as a primary goal, therapists should help them recognize the benefits of stopping binge eating. These benefits include ceasing to feel (and be) out of control, decreased preoccupation with thoughts about food and eating, and being in a better position to control body weight. A good way to introduce the benefits of stopping binge eating is to have patients complete an adaptation of Marlatt and Gordon's (1985) decision matrix. This involves identifying the positive and negative, short-term and long-term, consequences of stopping binge eating (Wilson & Pike, in press). Patients' responses to this task usually reveal unrealistic expectations that can then be addressed using cognitive techniques as opposed to didactic instruction by the therapist.

THE PATIENT'S ATTITUDE TO TREATMENT

Obese patients who binge eat typically have a long history of unsuccessful attempts at treatment. It is therefore not surprising that many come with a jaundiced view on the likelihood of success and this can undermine treatment. For example, it may make patients resistant to self-monitoring. It is therefore important to help them review their decision to seek treatment in order to engender enthusiasm, instill hope, and stress that they are responsible for change. As with CBT for bulimia nervosa, treatment requires full commitment: It needs to be given priority.

Some patients will have adopted the view that they are "addicted" to food or that they are "compulsive overeaters." Such patients make global internalized attributions about their perceived lack of control. Therapists must aim to modify this cognitive set. The goal is help patients shed the label of "addict" and assume responsibility for overcoming their eating problem (see Marlatt & Gordon, 1985, pp. 12–15).

EDUCATING THE PATIENT ABOUT OBESITY

In the course of discussing the goal of eliminating binge eating, it is important to provide patients with accurate information on obesity. Being overweight is not simply the result of eating too much. The causes are complex, with genetic factors being particularly important (Stunkard, Harris, Pedersen, & McClearn, 1990). While it is true that the genetic influence results in a predisposition rather than predestination, it nevertheless makes it difficult to maintain a low weight in a food-rich and sedentary environment such as ours. It limits, but does not entirely negate, the ability to have personal control over one's weight. Partly as a result, dieting is not only relatively ineffective in the long term (Garner & Wooley, 1991), but it can prove to be self-defeating, since, as discussed earlier, in certain individuals it encourages overeating.

One of the objectives in providing accurate information on obesity is to make patients aware that even the best dietary and behavioral treatments are ineffective in producing long-term maintenance of weight loss (Wadden, Sternberg, Letizia, Stunkard, & Foster, 1989). Thus, not only may restrictive dieting lead to binge eating, but it is unlikely to result in permanent weight loss. Patients need to accept the likelihood that they will always be overweight and therefore larger than average in size. This is difficult for some patients, but it is important for the long-term maintenance of change, since otherwise there is the risk that they will return to dieting and then binge eating.

It is also important to discuss societal prejudices against obese women, since these patients tend to incorporate such values into their already negative scheme for self-evaluation.

MODIFYING EATING

As with patients with bulimia nervosa, establishing a pattern of regular eating is of central importance. However, a different treatment emphasis is needed with obese binge eaters. In comparison with patients with bulimia nervosa, obese binge eaters show less dietary restraint. In addition, their bulimic episodes are less well defined. Rather than having an eating pattern characterized by extreme restraint punctuated by discrete bouts of uncontrolled overeating, they show a more general tendency to overeat. Therefore, when introducing a pattern of regular eating, it is important to pay attention to their overall eating behavior and not just their binge eating. Stimulus control techniques are of greater relevance to this group than they are to patients with bulimia nervosa. When addressing their eating habits, it is worth explaining that erratic eating tends to make matters worse, since it disrupts normal physiological controls over eating (see Blundell & Hill, Chapter 10, this volume; Tuschl, 1990).

Obese binge eaters often have little awareness of the amounts they eat and many say that they do not know what constitutes a normal intake. Although it is difficult to define normal, patients may be told that the average 200-lb woman consumes approximately 2,400 kcal/day to maintain a steady weight (12 kcal/pound/day). In contrast, the recommended daily caloric intake is roughly 1,500 to 2,000 kcal. Patients should be advised against having an intake below 1,500 kcal per day. (An occasional day under 1,500 kcal is acceptable, but regular attempts to restrict intake to below 1,500 kcal may promote binge eating.)

ADDRESSING NUTRITION

It is important with this group to provide sound nutritional information. Patients should be taught that fat has more calories per gram than carbohydrates or proteins, and that a healthy diet involves decreasing total fats and simple carbohydrates and increasing complex carbohydrates and fiber. Therapists should use the patient's monitoring sheets to make a general assessment of nutritional intake and on this basis make recommendations for dietary change. Patients should be reminded that occasionally eating desserts or other fattening foods is not inconsistent with healthy eating.

INTRODUCING REGULAR EXERCISE

Obese binge eaters are a relatively inactive group in comparison with patients with bulimia nervosa. A major goal of treatment is to help them become more active physically. The importance of increasing physical activity should be stressed from early on in Stage 1. Patients should be told that increased daily exercise can lead to modest weight loss independent of diet (Bray, 1990), that exercising is reliably associated with the maintenance of weight loss (Pavlou et al., 1989), and that it may have health benefits independent of weight loss (Blair et al., 1989). In addition, some patients derive a sense of control and general well-being (Fox, 1992).

Patients should be asked to begin a program of regular exercise based on walking, and they should monitor the time that they spend walking each day. Weekly goals should be set, and the amount of exercising gradually increased to a maximum of 45 minutes, five times a week. Patients should also be encouraged to increase their general activity level, for example, by using stairs instead of elevators.

Modifications to Stage 2

COGNITIVE RESTRUCTURING

As in the treatment of patients with bulimia nervosa, cognitive restructuring is used to modify problematic thoughts and attitudes. Many of these thoughts and attitudes are the same as those of patients with bulimia nervosa and may be addressed in the same way. However, obese binge eaters are particularly likely to view themselves as compulsive overeaters who are addicted to food. (Some will be veterans of treatment programs that explicitly adopt this view, such as Overeaters Anonymous.) Patients with this view are especially likely to resist the elimination of certain dietary rules; for example, many believe in the necessity of avoiding specific "toxic" foods, since they have been told that they trigger binge eating.

Therapists should acknowledge that this is a popular view in some quarters, and agree that there are commonalities between binge eating and problems such as alcohol and drug abuse. It should be pointed out, however, that there are important differences between eating disorders and addictive disorders (see Wilson, Chapter 6, this volume) and that there is no evidence that certain foodstuffs have toxic or addictive properties. Since total abstinence from food is impossible and undesirable, patients have no alternative but to develop flexible and healthy eating habits and to learn to cope with challenges that this presents.

Cognitive restructuring should be used to reinforce the distinction between the behavioral problem of binge eating (which patients should be able to control) and obesity (over which they can have only limited control). Cognitive procedures should also be used to address these patients' concerns about their shape and weight. Obese binge eaters are more concerned about their shape and weight than obese non-binge eaters, although most do not use shape or weight as the sole or main way of evaluating their self-worth, unlike patients with bulimia nervosa. For the most part, they realize that they will never meet today's ideal standards for shape and weight, but they do wish to weigh less. Body-image disparagement, which refers to feelings of revulsion toward one's body, is common.

One means of addressing body-image disparagement is to encourage patients to expand their definition of self-worth in order to diminish the importance attached to shape and weight. The therapist must not suggest that the patient must like her body if she does not. However, it is important for patients to accept that, although they are larger than they would like to be, self-contempt only increases their problems. Patients should learn that regardless of their weight, negative emotions and poor self-esteem intensify feelings of fatness and ugliness. In contrast, improving self-esteem and control over eating reduces the negative influence of their shape and weight. As part of this process of establishing a more balanced and positive scheme for self-evaluation, patients should be encouraged to behave in ways that counter their negative attitudes. For example, they should start attending social events that they otherwise would have avoided. The exercise program may also promote a positive body image. However, in contrast with the treatment of patients with bulimia nervosa, obese binge eaters should not be encouraged to compare their bodies with other women's. Such comparison is discouraged, since it triggers self-recrimination and may set off extreme attempts at weight control.

GUIDED EXPOSURE AND RESPONSE PREVENTION

Therapist-assisted exposure can be useful with those patients who are unable to resist eating in specific high-risk situations or who are unable to comply with the instruction to consume avoided foods. Unlike the use of this method with patients who purge, where the act of purging is the response that is prevented, obese binge eaters are exposed to specific food cues (e.g., a few bites of an avoided food) and then encouraged to resist further consumption. This method is most effective when conducted in vivo, but it can also be administered using imagery.

FURTHER MODIFICATION OF EATING HABITS

Even when their binges have been eliminated, many obese patients continue to overeat. They should be educated about how to moderate their eating in ways that do not provoke episodes of binge eating. If some form of dieting seems indicated, then it is important that it is the type of dieting least likely to provoke binge eating. For example, it may be reasonable to eliminate items that total about 100 kcal/day (e.g., eliminating two or three high-fat desserts or snacks during the week, changing from whole milk to low-fat or skim milk). The therapist must counter any tendency to adopt rigid dietary rules: Instead, the patient's eating should be governed by flexible guidelines.

Modifications to Stage 3

Treatment should follow the guidelines for bulimia nervosa except that it is usually extended by a month or more. This is because it takes time for the changes in eating to become established. During this phase sessions need not necessarily be frequent, every 2 or 4 weeks being adequate in the majority of cases.

During this phase there is continuing focus on moderating food intake. This may be reinforced by stressing the role of lifestyle moderation in general. Patients should be introduced to the concept of a balanced lifestyle, namely, one in which they balance the activities that they feel that they are obliged to engage in ("shoulds") with those that they want to engage in ("wants"). Eating, and binge eating in particular, is often viewed by these patients as one of their most important forms of self-gratification. Developing a broader range of satisfying activities can indirectly reduce the reinforcement value of binge eating. (For further details see Marlatt & Gordon's [1985, pp. 59–64] discussion of lifestyle balance as a global self-control strategy.)

ANOREXIA NERVOSA

Patients with anorexia nervosa have many features in common with those with bulimia nervosa: In particular, the specific psychopathology is very similar. In the region of a half are reported to have episodes of binge eating, although these have not been well characterized (see Garner, Chapter 4, this volume). Since the cognitive view of the maintenance of bulimia nervosa is likely to apply equally well to the maintenance of anorexia nervosa, and since the disorders have so many features in common, it is reasonable to expect that an adaptation of CBT for bulimia nervosa would benefit patients with anorexia nervosa.

Curiously, there have been few studies of the effectiveness of cognitive-behavioral techniques in the treatment of anorexia nervosa. Indeed, this treatment approach has yet to be properly described or evaluated. Cooper and Fairburn (1984) reported some success with those who binge eat, whereas restricting patients did poorly. Channon, de Silva,

Hemsley, and Perkins (1989) found that CBT was no better than a purely behavioral treatment or routine outpatient care. No distinction was drawn between those who ate in binges and those who did not.

For CBT for bulimia nervosa to be applied to anorexia nervosa, it needs to be modified and lengthened to accommodate two major problems. The first is poor motivation. Since the behavior of most patients with anorexia nervosa is consonant with their beliefs and values, many see no need for treatment. Garner and Bemis (1982) have described various ways of motivating these patients. They emphasize the importance of establishing a sound therapeutic relationship, accepting the patient's beliefs and values as genuine for her, and adopting an experimental approach in which the therapist and patient together explore the use of various different treatment strategies. In addition, at the outset of treatment it is worthwhile reviewing from the patient's standpoint the relative advantages and disadvantages of change. It is particularly important to identify issues that the patient regards as a problem. Such issues include starvation-related symptoms, for example, impaired concentration, sensitivity to cold, preoccupation with food and eating, and sleep disturbance. Once patients understand the origin of these symptoms, they are sometimes more willing to consider change. The issue of motivation is less problematic with those who binge eat, since the loss of control is usually a source of distress.

The second problem is the need for weight gain. Unless the weight loss is rapid or extreme, or the patient's health is endangered by physical complications, procedures for weight restoration can be incorporated into the outpatient regime. Before emphasizing the need for weight gain, however, it is best to devote several sessions to the establishment of a collaborative working relationship. Thereafter, weight gain must become a nonnegotiable part of treatment. However, patients must understand why they need to gain weight. They need to be informed of the physical and psychological effects of starvation, and they need to understand how these sequelae perpetuate the eating disorder (see Garfinkel & Garner, 1982). It is best to decide on a target weight range in excess of a body mass index of 18. Patients should be reassured that care will be taken to ensure that they do not exceed this weight range. The weight gain should be gradual and controlled (e.g., about 1 kg per week) and should occur within the context of the other components of the CBT program. In effect, this means that they must eat high-calorie foods as part of their planned meals and snacks. Alternatively, some patients find it easier to drink energy-rich preparations, labeling them as medicine. This is acceptable during the period of weight restoration, but once the target weight range has been reached, patients must maintain their weight without using dietary supplements. If weight gain does not occur, the therapist and patient must consider whether other treatment approaches are indicated including partial or full hospitalization. On the other hand, if the patient succeeds in gaining weight and reaches the target weight range, treatment can proceed thereafter exactly as for bulimia nervosa.

ACKNOWLEDGMENTS

Dr. Fairburn is supported by a Senior Lectureship award from the Wellcome Trust. This cognitive-behavioral treatment manual for bulimia nervosa was developed and evaluated with the support of grants from the Medical Research Council and Wellcome Trust. Its adaptation for obese binge eaters is supported by NIMH grant IROIMH4428, awarded to Dr. Marcus.

REFERENCES

Beck, A. T., Rush, A. J., Shaw, B. F., & Emery, G. (1979). *Cognitive therapy of depression*. New York: Guilford Press.

Blair, S. N., Kohl, H. W., Paffenbarger, R. S., Clark, D. G., Cooper, K. H., & Gibbons, L. W. (1989). Physical fitness and all-cause mortality. *Journal of the American Medical Association, 262*, 2395–2401.

Bray, G. A. (1990). Exercise and obesity. In C. Bouchard, R. J. Shephard, T. Stephens, J. R. Sutton, & B. D. McPherson (Eds.), *Exercise, fitness and health* (pp. 497–510). Champaign, IL.: Human Kinetics.

Channon, S., de Silva, P., Hemsley, D., & Perkins, R. (1989). A controlled trial of cognitive-behavioural and behavioural treatment of anorexia nervosa. *Behaviour Research and Therapy, 27*, 529–535.

Clark, D. M. (1989). Anxiety states: Panic and generalized anxiety. In K. Hawton, P. M. Salkovskis, J. Kirk, & D. M. Clark (Eds.), *Cognitive behaviour therapy for psychiatric problems: A practical guide* (pp. 52–96). Oxford: Oxford University Press.

Cooper, P. J., & Fairburn, C. G. (1984). Cognitive behaviour therapy for anorexia nervosa: Some preliminary findings. *Journal of Psychosomatic Research, 28*, 493–499.

Fairburn, C. G. (1981). A cognitive behavioural approach to the management of bulimia. *Psychological Medicine, 11*, 707–711.

Fairburn, C. G. (1985). Cognitive-behavioral treatment for bulimia. In D. M. Garner & P. E. Garfinkel (Eds.), *Handbook of psychotherapy for anorexia nervosa and bulimia* (pp. 160–192). New York: Guilford Press.

Fairburn, C. G. (1988). The uncertain status of the cognitive approach to bulimia nervosa. In K. M. Pirke, W. Vandereycken, & D. Ploog (Eds.), *The psychobiology of bulimia nervosa* (pp. 129–136). Berlin: Springer-Verlag.

Fairburn, C. G., Agras, W. S., & Wilson, G. T. (1992). The research on the treatment of bulimia nervosa: Practical and theoretical implications. In G. H. Anderson & S. H. Kennedy (Eds.), *The biology of feast and famine: Relevance to eating disorders* (pp. 317–340). San Diego: Academic Press.

Fairburn, C. G., & Cooper, P. J. (1989). Eating disorders. In K. Hawton, P. Salkovskis, J. Kirk, & D. M. Clark (Eds.), *Cognitive behaviour therapy for psychiatric problems: A practical guide* (pp. 277–314). Oxford: Oxford University Press.

Fairburn, C. G., Jones, R., Peveler, R. C., Carr, S. J., Solomon, R. A., O'Connor, M. E., Burton, J., & Hope, R. A. (1991). Three psychological treatments for bulimia nervosa: A comparative trial. *Archives of General Psychiatry, 48,* 463–469.

Fairburn, C. G., Jones, R., Peveler, R. C., Hope, R. A., & O'Connor, M. (in press). Psychotherapy and bulimia nervosa: The longer-term effects of interpersonal psychotherapy, behaviour therapy and cognitive behaviour therapy. *Archives of General Psychiatry.*

Fairburn, C. G., Kirk, J., O'Connor, M., Anastasiades, P., & Cooper, P. J. (1987). Prognostic factors in bulimia nervosa. *British Journal of Clinical Psychology, 26,* 223–224.

Fairburn, C. G., Peveler, R. C., Jones, R., Hope, R. A., & Doll, H. A. (in press). Predictors of twelve-month outcome in bulimia nervosa and the influence of attitudes to shape and weight. *Journal of Consulting and Clinical Psychology.*

Fairburn, C. G., Welch, S. L., & Hay, P. J. (in press). The classification of recurrent overeating: The "Binge Eating Disorder" proposal. *International Journal of Eating Disorders.*

Fennell, M. (1989). Depression. In K. Hawton, P. M. Salkovskis, J. Kirk, & D. M. Clark (Eds.), *Cognitive behaviour therapy for psychiatric problems: A practical guide* (pp. 169–234). Oxford: Oxford University Press.

Fox, K. R. (1992). A clinical approach to exercise in the markedly obese. In T. A. Wadden & T. B. Van Itallie (Eds.), *Treatment of the seriously obese patient* (pp. 354–382). New York: Guilford Press.

Garfinkel, P. E., & Garner, D. M. (1982). *Anorexia nervosa: A multidimensional perspective.* New York: Brunner/Mazel.

Garner, D. M., & Bemis, K. M. (1982). A cognitive-behavioral approach to anorexia nervosa. *Cognitive Therapy and Research, 6,* 123–150.

Garner, D. M., & Bemis, K. M. (1985). Cognitive therapy for anorexia nervosa. In D. M. Garner & P. E. Garfinkel (Eds.), *Handbook of psychotherapy for anorexia nervosa and bulimia* (pp. 107–146). New York: Guilford Press.

Garner, D. M., & Wooley, S. C. (1991). Confronting the failure of behavioral and dietary treatments for obesity. *Clinical Psychology Review, 11,* 729–780.

Garrow, J. S. (1988). *Obesity and related diseases.* Edinburgh: Churchill Livingstone.

Hawton, K., Salkovskis, P. M., Kirk, J., & Clark, D. M. (1989). *Cognitive behaviour therapy for psychiatric problems: A practical guide.* Oxford: Oxford University Press.

Jones, R., Peveler, R. C., Hope, R. A., & Fairburn, C. G. (in press). Changes during treatment for bulimia nervosa: A comparison of three psychological treatments. *Behaviour Research and Therapy.*

Marlatt, G. A. & Gordon, J. R. (1985). *Relapse prevention: Maintenance strategies in the treatment of addictive behaviors.* New York: Guilford Press.

Olmsted, M. P., Davis, R., Rockert, W., Irvine, M. J., Eagle, M., & Garner, D. M. (1991). Efficacy of a brief group psychoeducational intervention for bulimia nervosa. *Behaviour Research and Therapy, 29,* 71–83.

Pavlou, K. N., Whatley, J. E., Jannace, P. W., DiBartolomeo, J. J., Burrows, B. A., Duthie, E. A. M., & Lerman, R. H. (1989). Physical activity as a supplement to a weight-loss dietary regimen. *American Journal of Clinical Nutrition*, *49*, 1110–1114.

Smith, D. E., Marcus, M. D., & Kaye, W. (1992). Cognitive-behavioral treatment of obese binge eaters. *International Journal of Eating Disorders*, *12*, 257–262.

Stunkard, A. J., Harris, J. R., Pedersen, N. L., & McClearn, G. E. (1990). A separated twin study of the body mass index. *New England Journal of Medicine*, *322*, 1483–1487.

Telch, C. F., Agras, W. S., Rossiter, E. M., Wilfley, D., & Kenardy, J. (1990). Group cognitive-behavioral treatment for the non-purging bulimic: an initial evaluation. *Journal of Consulting and Clinical Psychology*, *58*, 629–635.

Tuschl, R. J. (1990). From dietary restraint to binge eating. *Appetite*, *14*, 105–109.

Wadden, T. A., Sternberg, J. A., Letizia, K. A., Stunkard, A. J., & Foster, G. D. (1989). Treatment of obesity by very low calorie diet, behavior therapy and their combination: A five-year perspective. *International Journal of Obesity*, *13*, 39–46.

Wilfley, D. E., Agras, W. S., Telch, C. F., Rossiter, E. M., Schneider, J. A., Cole, A. G., Sifford, L., & Raeburn, S. D. (in press). Group cognitive-behavioral therapy and group interpersonal psychotherapy for the nonpurging bulimic: A controlled comparison. *Journal of Consulting and Clinical Psychology*.

Wilson, G. T. (1988). Cognitive-behavioral treatments of bulimia nervosa: The role of exposure. In K. M. Pirke, W. Vandereycken, & D. Ploog (Eds.), *The psychobiology of bulimia nervosa*. (pp. 137–145). Berlin: Springer-Verlag.

Wilson, G. T., & Fairburn, C. G. (in press). Cognitive treatments for eating disorders. *Journal of Consulting and Clinical Psychology*.

Wilson, G. T., & Pike, K. (in press). Treatment of bulimia nervosa. In D. H. Barlow (Ed.), *Clinical handbook of psychological disorders* (2nd ed.). New York: Guilford Press.

INDEX